FRIENDSHIP IN JEWISH HISTORY, RELIGION, AND CULTURE

DIMYONOT דמיונות
Jews and the Cultural Imagination

Samantha Baskind, General Editor

EDITORIAL BOARD

Judith Baskin, University of Oregon
David Biale, University of California, Davis
Katrin Kogman-Appel, Ben-Gurion University of the Negev
Laura Levitt, Temple University
Ilan Stavans, Amherst College
David Stern, Harvard University

Volumes in the Dimyonot series explore the intersections, and interstices, of Jewish experience and culture. These projects emerge from many disciplines—including art, history, language, literature, music, religion, philosophy, and cultural studies—and diverse chronological and geographical locations. Each volume, however, interrogates the multiple and evolving representations of Judaism and Jewishness, by both Jews and non-Jews, over time and place.

OTHER TITLES IN THE SERIES

David Stern, Christoph Markschies, and Sarit Shalev-Eyni, eds.,
  The Monk's Haggadah: A Fifteenth-Century Illuminated Codex from the Monastery of Tegernsee, with a prologue by Friar Erhard von Pappenheim
Ranen Omer-Sherman, *Imagining the Kibbutz: Visions of Utopia in Literature and Film*
Jordan D. Finkin, *An Inch or Two of Time: Time and Space in Jewish Modernisms*
Ilan Stavans and Marcelo Brodsky, *Once@9:53am: Terror in Buenos Aires*
Ben Schachter, *Image, Action, and Idea in Contemporary Jewish Art*
Heinrich Heine, *Hebrew Melodies*, trans. Stephen Mitchell and Jack Prelutsky, illus. Mark Podwal
Irene Eber, *Jews in China: Cultural Conversations, Changing Perspectives*
Jonathan K. Crane, ed., *Judaism, Race, and Ethics: Conversations and Questions*
Yael Halevi-Wise, *The Multilayered Imagination of A. B. Yehoshua*
David S. Herrstrom and Andrew D. Scrimgeour, *The Prophetic Quest: The Windows of Jacob Landau, Reform Congregation Keneseth Israel, Elkins Park, Pennsylvania*
Laura Levitt, *The Afterlives of Objects: Holocaust Evidence and Criminal Archives*

Friendship in Jewish History, Religion, and Culture

EDITED BY LAWRENCE FINE

The Pennsylvania State University Press
University Park, Pennsylvania

Chapter 10 first appeared as Daniel Jütte, "Interfaith Encounters Between Jews and Christians in the Early Modern Period and Beyond: Toward a Framework," *American Historical Review* 118, no. 2 (2013): 378–400. Reprinted by permission of Oxford University Press and the American Historical Association.

Chapter 12 first appeared as Susannah Heschel, "A Friendship in the Prophetic Tradition: Abraham Joshua Heschel and Martin Luther King, Jr.," *Telos* 182 (Spring 2018): 67–84.

Library of Congress Cataloging-in-Publication Data

Names: Fine, Lawrence, editor.
Title: Friendship in Jewish history, religion, and culture / edited by Lawrence Fine.
Other titles: Dimyonot (University Park, Pa.)
Description: University Park, Pennsylvania : The Pennsylvania State University Press, [2021] | Series: Dimyonot: Jews and the cultural imagination | Includes bibliographical references and index.
Summary: "A collection of essays exploring the subject of friendship in Jewish culture, history, and religion from ancient Israel to the twenty-first century"—Provided by publisher.
  Identifiers: LCCN 2020043938 | ISBN 9780271087948 (hardback) | ISBN 9780271087955 (paper)
Subjects: LCSH: Friendship—Religious aspects—Judaism. | Jewish ethics.
Classification: LCC BJ1286.F75 F75 2021 | DDC 296.3/62—dc23
LC record available at https://lccn.loc.gov/2020043938

Copyright © 2021 The Pennsylvania State University
All rights reserved
Printed in the United States of America
Published by The Pennsylvania State University Press,
University Park, PA 16802-1003

The Pennsylvania State University Press is a member of the Association of University Presses.

It is the policy of The Pennsylvania State University Press to use acid-free paper. Publications on uncoated stock satisfy the minimum requirements of American National Standard for Information Sciences—Permanence of Paper for Printed Library Material, ANSI Z39.48–1992.

For happiness she required women to walk with. To walk in the city arm in arm with a woman friend . . . was just plain essential. Oh! Those long walks and intimate talks, better than standing alone on the most admirable mountain or in the handsomest forest . . . sometimes walking with a friend I forget the world.

—Grace Paley, *Midrash on Happiness*

Over the last few days, I have been able to see my life as from a great altitude, as a sort of landscape, and with a deepening sense of the connection to all its parts. . . . I feel intensely alive, and I want and hope in the time that remains to deepen my friendships, to say farewell to those I love.

—Oliver Sacks, *Gratitude*

CONTENTS

Acknowledgments (ix)

Introduction: Studying Friendship in Jewish History, Religion, and Culture (1)
Lawrence Fine

PART 1 LOVE, INTIMACY, AND FRIENDSHIP BETWEEN MEN

1   "Cherished in Life, for They Loved Each Other Exceedingly":
    Friendship in Medieval Ashkenaz (21)
    Eyal Levinson

2   God in the Face of the Other:
    Mystical Friendship in the *Zohar* (38)
    Eitan P. Fishbane

3   Friendship and Gender:
    The Limits and Possibilities of Jewish Philosophy (55)
    Hava Tirosh-Samuelson

PART 2 WOMEN AND THE BONDS OF FRIENDSHIP

4   "She and Her Friends":
    On Women's Friendship in Biblical Narrative (79)
    Saul M. Olyan

5   Friends and Friendship in the Memoir of Glückel of Hameln:
    Learning from Experience (89)
    Joseph Davis

6   "Got Yourself Some Friends? Now Build a Movement!" Friendship in the Jewish Women's Movement in the United States (106)
    Martha Ackelsberg

PART 3   FRIENDSHIP AND ITS CHALLENGES

7   Jacob and Esau: Twinship, Identity, and Failed Friendship (*129*)
    George Savran

8   *Hebraica Amicitia*: Leon Modena and the Cultural Practices of Early
    Modern Intra-Jewish Friendship (*145*)
    Michela Andreatta

9   Friendship and Betrayal: Hasidism and Secularism in Early
    Twentieth-Century Poland (*167*)
    Glenn Dynner

PART 4   CROSSING BOUNDARIES: FRIENDSHIP BETWEEN WOMEN
         AND MEN, AND BETWEEN JEWS AND GENTILES

10 Interfaith Encounters Between Jews and Christians in the Early
    Modern Period and Beyond: Toward a Framework (*185*)
    Daniel Jütte

11 Friendship, Jewish Female Philosophers, and Feminism (*212*)
    Hava Tirosh-Samuelson

12 A Friendship in the Prophetic Tradition: Abraham Joshua Heschel
    and Martin Luther King Jr. (*232*)
    Susannah Heschel

List of Contributors (*251*)

Index (*253*)

ACKNOWLEDGMENTS

It is my pleasure to express heartfelt thanks to those who have helped bring about this volume of essays. First and foremost, I wish to express my warm appreciation to Patrick Alexander, director of Penn State University Press, who supported this project with enthusiasm from its beginnings. My great appreciation goes as well to all those at the press who were responsible for the production of this book, including Laura Reed-Morrison, Jennifer Norton, Brian Beer, and Alex Ramos. I want to offer special gratitude to Jennifer Boeree for her meticulous work of copyediting.

I am much indebted to Professor Samantha Baskind, the general editor of the series of which this book is a part. Anyone who has ever edited a scholarly book knows that it is not unusual to experience various challenges along the way. Samantha provided wise and supportive counsel at a number of moments in the life of this project. I also offer thanks to Margaret Puskar-Pasewicz for the assistance she provided in the initial preparation of the manuscript.

Every edited volume is by the nature of things a collaborative scholarly process. I was fortunate to enjoy the collaboration of a group of distinguished scholars, representing a diverse and vast expanse of Jewish history and culture, from ancient Israel through the contemporary period. I am exceedingly grateful to each of them for their contributions to this collection of essays. This project represents scholarly collaboration at its best in another way. In the course of imagining a collection of essays on this subject, I consulted with numerous colleagues here and abroad. I am appreciative of all of them. I wish to express my special thanks to Professors Barry Holtz and George Savran, dear friends and colleagues with whom I had conversations about this project and who read and commented on a draft of the introduction to the book. My appreciation also goes to Professor Catherine Heszer, who generously provided me with a copy of her work on the topic of friendship in the Talmudic period.

It has been my exceptional good fortune to enjoy the warm collegiality of fellow members of the Mount Holyoke College Department of Religion for nearly three decades. My appreciation goes to Professors Jane

Crosthwaite, John Grayson, and Amina Steinfels and especially my friend and colleague Professor Susanne Mrozik, with whom I had conversations about this subject. This project was supported by a generous fellowship from the Sloan Foundation through the office of the Dean of Faculty of Mount Holyoke College.

I'm especially happy to have the opportunity to acknowledge members of my family, who make everything worthwhile: Jacob, Aaron and Emily, Julie, and my wonderful grandchildren, Ori and Nessa, Emet and Saphira. May their lives always be filled with deep and meaningful friendship. As always, my greatest encouragement and inspiration has come from my wife Deb. Words cannot express my gratitude for her lifelong gift of companionship, love, and deep friendship.

On behalf of all the contributors to this book, we dedicate it to our friends, for their support and all their kindnesses.

Introduction
Studying Friendship in Jewish History, Religion, and Culture

LAWRENCE FINE

Henry David Thoreau, the remarkable nineteenth-century New England transcendentalist philosopher, writer, and keen observer of the natural world and human nature, thought deeply about friendship. In his work *A Week on the Concord and Merrimack Rivers*, he wrote, "No word is oftener on the lips of men than Friendship, and indeed no thought is more familiar to their aspirations. All men are dreaming of it, and its drama ... is enacted daily. It is the secret of the Universe."[1] Yet despite friendship's ubiquity and familiarity, Thoreau lamented what he considered to be the scarcity of its consideration in literature: "Nevertheless, I can remember only two or three essays on this subject in all literature."[2]

While Thoreau certainly exaggerated the dearth of literature on friendship, the notion that it has not drawn the attention it deserves—at least in a scholarly way—is still pertinent long after he wrote about it. As one author put it, the study of friendship "is still compelled to justify its place in the history of ideas and the study of social institutions more frequently perhaps than its claims merit."[3] Based on the ethnographic record, friendship in human culture appears to be nearly universal and so commonplace that it may feel as if it may be taken for granted.[4] Indeed, friendship may seem to be in little need of serious scrutiny, particularly at the hands of scholars. After all, who doesn't know what friendship is or what friendship means? Or at least so it might seem, for when we do begin to inquire into the nature and meaning of friendship, we quickly discover how complex the questions actually are. If we were to gather a dozen people and ask each what it means to them, we would likely hear a dozen somewhat different thoughts and views. Even if we restrict ourselves to thinking about this in terms of the contemporary moment (in, say, American culture), the variables that can influence and shape views about friendship are numerous: one's age and stage of life, social and economic class, education, family, ethnicity, religious culture, sexual orientation, political and civic perspectives, and regional culture, not to mention one's temperament.

FRIENDSHIP IN HISTORICAL AND CULTURAL CONTEXT

If this is true with respect to one particular time and place, how much more so when we consider how different cultures and groups of people across time and space have conceived of friendship and engaged in its practice.[5] In his book *Friendship and Community: The Monastic Experience*, Brian Patrick McGuire writes, "Friendship is a subject that hardly seems conducive to academic treatment, and yet if we look back on the history of western culture we find friendship has been debated ever since the Greeks."[6] Friendship, like every kind of complex social relationship, has a rich and exceedingly varied history. This is true regarding the history of ideas about what friendship is or ought to be as well as its practice and its social history. In this light, the temptation to provide a universal definition or characterization is destined to fall short. Because friendship is historically and culturally situated, no sweeping or single idea can serve to inform its study without running the risk of simplifying complex matters or essentializing it. Social scientists of different types have taken an increasing interest in this subject as they investigate its nature with an eye toward its explanation and understanding.[7] While the results can certainly be valuable, the wide variety of approaches and conclusions in and of themselves attest to the fact that friendship resists fixed definitions and easy generalizations. As the editors of a collection of essays on anthropological studies of friendship have written, "The study of friendship is haunted by the problem of definition."[8]

All this is equally true with respect to the subject of this essay collection. We make no attempt to define friendship in Jewish culture or to conceive in advance what it connotes across the vast expanse of Jewish history and religious life. On the contrary, we are interested in the particulars. Our approach is based on the awareness that notions of friendship, as well as its practices, have varied considerably over time and are rooted in different intellectual, social, political, economic, and religious contexts. These contexts reflect the settings and circumstances in which Jews have lived with and among others, from ancient Israel to the Greco-Roman world, to the cultures of Islam and Christianity, to various parts of Europe and the Near East, to contemporary America. As the contributions to this book make clear, one does not have to look far to see the many ways in which conceptions and practices of friendship among Jews should be understood, at least in significant part, against the backdrop of the cultures among which they have lived. Does this mean that we can say nothing whatsoever of a generalizing nature? Are we altogether limited to many particulars without the ability to discern a larger and broader picture with some unifying features? We'll return to this question toward the end of these introductory remarks.

ATTENDING TO THE STUDY OF FRIENDSHIP

The scholarly literature on friendship in Jewish culture and history is exceedingly slim.[9] This would appear to be surprising, given the great importance of the interpersonal in Jewish religion and culture. After all, rabbinic tradition explicitly *names* the sphere of the interpersonal with the expression *ben adam le-ḥavero*, literally meaning "between a person and their fellow." This is in contrast to the category of *ben adam le-makom*, meaning the relationship "between a person and God." The former expression refers broadly to the obligations and responsibilities that govern the relationships between people, particularly in the realm of *halakhah*, or Jewish law. Rooted in biblical law and its sweeping social legislation and vastly elaborated on by the sages of the Talmudic period, *ben adam le-ḥavero* encompasses an enormous array of ethical *mitsvot*—that is, legal obligations. These include loving one's neighbor as oneself, loving the stranger, providing for the economically and socially marginal, releasing the financially indebted from their debts every seven years, being fair and honest in matters of business and law, not shaming another person in public, seeking and granting forgiveness for personal offenses, not bearing a grudge, and much more.

In addition to these ethically rooted halakhic obligations, rabbinic tradition insists on conduct that goes beyond what is sanctioned by Jewish law. The rabbinic language of *gemilut ḥasadim*, usually translated as "acts of loving-kindness," captures this category of behavior. As Michael Fishbane puts it, "*Gemilut ḥasadim* ... denotes gratuitous kindness (*ḥesed*); unrequited care; and superogatory acts. For the sages, such deeds were typified by clothing the poor; providing a dowry for indigent women; and burying the dead. The common core is that these actions express pure giving—works that cannot be repaid."[10] While there is a considerable body of scholarly literature that examines all these matters, the more specific subject of *friendship* has largely been neglected.[11] When it is occasionally discussed, it is typically subsumed under a more general discussion of ethics and the interpersonal rather than studied in its own right.

Why is this so? The most prominent reason is the privileging of *family* in the consciousness of Jewish tradition itself when it comes to the sphere of interpersonal and social intimacy. The narrative traditions of the Hebrew Bible, especially Genesis, provide the clearest evidence of this. We find numerous dramatic accounts of familial relations, particularly family conflict, but much less in the way of what we would identify as some form of friendship. And as we shall see, even the latter is usually associated with family ties. In postbiblical tradition, rules regulating the relationships between and among family members, wives and husbands, and parents and children, as well as extended relatives, continued to be a great focus of Jewish law (and nonlegal ethical literature) down through the rabbinic period, the Middle Ages, and beyond. Matters of betrothal, marriage, and divorce alone have occupied enormous attention on the part of legal authorities throughout Jewish religious history. Given all this, it is perhaps less surprising that scholars have shown little awareness of friendship as a category of inquiry.

Despite these considerations, the fact is that abundant evidence attests to rich and interesting notions and practices of friendship and to the fact that they have played a significant role in Jewish life. The studies in this collection amply demonstrate this reality. Our materials are diverse in a number of ways. First, they span the whole of Jewish historical experience, from the Hebrew Bible to the twenty-first century, as well as many of the different countries and regions where Jewish life has thrived. In addition, they include a wide range of types of evidence: narrative, legal, philosophical and kabbalistic, personal letters and diaries, and additional kinds of historical documentary materials. Further, our book is interdisciplinary and multidisciplinary in nature; contributors employ a variety of methodological approaches associated with the fields of history, religion, literary criticism, and feminist and gender studies, among others.

This book is divided into four parts representing a thematic approach in which we cluster together studies that bear on what we believe to be instructive and illuminating categories. Each of these categories helps identify and focus on a range of different questions that orient our study. To be sure, these essays could have been valuably organized in a strictly chronological way insofar as traditions build upon themselves over time. It is also the case that there is considerable overlap among these categories. Thus, for example, the question of gender is implicated to one degree or another in just about every chapter. Still, we believe that the approach we have taken will serve the reader well, as we hope the rest of this introduction will suggest.

LOVE, INTIMACY, AND FRIENDSHIP BETWEEN MEN

Discussions of friendship in late antiquity were predicated on the conviction that friendship was primarily, if not exclusively, a prerogative of men. This belief had enormous consequences for Jewish views of friendship for centuries. In his study of male friendship in medieval Germany (i.e., Ashkenaz), Eyal Levinson analyzes traditions that—in the rabbinic view—could only apply to males. The primary, but not exclusive, basis for friendship and intimate personal relations was the study of Torah (i.e., the study of sacred Jewish texts), something limited, at least formally, to men. This is dramatically brought home by Ashkenazi rules that encouraged males to study privately without the distraction of women and sexual temptation. Levinson demonstrates that in the early thirteenth century, R. Judah b. Samuel and his disciple R. Eleazar b. Judah, two leading Ashkenazi rabbis, emphasized the value of love and intimate friendship between two males and urged its cultivation by means of a number of strategies and practices. Male friendship was regarded as contributing to the spiritual development of the individuals involved as well as to the spiritual well-being of the community as a whole.

As historical background, Levinson points out that this is rooted in earlier talmudic teachings in which the disciples of master sages—always males—were enjoined to study together in pairs. An oft-cited passage in the popular rabbinic treatise *Pirkei Avot* (*Ethics of the Fathers*) 1:6 teaches, "Get yourself a teacher, and acquire a friend" (*aseh le-kha rav u-knei le-kha ḥaver*). *Avot de-Rabbi Natan* (*The Fathers According to Rabbi Natan*), a treatise closely related to *Pirkei Avot*, elaborates on this teaching in a way that explicitly encourages male intimacy around the study of Torah: "This teaches that a man should get a companion for himself, to eat with him, drink with him, study Scripture with him, study Mishnah with him, sleep with him, and reveal to him all his secrets, the secrets of the Torah and the secrets of worldly things."[12]

More generally, the entire rabbinic project in late antiquity was essentially a male phenomenon. Master sages and their students were exclusively male, and the numerous schools and academies, in both the Land of Israel and Babylonia, were composed entirely of men. Certainly, though, some women found less-formal ways to acquire rabbinic knowledge, especially but not exclusively in the home. The voluminous corpus of rabbinic literature, the *midrashim*, the two versions of the Talmud, and other cognate literature were produced by men and thus were written exclusively from their point of view. These sources provide abundant evidence concerning the nature of social relations, at least among the elite intellectual men who inhabited rabbinic culture.

I would like to expand briefly on the question of rabbinic friendship raised in Levinson's chapter. In what is the most detailed study of friendship in rabbinic tradition, Catherine Hezser—in a book dedicated to the relationship between the Jerusalem Talmud and Greco-Roman literature—explores different settings in which male friendship among the sages came to life.[13] Her work is especially valuable insofar as it does not limit itself to prescriptive traditions but draws primarily on anecdotal and narrative descriptions of different types of activities. As such, it offers a window onto the world of personal rabbinic relations as lived experience, at least to the extent possible based on ancient literary sources. Hezser tells us that in the Jerusalem Talmud, the noun *ḥaver*—which appears hundreds of times—can connote many different things depending on the context in which it is employed, but it is especially prominent in connection with the study of Torah.

In addition, there were other settings for close personal relationships. Similar to Greco-Roman practices, friendship also developed in connection to sages' visits to one another's homes and included the sharing of weekday meals as well as festive banquets. A closely related setting was participation in one another's family celebrations, such as weddings and circumcision ceremonies. Weddings, in particular, were occasions where fellow sages served as groomsmen and assistants in preparations for the wedding, as well as guests at wedding banquets. Similarly, the Talmud also provides numerous stories of rabbis visiting their friends at home when they were ill, accompanying them in mourning when members of their family died, and attending the funerals of rabbinic friends themselves. Still other narratives describe friendship among sages in a more public domain, in connection with working, traveling, visiting bathhouses together, and occasionally even going on journeys by ship to travel abroad. Finally, Heszer notes that rabbis also expressed friendship by giving gifts and supporting each other in moments of personal trouble, as well as by writing letters to each other when living at a distance.

All this is to say that interpersonal relations among rabbinic sages appear not to have been limited to intellectual and scholastic activities, as central as these were in rabbinic culture. Consistent with the intimation in the tradition cited from *Avot de-Rabbi Natan*, companionship among sages was holistic in nature. Rabbinic culture was unquestionably based on exceedingly strong hierarchical rules and customs—and our sources do not shy away from depicting competition and interpersonal conflict. Nevertheless, we find a model of friendship that involved concern for one another's well-being, mutual support, and engagement in a broad landscape of interpersonal and social activities.

As with rabbinic friendship in the talmudic period, Eitan Fishbane's study of the kabbalistic fellowship depicted in the *Zohar*, the great medieval work of Jewish mystical tradition, attests as well to the ideal of all-male companionship. In its fictive description of the second-century sage R. Shimon bar Yoḥai, the putative author of the *Zohar*, and his circle of disciples, the *Zohar* offers a dramatic picture of male fellowship. Walking on their mystical journeys in an idyllic imagined landscape in the Land of Israel, the members who compose the *Zohar*'s *ḥevrayya* (Aramaic, "fellowship") encounter one another on the road, greeting each other with extreme joy and enthusiasm. These emotions are characteristically expressed by how happy they are to see the divine Presence—in kabbalistic parlance, the *Shekhinah*—shining forth from each other's faces. Profound friendship, marked by an intense feeling of love and unity between individuals and among the companions as a whole, is absolutely central to the *Zohar*'s narratives and helps define the very essence of the companions' collective life. Fishbane explores this and other associated themes through a close textual reading of passages from the *Zohar*, drawing in part on a literary critical methodology.

These rich narrative traditions served as inspiration for later kabbalists, most notably Isaac Luria (d. 1572), by far the most influential figure in the great renaissance of kabbalistic community that developed in sixteenth-century Safed.[14] Luria was at the center of a fellowship that comprised about forty disciples, whom he enjoined to love and to support one another in every manner. In accordance with his teachings on the transmigration of souls (*gilgul neshamot*), Luria personally identified with the soul of R. Shimon bar Yoḥai and considered his closest disciples as soul incarnations of the other members of the zoharic *ḥevrayya*. Luria believed that he and his disciples were replicating and furthering the work of cosmic redemption in which the zoharic fellowship had been engaged. Among the most critical features of this work was his insistence that his disciples avoid anger, pettiness, and jealousy and instead cultivate a spirit of unity and love. Indeed, he taught that they should begin their morning prayers by contemplating their love and support for one another in times of trouble.

The Lurianic fellowship, in turn, influenced the development of other intentional kabbalistic groups with a similar commitment to interpersonal relationships. For example, in Jerusalem, the "Pietist's Study House of Bet El" (*Midrash Ḥasidim Bet El*) was established in 1737.[15] Four "contracts" or "bills of association" were produced over a series of years and signed by a small number of individuals within Bet El. In one of these pacts, the participants pledged uncompromising loyalty, love, and brotherhood toward one another. Aptly, they referred to their fellowship by the name *Ahavat Shalom* (Love of peace): "First, we the undersigned, twelve of us ... agree to love one another with great love of soul and body. ... Each man's soul will be bound to that of his companion (*ḥaver*) as if the latter were part of his very limbs, with all his soul and all his might, so that if, God forbid, any one of us will suffer tribulation all of us together and each one of us separately will help him in every possible way."[16]

Taken together, these and similar fellowships exemplify an intense and distinctive expression of interpersonal intimacy in medieval and early modern Judaism. We see that male companionship and friendship in the history of Jewish mystical tradition took place in the context of community or, more precisely, within the context of intentional communities. Love, humility, trust, honesty, mutuality, and unity were the social goals that defined the community and were intended to transcend any particular relationship between, say, two individuals.

In a wide-ranging study, Hava Tirosh-Samuelson explores ways in which friendship is treated in the Jewish philosophical tradition from late antiquity through the early modern period. She demonstrates the great influence of the Greek philosophical tradition, primarily Aristotelian, on Jewish philosophical views of friendship, just as it dominated Western discourse on this subject more generally. Medieval and early modern Jewish philosophers—as in the case of their Christian and Muslim counterparts—were generally far more focused on metaphysical questions than on ethical and interpersonal ones. Friendship was nevertheless a subject of considerable interest among a range of Jewish authors. By far, the most important of these was Maimonides (d. 1204), whose teachings on this subject—firmly rooted in Aristotle's conception of virtue friendship as articulated in the *Nicomachean Ethics*—exerted great influence over Jewish philosophical writing for the next several centuries. Other Jewish writers, especially figures living in Spain, Italy, and the Ottoman Empire, were influenced directly by Latin translations of Aristotle's *Ethics*, unmediated by Maimonides. In the course of her study, Tirosh-Samuelson simultaneously addresses the ways in which premodern Jewish philosophers sought to exclude women from philosophical life, which male philosophers believed to be necessary for acquiring friendships. She writes that despite the classical view of women that led Jewish philosophers to believe that only men could truly experience friendship, we have evidence that some teachers—including Maimonides himself—conceived of the possibility of women's friendship under certain circumstances. *Dialoghi d'amore*, by Judah Abravanel (d. ca. 1523), imagines women's friendships through its fictive account of an intellectual and emotional relationship between a male and a female philosopher. Beyond this, Tirosh-Samuelson points to several early modern Italian women who we know had friendships with men, including the notable Italian benefactor Sara Copia Sullam (d. 1641).

WOMEN AND THE BONDS OF FRIENDSHIP

As the example of Sara Copia Sullam makes evident, Jewish women were not necessarily paying attention to what philosophical men thought about their interest in or capacity for friendship. There is a documented history of friendship between and among Jewish women, as well as between women and men, even prior to the modern period. Even biblical authors had no trouble imagining friendship between women, as is clear from the narrative account of the relationship between Ruth and Naomi in the book of Ruth. True, theirs is also a familial relationship, as Ruth and Naomi are daughter-in-law and mother-in-law. However, as Saul Olyan shows in his exploration of women's friendship, Ruth and Naomi forge a relationship that goes far beyond what one would expect between female in-laws. Under circumstances that begin with extreme suffering, they develop a relationship characterized by trust, loyalty, intimacy, and radical kindness, the latter evidenced by the repeated employment of the language and social gestures of ḥesed. Olyan ultimately poses the question of how depictions of female friendship compare with accounts of male friendship, most notably the relationship between Jonathan and David.

The question of friendship among family members takes center stage in Joseph Davis's study of Glückel of Hameln, whose fascinating seventeenth-century story-filled memoir is a classic of early modern Jewish literature, among the first full-fledged autobiographies by a Jewish individual, man or woman.[17] Davis pays close attention to the (Yiddish) vocabulary Glückel uses to denote friendship in the course of her lively and poignant account of her life as wife, mother, and businesswoman. We learn that for her, friendship was largely, though not exclusively, associated with kin, near and extended. This was partly due to her conviction that while not perfect, kin were more likely to be trustworthy and reliable, especially when life was tough.

In her essay, Martha Ackelsberg explores the vital but complex role played by friendship and solidarity in the Jewish women's movement in the United States. In particular, she focuses on the origins of the movement in the 1970s. Here, as well, the relationship between family and friendship is a central question, but quite dissimilar to Glückel of Hameln's views. Ackelsberg describes the Jewish women's movement as creating a (necessary) space for social and personal intimacy *outside* of the family, something that goes to the very heart of a broader feminist critique of the constraints that traditional family structures have historically imposed on women's autonomy and agency.

The bond of friendship between women in the contemporary period is also exemplified in an especially compelling way in the writing—as well as in the life—of the great social activist and author Grace Paley (1922–2007). Through the voice of her semiautobiographical protagonist, Faith, Paley expresses the paramount importance of loving friendship among women: "By love she probably meant that she would *die* without being *in* love. By *in* love she meant the acuteness of the heart at the sudden sight of a particular person or the way over a couple of years of interested friendship one is suddenly stunned by the lungs' longing for more and more breath in the presence of that friend."[18]

FRIENDSHIP AND ITS CHALLENGES

Like every other type of social relationship, friendship is unquestionably a complicated matter, easily fraught for any number of reasons. It may be fair to say that the longer and deeper a relationship is, where much is at stake, the more likely there will be problems to navigate. Sometimes we stumble and have to repair a relationship. And naturally, even meaningful relationships sometimes come to an end. Glückel's memoir is filled with the turmoil and vicissitudes she experienced, frequently leading to disappointment, regret, and resentment. The several essays in this section speak as well to some of the challenges that come with friendship and the longing for it. In a study of the unique nature of twinship, George Savran explores the tense, complicated relationship between the biblical twins Jacob and Esau. While twins often have the very closest of friendships, at the same time they are susceptible to particularly intense rivalry and competition. Through a close reading of the Jacob and Esau narratives, Savran demonstrates how the possibility of intimacy and friendship between the two brothers ultimately fails.

Michela Andreatta's essay explores conceptions and practices of friendship among Jews during the Italian Renaissance, focusing particularly on one of the most famous rabbis of the seventeenth century, Leon Modena (d. 1648). In a way that is representative of broader sensibilities around friendship in early modern Italian literature, Modena speaks to concerns about the inconstant or fickle friend. Like Glückel, Modena worries about disloyalty, dishonesty, and untrustworthiness, whereas true friendship—ideal friendship—is known by sincerity and faithfulness. The strong bond of genuine friendship survives changes in the fortunes of its partners, often involves self-sacrifice, and may even transcend the death of one of them. For Modena, such friendship between two people is described in ways that verge on the erotic, the union of like souls.[19] Andreatta also provides an account of the relationship between Modena and Sara Copia Sullam.

Glenn Dynner's account of friendship among young Hasidim in early twentieth-century Poland navigates the question of challenges to friendship in the context of highly distinctive social and political circumstances. Dynner describes the traditional religious culture that originally served as the basis for interpersonal relations among Hasidim, going back to an earlier stage of the Hasidic movement beginning in the eighteenth century. Friendship was forged through comradery among fellow Hasidim in the daily practice of the community. What happens, though, when commitments to tradition and the ethos of the community begin to wane among some—in this case, among younger members of the community drawn to emerging intellectual, social, and political movements? Can friendships survive when individuals break from the community and seek a different life, as in post–World War I Poland?

CROSSING BOUNDARIES:
FRIENDSHIP BETWEEN JEWS AND CHRISTIANS, WOMEN AND MEN

How much similarity between individuals does friendship require? To put it historically, can we speak, for example, of friendships between Jews and Christians or between women and men in the Jewish world prior to the modern period? These are among the questions at the heart of the three essays that compose the final section of this volume.

In a broadly conceived programmatic essay, Daniel Jütte addresses the question of Jewish-Christian relationships by way of documentary sources from early modern Europe. He argues that while earlier historiography averred that genuine friendship between Jews and Christians was virtually unknown—according to some historians, even impossible—before the Enlightenment, considerable evidence proves otherwise. Jütte demonstrates his argument by unfolding the story of Hans Ulrich Krafft (d. 1621), a non-Jewish merchant from the region of Swabia in southern Germany, who found himself in dire straits, imprisoned in Tripoli. Over the course of several years in prison, Krafft, raised as a devout Lutheran, was befriended and assisted in critically important ways by two different Jewish men, including a certain Mayer Winterbach. Jütte provides evidence of other early modern Jewish-Christian friendships to support the argument that these relationships were not as implausible and uncommon as other historians have claimed. He illuminates the phenomenon of interreligious friendship by drawing attention to several early modern developments that helped enable them. These included the role played by increased mobility and travel, intra-Christian hostilities that made associating with members of the Jewish minority more appealing, and crucially, as in the case of Krafft and Winterbach, a shared cultural identity as fellow Swabians that transcended religious difference.

In the second of her two essays in this volume, Hava Tirosh-Samuelson continues her discussion of friendship and Jewish philosophical tradition by turning to the modern and contemporary periods. Her study shows how developments that had influenced notions and practices of friendship in the early modern period—as attested in the essays by Andreatta and Jütte—advanced dramatically, beginning in nineteenth-century Europe. Tirosh-Samuelson speaks to the crossing of old boundaries between genders as well as between Jews and Christians. Interestingly, these two types of boundary crossings would overlap and intersect. For example, the nineteenth-century salons of wealthy German-Jewish women—where art, philosophy, music, and literature were discussed—were spaces in which different types of people came together, such as Jews and Christians, men and women, artists, civil servants, aristocrats, and writers. Rahel Varnhagen (d. 1833) was perhaps the most important figure in this burgeoning cosmopolitan culture and a woman whose life inspired none other than Hannah Arendt. Not only did salon life result in the forging of personal relationships (including romantic ones), it also influenced newly emerging conceptions of friendship.

As for the twentieth century, the figures of Martin Buber (d. 1965) and Franz Rosenzweig (d. 1929) loom large in the development of philosophical views about friendship and the interpersonal, as Tirosh-Samuelson demonstrates. Buber and Rosenzweig, themselves friends and scholarly collaborators, forged a philosophy of the interpersonal rooted in the notion of dialogue. Buber's influence, in particular, has been immense, based on his classic work *I and Thou*. Tirosh-Samuelson also explores the continuing and especially prominent role played by intellectual Jewish women. No person exemplifies this better than the aforementioned German-Jewish émigré Hannah Arendt (d. 1975), philosopher and political theorist and one of the last century's most celebrated public intellectuals. Karl Jaspers, Arendt's doctoral advisor at the University of Heidelberg, spoke of her personal genius for friendship. Indeed, her large circle of friends comprised some of the great intellectual and literary figures beginning in the middle of the twentieth century: Martin Heidegger, Gershom Scholem, Walter Benjamin, Hans Jonas, Paul Tillich, Hans Morgenthau, Mary McCarthy, Salo and Jeanette Baron, Lionel and Diana Trilling, Randall Jarrell, Robert Lowell, and W. H. Auden, among others.[20] Moreover, as Tirosh-Samuelson shows, Arendt's penchant for attracting friends was matched by her highly influential philosophical thinking about friendship. Tirosh-Samuelson also reflects on the significance of the prominent and critical role of Jewish women in the contemporary feminist conversation around moral theory and the "ethics of care."

The crossing of boundaries in the name of friendship took on a literal meaning when Abraham Joshua Heschel (d. 1972) and Martin Luther King Jr. (d. 1968) marched together in protest across the Edmund Pettus Bridge in Selma, Alabama, in 1965. In her account of the extraordinary connection and collaboration between her father and King, Susannah Heschel explores the several bases for their friendship. In addition to their shared opposition to the Vietnam War, Heschel and King held remarkably similar theological views as well as an impassioned, existential commitment to bringing the teachings of the Hebrew prophets to bear upon the evils of racism and anti-Semitism. In light of the sometimes-fraught nature of relations between the African American and Jewish communities, the friendship between Heschel and King has, for many in both communities, served as inspiration and as a reminder that the two have an important history of friendship and cooperation.

If we cannot produce a definition of friendship that encompasses the many different conceptions and practices studied in these essays, I believe that we can, nevertheless, say some instructive things of a unifying nature. In the first place, in these studies we find a vast intertextual conversation through time in which the Jewish "language" of friendship resonates and reverberates across Jewish literature. For example, the biblical account of the relationship between David and Jonathan, as well as scriptural passages invoking the motif of friends and friendship found in Proverbs and Ecclesiastes, are cited again and again in subsequent discussions of this subject; these serve as grist for the development of new views and innovative interpretations. A surprising example of intertextual conversation may be found in the very title of Martha Ackelsberg's chapter, which begins with "Got Yourself Some Friends?" This unusual locution is a contemporary adaptation of the language of *Pirkei Avot* cited earlier: "Get yourself a friend." While this may be a whimsical example of what we have in mind, it nonetheless attests to the long career and endurance of a particular vocabulary, one that bears the signature and sensibility of Jewish religious culture.

Beyond a persistent vocabulary of friendship, many of the substantive conceptions and social practices discussed in these studies also reverberate over time. Maimonides's classic articulation of the nature of friendship, for example, influenced Jewish thinkers for centuries. Indeed, his views live on in certain contemporary Jewish understandings of friendship. For a completely different type of example, consider the fact that Arendt wrote a biography of Rahel Varnhagen. It is presumably no coincidence that Arendt—who identified so intimately with Varnhagen—created a latter-day salon of her own in her apartment on New York City's Upper West Side, home to the liveliest of conversation and to affection among friends.[21]

This collection of essays does not, by any means, constitute a comprehensive history of our subject. Many more examples of friendship in Jewish culture could easily be adduced. Taken together, however, we believe they represent and exemplify many of the most important themes and questions. We hope that this exploration will inspire further interest and provide the groundwork for future study of the nexus between Judaism and friendship.

NOTES

1. Henry David Thoreau, *A Week on the Concord and Merrimack Rivers* (New York: Penguin, 1998), 213.
2. Thoreau, *A Week*, 213.
3. Julian Haseldine, introduction to *Friendship in Medieval Europe*, ed. Julian Haseldine (Stroud, UK: Sutton, 1999), xvii.
4. On the question of whether friendship is attested universally, see Daniel J. Hruschka, *Friendship: Development, Ecology, and Evolution of a Relationship* (Berkeley: University of California Press, 2010), 50–55.
5. In a chapter entitled "Friendship Across Cultures" in his book *Friendship*, Hruschka provides compelling evidence

for dramatically diverse notions and practices of friendship among different cultures. These include types of friendships "unimagined by Westerners." This notwithstanding, Hruschka argues that "as one peels away those aspects of friendship that travel poorly to other societies, a core pattern is revealed that consistently appears in descriptions of friendship across a range of societies." According to him, "Mutual aid based on need, positive affect, and gift giving between partners—represent recurring parts of friendship-like relationships as they arise in numerous groups." See Hruschka, 68–75.

6. Brian Patrick McGuire, *Friendship and Community: The Monastic Experience* (Kalamazoo, MI: Cistercian Publications, 1998), vii. For a valuable overview of the history of friendship, at least in the West, see Barbara Caine, ed., *Friendship: A History* (London: Routledge, 2014).

7. For sociological studies, see, for example, Rebecca G. Adams and Graham Allan, eds., *Placing Friendship in Context* (Cambridge: Cambridge University Press, 1998); and Ray Pahl, *On Friendship* (Cambridge: Polity, 2000). Important anthropological studies include Evan Killick and Amit Desai, eds., *The Ways of Friendship: An Anthropological Perspective* (New York: Berghahn, 2010); and Hruschka, *Friendship*.

8. Killick and Desai, *Ways of Friendship*, 1.

9. Two important studies include Saul M. Olyan, *Friendship in the Hebrew Bible* (New Haven: Yale University Press, 2017); and Catherine Heszer, "Rabbis and Other Friends: Friendship in the Talmud Yerushalmi and in Graeco-Roman Literature," in *The Talmud Yerushalmi and Graeco-Roman Literature II*, ed. Peter Schafer and Catherine Heszer (Tubingen: Mohr Siebeck, 2000). An interesting (and rare) discussion of intra-Jewish friendship in the context of Jews of Arab lands may be found in S. D. Goitein, *A Mediterranean Society: The Jewish Communities of the Arab World as Portrayed in the Documents of the Cairo Geniza* (Berkeley: University of California Press, 1988), 5:72–97. For studies of friendship in Jewish mystical tradition, see the following by Lawrence Fine: "A Mystical Fellowship in Jerusalem," in *Judaism in Practice: From the Middle Ages Through the Early Modern Period*, ed. Lawrence Fine (Princeton: Princeton University Press, 2001), 210–14; "Spiritual Friendship as Contemplative Practice in Kabbalah and Hasidism," in *Meditation in Judaism, Christianity, and Islam*, ed. Halvor Eifring (London: Bloomsbury T&T Clark, 2013), 61–75; and "Spiritual Friendship: 'Go Among People Who Are Awake and Where a Light Shines Brightly,'" in *Jewish Mysticism and the Spiritual Life: Classical Texts, Contemporary Reflections*, ed. Lawrence Fine, Eitan P. Fishbane, and Or N. Rose (Woodstock, VT: Jewish Lights, 2011), 112–18. Certain contemporary French Jewish authors, most notably Emmanuel Levinas (1906–1995) and Jacques Derrida (1930–2004), manifested a particularly strong interest in the question and in the life of friendship. Levinas, Derrida, and the non-Jewish philosopher Maurice Blanchot (1902–2003) had intimate personal and intellectual friendships with one another. See, for example, Emmanuel Levinas, *Entre Nous: Thinking of the Other* (New York: Columbia University Press, 1998); Jacques Derrida, *The Work of Mourning* (Chicago: University of Chicago Press, 2001); Derrida, *Adieu: To Emmanuel Levinas* (Stanford: Stanford University Press, 1997); and William Young, *Uncommon Friendships: An Amicable History of Modern Religious Thought* (Eugene, OR: Cascade Books, 2009), 121–49. See also Alon Goshen-Gottstein, "Understanding Jewish Friendship, Extending Friendship Beyond Judaism," in *Friendship Across Religions: Theological Perspectives on Interreligious Friendship*, ed. Alon Goshen-Gottstein (Lanham, MD: Lexington Books, 2015). This book is the product of the Elijah Interfaith Institute, a project

dedicated to studying and promoting interreligious understanding. The present volume is the first scholarly book to address the subject of friendship in Jewish culture in a wide-ranging way.
10. Michael Fishbane, *Sacred Attunement: A Jewish Theology* (Chicago: University of Chicago Press, 2008), 152.
11. Scholarly works on Jewish ethics rarely even mention friendship. One generally looks in vain for the entry "friend" or "friendship" in indices to these works. Consider, for example, Elliot N. Dorff and Jonathan K. Crane, eds., *The Oxford Handbook of Jewish Ethics* (New York: Oxford University Press, 2013). This impressive book, comprising twenty-nine chapters and spanning 514 pages, contains no reference to our subject. One important exception to this general rule is Hava Tirosh-Samuelson, *Happiness in Premodern Judaism: Virtue, Knowledge, and Well Being* (Cincinnati: Hebrew Union College Press, 2003).
12. *Avot de-Rabbi Natan*, 8:3, translated by Judah Goldin as *The Fathers According to Rabbi Nathan* (New Haven: Yale University Press, 1955), 50. Concerning this book, see Jonathan Wyn Schofer, *The Making of a Sage: A Study in Rabbinic Ethics* (Madison: University of Wisconsin Press, 2005).
13. Heszer, "Rabbis and Other Friends." With respect to the relationship between sages and their disciples, see Moses Aberbach, "The Relations Between Master and Disciple in the Talmudic Age," in *Exploring the Talmud*, vol. 1, *Education*, ed. Haim Z. Dimitrovsky (New York: Ktav, 1978), 202–25.
14. See Lawrence Fine, *Physician of the Soul, Healer of the Cosmos: Isaac Luria and His Kabbalistic Fellowship* (Stanford: Stanford University Press, 2003).
15. See Fine, "Mystical Fellowship."
16. Fine, 212.
17. Concerning the general question of friendship among kin, see Hruschka, *Friendship*, 76–104.
18. Grace Paley, *A Grace Paley Reader: Stories, Essays, and Poetry*, ed. Kevin Bowen and Nora Wiley (New York: Farrar, Straus and Giroux, 2017), 315.
19. The relationship between friendship and the erotic is much discussed in the scholarly literature on friendship. See, for example, Hruschka, *Friendship*, 105–20. In Jewish literature, this matter figures prominently in medieval Hebrew poetry, where the popular themes of male friendship and love often resonate with erotic language. Some regard this as evidence of homosexual culture during the "Golden Age" of Spain, while others see it as an expression of intense homosociality. See, for example, Raymond Scheindlin, *Wine, Women, and Death: Medieval Hebrew Poems on the Good Life* (Philadelphia: Jewish Publication Society, 1986); and the bibliography on this question in Fine, *Physician of the Soul*, 406n59.
20. This illustrious circle of friends exemplifies the fact that by the twentieth century, intimate friendships between Jews and non-Jews (of all strata of society) had become altogether commonplace in Europe, the United States, and elsewhere.
21. Arendt wrote of Varnhagen that she is "my closest friend, though she died some hundred years ago." See Hannah Arendt, *Rahel Varnhagen: The Life of a Jewess*, ed. Liliane Weissberg, trans. Richard and Clara Winston (Baltimore: Johns Hopkins University Press, 1957), 5. It is exceedingly interesting that the close (though turbulent) friendship between Arendt and Scholem began, in part, over their mutual fascination with the life of Rahel Varnhagen. In their conversations in Paris in February 1938, Scholem took great interest in Arendt's project to write about Varnhagen. Arendt sent Scholem a draft manuscript of her work on Varnhagen the following year and encouraged him to help her seek its publication. See Marie Luise Knott, *The Correspondence of Hannah Arendt and Gershom Scholem*, trans. Anthony David (Chicago: University of Chicago Press, 2017), xi–xiv, letter 1.

PART 1
Love, Intimacy, and Friendship Between Men

CHAPTER 1

"Cherished in Life, for They Loved Each Other Exceedingly"
Friendship in Medieval Ashkenaz

EYAL LEVINSON

The Hebrew chronicles of the Crusades include a fascinating story about the love between two young men, a love nipped in the bud. According to Robert Chazan, this is "surely one of the most poignant tales in the entire record of 1096."[1] The incident occurred in the small German town of Wevelinghoven, located forty kilometers north of Cologne, where different groups of Crusaders gathered on the eve of the festival of Shavuot. Imbued with religious fervor, they were determined to convert the local Jews or annihilate them. Cologne's archbishop, Hermann III (period of office, 1089–99), along with some of the Christian townspeople, hid the Jews in the palace and in their homes. When it was no longer possible to hide the Jews, the archbishop sent them to seek shelter in seven villages near Cologne, among them Wevelinghoven. After three weeks, the Jews hiding in Wevelinghoven were discovered, and those who refused to convert were murdered or committed suicide. Scholars conclude that the chronicle was written fifty years after the events, between the years 1140 and 1146.[2] The story goes as follows:

> When the enemy came before the town, then some of the pious ones ascended the tower and threw themselves into the Rhine River that

flows around the town and drowned themselves in the river and all died. Only two young men did not die in the water, R. Shmuel the bridegroom ben R. Gedaliah and Yehiel ben R. Samuel. Cherished in life, for they loved each other exceedingly, they were not parted in death. When they decided to throw themselves into the water, they kissed one another and held one another and embraced one another by the shoulders and wept to one another and said: "Woe for our youth, for we have not been deemed worthy to see seed go forth from us or to reach old age. Nonetheless, let us fall into the hands of the Lord. He is a steadfast and merciful God and King. Better to die here for His great name and to stroll with the saintly ones in paradise than that these uncircumcised and unclean seize us and sully us against our will with their evil waters."[3]

The two young men jumped to their death but did not drown. They were found, still in the river and embracing each other, by the Jews who came out of the town. Yehiel was then slaughtered in the water by his father. When his friend Shmuel saw it, he asked Menahem, the sexton of Cologne's synagogue, to kill him as well, and Menahem complied. This description of intense love between two men is exceptional among Ashkenazi medieval sources, yet historians examining this story refrain from discussing the love of the two young men.[4]

This chapter argues that the story reveals a normative cultural conception of male friendship, a social institution that by the early thirteenth century was propagated by two leading German rabbis, Judah b. Samuel (d. 1217) and his student Eleazar b. Judah (1165–ca. 1240). It should be emphasized that this concept of friendship, however, did not negate or aim at replacing the rabbinic norm that prescribes a relationship between a husband and a wife for, among other things, procreation.[5] The words uttered by the two friends just before they jumped into the Rhine make this point clear: "Woe for our youth, for we have not been deemed worthy to see seed go forth from us or to reach old age." They say, in effect, "we are going to die young and not reach old age, and we will never fulfill our obligation as Jewish men to have children." This chapter also seeks to show that the language employed by the mid-twelfth-century chronicler to describe the love between the two young men is reminiscent of the poetic jargon often utilized by members of the Ashkenazi rabbinic elite in their exchange of letters.

In order to better understand this particular medieval idea of male-male friendship, the chapter begins with a brief discussion of three notions of friendship that influenced the various ways that friendships were conceptualized not only in medieval Ashkenaz but in subsequent Jewish thought as well. Two are biblical: the notion of friendship presented in Ecclesiastes and the friendship of David and Jonathan. The third is rabbinic, as found in *Avot de-Rabbi Natan*. This is followed by a discussion of male-male friendship propagated during the first half of the thirteenth century by the aforementioned two German rabbis and exemplified in the late eleventh century by the story of Shmuel and Yehiel. Apart from their love story and a fifteenth-century letter a young man wrote to his friend, to which I will return at the end of the chapter, this study focuses on social constructions of friendships encouraged by the medieval rabbinic elite.

When studying the concept of friendship in the premodern era, a time referred to by historians as "before sexuality," we need to remember that categories such as homosexuality and heterosexuality, with all their implications, did not exist until the end of the nineteenth century.[6] The social focus was on people's actions, whether they deviated from social conventions or remained within the boundaries of hegemonic sexual norms.[7] Before we explore these biblical, late antique, and medieval Jewish ideas of friendship, it should be emphasized that one basic assumption has remained constant in Western history until the nineteenth century: "true" friendship has always been conceptualized as a masculine activity.[8]

EXAMPLES OF FRIENDSHIP IN THE HEBREW BIBLE

In four verses, the book of Ecclesiastes delineates a notion of male friendship and its various characteristics, reminiscent of the one found in the Sumerian epic *Gilgamesh and Humbaba* and among Greek philosophers:[9] "Two are better off than one, in that they have greater benefit from their earning. For should they fall, one can raise the other; but woe betide him who is alone and falls with no companion to raise him! Further, when two lie together they are warm; but how can he who is alone get warm? Also, if one attacks, two can stand up to him. A three-fold cord is not readily broken!"[10] Mordechai Zer-Kavod points to four components on which this friendship is based: "a. for an increased income; b. for mutual assistance; c. for health reasons; d. for protection."[11] Unlike Zer-Kavod, Brian McGuire compares this idea of friendship to *Societas*—a partnership or alliance—comprising guidance, warmth, and defense.[12] The significant difference between Zer-Kavod and McGuire is their interpretation of the verse "Further, when two lie together they are warm; but how can he who is alone get warm?" Zer-Kavod refers to the mutual warmth resulting from the concern for the physical health of the two friends, while McGuire chooses a bolder interpretative approach that allows him to include an emotional aspect along with the physical. Neither commentator claims that this relationship includes a sexual component, but unlike McGuire, Zer-Kavod ignores the intimacy involved in the physical contact between the friends. The relationship described in Ecclesiastes seems to be egalitarian and nonhierarchical by either class or gender, and the mutuality of the relationship is emphasized. The author of Ecclesiastes does not explicitly address the emotional aspect involved in the relationship, nor does he expand on the two friends' commitment to each other. These, as we shall see, were the ideas that formed the basis for the well-known biblical account of the relationship between David and Jonathan.

David and Jonathan's friendship serves as a prototype in Western culture for a committed and intimate relationship between two men, a story William Burgwinkle describes as one of the most moving love stories in Western culture.[13] Alongside the friendships of Achilles and Patroclus, Glaucus and Diomedes, and Orestes and Pylades, the account of the love between the prince and the young redheaded shepherd has contributed greatly to how Western culture understands, defines, and circumscribes love in general and love among men in particular. To this day, their story is a source of inspiration for many. According to the biblical story, David and Jonathan's friendship included an alliance that was sanctified in a sacred rite. This covenant was based on loyalty and mutual support, and it continued to thrive despite great distance and even death, much like the ideal friendship described by Cicero and Aristotle.[14] Expressions of love, such as "Jonathan loved David as himself,"[15] were part of this friendship in both words and deeds as well as physical contact, kisses and embraces, and tears shed when parting from each other: "They kissed each other and wept together; David wept longer."[16] Their friendship could withstand jealousy, and each provided support to the other even when this opposed one's own wishes. The friendship also had an ingrained spiritual component, which sustained the relationship and allowed it to thrive, as Jonathan's words testify: "For we two have sworn to each other in the name of the Lord: 'May the Lord be [witness] between you and me, and between your offspring and mine, forever!'"[17] By late antiquity, as we will see, the understanding of friendship had somewhat changed.

THE CONCEPTION OF FRIENDSHIP IN THE RABBINIC TREATISES PIRKEI AVOT AND AVOT DE-RABBI NATAN

The rabbinic conception of male friendships underscored studying together as the main reason for forming such close relationships. There were, however, other components to the rabbinic notion of male bonding that contributed to the formation of an intimate relationship between two men.

The well-known dictum in tractate *Pirkei Avot* 1.6 to "make yourself a teacher and acquire a friend" provided the conceptual basis that the author of *Avot de-Rabbi Natan* later developed into a concise notion of friendship. This view of male friendship included a multifaceted social interaction, an intimate relationship, and mutual trust: "And GET THEE A COMPANION: how so? This teaches that a man should get a companion for himself, to eat with him, drink with him, study scripture with him, study Mishnah with him, sleep with him, and reveal to him all his secrets, the secrets of the Torah and the secrets of worldly things."[18] While this conception of friendship is not as comprehensive as the one found in Cicero's "On Friendship," a careful examination of it within the context of other rabbinic sources of late antiquity exposes a facet of rabbinic masculinity that was probably part of the social fabric of the intellectual elite. This notion of male bonding, which exerted its influence on Jewish thinkers throughout the ages, enumerates four activities that define the relationship: eating and drinking together, studying together, sleeping together, and confiding in each other.[19] The friendship includes the physical, emotional, and intellectual expressions involved in forging an intimate bond between two men. While David and Jonathan's relationship manifests the display of love in words and actions, the author of *Avot de-Rabbi Natan* does not list love as a component of male friendship. However, the activities that define the friendship and especially the suggestion that they share their secrets clearly reflect an emotional aspect of the relationship, and it stands to reason that feelings of affection and love were indeed intended to be part of it.

The author of *Avot de-Rabbi Natan* employs the concept of friendship found in Ecclesiastes as a basis for the advantages of learning together: "When two such friends study Torah together, if one of them should err regarding a *halakhah* (matter of law), or a premise; wrongly pronounce the pure impure, or the impure pure, permit the forbidden, or forbid the permitted, his friend can mend his mistake. For it is said: Two are better than one."[20] Studying in pairs diminishes the fear of making mistakes, such as confusing halakhic categories or crossing the lines of normative behavior. While the author of *Avot de-Rabbi Natan* does not limit the friendly interaction only to the realm of the dialectic, he does lead us to conclude that studying together is the main purpose of this friendship. As we will see, this idea was also a central component of the kind of friendship advocated by German rabbis in the early thirteenth century. According to *Avot de-Rabbi Natan*, the final component of friendship is the suggestion that friends confide in each other, emphasizing that the two should share secrets of the Torah as well as personal secrets. Sharing secrets is an act that necessarily calls for mutual trust and the expectation that these secrets will not be used to harm one's friend.

The representation of David and Jonathan's relationship in the Hebrew Bible and the notion of friendship in *Avot de-Rabbi Natan* are based on reciprocal trust and mutual feelings of confidence, intimacy, and a willingness to share secrets. Both also include a spiritual dimension that unites the two friends and maintains the friendship. For David and Jonathan, God was the binding force; in *Avot de-Rabbi Natan*, it is the Torah.

TYPES OF FRIENDSHIP IN THE WRITINGS OF R. ELEAZAR B. JUDAH

The late eleventh-century love story of Shmuel and Yehiel with which I began alludes to David and Jonathan's relationship by invoking a phrase from 2 Samuel 1:23: "Cherished in life, for they loved each other exceedingly, they were not parted in death."[21] And although the medieval story does not mention overcoming jealousy, altruistic motives as part of the friendship, or a covenant, it nonetheless resembles the biblical account in its intense love, in both words and deeds, in the physical contact between the two friends (embracing, kissing, holding hands, and crying together), in the spiritual dimension that bonded them ("let us fall into the hands of the Lord"), and in its enduring commitment in life and death. Was this type of intimate relationship a unique phenomenon in medieval Ashkenaz?

The sources indicate that the concept of a close, nonsexual friendship between two men was advocated in the early thirteenth century by two leading German rabbis, R. Judah b. Samuel and R. Eleazar b. Judah, who stressed the social value inherent in this type of relationship. For them, a close friendship between two men was a social institution that could contribute to a man's spiritual development while simultaneously serving as an effective tool to deal with sexual temptations. Moreover, both rabbis appropriated the institution of friendship in order to propagate a sharp gender segregation. While their writings do not present a detailed model of friendship such as the one in *Avot de-Rabbi Natan*, their writings do contain abundant references to the subject. We also find a recognition that this type of close relationship can contribute to individual pietistic disposition as well as to the community as a whole.

In his commentary on the prayer book, R. Eleazar names three types of friendships: those between acquaintances (*ḥaverim*), friends (*amitim*), and confidants (*rei'im*). The difference between them lies in the level of closeness and the frequency of their meetings: "An acquaintance is the one who leaves his place and befriends someone in another place, or reunites with someone after they were separated. A friend visits [his friend] infrequently. A confidant visits him [his friend] habitually and reveals his secret to him."[22] We may conclude, according to the order in which these three types of relationships are presented, that "acquaintance" represents the loosest relationship of the three. "Friend" indicates a more significant social bonding, though not a close one. "Confidant," however, may indicate an intimate relationship between two men based on trust and the confidence that the secrets the friends share will not be exploited. Although R. Eleazar does not mention that the two confidants study Torah together, in his pietistic circle, this traditional activity was one of the central reasons for forming male friendships.

FRIENDSHIP, CHERUBS, AND STUDYING TORAH

To emphasize that studying the Torah is one of the main purposes for forming close friendships between two men, R. Judah compares friends to the two cherubs (*keruvim*) who, according to the Torah, guarded the ark of the covenant: "And in resemblance to two cherubs, who shield the Torah, thus two [friends] should share words [of the Torah]."[23] For R. Judah, the intrinsic value of friendship transcends the physical and psychological realms; it generates metaphysical benefits for both friends, and perhaps more important, the Torah itself can benefit from her two guardians. While for R. Judah the cherubs symbolize two friends studying together, for R. Eleazar they represent a loving relationship between two men: "When a man loves his friend, he looks at him with a glowing face [*mabit panav be-kirun panim*] and speaks to him with affability, but when he does not love him [his friend], he looks to another direction and talks to him fiercely; that is why the cherubs were facing each other."[24] This idea contrasts with an earlier rabbinic view disseminated by the French commentator Rashi in the second half of the eleventh century, which portrayed the cherubs as a man and a woman embracing each other.[25]

For R. Judah, however, the idea of two friends studying together does not necessarily refer to scholars who dedicate all their time to learning. A good friend may also be of assistance to someone who is preoccupied with his economic livelihood and is incapable of devoting the necessary attention to studying: "And if his heart is overburdened with his business, he should study with his friend, because he who sits alone gets tired easily."[26] According to R. Judah, as long as the relationship protects the two men from sinning, the friendship will persist even when they are separated by a distance: "There are righteous men, who performed good deeds together, like two friends who consult each other to perform the *mitsvot*, or they are [physically] distant from each other but their actions are similar, and they avoid sinning; it is as if they are studying before the Glory."[27] Surprisingly, "studying together" does not necessitate the presence of friends in the same locality; by this, the author seems to imply the acquisition of common values and adherence to a similar world view. If they abide by the pietistic doctrines and practices, despite the distance between them, their friendship will be strong, and they will still be considered as "studying together." Furthermore, the advantages of friendship are not limited to scholarly interaction. This notion of friendship allows one of the friends to fully engage in studying Torah while the other tends to his livelihood.

FRIENDSHIP, TORAH STUDY, AND SEXUAL URGES

Torah study was a central reason for forming a friendship. Yet another prominent motive was to help the friends overcome their sexual urges. Torah study, for R. Judah and his students, was a major means to combat sexual temptation, and one way to pursue this activity was with a close friend.[28]

In contrast to R. Judah's encouragement of close friendship, Rashi, drawing upon a verse in Proverbs (25:17), warns against too much intimacy: "Just as, if you find honey, and it is sweet to your palate, you must not eat [too much] of it lest you become sated with it and vomit it, so should you visit your friend sparingly; although he is among [your kin], refrain from going there daily lest he become sated with you and hate you." R. Judah, however, uses the same verse from Proverbs to impart a very different message:

> [It is said in Prov. 25:17,] "Let your foot be seldom in your friend's house." However, the Sages said (*Pirkei Avot* 1.4): "May your house be a meeting place for the wise." But, *in your friend's house* [refers to] his wife. The rabbi should have a space for study separated [from the rest of the house], so that the incoming and outgoing students would not look at the rabbi's wife or his daughter or his daughter-in-law.... "Let your foot be seldom in your friend's house": so that you regularly study Torah and refrain from mundane talk. "Let your foot be seldom [in your friends' house]": should he visit his friend for many hours, he may need to use the toilet and thus be a burden on his friend. "Let your foot be seldom in your friend's house lest he be weary of thee." But all these [warnings] are not said about men such as Abaye and Rava in the house of R. Joseph, and R. Judah in the house of Shmuel, who studied together all day long.²⁹

If the words of Proverbs intended to prevent or reduce visits to a friend's home, then how could one fulfill the provisions of the Mishnah that a person's home should be "a gathering place for sages"? Attempting to settle this conflict, R. Judah summons an analogy used in rabbinic discourse—namely, the expression "his home is his wife"³⁰—to renounce the advice to avoid visiting a friend's home. In R. Judah's opinion, the words of Proverbs warn first and foremost against the visitor turning his attention to the rabbi's or friend's wife, as well as to the other women of the house, instead of focusing on the study of Torah. Thus R. Judah employs the warning issued by the author of Proverbs to advocate clear gender segregation.

There is another reference in *Sefer Ḥasidim* to the warning in Proverbs against frequently visiting a friend's house, and once again we see that R. Judah's major concern is that the visitor would be distracted by his friend's wife: "Let your foot be seldom [in your friends' house]. If two merchants are friends and one has a beautiful wife, better that he [who has the beautiful wife] come to your house."[31] Here we find a recommendation to avoid visiting a friend's home if his wife is beautiful and there is a chance that this might awaken the visitor's sexual urge. In this case, the friends should meet at the home of the one whose wife is not beautiful. R. Judah's reason stems from the concern that the study of Torah would be compromised. As long as the purpose of the visits is to study and not to engage in trivialities or be distracted by the presence of beautiful women, there is no reason to forbid or reduce the frequency of the visits. On the contrary, they should be encouraged. Around the same time that *Sefer Ḥasidim* was written, the communal ordinances (*takkanot ha-kahal*) of Speyer, Worms, and Mainz ruled that "every man shall set aside time for study."[32] It seems that for R. Judah and R. Eleazar, the preferred way to fulfill this communal ordinance and halakhic imperative was to find a good friend with whom to study.[33]

According to R. Judah, one could win the endless battle against sexual temptations through marriage. A man should marry as early as possible and could then satisfy his sexual desire with his wife in any way he wished:[34] "And no place is it written that a man may not enjoy his wife in any way he sees fit, lest he may look at other women."[35] This androcentric concept, originating in the Talmud (BT *Nedarim* 20a–b), also appears in the writings of R. Eleazar.[36] In a related attempt to overcome sexual urges, R. Judah and R. Eleazar encourage homosocial environments, such as the study hall in the rabbi's house, which should be, according to *Sefer Ḥasidim*, clearly separated from the rest of the house and the women in it. Yet it is hard to imagine that this recommendation could be practiced in the crowded and relatively small houses of medieval Ashkenaz, with its unavoidable gender interactions. However, even if this pietistic social vision never materialized, it was an idea advocated by an influential rabbi and must have had some influence on his followers. In any case, for R. Judah, the concept of friendship was directly linked to these imaginary and longed for homosocial spaces, where a man was expected to bond with another man and form a positive relationship with his teacher. In the words of *Sefer Ḥasidim*, "May he have a good friend and a good rabbi to beware of women."[37] In short, then, a man should seek to battle sexual temptation by way of an early marriage, male friendship, and association with his rabbi.

FRIENDSHIP, SHARING SECRETS, AND GENDER BOUNDARIES

For R. Judah, as we have seen, the concept of a close friendship between two men was linked to his vision of gender segregation. This was further emphasized by the idea that a central element of this kind of close friendship was the sharing of secrets, something we have already seen in both the biblical account of the relationship between David and Jonathan and the sort of friendship advocated in *Avot de-Rabbi Natan*. This was also a central characteristic of the relationship between two confidants described by R. Eleazar b. Judah. The recognition that revealing secrets could endanger the one who shares confidences with his friend, however, led some Talmudic-era and medieval rabbis to point to the risky nature of doing so. To the Talmudic advice "Let many be those who greet you; reveal your secrets to one in a thousand" (BT *Sanhedrin* 100b), Rashi added, "So you are loved by all, and nevertheless (*ve-af al pi khen*), you should not reveal your secret to everyone, but to one in a thousand."[38] In Rashi's view, a friendship between two men that is based on mutual trust is extremely rare, "one in a thousand." R. Eleazar, on the other hand, uses the same Talmudic phrase "Share your secret with one in a thousand" not so much to highlight the danger in sharing secrets but rather to stress the positive aspect of a relationship between two trusted friends. In R. Eleazar's words, "What only two know can be hidden, [if] three [know] everyone will know."[39] For R. Eleazar, this type of friendship offers a safe space that cannot exist in a group of three or more; in this way, secrets can be shared while withholding them from the rest of the community and avoiding unnecessary embarrassment. The idea that a relationship between two confidants allows a space where secrets may safely be shared appears again in R. Eleazar's writings: "If you have found a friend like yourself, share your secret with him."[40] Whether R. Eleazar is referring to sharing esoteric knowledge or secrets of the Torah, matters having to do with prayer, or personal secrets, this process entails a relationship based on trust and the assurance that these secrets will not be exploited.

It is important also to consider the gender aspect of sharing secrets, as secrets may be revealed only to other men. *Sefer Ḥasidim* says so explicitly: "Secrets should not be shared with women."[41] Similarly, the eleventh-century German rabbi Eliezer ha-Gadol b. Isaac of Mainz warns men against telling secrets to their wives while stressing the importance of concealing secrets shared by other men: "My son, do not reveal your secret to your wife, be trustworthy (*ne 'eman ruaḥ*) to every man, and do not reveal [his] secret when you fight with him, all the more so, when he is on good terms with you."[42] Even the marital bond was not viewed as a safe haven for sharing secrets. Only a trustworthy male friend could become the sole avenue for unburdening the heart. However, this trustworthy friend should be carefully selected.

The author of *Sefer Ḥasidim* suggests two ways of selecting a friend. The first is related to the manner in which the designated friend is treated by other members of the community: "If . . . you see a man who is despised [by members of the community] because he is manly and quiet [*gevartan ve-shatkan*] . . . , and he listens to you, him you should choose as your friend and pupil."[43] The instruction is to befriend a man who suffers scorn without reacting, but only if this man would be willing to listen to his new friend. In other words, the despised man should not only agree to be his new friend but also be willing to learn from his new friend the ways of the pious. Accordingly, *Sefer Ḥasidim* emphasizes elsewhere that "the righteous are glad to be humiliated and disgraced for God's sake."[44] This recommendation praises the ability to remain silent when being scorned and the ability to show self-restraint, which was considered a manly virtue. Not only should a man who is scorned remain silent but he also must ensure that his family, friends, and students do not react to the insults hurled at him.[45]

The second recommendation concerning how to select a friend is to inquire how he behaved in previous relationships. One should explore whether the intended friend ended the previous friendship with a dispute. If this was indeed the case, then further inquiries should be made. Did he reveal to others the secrets his companion shared with him while they were friends? In that case, he is untrustworthy. However, if the potential friend does not blame the ex-friend with false accusations, "him you should choose as your friend."[46] This warning in *Sefer Ḥasidim* is telling not only because it sheds light on the process of choosing a new friend and directs attention to potential hazards that might arise within the relationship but also because it emphasizes one of friendship's main purposes: to establish a safe zone for sharing secrets and having confidence that if the relationship turns sour, mutual trust will not be betrayed.

BETWEEN "FRIEND" AND "WIFE"

Another aspect of friendship advocated by R. Eleazar b. Judah can be found in his book *Hokhmat ha-Nefesh*. His interpretation of the centerpiece of Jewish liturgy, the *Shema Yisrael* (Deut. 13:7), presents a comparison between a man's wife and his best friend:

> For there are three human qualities. There is the one who never sins and does God's will, fearing calamities. And there is one who does God's will hoping for personal gain. And there is one who does [God's will] for pure love without anticipating a reward. And in the future, this attribute of not anticipating a reward [will prevail]....
> And you should love with all your heart, so that you will think how to conduct your own will thoughtfully. And with all your soul, [i.e.,] with your wife and your friend who is like your own soul.[47]

R. Eleazar distinguishes between three ways of worshiping God. Some avoid sinning because they are afraid of God's wrath, others hope that God will endow them with all that is good as a reward for their dedication, and some love God unconditionally. This latter type of love, according to R. Eleazar, will prevail in the future, but in the meantime, we may fulfill the Torah's commandment to love God "with all your soul" only within a conjugal relationship and with a trustworthy friend. Seemingly, by juxtaposing "wife" and "friend who is like your own soul" side by side and as equally important, R. Eleazar may mean that a "wife" and a "friend who is like your own soul" are two complementary ways to show love for God, through sexuality and the affective relationship of friendship. Procreation with one's wife is one way and the other is loving one's friend, whom you trust and to whom you can safely reveal your secrets. This may also mean that just as a wife is unique to a man in comparison to all other women, so does a "friend who is like your soul" denote the friend's exclusive status.[48]

CONCLUSION

The close friendship advocated by these two German rabbis was designed, first and foremost, to help friends bolster their worship of God in order to study the Torah and perform *mitsvot*, as well as to combat sexual temptation. It encouraged a meaningful and intimate relationship between two men, and it was part of their social vision for a community segregated by gender. The benefits of friendship transcended the walls of the study hall and were not based on scholarly interaction alone. Friendships were to be founded on trust, to serve as a channel for sharing secrets and to ensure that these confidences would not be exploited. Moreover, this intimate relationship could be sustained even when friends were separated by distance. Such a friendship was to be not a matter of whim or impulse but rather one of commitment and awareness of the effect of each person's behavior on the other.[49]

The tragic love story of Shmuel ben Gedaliah and Yehiel ben Samuel with which I began describes the two lovers as "Cherished in life, for they loved each other exceedingly, they were not parted in death."[50] Their story suggests that this type of special friendship was already a culturally accepted phenomenon in the Jewish community in Germany by the end of the eleventh century. By the end of the twelfth century and during the first half of the thirteenth century, R. Judah and his student R. Eleazar further encouraged this type of intimate relationship between two men. Finally, the language used by the chronicler to describe the love of Shmuel and Yehiel also reflects medieval rabbinic discourse employed in letters exchanged by the Ashkenazi rabbis. An earlier example of this literary genre from the late eleventh century is the response of R. Shlomo ben Shimshon to his student R. Yitzhak Bar Yitzhak, in which he appropriates the words of David in his lament to Jonathan, intertwined with the Song of Songs' language of erotic love: "How great is the pleasantness of my dear one because his wondrous love for me is better than the love of few, and numerous mighty may not be able to quench it because I desire him, I yearn for him since I met him."[51]

One of the more poetic examples in this genre is the response of R. Eliezer ha-Gadol of Mainz to his student R. Yitzchak Ben-Menahem, one of the better-known scholars of France in the third quarter of the eleventh century: "And I love him with pleasant and wondrous love and his soul is bound with mine."[52] Such expressions of love were common throughout the Middle Ages.[53] They contain expressions of intense love and sometimes homoerotic language.[54] We should, however, interpret these sources cautiously and not as necessarily indicating physically intimate relationships between two friends, unless additional evidence can support this claim. In many cases, these descriptions of love reflect a relationship between a rabbi and his student. However, while the words of love in these letters may be understood as manifesting conventional poetic discourse and do not necessarily indicate true feelings, the wording of the story of Shmuel and Yehiel suggests that the mid-twelfth-century chronicler did indeed perceive this friendship as a true relationship between friends.

The relationship between the two young men did not purport to be an alternative to a relationship between husband and wife. Instead, its purpose was to supplement the marital bond, fulfilling needs that were commonly unmet, including studying and performing *mitsvot* together and providing a safe space where secrets could be shared. Shmuel and Yehiel faced death willingly: "It is better for us to die here, honoring God, so that we may walk together in heaven."[55] They were only sorry that they would not be able to fulfill what was expected of them as Jewish men: to procreate and thus ensure the continuation of the Jewish people.

The notions of friendship discussed here are prescriptive in nature and aimed to mold appropriate male behavior. Except for the love story of Shmuel and Yehiel, I have found no descriptive textual evidence of similar friendships in Ashkenazi sources from the eleventh through fourteenth centuries. There is, however, an Ashkenazi source from the mid-fifteenth century, also from Germany, containing a letter in which an anonymous author was attempting to persuade his friend to join him on a journey to Erfurt, where a new Yeshiva had just opened:

> And now I have said I will ask you if you want to go with me, for my soul desires you and my love for you is eternal, and your soul is dear to me and I cannot be without you. Therefore, please let me know if you will go with me, and our strength will be together in one pocket, and your horse will be as mine and all your expenses will be on me. But there will always be a covenant between you and me, and no stranger shall intervene. Strong, we will get even stronger, stand by my side and be close to me, and we each will help each other, as two are better off than one. Therefore, prepare yourself to set out and come to me.[56]

Here we see once again how the words of Ecclesiastes "two are better off than one" exerted their influence on the conception of friendship in medieval Ashkenaz. The relationship portrayed in this letter, the love story of Shmuel and Yehiel, and the ideals of friendship advocated by R. Judah and R. Eleazar suggest that meaningful personal relationships between two men were an important and socially sanctioned form of practice in medieval Ashkenaz.

NOTES

1. Robert Chazan, *In the Year 1096: The First Crusade and the Jews* (Philadelphia: Jewish Publication Society, 1996), 44.
2. Regarding the dating of the chronicle, see Anna Sapir Abulafia, "The Interrelationship Between the Hebrew Chronicles on the First Crusade," *Journal of Semitic Studies* 27, no. 2 (Autumn 1982): 221–39.
3. Quoted in Chazan, *In the Year 1096*, 44.
4. Chazan presented the story in its entirety but did not interpret it (Chazan, 42–44). Israel Yuval defined Samuel and Yehiel as two friends but did not discuss the nature of the relationship. See Israel Yuval, "Vengeance and Damnation, Blood and Defamation: From Jewish Martyrdom to Blood Libel Accusations," *Zion* 58 (1993): 33–90, 69–70. Ezra Fleischer described them as brothers without providing evidence (Ezra Fleischer, "Yaḥasei Notsrim-Yehudim be-Yemei ha-Benayim be-Re 'i Akum," *Zion* 59 [1994]: 300–301).
5. BT *Yevamot* 63b.
6. See Froma Zeitlin, John Winkler, and David Halperin, introduction to *Before Sexuality: The Construction of Erotic Experience in the Ancient Greek World*, ed. Froma Zeitlin, John Winkler, and David Halperin (Princeton: Princeton University Press, 1990), 3–20. The term *heterosexuality* was coined toward the end of the nineteenth century and was first used in the 1920s. It only became part of public discourse in the 1960s. See Jonathan Katz, *The Invention of Heterosexuality* (Chicago: University of Chicago Press, 2007), especially chap. 2.
7. See Michel Foucault, *The History of Sexuality* (New York: Pantheon, 1978).
8. See Constant J. Mews and Neville Chiavaroli, "The Latin West," in *Friendship: A History*, ed. Barbara Caine (London: Equinox, 2009), 83.
9. The Sumerian epic tells of two friends who are making their way to save humanity from the monster Humbaba, but at the last minute, one of them, Enkidu, regrets his decision, and his friend Gilgamesh tries to change his mind. See Stephen Mitchell, *Gilgamesh: A New English Version* (New York: Free Press, 2004), 122. For the Aristotelian notion of friendship, see Aristotle, *Nicomachean Ethics*, trans. W. D. Ross (Kitchener, ON: Batoche Books, 1999), 127.
10. Ecclesiastes 4:9–12. Unless stated otherwise, all translated biblical quotes are from *Tanakh: The Holy Scriptures; The New JPS Translation According to the Traditional Hebrew Text*, 2nd ed. (Philadelphia: Jewish Publication Society, 1985).
11. Mordechai Zer-Kavod, *Da 'at Mikra: Ḥamesh Megillot* (Jerusalem: Mossad ha-Rav Kook, 1973), 25n21.
12. Brian P. McGuire, *Friendship and Community: The Monastic Experience, 350–1250* (Kalamazoo, MI: Cistercian Publications, 1988), xxii.
13. William E. Burgwinkle, *Sodomy, Masculinity and Law in Medieval Literature: France and England, 1050–1230* (Cambridge: Cambridge University Press, 2004), 33.
14. 1 Samuel 18:1–4. Aristotle, *Nicomachean Ethics*, 132; Cicero Marcus Tullius, *On Friendship*, trans. E. S. Shuckburgh (Urbana, IL: Project Gutenberg, 2009), http://www.gutenberg.org/files/2808/2808-h/2808-h.htm.
15. 1 Samuel 18:1.
16. 1 Samuel 20:41.
17. 1 Samuel 20:42. The story of David and Jonathan has historically served as an ideal of love in general and specifically between two men.
18. *Avot de-Rabbi Natan* 8.3, translated by Judah Goldin as *The Fathers According to Rabbi Nathan* (New Haven: Yale University Press, 1955), 50.
19. See, for example, *Sifrei on Deuteronomy* §305; *Midrash on Proverbs*, §§12 and 20; and *Yalkut Shimoni* on Torah Parashat Pinhas.

20. *Avot de-Rabbi Nathan* 8.3.
21. This biblical phrase is found in David's lament for Jonathan and his father, Saul. However, in the Middle Ages, this phrase was often associated with close friendships between two men, as it is in the story of Yehiel and Shmuel.
22. *Perushei Sidur ha-Tefilah la-Rokeah* (Jerusalem: Makhon ha-Rav Herschler, 1992), 372.
23. *Sefer Hasidim* §§1836 and 780 (unless specified otherwise, all quotes from *Sefer Hasidim* are from Cod. Parm. 3280).
24. *Perushei Siddur ha-Tefilah*, 357.
25. Rashi, *Yoma* 54a.
26. *Sefer Hasidim* §748.
27. *Sefer Hasidim* §1052.
28. See Eyal Levinson, "The Conceptualization of the Yetser and the Male Body in the Masculine Sexual Discourse in Sefer Hasidim" (master's thesis, Bar Ilan University, 2011).
29. *Sefer Hasidim* §800 (italics mine).
30. BT *Yoma* 2a (translation mine).
31. *Sefer Hasidim* §58.
32. Louis Finkelstein, *Jewish Self Government in the Middle Ages* (New York: Jewish Theological Seminary of America, 1924), 248.
33. This commandment is based on Joshua 1:8.
34. *Sefer Hasidim* §1084.
35. *Sefer Hasidim* §1111.
36. Eleazar of Worms, *Sefer ha-Rokeah ha-Gadol*, ed. S. Schneersohn (Jerusalem: Weinfeld Publishers, 1960), 23.
37. *Sefer Hasidim* §820.
38. Rashi, BT *Sanhedrin* 100b (translation mine).
39. Eleazar of Worms, *Sefer ha-Rokeah ha-Gadol*, 14.
40. Eleazar of Worms, *Hokhmat ha-Nefesh* (Lamberg: Lamberg Publishing, 1875), 3.
41. *Sefer Hasidim* §69.
42. *Orhot Hayyim hu Tsava'at Rabbi Eliezer ha-Gadol* (Venice, 1623), 6a.
43. *Sefer Hasidim* §781.
44. *Sefer Hasidim* §194.
45. *Sefer Hasidim* §118.
46. *Sefer Hasidim* §1253.
47. Eleazar of Worms, *Hokhmat ha-Nefesh*, 20b.
48. This idea echoes the well-known rabbinic saying "One who loves his wife as he loves his own soul, and who honors her more than his own body" (*Derekh Eretz Rabba*, chap. 2). This instruction can be found also in the Babylonian Talmud (*Yevamot* 62b), except that the word *soul* is replaced by the word *body*: "Who loves his wife as his own body, and honors her more than his own body."
49. *Sefer Hasidim* §1007.
50. Quoted in Chazan, *In the Year 1096*, 44.
51. *Teshuvot Hokhmei Tsarfat ve-Lutir*, ed. Yoel Hakohen Miller (Vienna: Alkala Publishers, 1881), 30.
52. *Teshuvot Hokhmei Tsarfat ve-Lutir*, 40.
53. Here are two examples from the thirteenth century: The Responsa of the Maharam of Rothenburg, part 3 §2; and *Shut Maharam Ohr Zarua* §191.
54. This form of expression was common in the Middle Ages not only among Jewish scholars but also among their Christian counterparts. See Julian Haseldine, "Friendship, Intimacy and Corporate Networking in the Twelfth Century: The Politics of Friendship in the Letters of Peter the Venerable," *English Historical Review* 519 (2011): 251–80.
55. Quoted in Chazan, *In the Year 1096*, 44.
56. *Igrot Shelomim* (Augsburg, 1534) §45. See also Israel Yuval, "An Ashkenazic Autobiography of the 14th Century," *Tarbiz* 55 (1986): 551.

CHAPTER 2

God in the Face of the Other
Mystical Friendship in the Zohar

EITAN P. FISHBANE

Since antiquity, the pursuit of wisdom has been deeply intertwined with ideals of fellowship and friendship. Perhaps nowhere more famously than in the dialogues of Plato, the quest for knowledge and understanding was bound up in the dynamics of interpersonal relations, the lived experience of camaraderie and love between friends. Indeed, the dialogic tales of the *Republic* and the *Symposium*, among others, situate the process of philosophizing within the organic give-and-take of companionship, the love cultivated between individual friends and the group of wisdom-seekers as a whole.[1] In the Platonic corpus, the narrative representation of master and disciples on a wandering journey is the setting for discussions of the just and the good, and it is precisely through the living experience of conversation—the face-to-face encounter with the friend who shares that irrepressible quest for wisdom—that true understanding is attained.[2] What is more, in the *Lysis*, Plato's early dialogue, the question of friendship itself is probed by the friends and their teacher in conversation,[3] laying the groundwork for the discussion of *eros* in the *Symposium*.[4] As other scholars have shown, this Socratic dimension of philosophy—this art of dialogue—reverberates in later medieval traditions, including the development of Jewish philosophy.[5]

For our purposes here, it is also important to note that Jewish mystical culture—and the search for the spiritual-theological wisdom that dwells at its heart—unfolded in the context of similar circles of fellowship. While there certainly were Jewish mystics who were more solitary in their practices, the history of Jewish mysticism is notably marked by a succession of social circles of spiritual companionship and shared purpose, usually centered on a master teacher. From the microcommunities of Heikhalot mystics[6] to the circles of medieval German pietists (Ḥasidei Ashkenaz),[7] late twelfth-century Provençal kabbalists,[8] and thirteenth-century groups in Iberian locales such as Gerona, Barcelona, Toledo, and Burgos,[9] mystical reflection and learning occurred deliberately in the context of interpersonal relationships, within brotherhoods of spiritual practice and theological rumination. But if the lived nature of such spiritual societies of learning and companionship was widespread among Jews in medieval Europe, the phenomenon was elevated to a fresh and vivid representation in the *Zohar*, the masterpiece of Jewish mysticism that was composed collaboratively by a series of Castilian kabbalists from approximately 1270 to 1330. Indeed, spiritual friendship lies at the heart of zoharic literary texture: the text features an episodic tale about the second-century sage Rabbi Shimon bar Yoḥai and his band of disciples wandering through the countryside of ancient Galilee in search of new-old mystical wisdom. In contrast to the purely metaphysical and exegetical nature of other contemporaneous kabbalistic books, the *Zohar* alternates between this narrative about the mystical companions and a mystical midrash that (partially) emulates ancient midrashic form—homilies that are framed as a sequence of hermeneutical discourses spoken by the friends on the road while traveling. The narrative genre of zoharic textuality, written pseudepigraphically and attributed to R. Shimon bar Yoḥai (RaShBY) himself, is a work of the medieval Jewish fictional imagination,[10] and this invented world centers on the passionate friendship between Bar Yoḥai's disciples, on the one hand, and the expressed love between the master and his pupils, on the other. Indeed, the dramatization of this *eros* in the spiritual friendships of RaShBY's circle, along with the texture of the creativity that emerges in the communal gathering before the master teacher, led one scholar to articulate a convincing phenomenological correlation between the *Idra Rabba* scene of the *Zohar* and the *Symposium* of Plato.[11]

Along the path of the mystics' wanderings in the zoharic story, the kabbalists meet various other characters, many of whom first appear to be simpletons of one sort or another and who often turn out to be great mystical sages in disguise. This feature of zoharic narrative is part of a literary phenomenon known to scholars of comparative literature as anagnorisis, the event and process of recognition and the discovery of a character's surprising true nature.[12] In this way, the *Zohar* may be located in the broader frame-tale tradition of medieval Iberian letters,[13] a literary genre that delights in the dramatization of friends traveling together from place to place in search of wisdom and in the pivotal narrative moments in which anagnorisis takes place. Thus in the same way in which historical circles of kabbalistic fellowship existed,[14] the fictional world of the *Zohar* represented a dynamic group of mystics who were devoted to a restless and collaborative search for the mysteries of the Torah. Indeed, this was one of the foundational insights advanced by Yehuda Liebes thirty years ago in a pioneering article claiming that the *Zohar*, long assumed to have been authored by one man (R. Moshe de Leon),[15] was in fact the work of a group of kabbalists in late thirteenth-century Castile.[16] Liebes argued that the circle of kabbalists represented in the zoharic frame-tale was a reflection of the real-life fellowship of Castilian Jewish mystics who authored the text.

For the purposes of this essay—leaving aside the question of collaborative authorship (or a cumulative compositional process)[17]—I posit that the spiritual life dramatized in the scenes of the *Zohar* is fundamentally relational and interpersonal. The various members of R. Shimon bar Yoḥai's group of disciples are ubiquitously depicted as delighting in the moment of encounter with their fellow mystics and in the uplifting and sacred joy of fellowship. The Aramaic term of choice for this cluster of mystical friends—*ḥevrayya*—appears well over four hundred times in the voluminous pages of the *Zohar*, underscoring the social and communal lens through which the zoharic characters consider their purpose. The third-person narrator of the text takes pains to emphasize the sense of celebration and gratitude felt by individual members of the group when they happen upon one another on the road in their quest for kabbalistic knowledge and discovery. These moments of greeting, along with responses to having heard a powerful mystical teaching, are frequently accompanied by theatrical bodily gestures and expressions of overwhelming emotion.[18] Whether it is a kiss,[19] prostration, the raising of hands in blessing, or weeping, the drama of human encounter—and the disclosure of secrets that takes place through it—constitutes the fulcrum of zoharic narrative representation. Integrated with this interpersonal drama is the sense, articulated frequently by the various zoharic speakers, that those who live in the generation of the extraordinary R. Shimon bar Yoḥai are privy to a singular, perhaps even messianic, level of revelation: the generation of RaShBY is believed to be unlike any other before the coming of the Messiah, an era when even the most hidden secrets are revealed and known.[20] In this way, the love of the master for his disciples and the reciprocal love of the disciples for their master dwell in the soul of zoharic representations of and reflections on spiritual friendship.

The heart of this relational structure—the drama of spiritual companionship, discipleship, and the celebration of strangers who turn out to be hidden mystic sages—is further described as a divine encounter. To meet the kabbalistic friend face-to-face is nothing less than a revelation of the divine Countenance. Various members of the *ḥevrayya* often greet one another with versions of the exclamation "How happy are we to behold the face of the *Shekhinah*!"[21] Mystical study and the sharing of secrets are likened to—and perhaps in some fundamental way *are*—a communion with the feminine dimension of divinity. As *Shekhinah* wanders the dusty road of Jewish exile with the people of Israel, She is incarnate in the face of the mystic friend and most especially in the event of shared Torah study. As such, the deepest mystery of friendship in the *Zohar* is that the love of one's fellow kabbalist opens into a devotional encounter with God.[22]

Let me turn now to a rich zoharic pericope that weaves together story and homily into a reflection on the nature and purpose of human friendship between the kabbalists. As we shall see, the face-to-face relations among the mystical companions—the cultivation of brotherhood and the love that emerges through shared study—are understood by the zoharic authors (and expressed through the authoritative voice of R. Shimon) to be a mirror image of the desired face-to-face harmony between the lower male and female dimensions of divinity, *Tif'eret* and *Shekhinah*, respectively. What is more, the metaphysical balance and loving unity of parts of the divine Self are damaged by strife between the friends and then healed through love and harmony. As such, the earthly relational harmony activates a theurgic effect above, but a certain fluidity is also implied here and elsewhere: the union of *Tif'eret* and *Shekhinah* are incarnate, to some degree, in the moment of harmonious and loving friendship between the mystical companions. In the following source, R. Shimon receives his devoted disciples and instructs them in the mysteries of this cosmic isomorphic principle:

> It has been taught [that] R. Yosi said: One time the world was in need of rain, so R. Yeisa, R. Ḥizkiyah, and others from among the friends came before R. Shimon. They found him setting out to see R. Pinḥas ben Ya'ir.[23] Because he saw them, he opened and said (Psalm 133:1): "A song of ascents. Behold how good and how pleasant it is when brothers dwell together! What is [the meaning of] when brothers dwell together? [It is like] what is said (Exodus 25:20): Their faces, each toward his brother.[24] When they were one-to-one, gazing face-to-face, [it was like what] is written, Behold how good and how pleasant! But when the male turns his face away from the female, woe to the world!"[25]

Here R. Shimon continues with a bit of creative exegesis on Psalm 89:15 ("Righteousness and justice are the foundation of Your throne" [*tsedek u-mishpat mekhon kis'ekha*]), in which righteousness (*tsedek*) is understood to symbolically represent the male *Tif'eret* and justice (*mishpat*) the female *Shekhinah*. They are the foundation for the higher *sefirah*, *Binah* (here represented by the throne). Thus the cosmos is woefully out of balance when justice withdraws from righteousness—when *Tif'eret* and *Shekhinah* are in a state of separation. Upon completing this segment of his symbolic and interpretative discourse, which serves as a mode of indirect greeting to his disciples, R. Shimon addresses them more directly: "'I now see that you have come because the male does not dwell with the female.' He said: 'If for this you have come to me, go back, for today I have seen that all will be restored to dwell face-to-face. But if you have come for Torah, stay with me.' They said to him: 'We have come to the Master for it all! Release one of us to bring the good news to our brothers, the other friends, and we will sit before the Master.'"[26]

The implication that the inner divine male and female, the *sefirot Tif'eret* and *Shekhinah*, are in a state of separation (i.e., are not face-to-face) is drawn by R. Shimon and the friends from the earthly condition of drought. Rain, the overflow of palpable energy from the heavens, is thus understood to be a mundane manifestation of generative unity within divinity, a state of flow and plenty that is a function of *hieros gamos* and erotic copulation. In this sense, rain represents the release of the nourishing and generative energies that result from face-to-face unity, the metaphysical *eros* of divine male and female. We may also note the significant portrayal of R. Shimon as one who is able to see clairvoyantly that the drought will end and the rain will soon come, a prophetic forecast in which he anticipates the imminent restoration of the procreative unity between *Tif'eret* and *Shekhinah*: "If for this you have come to me, go back, for today I have seen [*de-ha yoma istaklana*] that all will be restored to dwell face-to-face [*de-yithadeir kola le-mishrei apin be-apin*]." In and of itself, this is a tantalizing mythology that offers a radical and metaphysically allusive interpretation of the presence or absence of rain in the world. For my purposes here, however, we also learn a great deal about the correlations made by the zoharic kabbalists between that supernal mythic drama and the *eros* of friendship and brotherhood among the earthly mystics, characterized in the same "face-to-face" terms.

The state of *shevet ahim gam yahad* (when brothers dwell together) is clearly understood by R. Shimon to be related directly to the harmonious unity of the divine male and female in an ideal face-to-face condition, thereby implying that there is an incarnated male-female *eros* activated between the male friends within the fellowship. This homoerotic tone (here framed as the transformation of the two male companions into male and female, in parallel to *Tif'eret* and *Shekhinah*) is one that scholars have observed already,[27] and it is a clear extension of the previously discussed principle that the face of the encountered male friend is most often described as the face of *Shekhinah*.[28] As Elliot Wolfson has argued,[29] this dynamic reflects some gender fluidity and transposition among the zoharic companions; sometimes their masculinity is overt, while in other moments, they are feminized as receivers of masculine energy from another kabbalist or the divine *Tif'eret*. Even if we were to question whether R. Shimon makes a direct correlation between the notion that the drought is a reflection of the withdrawal of *Tif'eret* from *Shekhinah* and the need for face-to-face loving brotherhood between the disciples, we may nevertheless observe the narrative prompting for his theosophical homily: the arrival of his beloved disciples to sit together with him in the study of Torah. The narrator explains R. Shimon's exclamation, *hinei mah tov u-mah na 'im shevet ahim gam yahad*, as being the direct consequence of his having laid eyes on his arriving disciples ("Because he saw them, he opened and said" [*keivan de-hama lon, patah ve-amar*]).

It is also significant to note that this correlation between the *ḥevrayya* and male-female sefirotic relation is further textured by the exegesis of Exodus 25:20 ("Their faces, each toward his brother" [*ufneihem ish el aḥiv*]), a verse that refers to the face-to-face gaze of the two cherubim.[30] In the lines that immediately precede the passage cited earlier, the zoharic speakers reflect on the meaning of the joined male and female faces of the cherubim, and it is in this context that the character R. Yitsḥak asserts, "From here we learn that wherever male and female are not found, one is not worthy to see the face of *Shekhinah.*" This is, of course, an allusion to the imperative for the male kabbalist to be joined in sanctity with his female spouse to achieve self-completion through matrimony. But its mention here—combined with one's worthiness to behold the face of *Shekhinah*, the assertion that the cosmos is dangerously impaired when *Tif'eret* and *Shekhinah* are not face-to-face, the use of the verse referring to the cherubim, and R. Shimon's greeting of his disciples through his citation of the verse *hinei mah tov u-mah na 'im shevet aḥim gam yaḥad*—points to the conclusion that the friends' ideal relationship correlates directly with the face-to-face love between the divine male and female. This association is a function of the *Zohar*'s broader theomorphic conception of humanness; the individual person is a physical manifestation of divine metaphysical properties and so, therefore, is the nature of human relationships.[31] The face-to-face encounter of the mystic friends is an incarnation of the *Tif'eret-Shekhinah* relationship; the other male companion is thus *feminized* for the male kabbalist.[32] Indeed, this point is driven home by a passage found later on the same zoharic page. Following a homily on the romance of *Keneset Yisrael* (*Shekhinah*) and *Kudsha Brikh Hu* (*Tif'eret*) through a mystical-midrashic reading of the Song of Songs, R. Shimon teaches,

> "Alternatively: Behold how good and how pleasant it is when brothers dwell together! These are the friends (*ḥevrayya*), when they sit as one, and do not separate one from the other. At first, they appear as men waging war, wanting to kill one another. Afterward, they appear in love, in brotherhood. What does the Holy Blessed One say? Behold how good and how pleasant it is when brothers dwell together! [*Gam yaḥad*, also together]. Also [*gam*] including *Shekhinah* with them. What is more, the Holy Blessed One listens to their utterances and it is pleasing to Him and He delights in them. As it is

written (Malachi 3:16): Then those who revere YHVH spoke with one another; and YHVH listened and heard, and it was written in a book of remembrance before Him . . . And you, friends who are here, as you have been before this, from here forth do not separate from each other until the Holy Blessed One delights with you and calls peace upon you, and because of you peace will be present in the world. As it is written (Psalms 122:8): For the sake of my brothers and my friends, I speak a prayer that peace be upon you." They traveled on until they reached the house of R. Pinḥas. R. Pinḥas came out and kissed him. He said: "I have merited to kiss the *Shekhinah*! Happy is my portion!"[33]

Spiritual friendship, and particularly the fellowship marked by love and peace through mystical study, is here characterized as the ideal of kabbalistic practice; adversarialism, and even solitude for that matter, is viewed as a barrier to divine indwelling in the human realm. When the companions overcome the tensions of interpretative disagreement in their study,[34] when they are bonded in brotherhood and love with their fellow members of the *ḥevrayya*, then *Shekhinah* is included among them (*le-akhlela imahon Shekhinta*). What is more, then "the Holy Blessed One listens to their utterances and it is pleasing to Him and He delights in them." Indeed, in formulating this ideal of harmony and peace, the virtue of *connectedness* among the mystic friends, the zoharic homilist (through the authoritative voice of R. Shimon) interpretatively correlates the words of Psalm 133:1 (*hinei mah tov u-mah na'im shevet aḥim gam yaḥad* ["Behold how good and how pleasant it is when brothers dwell together!"]) with those of Psalm 122:8 (*le-ma'an aḥai ve-rei'ai adabrah na shalom bakh* ["For the sake of my brothers and my friends, I speak a prayer that peace be upon you"]). When the mystic friends overcome the opposition and conflict of their different exegetical opinions, when they attain the level of *reḥimuta* (love) and *aḥva* (brotherhood), then they are infused with a peace-bestowing divine Presence.

According to the homilist, the loving friendship between the mystics is the direct cause (and source of merit) for a broader peace that is called into the world by God ("the Holy Blessed One delights with you [*ad de-kudsha brikh hu ḥadei imakhon*] and calls peace upon you, and because of you peace will be present in the world [*ve-yishtakaḥ be-gineikhon shelama be-alma*]"). The very act of harmonious spiritual friendship, the relational event of mystical conversation among the bonded companions, is framed as a delightful and alluring phenomenon to God Him- or Herself (the plurality of divine gender reflected in the symbology of the *Zohar* itself, particularly in the passage previously cited). Playing with the quoted words from Malachi 3:16, the zoharic homilist states explicitly that divinity is drawn in by the interpersonal sharing of speech and learning (*az nidberu yir'ei YHVH ish el re'eihu*): it is the event of loving and brotherly dialogue, the discourse of Torah in spiritual friendship, that invokes the Presence of God. The attainment of peace (*shelama be-alma*), harmonious shared Torah speech (*nidberu...ish el re'eihu*), a sense of love (*reḥimuta*), brotherhood (*aḥva*), and bondedness (*la titparshun da min da*)—these are the qualities of mystical friendship idealized by the *Zohar* in this passage, and it is through these qualities of interpersonal relationship that God's Presence is disclosed, incarnated, and made immanent in the earthly space of human community. Divinity is revealed in the human moment of face-to-face loving friendship, centered on the disclosure of kabbalistic mysteries.

R. Shimon's hermeneutically rich homily on the nature of friendship, love, and peace—its fusion of anthropology and theology—immediately culminates in the arrival of the master and his disciples at the home of his father-in-law, R. Pinḥas ben Ya'ir. At the moment of their arrival, R. Pinḥas embodies the just-articulated teaching in the kiss and exclamation of his greeting: "I have merited to kiss the *Shekhinah* [*zakhiti le-nashka Shekhinta*]!" he effuses with the characteristic zoharic deployment of dramatic speech and physical gesture.[35] "Happy is my portion [*zaka'ah ḥulki*]!" R. Pinḥas proceeds to set up comfortable seating for his guests—a relatively rare scene in which the trappings of an indoor gathering and hospitality are depicted (given that the vast majority of such gatherings in the *Zohar* take place outdoors). Notably, R. Shimon responds to this gesture of welcoming by indicating a preference for simpler, perhaps more austere conditions for the learning of Torah, at which point R. Pinḥas responsively removes the comfortable seating.[36] All of this turns on the powerful reverence expressed for R. Shimon as the master of secrets, the one who speaks mysteries "without fear of those above or those below." Even leaving aside a more expansive consideration of this scene and its descriptive details, we may observe the manner in which story and homily are woven together in an overlapping tapestry[37]—an exegetical teaching about and a narrative representation of spiritual friendship. In concluding the pericope with R. Pinḥas's kiss and exclamation about kissing the divine face through the human face of the friend (or in this case, the son-in-law), the *Zohar* drives home a message not unlike the theological anthropology of Aelred of Rievaulx, the notion that a physical kiss between human spiritual friends is the embodiment of the divine-human kiss of mystical revelation.[38]

Having engaged in a deep dive into *Zohar* 3:59b, let us now briefly consider several additional textual instances that supplement and further nuance the conclusions previously discussed. First, we may note that the blurring of lines between interpersonal friendship/love and human-divine love (sometimes characterized as a modality of passionate friendship) is taken up elsewhere in the zoharic corpus. The height of interpersonal friendship for the *Zohar* is a devotional love—a friendship of ultimacy—with God. Musing on the meaning of Proverbs 17:17 ("At all times a friend loves, a brother is born for adversity" [*be-khol eit oheiv ha-rei ʿa, ve-aḥ le-tsarah yivaleid*]), the *Zohar* at 2:55b explicitly correlates the power and steadfastness of human friendship with the bond between the person and divinity. In another passage (*Zohar* 3:22a), the zoharic homilist asserts that through the study of Torah, the person becomes a "friend of God," bonded in love to *Tif'eret* and *Shekhinah* above (*ikri ḥaveirei de-Kudsha Brikh Hu ve-Keneset Yisrael*). What is more, the *Zohar* asserts in 2:55b, when the Jews are attacked by their enemies, God functions as a brother, defending them in adversity (*de-Yisrael ikrun aḥim le-Kudsha Brikh Hu*). The key prooftext used is once again Psalm 122:8, "For the sake of my brothers and my friends, I speak a prayer that peace be upon you" (*le-ma ʿan aḥai ve-rei ʿai adabrah na shalom bakh*), underscoring the core notion that the paradigmatic *eros* of friends—particularly the passionate companionship of mystical study partners, as well as their willingness to stand in support of one another in difficult times—is directly comparable to and, indeed, *is the embodiment of the devotional love of the mystic for God and of God for the kabbalist in return*. Put differently, the two modes of interpersonal relationship here—friendship and brotherhood—are understood to be mirrored in the bond between the human mystic and divinity. As we further find in *Zohar* 3:298a, "R. Yitsḥak was traveling on the way. He happened upon R. Ḥiyya, who said to him: 'I see in your face that you abide in the abode of *Shekhinah*.'"[39] . . .

He said to him: 'Surely in every place where Israel dwells, the Holy Blessed One is among them, and wherever the wise of the generation go, the Holy Blessed One goes with them.'... Now let us join as one, and let us travel on the way, for I know we are going to one [the same] place—to receive the face of *Shekhinah*."

Daniel Matt has suggested that this reference to R. Yitshak abiding in the abode of *Shekhinah* may be an expression on R. Hiyya's part of how frequently R. Yitshak dwells in the presence of R. Shimon, their master— that is, R. Shimon is the paradigmatic human embodiment of the face of *Shekhinah*, and his dwelling place is Hers.[40] This is certainly a plausible reading. However, leaving aside the fact that R. Shimon is also often associated with the masculine *sefirah Yesod*—that he, no less than the biblical Moses, sees uniquely through the illumined lens of prophecy (*ispeklaria ha-me'irah*)[41]—R. Hiyya's proclamation may instead be an instance of the more general and widespread correlation of various members of the *hevrayya* with the face of *Shekhinah*. So interpreted, R. Hiyya's exclamation would indicate his friend's taut connection to *Shekhinah* ("that your dwelling-place is within the dwelling of *Shekhinah*"), discerned directly from R. Yitshak's visage. This point—that the encountered friend reflects the presence of divinity, that he is circumscribed by the metaphysical space of God—is reinforced hermeneutically by R. Hiyya through the invocation of a zoharic dictum clearly based on established rabbinic tradition: "Surely in every place where Israel dwells, the Holy Blessed One is among them [*adai be-khol atar de-Yisrael sharyyan Kudsha Brikh Hu beinayyhu*], and wherever the wise of the generation go, the Holy Blessed One goes with them [*ve-khol atar de-hakimei dara azlin, Kudsha Brikh Hu azil imahon*]."[42] Divinity is present among the Jewish people in exile, and most vividly "wherever the wise of the generation go." Their joining as one in companionship following this encounter on the road is framed by the characters as a pivot from solitary journeying to sacred friendship with a shared devotional purpose. This may be (along the lines of Matt's reading) a bondedness in pilgrimage to R. Shimon, their teacher (who is the earthly font of divine revelation), but it may also reflect the sense that together they will set out to further receive the face of *Shekhinah* through the companionship of mystical dialogue and Torah study along the way.

It is important to note at this juncture that a dominant feature of spiritual friendship in the *Zohar* is not only the vision of divine Presence in the face of the kabbalistic companion but also a shared purpose among the friends that their holy practice of study and disclosure of mysteries serves theurgically to facilitate and cultivate *Shekhinah*—to stimulate Her reunion with *Tif 'eret* above and to draw Her indwelling into the earthly realm below. Consider, for example, *Zohar* 1:181a, in which the homilist speaks of the human love of God, the love of *Shekhinah*, as one that involves participatory suffering—enduring *yisurin shel ahavah*, or suffering for the sake of one's love of God, in solidarity with *Shekhinah*. By experiencing and participating in the downtrodden suffering of *Shekhinah*, the mystics are transformed into Her "friends."[43] "Those who suffer with Her, will rejoice with Her (*inun de-savlu imah, yithadetun imah*)," the text asserts—and "these are called *yisurin shel ahavah*." In this way, these individuals are "friends who participate/join with Her (*ilein inun ḥaveirim meshutafin be-hadah*). Happy is their portion in this world and in the world to come! For they have merited [or attained] this, to be friends with Her (*le-mehevei ḥaveirim be-hadah*). About them it is written (Psalm 122:8): 'For the sake of my brothers and my friends, I speak a prayer that peace be upon you.'" This verse is used here to speak directly about the human-divine friendship; unlike the previous cases, where an interpersonal friendship opens into relation with divinity, here it is only the human-divine relationship that is discussed, for God draws close to the brokenhearted, as the zoharic homilist opens this passage: when the human mystic experiences brokenheartedness through participatory suffering with *Shekhinah*, then the intimate friendship between the person and divinity is activated.

This motif of theurgic participation with *Shekhinah*—linked, as we shall see, to our previously studied themes of shared mystical Torah study and passionate interpersonal friendship—may be observed in the famous and influential zoharic depiction of all-night Torah study on the eve of the festival of Shavuot (*Leil Shavuot*), one of the texts that shaped the liturgical formation of *Tikkun Leil Shavuot* as it was developed and practiced by the sixteenth-century kabbalists of Safed. In that passage in *Zohar* 1:8a, R. Shimon and his disciples are depicted as staying up through the night (as they are on other occasions in the *Zohar*) studying Torah as a way of accompanying and adorning the divine Bride (*Shekhinah*) for Her wedding and unification with *Tif 'eret* the following morning of Shavuot. R. Shimon and the friends are depicted here as "singing the song of Torah," "innovating words of Torah," and "rejoicing" together in the shared fellowship of this theurgic drama, the mythic preparation of *Shekhinah* for the bridal canopy.

In this brief narrative and the accompanying mythic discourse, the event of group fellowship and mystical study is framed explicitly as a time of once again participating in the theosophic process of *Shekhinah*. Through the passionate friendship of joyous midnight learning, the *ḥevrayya* facilitate and cultivate the metaphysical *eros* of feminine *Shekhinah*'s anticipated union with masculine *Tif'eret*. They, the friends, are in service of *Shekhinah* through the very nature of their Torah study and spiritual companionship. In these ways, mystical friendship in the *Zohar* is a relational process within which the kabbalist crosses the physical-metaphysical boundary, a state of interpersonal connection whereby the human mystic becomes an active participant in the mythology of *hieros gamos* that lies at the very heart of the *Zohar*.

Let me conclude with one last passage that depicts the love between members of the zoharic friendship circle, and particularly between R. Shimon bar Yoḥai and his disciples. Tormented over the dilemma of whether to reveal exalted secrets or to keep them hidden from his beloved students, R. Shimon is overwhelmed by his soul-love for his disciples:[44]

> Because [R. Shimon] saw a sign on their faces and told them so, they said to him: "Surely the spirit of prophecy is upon the Holy Light, and we therefore must know." R. Shimon wept and then said one of those words whispered to him from the head of the Academy of the Garden of Eden, [but] not said in a revealed way. "This word is a secret, but I will tell it to you, my beloved sons—my sons, the love of my soul. What shall I do? They spoke to me in a whisper, yet I am speaking openly!"[45]

As elsewhere in the *Zohar*, the act of speaking secrets—of mystical Torah study more generally—is an expression of interpersonal love between members of the *ḥevrayya*. In this case, despite his trepidation that he is violating the seal of secrecy bestowed by the head of the heavenly academy, R. Shimon is overcome with love for his disciples—characterized here as sons to the father-like master teacher—and the urge to reveal the mysteries as a result of that love. As observed earlier, it is the *love* of mystical friendship that most consistently marks their relational bond—one in which the face of *Shekhinah* is greeted and kissed and where the human mystics are intimately involved in the internal *hieros gamos* of the dynamic divine Self.

NOTES

1. See A. W. Price, *Love and Friendship in Plato and Aristotle* (Oxford: Oxford University Press, 1989); and Charles H. Kahn, *Plato and the Socratic Dialogue: The Philosophical Use of a Literary Form* (Cambridge: Cambridge University Press, 1996), especially xiii–xv, 258–59.
2. Consider, for example, the opening description and dialogue of the *Lysis*, which combines narration of the character's journey, the encounter of one character with another along the way of travel, and the prompt to philosophize through the relational experience of companionship. See David Bolotin, *Plato's Dialogue on Friendship: An Interpretation of the Lysis, with a New Translation* (Ithaca: Cornell University Press, 1979), 17.
3. See Bolotin, *Plato's Dialogue on Friendship*; and Mary P. Nichols, "Friendship and Community in Plato's 'Lysis,'" *Review of Politics* 68, no. 1 (Winter 2006): 1–19.
4. See Kahn, *Plato*, 264–65.
5. See Aaron W. Hughes, *The Art of Dialogue in Jewish Philosophy* (Bloomington: Indiana University Press, 2008), especially 1–16.
6. See, for example, the formulation in Ra'anan S. Boustan, *From Martyr to Mystic: Rabbinic Martyrology and the Making of Merkavah Mysticism* (Tübingen: Mohr Siebeck, 2005), 148.
7. See, as a select example, Ivan G. Marcus, "Religious Virtuosi and the Religious Community: The Pietistic Mode in Judaism," in *Take Judaism for Example: Studies Toward the Comparison of Religions*, ed. Jacob Neusner (Chicago: University of Chicago Press, 1983), 93–115.
8. See Mark B. Sendor, "The Emergence of Provençal Kabbalah: Rabbi Isaac the Blind's Commentary on Sefer Yeẓirah" (PhD diss., Harvard University, 1994), 1:40–42; and Haviva Pedaya, *Ha-Shem ve-ha-Mikdash be-Mishnat R. Yitsḥak Sagi Nahor* [Name and sanctuary in the teaching of R. Isaac the Blind] (Jerusalem: Magnes, 2001), 3–69.
9. See Moshe Idel, "Nahmanides: Kabbalah, Halakhah, and Spiritual Leadership," in *Jewish Mystical Leaders and Leadership in the 13th Century*, ed. Moshe Idel and Mortimer Ostow (Northvale, NJ: Jason Aronson, 1998), 15–96; and Idel, "Kabbalah and Elites in Thirteenth-Century Spain," *Mediterranean Historical Review* 9, no. 1 (1994): 5–19. Cf. the observations in Philip Wexler, "Mystical Jewish Sociology," *Journal for the Study of Religions and Ideologies* 6, no. 18 (2010): 206–17. For earlier, classic reflections on this subject, see Gershom G. Scholem, *Origins of the Kabbalah*, ed. R. J. Zwi Werblowsky, trans. Allan Arkush (Princeton: Princeton University Press, 1987), 199–231, 365–72.
10. See Eitan P. Fishbane, *The Art of Mystical Narrative: A Poetics of the Zohar* (New York: Oxford University Press, 2018), 22.
11. See Yehuda Liebes, "Zohar ve-Eros" [Zohar and Eros], *Alpayyim* 9 (1994): 112–17.
12. On this literary phenomenon, first discussed substantially by Aristotle in his *Poetics*, see the extensive analysis in Terence Cave, *Recognitions: A Study in Poetics* (Oxford: Oxford University Press, 1988). For a detailed study of anagnorisis in zoharic narrative, see Fishbane, *Art of Mystical Narrative*, 128–52.
13. See Fishbane, *Art of Mystical Narrative*, chap. 6.
14. On possible social configurations of the Castilian zoharic kabbalists and the context for their cultivation of a living ḥavurah of spiritual fellowship, see Hartley Lachter, "Charity and Kabbalah in Medieval Spain: Possible Evidence from Isaac ibn Sahula's Meshal ha-Kadmoni," *Iberia Judaica* 6 (2014): 119–26.
15. For the classic and highly influential formulation of this theory, see

Gershom Scholem, *Major Trends in Jewish Mysticism* (1941; repr., New York: Schocken Books, 1974), 156–204.

16. Liebes, "Keizad Nitḥaber Sefer ha-Zohar" [How the *Zohar* was written], *Meḥkarei Yerushalayim be-Maḥshevet Yisra'el* 8 (1989): 1–71.

17. See an overview of this scholarship in Daniel Abrams, *Kabbalistic Manuscripts and Textual Theory: Methodologies of Textual Scholarship and Editorial Practice in the Study of Jewish Mysticism* (Jerusalem: Magnes, 2010), 303–428.

18. See Fishbane, *Art of Mystical Narrative*, 58–127.

19. On the kiss between members of the *ḥevrayya* in zoharic narrative and its relational aspects among the mystic friends, see Joel Hecker, "Kissing Kabbalists: Hierarchy, Reciprocity, and Equality," in *Love—Virtual and Real—in the Jewish Tradition*, ed. Leonard J. Greenspoon, Ronald A. Simkins, and Jean A. Cahan (Omaha: Creighton University Press, 2008), 171–208.

20. On this motif, see Yehuda Liebes, "Ha-Mashiaḥ shel ha-Zohar: Le-Demuto ha-Meshiḥit shel R. Shimon bar Yoḥai" [The Messiah of the *Zohar*: Toward the messianic image of R. Shimon bar Yoḥai], in *Ha-Ra'ayon ha-Meshiḥi be-Yisra'el* (Jerusalem: Israel Academy of Sciences and Humanities, 1982), 87–236, and especially 146–51; Melila Hellner-Eshed, *A River Flows from Eden: The Language of Mystical Experience in the Zohar*, trans. N. Wolski (Stanford: Stanford University Press, 2009), 99–104; and Hellner-Eshed, *Mevakshei ha-Panim: Mi-Sodot ha-Idra Raba she-be-Sefer ha-Zohar* [Seekers of the face: The secrets of the Idra-Rabba (the Great Assembly) of the *Zohar*] (Rishon le-Tsiyon: Yedi'ot Aḥaronot and Sifrei Ḥemed, 2017), especially 104–6.

21. See previous reflections on this zoharic phenomenon in Liebes, "Zohar ve-Eros," 104–12; Elliot R. Wolfson, *Through a Speculum That Shines: Vision and Imagination in Medieval Jewish Mysticism* (Princeton: Princeton University Press, 1994), 368–72; Hellner-Eshed, *River Flows from Eden*, 108; Joel Hecker, *Mystical Bodies, Mystical Meals: Eating and Embodiment in Medieval Kabbalah* (Detroit: Wayne State University Press, 2005), 140–41; and Fishbane, *Art of Mystical Narrative*, 58–60, 83–84, 99–100, 138–39, 187.

22. Indeed, in his remarks cited above in note 21, Elliot R. Wolfson characterizes "mystical fellowship as constitution of the divine face." See Wolfson, *Through a Speculum*, 368–77.

23. Or, perhaps, "as he was traveling to see R. Pinḥas ben Ya'ir" (*de-hava azil le-meḥmei*).

24. As I will discuss, it is important to note that this verse is talking about the two cherubim facing one another.

25. *Zohar* 3:59b.

26. *Zohar* 3:59b.

27. See, for example, Elliot R. Wolfson, *Circle in the Square: Studies in the Use of Gender in Kabbalistic Symbolism* (Albany: State University of New York Press, 1995), 107–8; and Wolfson, "Coronation of the Sabbath Bride: Kabbalistic Ritual and the Myth of Androgynisation," *Journal of Jewish Thought and Philosophy* 6, no. 2 (1997): 305n15. Also see the remarks of Liebes, "Zohar ve-Eros," 104.

28. An intriguing parallel to several intersecting elements here—passionate friendship, semiveiled homoeroticism, mystical experience, messianic overtones (which have been observed with respect to the zoharic fellowship), and the physical gesture of the kiss—may be found in Juan A. Herrero Brasas, *Walt Whitman's Mystical Ethics of Comradeship: Homosexuality and the Marginality of Friendship at the Crossroads of Modernity* (Albany: State University of New York Press, 2010), 83–116. Despite the anachronistic nature of such a comparison, the phenomenological and literary correlations are striking indeed.

29. See Wolfson, *Through a Speculum*, 368–89.

30. There is a widespread association in Jewish mystical sources between the two cherubim and the *du-partsufin* of the *sefirot* (a common cognomen for the unity of *Tif'eret* and *Shekhinah*), on the one hand, and other supernal dimensions, on the other (as in the case of the Ḥasidei Ashkenaz). See my discussion of this question in Eitan P. Fishbane, *As Light Before Dawn: The Inner World of a Medieval Kabbalist* (Stanford: Stanford University Press, 2009), 129–34, 214n86, 218–22. Also see Daniel Abrams, "The Evolution of the Intention of Prayer to the 'Special Cherub': From the Earliest Works to a Late Unknown Treatise," *Frankfurter Judaistische Beiträge* 21 (1995): 1–26. Cf. Elliot R. Wolfson, *Language, Eros, Being: Kabbalistic Hermeneutics and Poetic Imagination* (New York: Fordham University Press, 2005), 70, 349.

31. We would do well here to compare this kabbalistic conception of human friendship (as a path to a devotional encounter with divinity) with the influential writings of Aelred of Rievaulx (ca. 1110–1167), an English Christian mystic, thinker, and disciple of Bernard of Clairvaux who adapted elements of Cicero's classic dialogue on friendship to the conceptual and practical context of Christian mystical piety (in a work entitled *Spiritual Friendship* [*Amicitia Spiritualis*]). As Bernard McGinn has characterized the matter, "Like all Cistercians, Aelred rooted his spiritual teaching in a theological anthropology based on the understanding of humanity as the *imago et similitudo Dei*." See McGinn, *The Growth of Mysticism: Gregory the Great Through the 12th Century* (New York: Crossroad, 1994), 311. But as McGinn explains, in Aelred's hands, this idea came to mean that it was through the event of Christian friendship that a path ultimately leading to a mystical union with God is opened. What is more, and particularly relevant in comparison to the zoharic texts discussed throughout this chapter, the kiss of spiritual friendship between human beings (distinguished from the kiss of erotic lust) is understood to be nothing less than the kiss of God (a reverberation of the Cistercian focus on the erotic symbolism of the Song of Songs). Again to quote McGinn on Aelred (*Growth of Mysticism*, 319), "The spiritual kiss, which is the proper expression of spiritual friendship, is described as 'the kiss of Christ, one that he does not offer from his own mouth but from that of another, breathing that most holy attraction into his lovers so that it seems to them there is but one soul in different bodies.' . . . This kiss, since the soul knows that it comes from Christ, leads to longing for the intellectual kiss to be given directly by the Divine Lover 'when all worldly thoughts have been put to rest.'" Also see the remarks with respect to Jewish material in Michael Fishbane, *The JPS Bible Commentary: Song of Songs* (Philadelphia: Jewish Publication Society, 2015), 26–28.

32. In addition to the previous references, see the reflections on this dynamic in Wolfson, *Language, Eros, Being*, 49, 109, 167, and especially 325. Cf. Shaul Magid, "Constructing Women from Men: The Metaphysics of Male Homosexuality Among Lurianic Kabbalists in Sixteenth-Century Safed," *Jewish Studies Quarterly* 17, no. 1 (2010): 4–28; and Hartley Lachter, "Jewish Bodies in Divine Form: Jewish Difference and Historical Consciousness in Medieval Kabbalah," *Journal of Jewish Identities* 11, no. 1 (2018): 123–42.

33. *Zohar* 3:59b.

34. This is also how Daniel Matt reads the line: "At first, they appear as men waging war, wanting to kill one another (*de-va'ei le-katla da le-da*)." See Matt, *The Zohar: Pritzker Edition* (Stanford: Stanford University Press, 2012), 7:386n91.

35. See Fishbane, *Art of Mystical Narrative*, chap. 1.

36. Also see the observations of Matt, *Zohar*, 7:387–88n94, and his use of

the words *simple* and *austere* in his commentary.
37. On the interplay of narrative and exegesis in the *Zohar*, see Fishbane, *Art of Mystical Narrative*, chap. 3.
38. See Michael Fishbane, *The Kiss of God: Spiritual and Mystical Death in Judaism* (Seattle: University of Washington Press, 1994), 19–20, 24–43; Hecker, "Kissing Kabbalists," especially 171; and Fishbane, *Art of Mystical Narrative*, 64–66.
39. Or perhaps more literally, "that your dwelling-place is within the dwelling of Shekhinah."
40. See Matt, *Zohar*, 9:859–60nn30–31. Also see this reference for Matt's discussion of the older rabbinic sources for the idea that to welcome the human other is to simultaneously welcome the divine Shekhinah.
41. See discussion in Hellner-Eshed, *River Flows from Eden*, 33–34.
42. This statement is founded on the classic formulation in *Mekhilta*, *Pisḥa* 14, and elsewhere. Cf. Matt, *Zohar*, 9:393n318.
43. On the kabbalistic development of the theme of divine participation in the suffering of Israel and vice versa, see Elliot R. Wolfson, "Divine Suffering and the Hermeneutics of Reading: Philosophical Reflections on Lurianic Mythology," in *Suffering Religion*, ed. Robert Gibbs and Elliot R. Wolfson (London: Routledge, 2002), 109–70.
44. On friendship as a bonding of souls, particularly as represented in the arts, see Alexander Nehamas, *On Friendship* (New York: Basic Books, 2016), 65–98.
45. *Zohar* 2:190b. Cf. my further discussion of this passage in Fishbane, *Art of Mystical Narrative*, 104–6.

CHAPTER 3

Friendship and Gender
The Limits and Possibilities of Jewish Philosophy

HAVA TIROSH-SAMUELSON

As a topic of philosophical analysis, friendship has not fared well in Jewish philosophy.[1] With the notable exception of Judah Abravanel's *Dialogues on Love*, there has been no philosophic treatise devoted to friendship in the long history of Jewish philosophy.[2] Jewish philosophers did not produce sustained discourses on friendship comparable to books 8 and 9 of Aristotle's *Nicomachean Ethics*, Plutarch's essays *How to Tell a Flatterer from a Friend* and *On Having Many Friends*, Cicero's *Of Friendship*, Aelred of Rievaulx's *Spiritual Friendship*, Michele de Montaigne's *Of Friendship*, Francis Bacon's *Of Friendship*, Immanuel Kant's *Lecture on Friendship*, or Søren Kierkegaard's *Works of Love*.[3] This lacuna, however, does not mean that the theme of friendship was irrelevant to Jewish philosophy or that Jewish philosophers contributed nothing to Western philosophic discourse on friendship. This chapter focuses on premodern Jewish philosophic reflections on friendship and shows how these relate to Western discourses on happiness.

I argue that the philosophical discourse on friendship and happiness has always been gender inflected: until the modern period, true virtue friendship and true happiness were reserved for men only. Women as a class were excluded from both because they were considered to be rationally inferior and unable to engage in philosophy. Nonetheless, while Jewish philosophers highlighted the presumed intellectual limitations of women, a few Jewish philosophers also entertained the possibility of women as philosophers. This possibility was realized only in the modern period with the emancipation of the Jews and the admission of women and Jews to universities, which will be discussed in chapter 11 in this volume. Together these chapters illustrate how the philosophic discourse on friendship captures the dialectics of equality and difference, of inclusion and exclusion, of universality and particularity.

FRIENDSHIP, VIRTUE, AND HAPPINESS IN ANCIENT PHILOSOPHY

Friendship took center stage in ancient moral philosophy because it was viewed as the social context for the cultivation of virtues without which human beings could not flourish. Ancient philosophers thought an act was right or wrong depending on whether it was in accordance with or contrary to a virtue (*arête*). The virtues are the excellences of character that constitute the well-functioning person, whose life is happy or flourishing. In this approach, the starting point of the moral life is the individual and the individual's concern to live well, but the individual pursuit of one's virtue is directly related to the pursuit of virtue by others. Friendship is thus the bridge that links together the individual and others—and even other groups to which the individual belongs. The cultivation of virtue is thus a social process that can be accomplished only through interaction with other individuals, especially friends.

Western philosophic discourse on friendship began with Plato, who distinguished between love (*eros*) and friendship (*philia*). Both are rooted in a desire of some kind, and both "involve relations primarily between men," but desire could also "foster competition, jealousy, or enslavement of one person to another."[4] Plato's metaphysical concept of *eros* as the love of the Good would undergird Western moral philosophy, but it was Aristotle's systematic analysis of friendship in the *Nicomachean Ethics* (NE) that dominated Western discourse on friendship until the Renaissance.[5] In books 8 and 9 of the *Nicomachean Ethics*, Aristotle explains why friendship is necessary for human beings, even with respect to the virtuous person (for whom friendship seems unnecessary) or the vicious person (for whom friendship seems impossible). The essence of friendship is wishing good things for the other person, but only if it is reciprocated. The core of friendship is "the specific situation where two individuals have this good will for one another, are aware of it, and actually start becoming friends."[6]

In ancient Greece, the term *philia* covered a wide range of social relations. Aristotle's analysis of these diverse relations concluded that there are three basic types of friendship: friendship based on utility or benefit, friendship based on pleasure, and friendship based on virtue or character. The first two types of friendship are shown to be imperfect and inferior to the third because they are temporary and undertaken not for their own sake. Only virtue friendship can count as true or perfect friendship because the bond of virtues is permanent or at least long lasting. In virtue friendship, each person is a friend to the other because of that person's intrinsic goodness; attracted to each other's character, friends influence the shape of each other's life, spend time doing things together, and are disposed toward each other as they are disposed toward themselves. In such friendship between intrinsically good people, the friend is "another self" (NE 1166a). For Aristotle, friendship was a necessary ingredient of the intrinsically good life that enables humans to flourish qua humans. But Aristotle complicated matters when he claimed that the life of moral virtue is happy only in a "secondary way"—that is to say, a happy life with friends is only "second best" (NE 1178a9). To achieve "complete happiness" and experience the best life possible, the virtuous person turns inward to engage in the intellectual activity of contemplation (*theoretike*; NE 1177a18–19). While in books 8 and 9 Aristotle extolls the merits of friendship as an ingredient of the good life, in book 10 he advocates contemplation rather than friendship as the happiest way of life for humans.

Aristotle's ambiguous position gave rise to conflicting interpretations.[7] According to one interpretation (known as the "exclusive" view), Aristotle privileged the philosophic life of contemplation (*bios theoretikos*) as the happiest or best life for humans that does not include friends, but according to the other interpretation, Aristotle promoted an "inclusive" conception of happiness for which the best life for humans is a political life (*bios politikos*) with friends and several other external goods. Are the theoretical life and the political life in conflict with each other, or are they complementary? For our purpose, the crucial question is whether Aristotle included women in his analysis of the nexus among friendship, contemplation, and happiness. Did Aristotle envision women as virtue friends? Could women study philosophy and take part in the life of contemplation? Could women experience equality (moral and intellectual) in their relations with men? The answer to all three questions is a resounding no.

Although *philia* covered the relations between husbands and wives, Aristotle did not consider it an example of perfect friendship because men and women are inherently unequal. Aristotle held that "females are weaker and colder in their nature; and we should look upon the female state as being as it were a deformity, though one which occurs in the ordinary course of nature" (*Generations of Animals* 4.6.755a). The biological differences between males and females had wide-ranging social implications: because women were seen as "deformed males" or "incomplete males," women were excluded from formal education, especially philosophic education, and from political citizenship. Within the institution of marriage, women's exclusive roles were mothering and child-rearing, and they were subordinate to their husband's authority. In the ancient Greek polis, men and women could not be virtue friends because they were not equal, just as parents and children could not be virtue friends.[8] Perfect friendship is reserved for men of virtue; they alone could thrive in the political sphere and in the life of contemplation. Only a good man can love his friend for the friend's own sake and not only for qualities associated with utility and pleasure.

Aristotle's ethics framed the Western discourse on friendship, virtue, and happiness for centuries. After his death in 322 BCE, pagan philosophical schools continued to reflect on friendship with various nuances. The Stoics "recognized friendship as a kind of knowledge of a most general type that does not really instruct us about the particulars of how to be a friend. They did, however, acknowledge virtue as an art of how to make friends."[9] The other leading philosophical school in antiquity, the Epicureans, also considered friendship to be rationally based, but they valued freedom from care and anxiety (*ataraxia*) above all else. For the Epicureans, friendship played a crucial role in securing freedom from pain and anxiety, and philosophizing could only be undertaken among friends who were committed to frank speech, a commitment between people who can trust each other absolutely. In the Epicurean community of like-minded sages, "friendship involved mutual enjoyment of each other's company, mutual activities, mutual help and cooperation, whatever the sacrifices involved,"[10] and friendship, in contradistinction to *eros*, was not an emotion but a virtue and an art.

PHILO: CONTEMPLATION AND FRIENDSHIP WITH GOD

Greek philosophizing about friendship, virtue, and happiness was given a Judaic twist with the Hellenization of the Near East after the conquests of Alexander the Great. As early as the second century BCE, Greek-speaking Jews began to reconcile Greek philosophy with biblical religion by identifying the life of Torah with the pursuit of wisdom and by interpreting the biblical text allegorically.[11] Philo of Alexandria was a member of the social elite in Roman Egypt, where Jews constituted a significant minority, enjoying a large degree of autonomy and participating in Greek education of the gymnasium but not possessing full citizenship. Philo's gendered view of friendship illustrates how philosophy marks both limits and possibilities for women.

Philo did not write a special treatise on friendship. The closest he came to reflecting systematically on friendship was in the discussion of the virtue of humanity (*philanthropia*) in his *On Virtues*. When the entire Philonic corpus is consulted, Philo's dispersed remarks on friendship do add up to a consistent position that is deeply indebted to the Stoic view.[12] Philo was most familiar with the philosophic discourse on friendship in Aristotle, Cicero, and Plutarch, which he utilized in his allegorical interpretation of the Bible, known to him only in the Greek translation, the Septuagint. Philo adopted Aristotle's definition of a friend as "another self," saying that "in the works of Moses a friend is so near that he does not differ from a person's own soul."[13] As for the practice of friendship, Philo applied conventional philosophic motifs to the Bible. Thus the commandments concerning conduct in a war on a besieged city (Deut. 20:10–13) provided an occasion to reflect on the relationship between friends and enemies, the prohibition on taking God's name in vain (Exod. 20:7) enabled him to reflect on friendship and false testimony, and most importantly, God's revelation to Moses (Exod. 33:11) was the context for reflection on the well-known proverb that "the possessions of friends are held in common."[14] Philo interpreted the verse to mean that as his friend, God shared His possessions with Moses. Philo spoke as well about God's friendship with Abraham and Jacob.

As a member of the Jewish *politeuma* (citizenry), Philo took it for granted that all Israelites or Hebrews were "relatives and friends" (*Special Laws* 1.69–70), but Philo also referred to proselytes as "friends," since "they have demonstrated a disposition for friendship with God, which above all leads to friendship and affinity."[15] Friendship with God is the "basis for the common bond among Jews and proselytes," and all friends of God share in the divine attributes.[16] Devotion to God creates a universal bond of friendship among all people, a bond that is implanted in the hearts of human beings by nature, as the Stoics already noted.

What does it mean to live a life as God's friend? In *On the Contemplative Life*, Philo addresses this question by describing a group of Jews who departed from Alexandria to settle by Lake Mareotis, where they lived an austere life devoted to meditation, the study of philosophy, biblical exegesis, and music, all in dedication to God. Calling them "Therapeutae" because they engaged in the "healing of souls," Philo describes how these Jews acquired not only the moral and intellectual virtues as understood by pagan moral philosophers but also the religious virtue of faith (*pistis*) that culminates in the contemplative experience of "seeing" the "immaterial and transcendent" God.[17] Remarkably, the community of Jewish contemplatives included women![18] If so, does that mean that Philo considered men and women to be equal? Not necessarily. In accord with the philosophic conventions of his day, Philo thought that the male represented the standard of humanity (reason and intellect), whereas the female always stood for that which the male had to transcend (embodiment and materiality). In Lake Mareotis, gender hierarchy was somewhat attenuated because the women ascetics chose to be celibate and renounced sexuality, marriage, and family life. Hence Philo refers to the women contemplatives as "virgins." They could live the life of contemplation only because they had transcended what made them distinctly female—namely, embodiment and sexuality.[19] The very fact that Philo imagined a possibility of Jewish female contemplatives suggests that in Greco-Roman Judaism, philosophy was available to highly educated Jewish women. They could have chosen to pursue philosophy in order to become "friends of God."

RABBINIC JUDAISM AND THE
EXCLUSION OF WOMEN FROM TORAH STUDY

Philo's philosophical interpretation of the Hebrew scriptures did not become normative Judaism. Indeed, his works were preserved for posterity by Christians in either the original Greek or Latin translations, and they were largely unknown to Jews until the fifteenth century, when Jewish humanists "rediscovered" Philo. Nonetheless, the Philonic approach to the harmonization of the scriptures and Greek philosophy influenced medieval Jewish philosophy indirectly through the mediation of Muslim thinkers, and the entire project of medieval Jewish philosophy could be seen as a Philonic one. But whereas in Philo's day "Judaism" encompassed only the Hebrew scriptures, in the Middle Ages "Judaism" included the entire rabbinic corpus as well. The discourse on friendship in medieval Jewish philosophy and the place of women within it was thus shaped by the rabbinic tradition as well as by Aristotle.

Rabbinic Judaism articulated a comprehensive way of life in pursuit of wisdom, which the rabbis equated with "Torah." Like their Greco-Roman counterparts, the rabbis endorsed the nexus of virtue, knowledge, and well-being (i.e., happiness), but they gave it a distinctive Judaic meaning by framing it within the myth of Torah and the eternal love relationship between God and Israel. Happiness was thus understood as a personal relationship with God, manifested in following divine commandments as spelled out by rabbinic law. In other words, the best life for Israel is the life of the unconditional love of God in which the believer lives the life of Torah for its own sake and strives to imitate God through good deeds toward others. Like Philo before them, the rabbis integrated virtue ethics with the ethics of duty to divine commands. Whereas for the Greek philosophers, well-being is a direct result of human efforts through the acquisition of virtues, in the rabbinic perspective, happiness is relational: one is happy to the extent that one is properly related to God and, through God, to other persons. Most importantly, in contrast to the Greco-Roman philosophical schools, the rabbinic culture of learning privileged speech over contemplation because the rabbis considered that "God's words were part and parcel of God's essence."[20] For the rabbinic sages, "dialogue and even monologue would take preference over contemplation."[21]

Friendship played a critical role in the rabbinic culture of learning, since friendship was the context for the cultivation of virtues.[22] The rabbinic list of virtues, chief among them humility, expressed the culture of learning in the rabbinic academy as well as the religious ideals of the Judaic tradition. However, when the rabbis reflected on the merits of friendship, they only had in mind friendship between male scholars, since women were categorically excluded from rabbinic academies. Departing from practices and norms in Second Temple Judaism, rabbinic Judaism restricted women from participation in public and private life.[23] Most relevant to our discussion was the fact that women as a class were exempted from Torah study, even though a few outstanding women did master rabbinic oral discourse. But they were the exception that proved the rule.[24] The exemption of women from Torah study eventually led to barring them from all formal participation in Jewish learning (BT Kiddushin 30a), which meant that Jewish women who lived the life of Torah did not do so as searchers of wisdom, nor could they express themselves as lovers of Torah/wisdom.

WOMEN, JEWISH EDUCATION, AND PHILOSOPHY IN THE MIDDLE AGES

The exclusion of women from formal Jewish education was exacerbated in the Middle Ages, especially for Jews in the orbit of Islam.[25] From the tenth century onward, Jews expanded the scope of Torah/wisdom by encompassing philosophy and science written by non-Jews. The study of philosophy and science, however, was not part of the rabbinic curriculum and was cultivated privately by Jews who functioned primarily as physicians and financiers. Although not all Jewish men studied philosophy, all women as a class were categorically excluded from it because women had already been excluded from the study of Torah/wisdom. Consequently, there were no female Jewish philosophers, and no philosophic texts were written by a Jewish woman in the Middle Ages. Moreover, because Aristotelian philosophy associated women with matter and men with form, it not only rooted social hierarchies in metaphysical differences but also considered women to be intrinsically evil because of their presumed inherent materiality. A few authors rose to defend women, but the ensuing literary debate about the merits and demerits of women, which lasted from the thirteenth to the sixteenth centuries, was overtly misogynistic, as humor and rhetorical wit were employed to entertain Jewish men. Undoubtedly, medieval philosophy exacerbated the perceived intellectual inferiority of women and their social marginalization in traditional Jewish society. And yet at least two Jewish thinkers—Moses Maimonides (d. 1204) and Judah Abravanel (d. ca. 1530)—considered the egalitarian potential of philosophy. Philosophy, which was viewed by its opponents as "alien wisdom," offered women a path toward intellectual life not available to them within rabbinic Judaism.

MOSES MAIMONIDES:
FRIENDSHIP AND THE INTELLECTUAL LOVE OF GOD

Maimonides was the first to systematically reinterpret rabbinic Judaism in light of Aristotle's philosophy. Aristotle's *Nicomachean Ethics* framed Maimonides's ethical teachings in the *Eight Chapters* (Maimonides's introduction to the *Commentary on Tractate Avot*), in the *Mishneh Torah: Hilkhot De'ot* (Laws concerning character traits), and in the *Guide of the Perplexed*.[26] It was only after he settled in Egypt in 1167 that Maimonides became acquainted with the Arabic translation of the *Ethics* and then cited it in the *Guide of the Perplexed*.[27] Aristotle's *Ethics* was the main source for Maimonides's statements on friendship. In his *Commentary on Avot* (1.6), Maimonides cites "friendship of the student for his teacher and vice versa as the highest kind of friendship."[28] Like Aristotle, Maimonides recognized the human need for companionship, and he valued a "friendship of trust" in which "a person does not withhold anything from what he tells his friend."[29] Maimonides regarded virtue friendship as the only true kind of friendship, and he agreed with Aristotle that virtue friends devote their lives to the acquisition of knowledge. But did the life of friendship and moral virtue constitute the best life for humans? Did Maimonides consider the *vita activa* or the *vita contemplativa* to be the ultimate end of human life? Maimonides stated that contemplation of God was the highest form of worship. In Maimonides's words, "It is clear that after apprehension, total devotion to Him and the employment of intellectual thought in constant passionate love for Him should be aimed at."[30]

Where do women fit into Maimonides's lofty vision? Maimonides regarded women as rational creatures because they were created in the "image of God." Hence women were moral agents who were obligated to live by Jewish law and who should cultivate the virtues necessary for human flourishing. However, because Maimonides accepted the gendered metaphysics of Aristotle that associated form with "male" and matter with "female," Maimonides also regarded females as "incomplete males" because their rational power "lack[ed] authority."[31] Less rational than men, women were deemed to be more prone to anger, more gullible, and more susceptible to depression. Because of their "feeble mind[s]," Maimonides agreed with the rabbinic ruling to exempt women from the commandment of Torah study. Siding with Rabbi Eliezer in the famous rabbinic dispute (Mishna

Sotah 3.4), Maimonides stated that "a man shall not teach his daughter Torah, for the mind of the majority of women is not adapted to be taught, rather they turn the words of the Torah into words of nonsense according to the poorness of their mind."[32] But if we accept Warren Zev Harvey's argument, Maimonides did not exempt women from the obligation to study "Talmud," or "Gemara," "even though this obligation is not within the framework of the commandment of Talmud Torah."[33] Therefore, it is reasonable to conclude that "Maimonides wanted women to acquire knowledge not only of physics and metaphysics, but also of 'what is forbidden, permitted and the like, with regard to other commandments.'"[34] Because he thought that women should be taught philosophy, Maimonides could consider the possibility of a female philosopher-prophet. Maimonides cited a rabbinic Midrash that depicted Miriam, along with her brothers, Moses and Aaron, as an intellectually perfect prophet who experienced "death by a kiss" from God.[35] Like Philo before him, Maimonides held that Miriam, although female, transcended her materiality and sex difference and attained intellectual perfection.

What Maimonides gave with one hand, he took away with the other, so to speak. Miriam was a theoretical possibility rather than a social reality. In traditional Jewish society, women were not actually taught philosophy, and within the institution of marriage, wives were to be ruled by their husbands, according to Maimonides. There is thus no evidence that Maimonides believed in virtue friendship between husbands and wives; their relationship was at best a friendship of utility.[36] The ideal "woman of virtue" was the person whose practical household management freed her husband to acquire intellectual virtues.

FRIENDSHIP IN POST-MAIMONIDEAN PHILOSOPHY:
THE NEGATION OF WOMEN

Maimonides's legacy shaped Jewish philosophy for the subsequent three centuries, although his philosophic interpretation of Judaism was vigorously debated. Those who accepted Maimonides as authoritative endorsed his view that Torah is a philosophic-scientific text whose esoteric meaning accords with the philosophy of Aristotle, that to worship God correctly Jews must know philosophy, and that the ultimate end of human life is the intellectual love of God, by which the human intellect attains immortality.

Because friendship belonged to moral perfection, which was lower in rank than intellectual perfection, medieval Jewish philosophers paid only limited attention to the theme of friendship. In the schema of sciences, ethics and politics were clearly secondary in importance to physics and metaphysics. Philosophical discourse on friendship appeared in two main contexts: commentaries on the Bible, especially on the book of Proverbs, and commentaries on the *Nicomachean Ethics*.

The book of Proverbs was the main biblical text that expressed the connection among friendship, virtue, and happiness characteristic of ancient philosophy. The book instructs the "wise man" to appreciate the value of friendship. Thus Proverbs teaches, "A friend is devoted at all times / A brother is born to share adversity" (Prov. 17:17). It instructs, "A righteous man gives his friend direction / But the way of the wicked leads astray" (Prov. 12:26), and it counsels, "Do not desert your friend and your father's friend / Do not enter your brother's house in time of misfortune" (Prov. 27:10). Conceptually, medieval Jewish philosophic discourse on friendship added little to the Aristotelian analysis, and certain themes became standard tropes in post-Maimonidean Jewish philosophy, but the commentaries on Proverbs were instrumental in popularizing the notion that friendship is necessary for the moral life of the man who seeks intellectual perfection.[37]

The reception of Aristotle's *Ethics* among Jewish intellectuals was the other factor that shaped philosophic discourse on friendship in the late Middle Ages.[38] As noted, because ethics and politics were ancillary to physics and metaphysics, there were only sporadic discussions of friendship in Jewish philosophy of the thirteenth and fourteenth centuries. That began to change in the fifteenth century, when Jewish philosophers in Spain availed themselves of Latin translations of the *Ethics* along with their scholastic commentaries, chief among them the commentary of Thomas Aquinas. The rise of humanism, first in Italy and later in Spain, generated a new appreciation of civic life and involvement in politics that further enhanced the interest in Aristotle's *Ethics* among Jewish intellectuals. In 1435, Meir ben Solomon Alguades composed a new translation of the *Ethics* into Hebrew at the request of Don Samuel Lavi of Aragon. In the fifteenth century, Jewish courtiers lost much of their previous social status and political power, leaving them in need of an ideology to boost their self-esteem. The virtue ethics of Aristotle, with its focus on civic friendship, the virtue of magnanimity, and the "great-souled man," was most appealing to the aristocratic self-perception of this class. As a result, through the fifteenth and the first half of the sixteenth centuries, we find more references to Aristotle's discourse on friendship among Jewish writers.

I wish to illustrate the discourse on friendship among Sephardic intellectuals by reference to Isaac Abravanel (d. 1508). Attuned to the Aristotelian understanding of civic friendship, Abravanel cited Aristotle's discourse on friendship in his *Naḥalat Avot* (the commentary on Tractate Avot) and in his commentary on Deuteronomy.[39] In the service of kings in Portugal and Castile, Abravanel's life exemplified the *vita activa* in which civic friendship plays a crucial role. Abravanel also echoed Aristotle's views of friendship when he presented the relationship between Moses and Jethro as one of virtue friendship. In his commentary on Exodus 18:7, Abravanel states that in "the shared love of wisdom and admiration for each other's goodness Moses and Jethro were friends."[40] Abravanel might have experienced such virtue friendship with the Italian Jewish loan banker and scholar Yeḥiel da Pisa (d. 1490), the leading banker in Florence, with whom Abravanel corresponded.[41] In this epistolary friendship, the two Jewish scholars and communal leaders not only shared their intellectual and religious values but also were able to support each other in times of need. For example, Abravanel consoled Yeḥiel after his daughter Clemenza married outside the faith and converted to Christianity and after the death of Yeḥiel's wife, Ricca. The letters deflect Yeḥiel's suffering and anguish by referring to God's trial of the chosen and finding consolation in divine providence. Such letters were the main venue for the expression of personal friendship.

After the expulsion of 1492, the Iberian cultural legacy was perpetuated in the new homes of the Sephardic exiles in Italy and in the Ottoman Empire, where distinguished Jews continued to render services to rulers as financiers, physicians, and diplomats. Aristotle's *Ethics* and its sociopolitical understanding of friendship continued to inform elite Sephardic culture well into the sixteenth century, as is demonstrated in the works of Moses ben Baruch Almosnino, the leader of the Jewish community in Salonica. In *Penei Mosheh*, his commentary on the *Ethics*, and in *Sefer Hanhagat ha-Ḥayyim* (*Regimiento de la Vida*), a manual for ethical education of young men, Almosnino elaborated on friendship, summarizing standard themes of Aristotelian moral philosophy. Part 2 of the composition provides an "extensive explanation of the existence and essence of ten ethical virtues, universal in the human species for their benefit and welfare to keep back their souls 'from the pit' (Job 33:18), and to diminish the diverse vices that link them to matter."[42] These include "courage," "temperance," "liberality," "magnificence and magnanimity," "humility," "patience," "affability," "courtesy," and "truthfulness." Almosnino then presents "friendliness" and "justice" as "two great virtues that subsume all of the ethical virtues" and moves on to explain how these two virtues are the foundation of the five intellectual virtues—namely, "science," "intelligence," "wisdom," "prudence," and "art."[43] Because the text was intended exclusively for the moral training of young men, presumably those being prepared for communal leadership, Almosnino makes no reference to women, as the virtue of friendship was deemed relevant only to men.

JUDAH ABRAVANEL:
FRIENDSHIP, LOVE, AND A FICTIONAL FEMALE PHILOSOPHER

In Italy at the beginning of the sixteenth century, a different view of friendship was elaborately articulated by Isaac Abravanel's son, Judah Abravanel, in his *Dialoghi d'amore*.[44] The text consists of three discourses on love: the first dialogue is on love and desire, the second is on the universality of love, and the third is on the origins of love.[45] Aristotle's distinction among three types of friendship—utility, pleasure, and virtue—is but the point of departure for an elaborate discourse on love as a cosmic energy that originates in God and pervades all levels of existence. While friendship is discussed only at the beginning of the book,[46] the first dialogue explicates the conceptual connection among desire, love, and friendship; it shows how Aristotle's discussion of friendship in the *Nicomachean Ethics* could be integrated with Plato's discussion of love in the *Symposium*. But instead of theorizing about these issues in the abstract, Abravanel offers a lively conversation between a man and a woman who act as intellectual friends. Given the unusual impact of the *Dialoghi d'amore* on Western philosophy, this text merits a closer look.

Judah Abravanel composed the *Dialoghi d'amore* in the first decade of the sixteenth century.[47] At that time he resided in Naples, where he and his father, Don Isaac Abravanel, were welcomed into the court of Ferdinand I. The original language of the *Dialoghi* has long been disputed: while there are reasonable arguments in favor of Hebrew as the original language of composition, it seems more likely that the text was composed in Italian, the vernacular.[48] The text was published posthumously in 1535 in Rome, brought to press by the humanist Mariano Lenzi, a member of a group of intellectuals who fled Sienna for Rome to escape political turmoil. This group of non-Jewish displaced intellectuals, with whom Abravanel had close contacts in the 1520s, did not consider the Jewishness of the author a problem. It appears that in the courts of Renaissance Italy, especially in Rome, intellectual friendship between Christians and Jews was not impossible, and friendship between learned courtiers and courtesans was the norm.

Theorizing about love preoccupied philosophers and literati in Renaissance Italy. This interest in the topic reflected the revival of Platonism, inaugurated by Marsilio Ficino's translations and commentaries on Plato's works, most importantly the *Symposium*. Ficino harmonized Platonism with Christianity and with the humanist concept of humankind at the center of creation. For Ficino, love is a universal force binding the world and divinity together, for God has created the world and governs it through an act of love, and through love, the world returns to the godhead. In the earthly realm, the human soul progresses from love of earthly beauty to the ecstatic contemplation of the divine. Thus Ficino "regards love for another human being as merely a preparation, more or less conscious, for the love of God, which constitutes the real goal and true content of human desire, and which is merely turned toward persons and things by the reflected splendor of divine goodness and beauty as it may appear in them."[49] In Ficino's Platonically inspired philosophy, beauty serves as the origin and the telos of character development and human perfection: the purpose of love is the enjoyment of beauty.

Ficino's philosophy of love generated numerous texts on the subject, most of which were written in dialogue form. Dialogue was the literary genre most apt to negotiate cultural and ideological conflicts, propose possible solutions, and minimize contrasts between irreconcilable positions. Abravanel's work was not just one more dialogue on love among many but the most popular of these texts. Between 1535 and 1607, it was published in sixteen separate editions in Italy alone, and it was eventually translated into several other languages. As a result, more people, including women, could have read the text and joined the debate about love. Most important to us, the dialogical form of the text—which dramatized abstract principles through an interaction between two fictional characters, Philo and Sophia—made it immensely appealing because it explored the emotional dimension of friendship, which the Aristotelian understanding of civic friendship had neglected.[50]

Abravanel dramatized the pursuit of wisdom as a courtship between Philo, the male lover, and Sophia, the female beloved. While the *Dialoghi d'amore* is an allegory about the pursuit of wisdom, treating Greek mythologies as well as biblical narratives as philosophical allegories, the dynamic relationship between the protagonists subverted traditional social conventions concerning the pursuit of philosophic wisdom as well as gender relations. Thus Philo, the male lover of wisdom who patiently explicates subtle philosophical points, is in fact interested not in abstract knowledge so much as in expressing his bodily passion for Sophia, whereas she resists his amorous advances by posing philosophical questions that keep the conversation going and delay his desire to conquer her. With great philosophical acumen and much humor, she challenges, contradicts, and occasionally defeats Philo, giving us the first literary representation of a female Jewish philosopher in action.[51]

In Abravanel's literary depiction, the fictional Sophia is a woman who actively engages in the act of philosophizing as an intellectual equal to her male counterpart. In this dramatization of the pursuit of philosophy, gender stereotypes are reversed: the female who was presumed to be the passive beloved is in fact the active partner of the dialogue, and it is the man who is more interested in bodily pleasures. To the courtiers and courtesans in Naples and Rome, such a reversal of gender dynamics may not have been outlandish but more of a reflection of real relations between philosophically educated men and women.

That the interlocutors of the *Dialoghi d'amore* are a man and a woman was germane to the argument of the book: Love is a creative force that originates in the androgynous divine realm and descends through the Great Chain of Being to encompasses all levels of the hierarchical cosmos. Therefore, love of the beautiful moves the souls of created beings to be reabsorbed into the divine source. The ideal that accounts for creative love is not truth but beauty, for "it is beauty which engenders universal and productive affections, which thereby ensures the unity of the universe."[52] If previous philosophers regarded the pursuit of philosophic wisdom as the ascent of the soul and its liberation from imprisonment in the material body, Abravanel offered a positive valuation of the earthly world, human embodiment, sexuality and sensuality, the imagination, and art.⁵³ In this theory of the circle of love, body and mind, male and female, intellect and imagination are all reciprocal and complementary, necessary for the attainment of perfection, as God encompasses all of them. God is not the abstract simplicity of the intellect as Jewish Aristotelians held but a unity within the multiplicity of androgynous forces whose center is beauty (*Tif'eret*). In Kabbalah, love is creative as well as procreative.⁵⁴ The rising importance of Kabbalah in early modern Judaism contributed to the shift from *philia* as the context for character formation to focusing on *eros* as a cosmic principle.

The *Dialoghi d'amore* marked the culmination of the medieval discourse on friendship and love as well as important new developments that would characterize the discourse on friendship in the modern period. In Abravanel's Platonic and kabbalistically inspired philosophy, human friendship instantiates a universal metaphysical principle that transcends politics and ethics. By depoliticizing friendship, Abravanel suggested that it could be experienced not only by men (the dominant agents of politics) but also by women, that friendship could be exercised not only in the public arena but in the private sphere as well. Moreover, Abravanel taught that friendship has an erotic and emotional depth that goes beyond the rational cultivation of virtues. The *Dialoghi d'amore* integrated Greek, Christian, Muslim, and Jewish reflections on friendship and love while creating space for a new understanding of friendship. In this view, egalitarian relations were possible between men and women and possibly even between Jews and non-Jews. By dramatizing his theory of love in the context of relations between a male and female philosopher, the *Dialoghi d'amore* made it possible for readers to envision intellectual friendship between a man and a woman who are not married to each other and who act as equal seekers of wisdom.

In the courtly circles of Rome and Naples, where Platonism flourished, such intellectual friendship between educated men and women was common. But what about Italian Jewish women? Although they could not enroll in advanced rabbinic training, a few upper-class Jewish women engaged in the private study not only of Judaic texts but also of philosophy and secular literature.⁵⁵ Laura, the wife of the banker Samuel ben Yeḥiel of Pisa and the mother of the aforementioned Yeḥiel Nissim of Pisa, was a case in point. Like her Christian cohorts, she functioned as a patroness of learning, and it was to her that David Messer Leon composed his *Shevaḥ Nashim* (Praise of women). In this work, he requests financial support while singing her praises as an "intellectual woman" (*ishah maskelet*) and offering a spirited defense of the merits of women in general by invoking Jewish and non-Jewish sources.[56]

Precisely because of the prevalence of traditional gender expectations, the case of the Italian woman Sara Copia Sullam (d. 1641) is so intriguing. She was the first Jewish female poet-philosopher to publish her own poetry; run a literary salon for Jews and Christians, men and women; and engage in a public philosophic debate about the immortality of the soul.[57] An immensely talented woman who mastered music, literature, and philosophy, Copia Sullam corresponded with the much older Christian humanist Ansaldo Cebà, whom she admired but never met; their literary relationship illustrates the power of intellectual friendship to cross religious boundaries.[58] The fact that Cebà expected his Jewish interlocutor to convert to Christianity and that she successfully rejected his pressure reminds us that friendship across religious boundaries had its limits. That intellectual friendship could cross religious and cultural boundaries would become most evident in the modern period, which I discuss in chapter 11 in this volume.

In sum, this chapter has shown the importance of friendship in Jewish philosophical discourse on happiness from antiquity through the early modern period. From Philo to Judah Abravanel, Jewish philosophers were deeply aware of the non-Jewish philosophic discourse on happiness, virtue, and friendship, especially Aristotle's *Nicomachean Ethics*, which they reframed and reinterpreted in the context of Judaic theology and the myth of Torah/wisdom. Here I have documented the gender inflection of the discourse on friendship, which was decidedly androcentric: virtue friendship was for men only, as women were categorically excluded because their intellect was deemed to be inferior, more dominated by their materiality. The chapter considered the formal exclusion of women from the life of the mind (be it Torah study or the study of philosophy and science) in the context of Greco-Roman, Muslim, and Christian societies, where hierarchy and inequality were the norm. Yet despite the perceived inferiority of women, I have also shown that at least three Jewish philosophers—Philo, Maimonides, and Judah Abravanel—entertained the possibility of women as philosophers. As such, they posed the cultivation of philosophy as a path toward intellectual equality between the sexes, the inclusion of women in education, the love of God, and the attainment of certain types of friendship.

NOTES

1. For recent philosophic analyses of friendship, see Neera Kapur Badhwar, ed., *Friendship: A Philosophical Reader* (Ithaca: Cornell University Press, 1993); Mark Vernon, *The Philosophy of Friendship* (New York: Palgrave Macmillan, 2005); Sandra Lynch, *Philosophy and Friendship* (Edinburgh: University of Edinburgh Press, 2005); and Alexander Nehamas, *On Friendship* (New York: Basic Books, 2016).
2. Jacques Derrida, *The Politics of Friendship*, trans. George Collins (London: Verso, 1997), may be another exception to this generalization, but whether Derrida should be considered a "Jewish philosopher" (and not only a philosopher who was a born Jew) is open to debate.
3. For an overview of these books, see Michael Pakaluk, *Other Selves: Philosophers on Friendship* (Indianapolis: Hackett, 1991).
4. Lynch, *Philosophy and Friendship*, 12.
5. The scholarship is extensive. Important works include A. W. Price, *Love and Friendship in Plato and Aristotle* (Oxford: Clarendon, 1989); Suzanne Stern-Gillet, *Aristotle's Philosophy of Friendship* (Albany: SUNY Press, 1995); and Lorraine Smith Pangle, *Aristotle and the Philosophy of Friendship* (Cambridge: Cambridge University Press, 2003). On the reception of the Aristotelian conception of happiness and virtue in Judaism, see Tirosh-Samuelson, *Happiness in Premodern Judaism: Virtue, Knowledge and Well-Being* (Cincinnati: Hebrew Union College Press, 2003); and Hava Tirosh-Samuelson, "Virtue and Happiness," in *Cambridge History of Jewish Philosophy from Antiquity Through the Seventeenth Century*, ed. Steven Nadler and T. M. Rudavsky (Cambridge: Cambridge University Press, 2009), 707–67.
6. Gary M. Gurtler, "Aristotle on Friendship: Insights from the Four Causes," in *Ancient and Medieval Concepts of Friendship*, ed. Suzanne Stern-Gillet and Gary M. Gurtler (Albany: SUNY Press, 2014), 35–50; quotation from 37.
7. For a recent review of these two approaches and an attempt to reconcile them, see Ann Ward, *Contemplating Friendship in Aristotle's Ethics* (Albany: SUNY Press, 2016).
8. Recent feminist readers have returned to Aristotle in an attempt to show that his philosophy would benefit from a more egalitarian reading. Thus Ann Ward argues that mothering, according to Aristotle, was "a model of friendship" and that the relationship between mothers and their children "bears some similarity to perfect friendship." See Ward, *Contemplating Friendship*, 17–18. Ward's strong misreading illustrates how much feminists wish to use Aristotle as a source for their egalitarian philosophy.
9. Bernard Collette-Ducic, "Making Friends: The Stoic Conception of Love and Its Platonic Background," in Stern-Gillet and Gurtler, *Ancient and Medieval Concepts*, 87.
10. Harry Lesser, "Eros and Philia in Epicurean Philosophy," in Stern-Gillet and Gurtler, *Ancient and Medieval Concepts*, 117–31, quote on p. 126.
11. See Tirosh-Samuelson, *Happiness*, 9–54.
12. Gregory E. Sterling, "The Bond of Humanity: Friendship in Philo of Alexandria," in *Greco-Roman Perspectives on Friendship*, ed. John T. Fitzgerald (Atlanta: Scholars Press, 1997), 203–23.
13. Sterling, "The Bond of Humanity," 209.
14. This proverb is attributed to Pythagoras, who was also the first to coin the saying "friendship is equality" (*philotes isotes*).
15. Sterling, 218.
16. Sterling, 218.
17. See Ellen Birnbaum, *The Place of Judaism in Philo's Thought: Israel, Jews and Proselytes* (Atlanta: Scholars Press, 1996).

18. For a detailed analysis of Philo's depiction of this community, consult Joan E. Taylor, *Jewish Women Philosophers of First Century Alexandria* (Oxford: Oxford University Press, 2003).
19. The point is elaborated in Ross Kraemer, "Monastic Jewish Women in Greco-Roman Egypt: Philo Judaeus on the Therapeutrides," *Signs* 14, no. 2 (1989): 342–70.
20. Marc Hirshman, *The Stabilization of Rabbinic Culture 100 C.E.–350 C.E.: Texts on Education and Their Late Antique Context* (Oxford: Oxford University Press, 2009), 22.
21. Hirshman, *The Stabilization of Rabbinic Culture*, 26.
22. A very useful conceptual analysis is offered in Alon Goshen-Gottstein, "Understanding Jewish Friendship: Extending Friendship Beyond Judaism," in *Friendship Across Religions: Theological Perspectives on Interreligious Friendship*, ed. Alon Goshen-Gottstein (Lanham, MD: Lexington Books, 2015), 1–35.
23. See Judith Romney Wegner, "The Image and Status of Women in Classical Rabbinic Judaism," in *Jewish Women in Historical Perspective*, 2nd ed., ed. Judith R. Baskin (Detroit: Wayne State University Press, 1999), 73–100. For a more nuanced and sympathetic treatment, see Judith Hauptman, "Women and Jewish Law," in *Women and Judaism: New Insights and Scholarship*, ed. Frederick E. Greenspahn (New York: New York University Press, 2009), 64–87.
24. See Tal Ilan, "'Beruria Has Spoken Well' (Tosefta Kelim Bava Metzia 1:3): The Historical Beruria and Her Transformation in Rabbinic Corpora," in Ilan, *Integrating Women into Second Temple History* (Peabody, MA: Hendrickson, 2001), 175–94.
25. There has not been a comprehensive study of the education of Jewish women in medieval Islam. Renee Levin-Melamed, who has written on Jewish women in Islamic societies, has been too eager to prove female agency and economic activities and therefore has not addressed the exclusion of women from advanced Torah study. See Renee Levin-Melamed, "Sephardi Women in the Medieval and Early Modern Periods," in *Jewish Women in Historical Perspective*, ed. Judith Baskin (Detroit: Wayne State University Press, 1999), 128–49.
26. Raymond Weiss, *Maimonides' Ethics: The Encounter of Philosophic and Religious Morality* (Chicago: University of Chicago Press, 1991); Tirosh-Samuelson, *Happiness*, 192–245.
27. See Steven Harvey, "The Sources of the Quotations from Aristotle's *Ethics* in the *Guide of the Perplexed* and the *Guide to the Guide*," in *Joseph Baruch Sermoneta Memorial Volume*, ed. Aviezer Ravitzky (Jerusalem: Jerusalem Studies in Jewish Thought, 1998), 87–102.
28. Weiss, *Maimonides' Ethics*, 182.
29. Weiss, 183. Self-disclosure and openness between friends was emphasized especially in Epicurean sources.
30. Moses Maimonides, *Guide of the Perplexed* 3:51; Shlomo Pines, ed. and trans., *Moses Maimonides: The Guide of the Perplexed* (Chicago: University of Chicago Press, 1963), 2:621.
31. See Idit Dobbs-Weinstein, "Matter as Creature and Matter as the Source of Evil: Maimonides and Aquinas," in *Neoplatonism and Jewish Thought*, ed. Lenn E. Goodman (Albany: SUNY Press, 1995), 217–35; and Susan Shapiro, "A Matter of Discipline: Reading for Gender in Jewish Philosophy," in *Judaism Since Gender*, ed. Miriam Peskowitz and Laura Levitt (New York: Routledge, 1997), 158–78.
32. Maimonides, *Mishneh Torah*, Hilkhot Talmud Torah, 1.13; Eliyahu Touger, trans. and ed., *Mishneh Torah* (New York: Moznaim, 1998), 366.
33. Warren Zev Harvey, "The Obligation of Talmud on Women According to Maimonides," *Tradition: A Journal of Orthodox Jewish Thought* 19, no. 2 (1981): 124.
34. Harvey, "Obligation," 125.

35. Maimonides, *Guide of the Perplexed* 3:51; Pines, *Moses Maimonides*, 627–28.
36. Hava Tirosh-Samuelson, "Gender and the Pursuit of Happiness in Maimonides Philosophy," in *Tov Elem: Memory, Community and Gender in Medieval and Early Modern Jewish Societies, Essays in Honor of Robert Bonfil*, ed. Elisheva Baumgarten, Amnon Raz-Krakotzkin, and Roni Weinstein (Jerusalem: Bialik Institute, 2012), 55–78.
37. Thus the Aristotelian differentiation among the love of the pleasant, the useful, and the good, which is the basis for the three types of friendships, became a standard trope in medieval Jewish philosophy. See Abraham Melamed, "The Metamorphosis of the Motif of Love of the Pleasant, the Useful and the Good in Albo, Alemanno, Judah Abravanel, and Muscato" [in Hebrew], in *Yehuda Abravanel's Philosophy of Love*, ed. Menachem Dorman (Haifa: University of Haifa Press, 1985), 57–72.
38. For an overview of the reception of Aristotle's *Nicomachean Ethics*, see Tirosh-Samuelson, "Virtue and Happiness," 707–67.
39. Isaac Abravanel, *Naḥalat Avot* (Venice, 1545; repr., Jerusalem: Zilberman, 1970), 356–57; Abravanel, *Commentary on the Torah: Deuteronomy* (Venice 1579; repr. Jerusalem: Benei Arabel, 1964), 74–75.
40. See Eric Lawee, *Isaac Abravanel's Stance Toward Tradition: Defense, Dissent, and Dialogue* (Albany: SUNY Press, 2001), 120.
41. For a critical edition of three of Abravanel's letters and analysis of their historical context, see Cedric Cohen Skalli, ed. and trans., *Isaac Abravanel, Letters* (Berlin: Walter de Gruyter, 2007).
42. John M. Zemke, ed. and trans., *Mose ben Baruk Almosnino, Regimiento de la vida; Tratado de los suenyos (Salonika, 1564)* (Tempe: Arizona Center of Medieval and Renaissance Studies, 2004), 50.
43. Almosnino's theory of human perfection moved beyond the Maimonidean-Aristotelian tradition, as it included not only the perfection of the intellect but also the perfection of the will. See Tirosh-Samuelson, *Happiness*, 394–498.
44. For a new English translation, biographical information on the author, and analysis of the cultural context of the *Dialoghi d'amore*, see Rosella Pescatori, ed., *Dialogues of Love: Leone Ebreo*, trans. Damian Bacich and Rosella Pescatori (Toronto: University of Toronto Press, 2009), especially 3–19.
45. A good summary of the arguments of each of the three dialogues is provided by T. Anthony Perry, *Erotic Spirituality: The Integrative Tradition from Leone Ebreo to John Donne* (Tuscaloosa: University of Alabama Press, 1980), 10–24.
46. Pescatori, *Dialogues of Love*, 28–71.
47. The date of composition of the *Dialogues of Love* is still unclear. For a long time, it was held that Abravanel composed the text from 1501 to 1502, but Barbara Garvin has made a strong argument in favor of dating the text to 1512. See Barbara Garvin, "The Language of Leone Ebreo's *Dialogi d'amore*," *Italia* 13–15 (2001): 181–210.
48. Compelling arguments in favor of Italian as the language of composition are given by Barbara Garvin, as previously cited. In my earlier work, I held that Hebrew was the language of composition, but I am now persuaded that this is not the case.
49. Paul Oscar Kristeller, "Ficino," in his *Eight Philosophers of the Italian Renaissance* (Palo Alto: Stanford University Press, 1964), 47.
50. On the dialogue form in Jewish philosophy and its cultural significance for relations between Jews and non-Jews, see Aaron W. Hughes, *The Art of Dialogue in Jewish Philosophy* (Bloomington: Indiana University Press, 2008).
51. This point was already noted by Abraham Melamed, "The Woman as Philosopher in Y. Abravanel's Dialoghi

d'Amore" [in Hebrew], *Jewish Studies* 40 (2000): 113–30.
52. Sergius Kodera, "The Idea of Beauty in Leone Ebreo (Judah Abravanel)," in *The Jewish Body: Corporeality, Society, and Identity in the Renaissance and Early Modern Period*, ed. Giuseppe Veltri and Maria Diemling (Leiden: Brill, 2009), 307.
53. See Aaron W. Hughes, "Transforming the Maimonidean Imagination: Aesthetics in the Renaissance Thought of Judah Abravanel," *Harvard Theological Review* 97, no. 4 (2004): 461–84.
54. For an overview, see Moshe Idel, *Kabbalah and Eros* (New Haven: Yale University Press, 2005).
55. See Howard Adelman, "Italian Jewish Women," in *Jewish Women in Historical Perspective*, 2nd ed., ed. Judith R. Baskin (Detroit: Wayne State University Press, 1999), 150–68. In Italy there were female Jewish medical practitioners, but the depth of their knowledge of professional medical literature is not clear to me. A female medical practitioner could engage in healing without formal knowledge of the philosophical-medical tradition that was accessible to men. In Italy the very cultivation of philosophy reflected gender differences: men studied philosophy as part of their training to become physicians and had access to Aristotelianism as practiced in universities. By contrast, women cultivated philosophy as part of their exposure to the *studia humanitatis*, especially rhetoric and poetry, as practiced in princely courts.
56. On this text and its female addressee, see Hava Tirosh-Rothschild, *Between Worlds: The Life and Works of David ben Judah Messer Leon* (Albany: SUNY Press, 1991), 61–66.
57. Don Harrán, ed. and trans., *Sarra Copia Sulam, Jewish Poet and Intellectual in Seventeenth Century Venice* (Chicago: University of Chicago Press, 2009), especially the "Editor's Introduction," 1–90. Harrán correctly notes that the salon of Copia Sullam predated and anticipated the salons of educated Jewish women in Berlin and Vienna.
58. The religious tension in the epistolary relationship between Cebà and Copia Sullam is analyzed in Giuseppe Veltri, "Body of Conversion and Immortality of the Soul: Sara Copio Sullam, the 'Beautiful Jewess,'" in *Renaissance Philosophy in Jewish Garb* (Leiden: Brill, 2009), 226–47. See also Lynn Lara Westwater, *Sara Copia Sulam: A Jewish Salonniere and the Press in Counter-Reformation Venice* (Toronto: University of Toronto Press, 2020).

PART 2

Women and the Bonds of Friendship

CHAPTER 4

"She and Her Friends"
On Women's Friendship in Biblical Narrative

SAUL M. OLYAN

It is often noted that biblical representations of friendship are mainly concerned with men. David and Jonathan, Job and his three comforters, the friend of Proverbs 17:17 who loves at all times and is compared implicitly to a brother, the anonymous disloyal friends of the psalms of individual complaint—all of these contribute to our understanding of friendship between men as it is represented in the various literary genres of the Hebrew Bible. In comparison, texts that portray friendships between women are few in number and restricted to narrative.[1] Nonetheless, they are rich and warrant careful consideration because of what they might tell us about how some biblical authors conceive of such friendships. Two texts will be my focus in this essay: the narrative of Jephthah's daughter in Judges 11:29–40 and the book of Ruth. After considering the portrayal of Jephthah's unnamed daughter and her friends and that of Naomi and Ruth, I shall compare the presuppositions about friendship that characterize these two narratives with those that are characteristic of men's friendships in narratives such as the prologue to the book of Job and the Jonathan-David stories, as well as in poetic texts such as Proverbs, the dialogues of the book of Job, and the psalms of individual complaint.

JEPHTHAH'S DAUGHTER AND HER FRIENDS

Judges 11 tells of the Gileadite military leader Jephthah's impulsive vow and its catastrophic consequences. As Jephthah prepares for war with the Ammonites, he vows to Yhwh, "If you will give the Ammonites into my hand, whoever comes forth from the doors of my house to meet me when I return safely from the Ammonites will be Yhwh's and I will offer him up as a whole burnt offering" (11:30–31).[2] After a resounding victory, Jephthah returns home to find his only child, a daughter, coming out to meet him, dancing and beating a hand drum in celebration. Victory, however, is turned to mourning for Jephthah, who rends his garments, stating that his vow cannot be undone (11:34–35).[3] Jephthah's daughter, who remains anonymous throughout the narrative, urges Jephthah to follow through with his vow, given that Yhwh has granted him vengeance against the Ammonites, his enemies (11:36). Nonetheless, she asks one thing of her father: "Give me leave for two months that I might go and descend upon the mountains and that I might weep over my virginity, I and my friends (*anokhi ve-reʿotay*)" (11:37).[4] He does so, "and she went—she and her friends—and she wept over her virginity upon the mountains" (11:38). When the two-month-long reprieve is complete, Jephthah's daughter returns to her father, and he sacrifices her, fulfilling his vow.

One of the most striking things about this narrative is the evident supplementation that the narrative has experienced. Although the friends of Jephthah's daughter play an important role in the final form of the text, each of the two times they are mentioned appears to be an expansion of the narrative. In verse 37, "I and my friends" reads as a somewhat awkward addition tacked on to the end of the verse, which otherwise concerns only Jephthah's daughter ("that I might go and descend upon the mountains and that I might weep over my virginity, I and my friends"). Were we to remove the supplement, the text would read more smoothly. I suspect that verse 38 has also undergone expansion under the influence of verse 37, with "she and her friends" apparently added to a sentence that otherwise concerned Jephthah's daughter alone: "And she went—she and her friends—and she wept over her virginity upon the mountains."[5] The addition tacked on to verse 37 is much like that of Leviticus 20:10 in form: "As for the man who commits adultery with the wife of his neighbor, he shall surely be put to death, the adulterer and the adulteress." This text states that the man who commits adultery with his neighbor's wife shall certainly be executed; it then adds, rather awkwardly, "the adulterer and the adulteress," thereby expanding the penalty to include the woman, who is not otherwise mentioned in the penalty formulation.[6] In the case of Judges 11:37, it is not a penalty that is expanded but the characters of a narrative that would otherwise concern Jephthah's daughter alone.

According to the final form of Judges 11, Jephthah's daughter spends her two-month-long reprieve in the company of her friends rather than in isolation. How do the daughter's friends function in the story, and what might have motivated their inclusion by a later hand? Those who mourn the dead, petitioners who embrace mourning behaviors and those utilizing mourning rites to mark a calamity, typically do so in company, as the Job prologue aptly illustrates.[7] When Job's three friends hear of his misfortune, they join him physically, embracing his mourning rites and playing the role of comforter (*menaḥem*): "When the three friends of Job heard [about] all this evil that had come upon him, each came from his place: Eliphaz the Temanite, Bildad the Shuhite and Zophar the Naamite. They took counsel together to come to move back and forth (*lanud*) for him and to comfort him" (Job 2:11).[8] They also weep, tear their garments, and strew dirt upon their heads as mourners typically do. Various texts suggest that it is unusual to be isolated while mourning, whether one is mourning the dead, petitioning the deity, or reacting to or anticipating a personal or corporate calamity. Friends, allies, and family members are expected to be present and function as comforters (e.g., Gen. 37:35; 2 Sam. 10:2; Jer. 16:7; Ps. 69:21).[9] To comfort can mean several things: to join the mourner in the mourner's ritual behavior, to console the mourner, or in the case of mourning the dead, to end a mourner's period of mourning.[10] According to the final form of Judges 11, Jephthah's daughter's friends join her in her time of calamity, weeping with her just as male comforters are said to do according to Job 2:12 and a number of other texts.[11] Nothing is said directly about the friends offering consolation to Jephthah's daughter, but it is possible that we are intended to assume that they do so because of their very presence with her.[12] Although the technical term *comforter* and the verb *to comfort* are not used in the narrative of Judges 11, the daughter's friends nonetheless function just as male comforters would in a typical context of male mourning, including mourning tied to a calamity. They are physically present with Jephthah's daughter, they weep with her, and the author may intend that we assume that they offer her consolation.

Why might the writer who evidently added the friends to this narrative have done so? It may be that the writer felt that the presence of comforters was appropriate for a woman experiencing a personal catastrophe as much as for a man in the same situation and that the story in its penultimate form was incomplete without them. Although this must remain at best a speculation, it does have significant implications for our understanding of the literary representation of mourning in the Hebrew Bible, as biblical texts do not otherwise mention women comforting women in a mourning context.[13] More important for our purposes, it also has significant implications for our understanding of how our authors represent friendship between women. If my reading of Judges 11 is correct, the writer who added the friends to the narrative of Jephthah's daughter conceives of women's friendship in terms not unlike that of men with one another, at least with respect to the obligations incumbent upon friends at the time of a friend's personal misfortune. Just as Job's three friends in the Job prologue are loyal to him at a time of calamity, joining him physically and embracing his ritual state by undertaking mourning rites, so the daughter's friends are faithful to her in her time of need, accompanying her on her journey and joining her in her mourning behavior.[14]

RUTH AND NAOMI

The focus of the book of Ruth is the evolving relationship between Naomi and her daughter-in-law Ruth. Set at first in Moab, where Naomi; her husband, Elimelech; and her two sons, Mahlon and Kilyon, are refugees from a famine in Judah, the narrative tells of the deaths of Naomi's husband and sons and Naomi's return to Bethlehem accompanied by Ruth. Although Naomi and Ruth are relatives by marriage, the narrator goes to great lengths to emphasize that Ruth and Orpa, Naomi's other daughter-in-law, have fulfilled every obligation incumbent upon them as daughters-in-law, both to their dead husbands and to Naomi. They have been models of loyalty; they owe Naomi nothing. Thus they should return to their natal families and find new husbands: "Go, return each woman to her mother's house! May Yhwh be loyal to you [*asah ḥesed*] as you have been with the dead and with me! May Yhwh grant to you that you may find a place of repose, each in the house of her husband" (1:8–9). At first, both Orpa and Ruth refuse to leave Naomi and begin the trek to Judah with her. After much urging, Orpa relents and returns to her family of origin, but Ruth "clings" to Naomi, refusing to leave her (1:14; figure 4.1). To "cling" (*davak*) is an idiom of loyalty used elsewhere to describe the exceptional male friend: "There are friends for friendly exchanges, // And there is a friend who clings more closely than a brother" (Prov. 18:24).[15] Ruth's continuing loyalty to Naomi, expressed using the verb *davak*, is clearly based on choice rather than obligation, as she has fulfilled all familial expectations according to 1:8. In contrast to the mother-in-law / daughter-in-law relationship, which is said to have reached an endpoint once all obligations have been met, the new relationship between the women is unaffected by circumstances and has no endpoint whatsoever as far as Ruth is concerned: "Where you go, I will go and where you lodge, I will lodge; your people will be my people, and your god my god. Where you die, I will die and there I will be buried" (1:16–17).[16] Thus I understand the relationship of Ruth and Naomi to have evolved into a new, voluntary association characterized by loyalty that fulfills no familial obligations. This new bond of choice is best described as a friendship.[17] As the story unfolds, other features of biblical friendship in addition to loyalty and choice come to characterize the relationship between Naomi and Ruth.[18] These include shared trust, mutual affection, and reciprocal support.[19]

As in biblical representations of friendship between men, the new bond between the women is not only a bond of choice; it is also reciprocal, characterized by what I call behavioral parity. Ruth insists on accompanying Naomi to Bethlehem; Naomi accepts Ruth's decision to do so. Ruth supports Naomi and herself by providing food for the two of them (2:2, 17–19; 3:17); Naomi aids Ruth by helping secure her a husband (3:1–4). Both are widows, yet they are of different generations and therefore not formally equal in terms of all personal characteristics. Nonetheless, their behavior toward one another is that of peers: each looks out for the well-being of the other, "repaying" "that which is good" to the other.[20] Behavioral parity, rather than parity of life stage, social status, wealth, or some combination of personal attributes, is also characteristic of ideal male friendship, as texts such as Psalms 35:12–14, 88:19; Job 19:19; and Proverbs 17:17 illustrate, mostly in the breach. Although friends might also be peers with respect to one or more personal characteristics, they need not be in order to be friends. Like Naomi and Ruth, male friends such as Jonathan and David are not

FIGURE 4.1 Simeon Solomon, *Ruth, Naomi, and the Child Obed* (1860). Courtesy of the collection of Carolyn Conroy.

necessarily portrayed as equal in terms of status—Jonathan is the king's son and heir—or other personal characteristics, yet they are portrayed as peers in terms of their treatment of one another. For example, in 1 Samuel 20:41, David and Jonathan exchange reciprocal ritual acts of affection, kissing each other and weeping together. They do this even though they are not formally equal in terms of status. Although the Ruth narrative does not speak explicitly of the expectation of behavioral parity between friends, the assumption that behavioral parity is a norm of friendship is implicit in the story's emphasis on the reciprocal acts of caring each woman undertakes on behalf of the other.

What do we learn of the biblical representations of friendship between women from the narrative of Jephthah's daughter and her friends and that of Ruth and Naomi? Furthermore, how do the presuppositions implicit in these texts compare with assumptions about male friendships elsewhere in the Hebrew Bible? The final form of the narrative of Jephthah's daughter and her friends portrays women who are loyal to their friend in her time of need, behaving as comforters are expected to behave according to other texts that treat the mourning obligations of male friends. The daughter's friends not only accompany her on her journey; they also embrace her ritual behavior, weeping with her. It is possible that we are also meant to assume that the friends console Jephthah's daughter, given that consolation is an important component of comforting according to other biblical texts.

Loyalty also characterizes the relationship of Ruth and Naomi, but this narrative portrait of women's friendship brings other aspects of friendship into relief as well: its voluntary nature, which is particularly emphasized in Ruth 1, as well as mutual affection, reciprocal support, and shared trust, all aspects of behavioral parity in a friendship. Jephthah's daughter and her friends are very likely life-stage peers and may share other characteristics, such as wealth; like some male friends, they appear to be peers in most or all respects (compare the male friends of Ps. 55:14, one of whom describes the other as "a man like myself" [*enosh ke 'erki*]). In contrast, Naomi and Ruth belong to different generations, though they share widowhood in common. Like some male friends in biblical texts, they are not peers in all or even most respects (e.g., Prov. 19:4, which states that "wealth adds many friends," implying that riches attract those who have less). Yet like ideal male friends, the relationship of Naomi and Ruth is characterized by behavioral parity.

The portrayals of women's friendship in the book of Ruth and in Judges 11:29–40 suggest that many of the characteristics associated with male friendship as it is represented in other biblical texts are shared in common with friendship between women. These include mutual choice, affection, trust, loyalty, support, and other elements of behavioral parity, as well as a potential range of possible shared personal characteristics between friends (from none at all to several). Judges 11:29–40 brings into relief the obligation of the friend to function as a comforter at a time of personal calamity, well known from other texts that speak of men's friendships (e.g., Ps. 35:13–14; Job 2:11–13). The book of Ruth emphasizes both the voluntary nature of friendship and various aspects of behavioral parity, including reciprocal loyalty. The main difference I discern between the biblical representation of women's friendships and those between men is a lack of evidence for the formalization of friendship through covenant-making in the case of friendship between women, a characteristic of a few biblical texts treating male friendship. These include the narratives of Jonathan and David (e.g., 1 Sam. 18:1–4, where the two cut a covenant) and Psalm 55:21, which speaks of the psalmist's friend violating his covenant (*ḥll berit*) with the psalmist. It is no surprise that friendship between women lacks evidence of formalization through covenant-making, given that women are not portrayed in biblical texts as treaty partners.

NOTES

I would like to thank Yale University Press for permission to rework material from my book *Friendship in the Hebrew Bible* (New Haven: Yale University Press, 2017).

1. Friendship between women and men is not attested in biblical texts, although friendship rhetoric is used for erotic relations between the sexes, not unlike familial rhetoric (e.g., Song of Songs; Jer. 3:4). On this, see Olyan, *Friendship*, 8–9, 113.
2. All translations in this essay are my own.
3. Mourning rites such as the tearing of clothing are used not only for mourning the dead but also to mark a personal or corporate calamity—either anticipated or after the fact—as Esther 6:12 illustrates. After having been forced by the Persian king to honor his archenemy Mordecai in a most public way, Haman retreats to his house "in mourning (*abel*) and with [his] head covered." Other contexts in which mourning is embraced include petitioning of the deity (as in Joel 2:17 or Ps. 69:11–12) and the rites of the person afflicted with skin disease (Lev. 13:45–46). On these four distinct types of mourning, see my discussion in *Biblical Mourning: Ritual and Social Dimensions* (Oxford: Oxford University Press, 2004), 25–27.
4. Reading with the *qere*. Weeping over her virginity presumably means to bewail the fact that she will die without

experiencing sexual intercourse with a man, as the text emphasizes in verse 39: "And as for her, she did not know a man." Such a death also implies that Jephthah's daughter will never bear children, a central role of a woman according to biblical texts.
5. There are many examples of the syntactical construction singular verb + subject (often represented by a singular independent pronoun, or PN) + additional subject, sometimes a plurality. For discussion of this construction, see, for example, Bruce K. Waltke and M. O'Connor, *An Introduction to Biblical Hebrew Syntax* (Winona Lake, IN: Eisenbrauns, 1990), 16.3.2c, who cite comparable examples, such as Ruth 1:6. See also Paul Joüon, *Grammaire de l'hébreu biblique* (Rome: Institut biblique pontifical, 1923), 146c; and E. Kautzsch, ed., *Gesenius' Hebrew Grammar*, trans. A. E. Cowley (Oxford: Clarendon, 1910), 146 f and g. Though commonplace and not usually understood to be an indicator of supplementation in itself, the presence of this construction in verse 38 is very likely supplementary, given the more obvious addition to the text in verse 37.
6. On the expansion of this verse to include the adulteress, see, for example, the discussion of Jacob Milgrom, *Leviticus 17–22: A New Translation with Introduction and Commentary*, AB 3A (New York: Doubleday, 2000), 1747, who cites the relevant bibliography.
7. Contrast the person afflicted with skin disease (the *tsarua'*), whose isolation is mandated according to Leviticus 13:44–45. This person is the only type of mourner who is not entitled to comforters. For the four types of mourners, see further Olyan, *Biblical Mourning*, passim.
8. To "move back and forth" (*lanud*) is one of a number of mourning rites (e.g., Isa. 51:19; Jer. 15:5, 16:5, 22:10; Nah. 3:7), perhaps intended here as a synecdoche.
9. Again, the exception to this pattern is the person afflicted with skin disease, who must remain isolated as previously noted.
10. Olyan, *Biblical Mourning*, 46–49. On comforters ending mourning, see Gary A. Anderson, *A Time to Mourn, a Time to Dance: The Expression of Grief and Joy in Israelite Religion* (University Park: Penn State University Press, 1991), 84–87.
11. The weeping of the friends is implied by the additions to the narrative at the end of verse 37 and in verse 38.
12. The consoling role of the comforter is illustrated by texts such as Isaiah 40:1; Jeremiah 16:7; Job 16:5; and Lamentations 1:16, 2:13. In Lamentations 1:16, the comforter is "one who restores my spirit (*nefesh*)"; in Lamentations 2:13, comforting is associated with healing. On the consoling role of the comforter, see further my discussion in *Biblical Mourning*, 48.
13. Other biblical texts do mention women comforting men or being comforted by men. Among these, see, for example, 2 Samuel 12:24; Isaiah 66:13; Job 42:11; and Ruth 2:13.
14. That friends are expected to comfort their friends at a time of personal calamity is illustrated by a text such as Psalm 35:13–14, where the psalmist excoriates disloyal friends who do not reciprocate support in his time of need, although he had supported them ritually when they were ill: "As for me, when they were sick, // my clothes were sackcloth; // I afflicted myself with fasting ... // I walked around like one mourning [his] mother; // I was prostrated, a mourner." Although the vocabulary of comforting is not used here, the actions are those of comforters.
15. Derivatives of *davak* are used to describe loyalty in a number of different contexts, including the loyalty of intimate male friends and brothers to one another (Prov. 18:24); that of the people of Judah to their king, David, at a time of rebellion against him (2 Sam. 20:2); and that expected of Israelites in

their relations with their divine suzerain Yhwh (e.g., Deut. 4:4, 11:22; Josh. 22:5). In other contexts, the verb *davak* has meanings other than to be loyal: it may suggest physical proximity (Ruth 2:8, 21, 23) or sexual-emotional intimacy (Gen. 2:24, 34:3; 1 Kings 11:2).
16. For detailed analysis of Ruth's declaration and its various resonances, see my discussion in *Friendship*, 63–65, 143–45.
17. It is noteworthy that the idiom used for Ruth's loyalty to Naomi after all familial obligations are fulfilled—the verb *davak*—differs from that used of fulfilling those obligations (*asah ḥesed*). Perhaps the change of idiom is intentional, meant to signal the transition to the incipient, voluntary bond between Ruth and Naomi.
18. The voluntary nature of biblical friendship comes into relief when one observes how easily it is terminated in contrast to familial relations. Disloyal friends are a topos of the psalms of complaint, as Psalms 35:12, 15, 19; 38:12; and 88:9 illustrate. They are also mentioned in other poetic texts (e.g., Job 19:19), in prophetic materials (Jer. 9:7), and in prose narratives such as the story of Amnon, Jonadab, and Absalom (2 Sam. 13). Loyalty as a cornerstone of friendship is suggested by texts such as Jeremiah 9:7; Psalm 35:13–14; Job 19:19, 21–22; and Proverbs 17:17, 18:24.
19. On these characteristics, see further Olyan, *Friendship*, 29–33.
20. Implicit in texts such as Psalms 7:5, 35:12, 38:21, and 109:5 is the expectation that friends and family members should repay "that which is good" rather than "that which is evil." This rhetoric captures nicely the presuppositions of behavioral parity.

CHAPTER 5

Friends and Friendship in the Memoir of Glückel of Hameln
Learning from Experience

JOSEPH DAVIS

The memoir of the German-Jewish woman Glückel of Hameln (1645–1724) represents a novelty in Jewish literature, as it is the first complete life story written by a Jewish woman.[1] A contemporary of pioneering women authors, such as Madame de Sévigné (1626–1696) and her friend Madame de La Fayette (1634–1693), Glückel was indeed one of the first Jewish women to write a book of any sort. As she began to write the Yiddish memoir that would later bring her fame, shortly after the death of her husband, Chaim, in 1689, Glückel was thinking a great deal about friendship.

Her thoughts are bitter, and she gives voice to them in a number of places throughout the memoir. They are crystallized with special urgency in a parable that she retells: a story of a prince and his three faithless friends. In this story, a prince tests the loyalty of his three closest friends, but each of them fails the test. The moral of the story is that "a friend [Yiddish, *oy(h)ev*, from Hebrew] cannot be known until he has been proven."[2] Addressing her children, as she did frequently throughout the memoir, Glückel applies the lesson of the story: "Look after yourselves, dear children, for you have no one, no friends [Yiddish, *fraynt*, from German], on whom to depend, and even if you have many friends, when you need them, you cannot depend on them.... When they are wanted, they cannot be found.... There is no friend to rely on save the Holy One, blessed be He."[3] In writing about her late husband, however, Glückel takes a more optimistic view of the possibilities of friendship: "He was such a loving and faithful husband and father.... I had had my husband thirty years and had enjoyed through him all the good that a woman could wish for."[4] Throughout the memoir, the only person on whom she bestows the common trebled endearment *hertsigen liben fraynd* (dear beloved friend) is her husband, Chaim.[5]

Many Jewish writings of the sixteenth and seventeenth centuries included discussions of friendship. Many are incorporated into works of Jewish law or moral instruction (*musar*), and they are mostly prescriptive. For example, Moses Hanokh Altschul warned the readers of his late sixteenth-century *Brantspigel* that a friend should not wear out his welcome by spending too much time at his friend's house.[6] A generation later, the great rabbinic scholar and pietist Isaiah Horowitz (d. 1630), whose *Shenei Luḥot ha-Berit* was a favorite of Glückel's husband, Chaim, urged his readers to prefer the friendship of the learned, as well as the friendship of the poor and needy, to that of pleasure seekers, sinners, and women.[7] Glückel takes a different approach to thinking about friendship, an approach that is empirical and in a sense skeptical.[8] Glückel's account of friendship is descriptive, and she expresses disappointment in her friends as often as she expresses appreciation.

FAMILY AS THE CLOSEST FRIENDS

To understand Glückel's views concerning friendship, it is imperative to understand that in early modern Yiddish, and indeed in early modern German, a "friend" was often a member of the family. Indeed, in many contexts, the main connotation of the word *friend* was kinship rather than affection or loyalty. In ordinary English usage and some other contemporary languages, a "friend" is not a member of the "family" and vice versa.[9] For Glückel, by contrast, the linguistic situation is almost the opposite.[10] Glückel could certainly imagine friends who were not related by blood or even by marriage. On the other hand, Glückel often uses *fraynt* as a synonym for the Hebrew-derived *kroyvim*, meaning precisely "kinsmen."[11] Most commonly, the exact connotation of the word is ambiguous, and it might include either kin or nonkin friends.[12] For example, the prince's three friends in Glückel's story might or might not be his kinsmen. "Friends" and "family," in Glückel's world, were overlapping categories, and indeed many of the "friends" who appear in her memoir are members of her family.

The issue here is not merely semantic; it involves the very categories by which Glückel thought about the people around her. "Friends" for Glückel meant people with whom one has ties of affection but also, as we will see, ties of reciprocal responsibility, shared sociability and hospitality, and, above all, closeness or social connection. This was a group that consisted mainly of family and in-laws. Not all the people whom Glückel labels in the memoir as her friends can be identified, but all the ones who can be identified were her kinsmen and kinswomen. For example, there is Breinelé, one of Chaim's first cousins. "We were always good kinsfolk and friends—*gute fraynt un' bakante*," Glückel writes.[13] According to her, Chaim's nephew Jacob Hanover "was a close friend of my family."[14] Alas, he was no help when Glückel's son Leib was in straits. "From this we can see again that we should hold no one to be a true friend until he has been proved," Glückel repeats.[15] Glückel believed that one's closest kin are almost inevitably one's best friends and perhaps one's only true friends; that is the point she makes to her children in the pessimistic quote with which the chapter began.

GLÜCKEL'S SECOND MARRIAGE

The severest test of Glückel's views on friendship and its relationship to marriage was her second marriage, to Hirsch (or Herz) Levy of Metz. Although she had chosen her second husband herself (unlike her first husband, to whom she was betrothed before the age of twelve) and had consulted carefully with her family and her circle of advisers, and while indeed her future husband had himself written to her, urging his proposal, it was not a happy marriage. She was convinced in retrospect that her second marriage was a mistake. Glückel draws a cruel contrast between the outward trappings of the grand wedding and the decorous attention to gifts, feasts, and other formal marks of friendship that her husband provided at the time of their marriage and her inward feeling of unhappiness. She accuses her husband of having deceived her in his letters of courtship and imagines that his intentions in the marriage were essentially mercenary. In truth, she admits that her own motives were not much different. She had hoped that she would share his wealth, but instead he went bankrupt, and they lived together in poverty.[16]

Glückel tells a series of anecdotes expressing her sense of alienation from her new stepchildren and the new family she has joined. She suggests that the members of her new household, and perhaps Hirsch as well, were cold and materialistic and not accommodating toward her. The best that Glückel will admit is that Hirsch treated her honestly and fulfilled his financial responsibilities.[17]

As many of her readers have surely noticed, these unhappy experiences did not lead Glückel to endorse a model of companionate marriage. She had arranged marriages for each of her children, based almost strictly on the wealth and good reputation of her prospective in-laws. She expresses no uneasiness about this. Her conclusion from her unhappy second marriage is not that arranged marriages are risky but that she would have been better off remaining a widow.[18]

GLÜCKEL AND HER IN-LAWS

The middle section of Glückel's memoir focuses on her long and ultimately successful effort to arrange marriages for each of her twelve children. As they married, Glückel inevitably developed a growing circle of in-laws—in Yiddish, *mekhutonim*. The Yiddish word has two senses: a narrower sense and a wider one. In the first, *mekhutonim* refers specifically to the parents of one's son-in-law or one's daughter-in-law (*gegenschwäher* in some German dialects). The respective parents of a married couple were regarded as especially closely linked. "There are no friends [Hebrew, *re'im*] greater than these," declared Rabbi Meir of Lublin in the early seventeenth century.[19] But in a broader sense, *mekhutonim* could include any sort of relative by marriage.[20] Beyond the immediate circle of close in-laws was a range of secondary in-laws and kin. Early modern Yiddish had no specific name for this kind of in-law, which combined an in-law relationship with a blood relationship, such as the nephew of a sister-in-law or the son-in-law of a cousin. They, too, are *mekhutonim*. By today's standard, this might seem a very distant relative. Nevertheless, this type of second-degree family connection—the blood relatives of in-laws and the in-laws of blood relatives—seems to have been an important one in Glückel's world.[21] For example, Judah Berlin, one of the major characters in the memoir, was a cousin of one of Glückel's eleven brothers-in-law.[22] Including these more distant relatives, Glückel mentions more than one hundred relations by name in the memoir. Given the size of this clan, one might even ask how much time or space Glückel had in her life for nonkin friends.

Many of Glückel's new in-laws were chosen from within her own extended family or from among friends of the family. Glückel's daughter Hannah was married to one of her first cousins, while another daughter Freudchen was matched with one of her second cousins.[23] Her son Zanvil married the daughter of Moses Bamberg, a "faithful friend" of Glückel's brother-in-law Joseph.[24] Such a strategic selection of in-laws did not, however, always succeed. Hirschel Ries, the father-in-law of Glückel's son Leib, was the brother-in-law of Glückel's sister Mattie. Glückel's criticism of Hirschel returns to the themes of betrayal and false friendship that are spelled out in her story of the prince's false friends. Leib went to live with Hirschel in Berlin. But when Leib encountered financial difficulties, Hirschel, as Glückel saw the matter—far from fulfilling his sworn promises to look after the boy—showed himself to be rapacious and untrustworthy: "His father-in-law would sooner see him rotted and wasted in [debtors'] prison than help him with a hundred... *reichstaler*."[25] All of which is to say that kinship does not ensure reliable friendship.

JUDAH BERLIN, UNTRUSTWORTHY FRIEND

Glückel, as noted, generally took a pessimistic view of friendship, and she did not believe that generosity among friends was reciprocated very often. Nor did she believe that her own friends had shown proper loyalty to her and her children after Chaim's death.[26] She writes, "We helped many and—before God—all those with whom we had business dealings became rich as kings, but... many to whom we did good repaid our children with evil.... Those to whom we did good do not remember and do not care to know my children, who losing their pious father are like sheep without a shepherd. They could help them a little. May God have mercy on them, they do the reverse."[27]

Glückel's thoughts about loyalty, reciprocity, and friendship, as well as the complex ways that these could be tied to kinship, are apparent in her story of Judah Berlin (Jost Liebmann).[28] When Judah first appeared in Hamburg, as Glückel tells the story, he was a poor Polish Jew, possessing only twenty to thirty *reichstaler*, as Glückel states, with her usual precision in matters of money. He was, as mentioned, a sort of in-law of Glückel and

Chaim, and they offered him hospitality. Then, having appraised his talent, they offered him employment, and he worked for them both in their home as a sort of servant and in their business in jewels, jewelry, and precious metals. Subsequently, Chaim and Judah became partners. Moreover, a marriage was arranged between Judah and one of Chaim's nieces, cementing the family bond. Eventually, however, the partnership broke up. There were recriminations and eventually a lawsuit in a rabbinic court. Judah won the suit, but Glückel suggests that the rabbinic judges were corrupt.[29] Later on, Judah became one of the richest men in Germany, and in spite of the lawsuit and Glückel's continuing bitterness, social relations were maintained between her family and Judah. Once when Glückel visited Berlin for the wedding of one of her sons, Judah, she says, "sent me Sabbath gifts . . . and . . . made a great feast in my honour." When Glückel held another wedding celebration, some time afterward, for her daughter Hendelé, Judah attended the wedding and once more hosted a meal for Glückel and the bride and groom.[30]

Judah Berlin was a "good friend" of Glückel and Chaim—more than a mere servant, more than a talented business partner, and much more than a distant relative.[31] Glückel recounts how he and Chaim used the language of brotherhood for the bond between them.[32] Yet Judah does not fall easily into the simple categories of "false friends" and "true friends" that Glückel establishes in her parables. Glückel naturally wished to be able to claim the friendship of wealthy men such as Judah Berlin, which was worth much for the commercial reputation of her family.[33] Nor did she forget that at the time of the quarantine of Glückel's oldest daughter, Zipporah, Judah—then still a young man, living as a part of Glückel's household—acted with courage and devotion.[34] But she also expresses her sense that her family's generosity to the impoverished youth from Poland had never been properly repaid. She writes, "We have all forgiven [Judah]. . . . He always did business with my children, and we had no cause to grumble at him."[35] And yet grumble she did.

WOMEN'S FRIENDSHIP OVER TIME:
GLÜCKEL AND MISTRESS JACHET

Premodern Jewish writings about friendship focus mainly, or even overwhelmingly, on friendships among men. Glückel's memoir also focuses on her interactions with men, while those with women are more rarely mentioned. Glückel does include one substantial narrative of a friendship with another woman—namely, the story of her relationship with her in-law, Mistress Jachet. It was not her deepest friendship—that was with her first husband, Chaim—but it is the relationship whose development over time Glückel describes with the greatest detail, nuance, and brio.[36] Glückel understood that relationships with in-laws required nurturing and that in-laws are not inevitably friendly toward one another, as we have seen. In recounting her own wedding, she recalls that her mother did not take immediately to Chaim's family, and she retells a self-deprecating story that her father-in-law told in order to mollify Glückel's mother: "Ill-humour was dissolved in joyous laughter and friendship, and the marriage was celebrated with hearty good cheer."[37] Similarly, although over a much longer period, Glückel's relationship with Jachet began in distrust but gradually developed in a friendlier direction.

Jachet was the sister of Kossman, who was married to Glückel's oldest daughter, Zipporah.[38] Jachet's son, Moses Krumbach, was just a little older than Glückel's younger daughter Esther, and a number of years after the Zipporah-Kossman wedding, a match between Moses and Esther was proposed. But as the two families were making preliminary arrangements for the wedding, Glückel heard rumors ("from some very good friends," whom Glückel leaves unnamed) that Moses was unsuitable for her daughter in some way.[39] Glückel thereupon wrote an unfriendly letter to Jachet, and this was followed by a "vain, angry" correspondence. Glückel wrote that young Moses must come to Hamburg for Glückel and Chaim to approve or disapprove him. Jachet wrote back that if there was to be a marriage, Esther would have to come to Metz, where Jachet and her family lived. While these negotiations were going back and forth, Chaim passed away. After a time, Glückel, now a widow, renewed her correspondence with Jachet, but it continued to be "contrary," she writes.[40] Eventually, however, a compromise was reached, Esther and Moses were married, and Jachet's status relative to Glückel changed from being an in-law in the broader sense to being one in the narrower sense—that is, from being merely the *sister* of Glückel's son-in-law Kossman to being the *mother-in-law* of Glückel's daughter Esther.[41]

Glückel's relationship to Jachet drew closer still a few years later. Glückel, as mentioned earlier, received a proposal of marriage from a wealthy widower in Metz, Hirsch Levy. After consulting with her family and friends, Glückel moved to her new home to be wed.[42] Jachet was among the small group who traveled out to greet Glückel when she arrived in Metz, and Jachet was something like a matron of honor at the wedding.⁴³ Glückel was certainly flattered by these gestures, as being shown respect (Yiddish, *koved*) was exceedingly important to her. Glückel and Jachet, if not yet the best of friends, were certainly no longer enemies.

Glückel lived in Metz for twenty-five years, and her doubts about her son-in-law Moses, Jachet's son, reemerged as she spent time with him. "My son-in-law was like other people who are very keen on . . . money," Glückel writes.⁴⁴ But in her perception, Moses's character improved over the years: "He received a new heart, so that he does much good to the family on both sides, his own and Esther's. His door is wide open to the poor, and he is now parnass [a leader] of the Community."⁴⁵ Jachet appears to have also made efforts to advance the relationship: "Mistress Jachet often spoke to me of [Glückel's daughter Esther's] good cooking and fine household arrangements, saying, 'I must confess that Esther can cook better than I.'"⁴⁶ Thus both mothers began to share satisfaction in both of their married children.

Jachet appears only once more in the memoir. Jachet died, and her family gave money for Psalms to be recited every morning in synagogue for the benefit of her soul. Glückel writes that she attended that service regularly. This is what is characterized in Jewish tradition as a *ḥesed shel emet*, an altruistic deed that one does for the dead because the responsibilities of kinship and friendship extend to the dead as to the living.⁴⁷

NONKIN FRIENDS:
SERVANTS, EMPLOYEES, AND BUSINESS PARTNERS

For early modern people of all sorts, Jews and non-Jews, and for Glückel as well, it was axiomatic that one's household, kin, in-laws, and friends (kin and nonkin) would all be economically active and instrumentally useful. Recent scholarship has emphasized that ties of kinship and friendship undergirded the networks of commercial trust and credit in early modern Europe.⁴⁸ The business network of Glückel and her husband consisted in large part of a network of kin, in-laws, and friends. Indeed, Glückel often returns implicitly to the question of whether friendship, kinship, and marriage are merely commercial relations; this is particularly the point at issue in her description of her second husband, Hirsch.⁴⁹

The nonkin who figure most prominently in Glückel's memoir are a series of servants, employees, and business partners, whose stories are told in the middle sections of the memoir. Several were members of Glückel's household (*bnei bayis* in Yiddish), and Glückel seems to have counted them, as she did Judah Berlin, among her friends.[50] For example, Abraham Kantor (like Judah Berlin) performed household and commercial services. Another young employee, Issachar Cohen, by contrast, seems never to have lived within the household. But in the early modern period, steady employment or service of any kind, whether in the household or outside it, had some of the character of a personal relationship. So did business partnerships, such as Glückel and Chaim's partnership with Moses Helmstadt.[51]

Glückel's retrospective attitude toward these associates varies greatly. She makes no effort to hide her contempt for Moses Helmstadt, another "false friend." He became partners with Chaim but never paid Chaim his fair share. In Glückel's telling of events, he addresses Chaim as his "brother" and swears on a Torah scroll to deal honestly with him, but "he was false, and dishonest hearts have no rest."[52] Glückel's anger and scorn should not hide from us that she takes the rhetoric of kinship seriously and regards its misuse as wicked.[53] At the other extreme, she shows a fondness for an old retainer of her husband's family, nicknamed "Shot" Jacob, because he was once shot with a bullet. She tells a long story, one of the longest narratives in the book, of how he was once dispatched to be her escort when she was returning to Hamburg by coach with some of her children. "My good Jacob," she calls him, expressing a combination of affection and exasperation, got drunk, and Glückel found herself protecting him instead of the other way around.[54]

Between these extremes of affection and betrayal lies the story of Issachar Cohen. Like Judah Berlin, Issachar was first an employee and then left Hamburg to found his own business. As she does in writing about Judah, Glückel expresses her anger and disappointment at what she sees as Issachar's ingratitude and stinginess. Even after leaving his partnership with Chaim, however, Issachar continues to appear in the memoir, accompanying Chaim in his travels as a business companion. In one anecdote, Glückel herself begs Issachar to escort her husband. Showing "his wickedness then as always," Glückel says, Issachar insists on a share of Chaim's profits.[55] Issachar appears one last time after Chaim's death when he accompanies Glückel to the wedding of one of her sons. The wedding invitation is a formal sign, as the shared travels are the informal sign, that Issachar remained a friend of the family in spite of Glückel's disapproval of his character.[56]

GLÜCKEL'S RELATIONSHIPS WITH NON-JEWS

In Glückel's memoir, beyond that outermost circle of Jewish acquaintances lies the world of non-Jews. Did Glückel have any non-Jewish friends?[57]

We should not imagine Glückel as living in isolation from non-Jews. The reverse is true, as her very household included non-Jewish servants. Glückel tells a story, for example, of a craving she had once when she was pregnant; she sends an unnamed non-Jewish servant (the *shabbes-froye*) out into a stormy night to buy a particular fruit. Interestingly, Glückel never lists any non-Jews among her travel companions. The one exception proves the rule: an army corporal who is enlisted by her husband as an escort when they travel through a dangerous area.[58]

Nonetheless, Glückel had extensive business ties with non-Jews. Doubtless she regarded some of them as her friends, at least in a certain sense. Her son Leib, she writes in one place, was "well regarded by Jews and non-Jews," and she says the same of her second husband, Hirsch Levy, and her in-law Elia Ballin.[59] She describes herself as having "extensive credit with Jews and non-Jews."[60] Did she see herself as bound to these non-Jews, and them to her, by ties of affection, gratitude, and loyalty? Did she esteem their counsel? Was the unidentified "good friend" who offered Glückel news and advice about Leib's dangerous financial situation a non-Jew?[61] Were any of the unnamed non-Jews in the memoir "friends" of the author?[62] It is possible that they may have been. At the same time, we should not ignore Glückel's presentation of her own social world. Even Jewish friends who were not her kinsmen or kinswomen or members of her household or employees occupy only a small place in her account of her life, and she is openly skeptical of the power of such distant ties.

Glückel does tell several stories of Jewish-Christian friendship in the memoir. None of them, however, involve her own friends, and some of them are quite alarming. Two princes of Brandenburg attended Zipporah and Kossman's wedding. As they were standing there, Glückel's relative Elia Cleve missed an opportunity to give one of the princes an expensive gift. Gift giving was one of the crucial formal gestures of friendship in Glückel's world as in our own. In telling the story of her servant "Shot" Jacob, Glückel draws special attention to Jacob's non-Jewish "drinking partner" or "drinking-brother" (*zoyf bruder*), a postmaster named Petersen, who does Jacob no good but leaves him drunk and alone on the road.[63] The story of Jacob and Petersen calls to mind the other "drinking brothers" in the memoir—namely, the prince and his three friends in Glückel's parable. Drinking friends are not true friends, in her view, but she may also have been more generally skeptical that Jews and non-Jews could be true friends. In another anecdote, two Jews feign friendship with a non-Jewish baker in order to rob his house.[64] In yet another, a non-Jew again feigns friendship with a Jew. They drink together at a tavern—once again an unhealthy type of friendship in Glückel's view—and then the non-Jew murders him.[65] What indeed did Glückel's experience, as she interpreted it, teach her about the friendship of non-Jews?

GLÜCKEL'S FRIENDS: THEORY VERSUS EXPERIENCE

Near the beginning of the memoir, Glückel tells a story of a father bird and his young. Like the story of the prince and his three friends, it involves a series of tests concerning friendship and love. The father bird asks each of his goslings whether he will support him in old age. The young birds who fail the test claim that they will reciprocate his love and support him. The father kills them because they are lying. The one who passes the test gives the true answer—at least what Glückel regards as the true answer—which is that the kindness of parents is never reciprocated by their children, since children are always ungrateful.[66] Like all Glückel's parables, this one expresses her most general thoughts, and like so many of the parables, it focuses on love and friendship. Glückel's own experiences, however, as she narrates them in the memoir, did not altogether confirm these gloomy generalizations about the ingratitude of children. After the death of her first husband, her sons Nathan and Mordecai were helpful to her, and after the death of her second husband, Glückel was supported for years by her daughter Esther and son-in-law Moses.[67]

Glückel's parables, with their sharp differentiation of reciprocated and unreciprocated help, of mere sociability and true loyalty, express her guiding principles. But her reminiscences of her relationships with her friends show a more complex tangle of motives and possibilities. Glückel's thoughts on reciprocated and unreciprocated benefits were in fact ambivalent. She admired true generosity—generosity without thought of reciprocation. She expresses regret that, in this respect, she was not the equal of her self-sacrificing and generous husband Chaim.[68] Moreover, although she laments that friends can never be relied on, she also depicts herself, after Chaim's death, throughout the second half of the memoir, as receiving aid from both kin and nonkin. She is assisted by men such as Rabbi Mendel Rothschild and Leib Biber of Bamberg, with whom Glückel deposited money, or from Gabriel Levy, who not only did some banking for Glückel but refused the customary commission.[69]

The story of the prince and his three friends deprecates shared sociability while extolling true friendship. This contrast is repeated in Glückel's anecdote of her servant Jacob and his drinking brother. Nevertheless, Glückel herself was far from unsociable, and many of her stories center on moments of happy sociability, particularly weddings, and also journeys that are shared with traveling companions.[70] Hospitality is a frequent motif in the memoir; Glückel mentions more than a dozen households, nearly all of them kin, where she was a guest, and she invariably depicts her visits as happy.[71]

In one particularly revealing incident during one of their journeys, Glückel and Chaim find themselves by accident in a strange town, and they are forced to search for a Jewish family who will take them in. It turns out, as Glückel explains at length, that their host is the brother-in-law of the daughter of a wealthy Hamburg Jew named Chaim Fürst, a close associate of Glückel's father.[72] It is hard to judge whether, in her own terms, Glückel would have called her accidental host a "friend," since he was not a relative of hers or even a relative by marriage. It is clear, however, that the chain of connections and relationships, tenuous though it might seem, by which she saw him as connected to herself brought him within what she regarded as sort of a social network. This network extended beyond her own immediate family, and that included the friends of her kin (i.e., their "friends" in our terms), such as Chaim Fürst, and the kin of those friends, such as her host.

Glückel's memoir is a unique document in Jewish literature, but it is typical of the early modern era in its pioneering efforts at the realistic portrayal of experience. It is focused significantly on Glückel's experiences of friendship—that is, what she considered to be friendship. As we have seen, her experiences were mixed and followed no fixed rule. The memoir contrasts the close and loving relationship that Glückel enjoyed with her first husband, Chaim, to her much chillier relationship with her second husband, Hirsch. As a widowed mother struggling to marry off her younger children, Glückel relied on her wide network of friends—that is, her household, kin, and in-laws, as well as servants and other business associates. But they often disappointed her as well. Indeed, her memoir is, in part, a broad portrayal of those relationships and a guide to the pitfalls and blessings of friendship.

NOTES

1. All references to Glückel's memoir are to the edition of the Yiddish text published by Chava Turniansky together with her Hebrew translation: *Glikl: Zikhronot 1691–1719* (Jerusalem: Merkaz Zalman Shazar le-Toldot Yisra'el, 2006), henceforth Turniansky, *Zikhronot*. All the translations here, except as noted, are from Beth-Zion Abrahams, trans., *The Life of Glückel of Hameln 1646–1724: Written by Herself* (London: Horovitz, 1962), henceforth Abrahams, *Glückel*. Abrahams's translation is not absolutely complete, nor is it as accurate or literal as Turniansky's Hebrew translation. Digital images of the manuscript of the memoir are online at the website of the Frankfurt Universitätsbibliothek (http://sammlungen.ub.uni-frankfurt.de/mshebr/content/titleinfo/1759801). The 1896 edition of the Yiddish text, edited by David Kaufmann, is also available online at the Frankfurt Universitätsbibliothek (http://publikationen.ub.uni-frankfurt.de/frontdoor/index/index/docId/10522). There is a growing scholarly literature on Glückel and her memoir. See Monika Richarz, ed., *Die Hamburger Kauffrau Glikl: Jüdische Existenz in der Frühen Neuzeit* (Hamburg: Christians, 2001); and Natalie Zemon Davis, *Women on the Margins: Three Seventeenth Century Lives* (Cambridge, MA: Harvard University Press, 1995), 5–62. On the genre of Glückel's memoir and its novelty, see, for example, Marcus Moseley, *Being for Myself Alone: Origins of Jewish Autobiography* (Stanford: Stanford University Press, 2006). The sobriquet "of Hameln" is deceiving. Glückel was born in a suburb of Hamburg, and she lived in Hamburg most of her adult life. Her husband, Chaim, was born in Hameln. Spellings of all names (including Glückel's—or Glikl's—own name) will follow Abrahams's translation.

2. Abrahams, *Glückel*, 111–13; Turniansky, *Zikhronot*, 382. The memoir has many parables or stories interspersed within it. Turniansky discusses Glückel's version of this story and compares it to earlier versions in other texts: "Sipurim be-Yetsiratah shel Glikl Hamel u-Mekoroteihem," *Meḥkerei Yerushalayim be-Folklor Yehudi* 16 (1994): 59–61. Yiddish offers several words for friends, including the Hebrew-derived *oyhev* and the German-derived *fraynt* or *fraynd*, which is Glückel's usual term for "friend," but also German-derived *gizele* (*gesselle*) and *bakante* (*bekannte*). Glückel also has special terms for drinking partners. See note 63. She uses the Hebrew-derived *khevrusa* for various sorts of relationships: a group of traveling companions (e.g., Turniansky, *Zikhronot*, 112), a business partnership (118), or alternatively, a gang of thieves (248) or a pious confraternity of women (602, cf. 426). On concepts of kinship and friendship among seventeenth-century Yiddish-speaking Ashkenazic Jews in general, see also Joseph M. Davis, "Concepts of Family and Friendship in the 1619 Letters of Prague Jews," *Judaica Bohemiae* 49 (2014): 27–58.

3. Abrahams, *Glückel*, 109–11; Turniansky, *Zikhronot*, 374.

4. Abrahams, *Glückel*, 38, 109, 111. "Spouses are often called friends." For example, in the *Brantspigel*, a good wife is said to be a *getroyer khover* or a *guten khover*, a

"true friend." See Altschul, *Brantspigel*, chap. 7 (in the transcription published by Sigrid Riedel, 41, 50). Cf. the *tekhine* of Jacob b. Elijah (Prague, 1615), trans. Debra Kay, *Seyder Tekhines* (Philadelphia: Jewish Publication Society, 2004), 230–35.
5. Turniansky, *Zikhronot*, 372.
6. Altschul, *Brantspigel*, chap. 21.
7. Abrahams, *Glückel*, 109; Isaiah Horowitz, *Shenei Luḥot ha-Berit* (Warsaw: Zysberg, 1862), "Sha'ar ha-Otiyot," 1:48a.
8. In this respect, Glückel fits into generalizations about early modern discussions of friendship in European literature in Ullrich Langer, *Perfect Friendship: Studies in Literature and Moral Philosophy from Boccaccio to Corneille* (Geneva: Droz, 1994), 28. Cf. Daniel Lochman and Maritere López, "The Emergence of Discourses: Early Modern Friendship," in *Discourses and Representations of Friendship in Early Modern Europe, 1500–1700*, ed. Daniel T. Lochman, Maritere López, and Lorna Hutson (London: Routledge, 2011), 9–10. There has been much recent scholarship on friendship in early modern Europe. See, for example, Albrecht Classen and Marilyn Sandidge, *Friendship in the Middle Ages and the Early Modern Age: Explorations of a Fundamental Ethical Discourse* (Berlin: De Gruyter, 2010). Pessimism about friendship is not uncommon in this period. For example, see Francis Bacon's 1597 essay "Of Followers and Friends: There Is Little Friendship in the World, and Least of All Between Equals."
9. For contemporary English usage, see, for example, Mark Peel with Liz Reed and James Walter, "The Importance of Friends: The Most Recent Past," in *Friendship: A History*, ed. Barbara Caine (London: Equinox, 2009), 317–56; and Anna Wierzbicka, *Understanding Cultures Through Their Key Words: English, Polish, Russian, German, and Japanese* (Oxford: Oxford University Press, 1997). On the formation of a modern concept of friendship as disinterested, private, voluntary, and independent of both commerce and kinship, see, for example, Allan Silver, "'Two Different Sorts of Commerce': Friendship and Strangership in Civil Society," in *Public and Private in Thought and Practice: Perspectives on a Grand Dichotomy*, ed. Jeff Weintraub and Krishan Kumar (Chicago: University of Chicago Press, 1997), 43–74.
10. In examining Glückel's own social categories, rather than using strictly academic categories, I am following the methodological lead of Naomi Tadmor, *Family and Friends in Eighteenth Century England: Household, Kinship, and Patronage* (Cambridge: Cambridge University Press, 2001). As Tadmor shows in detail, in eighteenth-century England, "family" often includes nonkin, especially nonkin members of the household, and conversely, "friend" can refer to kin. In early modern German, similarly, *freund* is often a synonym for "kinsman." See also Johannes Erben, "Freundschaft—Bekanntschaft—Verwandtschaft: Zur Bezeichnungsgeschichte der Ausdrucksformen menschlicher Verbundenheit im frühen Neuhochdeutschen," in *Vielfalt des Deutschen: Festschrift für Werner Besch*, ed. Klaus J. Mattheier, Klaus-Peter Wegera, Walter Hoffmann, and Jurgen Macha (Frankfurt am Main: P. Lang, 1993), 111–21. Cf. Manuel Braun, *Ehe, Liebe, Freundschaft: Semantik der Vergesellschaftung in frühneuhochdeutschen Prosaroman* (Berlin: De Gruyter, 2001).
11. In fact, Turniansky frequently translates Glückel's *fraynd* as "kin" (Hebrew, *karov*). See her explanation in Turniansky, *Zikhronot*, 23n72. The usage can be found in many other Yiddish texts. See, for example, in the *Ma'aseh Bukh*, *kroyvim* and *fraynd* are used as synonyms in Astrid Starck's edition of *Un beau livre d'histoires* (Basel: Schwabe, 2004), 739 (p. 180b of the first 1602 edition). The term *fraynd* carried connotations of both kinship and affection. On kinship

terms in Yiddish, see Erika Timm, "Verwandtschaftbezeichnung in Jiddischen, kontrastiv zum Deutschen betrachtet," in *Röllwagenbüchlein: Festschrift für Walter Röll zum 65*, ed. Jürgen Jaehrling, Ewe Meves, and Erika Timm (Tübingen: Max Niemeyer Verlag, 2002), 443–64; and Beatrice Weinreich, "Kinship Terminology in a Modern Fusion Language," in *Working Papers in Yiddish and East European Jewish Studies*, no. 11 (New York: Max Weinreich Center for Advanced Jewish Studies of the YIVO Institute for Jewish Research, 1975).
12. See Davis, "Concepts," on the utility of vague social categories.
13. Turniansky, *Zikhronot*, 282 (translation mine). Abrahams, *Glückel*, 83: "always on good terms with my husband."
14. Abrahams, *Glückel*, 123. See also Turniansky, *Zikhronot*, 409: Yiddish, "mayn kinder nahnter fraynt"; Turniansky understands this as "close kin of my children."
15. Abrahams, *Glückel*, 123; cf. 7, 152.
16. Abrahams, 149–52, 160–62.
17. Abrahams, 163, 170.
18. Abrahams, 149.
19. *Responsa*, no. 63 (translation mine). Cf. Yair Bacharach, *Ḥavvot Yaʾir*, no. 2 and no. 17.
20. See Beatrice Weinreich, "Kinship Terminology," 16–18; Israela Klayman-Cohen, *Die hebräische Komponente in westyiddischen am Beispiel der Memoiren der Glückel von Hameln* (Hamburg: Buske, 1994), 149; and Timm, "Verwandtschaftbezeichnung," 447–48. Cf. Turniansky, *Zikhronot*, 60n87, and the reference there to Elijah Levita's *Sefer ha-Tishbi*.
21. On this category of distant relatives, see Davis, "Concepts," 35–38.
22. Abrahams, *Glückel*, 44. Glückel's husband Chaim had seven brothers and sisters, while Glückel herself had four married sisters. See the genealogical tables in Alfred Feilchenfeld, *Denkwürdigkeiten der Glückel von Hameln* (Berlin: Jüdischer Verlag, 1913), 326–28, also the appendix of Turniansky, *Zikhronot*.
23. See the genealogical tables in Turniansky, *Zikhronot*, and Feichenfeld, *Denkwürdigkeiten*.
24. Abrahams, *Glückel*, 137. Again, one should not rule out that Bamberg was a relation of Joseph's.
25. Abrahams, 122.
26. That is, her immediate family; the friends were themselves members of the extended family.
27. Abrahams, *Glückel*, 67, 69.
28. Abrahams, 44–45, 59–67.
29. Abrahams, 67.
30. Abrahams, 124.
31. Abrahams, 59.
32. Abrahams, 63.
33. Compare Alexander b. Isaac Pfaffenhofen, who places effusive assertions of friendship in the mouth of a rich man's poorer host: "Mayn khover ... mayn hertser liber guter fraynt." *Sefer Masah u-Merivah*, ed. Chava Turniansky (Jerusalem: Magnes, 1985), 252. In the parallel Hebrew text, *reʾi ve-ohevi*.
34. Abrahams, *Glückel*, 50–51.
35. Abrahams, 66–67. Such "grumbling" is sometimes seen as sinful in Jewish religious tradition because it shows a lack of faith in Providence. Glückel is especially self-conscious because she is not only grumbling but recording her complaints in writing.
36. Contrast, for example, the many female friends of Madame de Sévigné. Cf. Lewis Seifert and Rebecca Wilkin, eds., *Men and Women Making Friends in Early Modern France* (London: Routledge, 2015). On a female Jewish confraternity in eighteenth-century Modena, see Federica Francesconi, "Confraternal Community as a Vehicle for Jewish Female Agency in Eighteenth Century Italy," in *Faith's Boundaries: Laity and Clergy in Early Modern Confraternities*, ed. Nicholas Terpstra, Adriano Prosperi, and Stefania Pastore (Turnhout: Brepols, 2013), 251–76. The story of Jachet is in Abrahams, *Glückel*, 98–99; see the other references to Jachet in

the index. The other main female-female relationships in the memoir are mother-daughter. Glückel tells a couple of long anecdotes in which her mother is a major character. In the last books of the memoir, readers can see Glückel's developing relationship with her daughter Esther, with whom she reluctantly goes to live toward the end of her life. In one place, Glückel recounts a friendly visit to a kinswoman, Jachet's mother, Miriam Gompertz (Abrahams, 116–17).

37. Abrahams, 32–33.
38. More properly, Zippor; see Turniansky, *Zikhronot*, 138n478. Kossman and Jachet were already in-laws of Glückel—the nephew and niece, respectively, of one of Glückel's many brothers-in-law.
39. Abrahams, *Glückel*, 99.
40. Abrahams, 114.
41. Abrahams, 116. On Glückel as a letter-writer, see Eric Henriksen and Mark Zelcer, "'Much Could Be Written': Glikl of Hameln's Life in Writing," in *Women's Letters Across Europe 1400–1700: Form and Persuasion*, ed. Jane Couchman and Ann Crabb (Aldershot: Ashgate, 2005), 56–70. Long-distance friendships in the early modern period were maintained by writing letters.
42. Abrahams, *Glückel*, 152. "My children ... and my brothers and sisters and friends ... had all advised me to [accept the proposal]."
43. Abrahams, 160–62.
44. Abrahams, 165–66. Glückel herself is far from indifferent to money and argues here for "moderation in all things."
45. Abrahams, 171.
46. Abrahams, 164.
47. Abrahams, 175.
48. On the role of kinship, trust, and friendship in early modern commerce, see Francesca Trivellato, *The Familiarity of Strangers: The Sephardic Diaspora, Livorno, and Cross-Cultural Trade in the Early Modern Period* (New Haven: Yale University Press, 2009); Cornelia Aust, "Jewish Mobility in the Eighteenth Century: Familial Networks of Ashkenazic Merchants Across Europe," *Jahrbuch für Europäische Geschichte* 16 (2015): 15–32; Aust, "Daily Business or an Affair of Consequence: Credit, Reputation, and Bankruptcy Among Jewish Merchants in Eighteenth-Century Central Europe," in *Purchasing Power: The Economics of Modern Jewish History*, ed. Rebecca Kobrin and Adam Teller (Philadelphia: University of Pennsylvania Press, 2015), 71–90; and Francesca Bregoli, "'Your Father's Interests': The Business of Kinship in a Trans-Mediterranean Jewish Merchant Family, 1776–1790," *Jewish Quarterly Review* 108 (2018): 194–224. Bregoli offers a keen analysis of the interweaving of affection, family bonds, and family business in a Jewish mercantile family similar to Glückel's.
49. Notice Glückel's distinction between the sentimental value of a gift from her father-in-law and its monetary value. See Abrahams, *Glückel*, 77; cf. 162. Notice also her distinction between a paid escort and a traveling companion (158–59).
50. Contrast Judah Loew of Prague, who argues that the term *friend* excludes members of one's household. See his commentary *Derekh Ḥayyim* on Pirkei Avot 1:6 (Tel Aviv: Chaim Pardes, 1975).
51. In Glückel's Yiddish, a business partnership is a *khevrusa*, or a "fellowship." See note 2.
52. Abrahams, *Glückel*, 87.
53. Cf. in the story of Judah Berlin (Abrahams, 63).
54. Abrahams, 55–59.
55. Abrahams, 89; cf. 96. Glückel calls him "the real Herod of my whole family" (66). Note the connection of friendship and travel companionship in many of Glückel's stories.
56. Abrahams, 115.
57. Nonkin Jewish friends appear rarely in the 1619 letters of Prague Jews and in Jewish texts of this period from central and eastern Europe. Non-Jewish friends hardly appear at all. See Davis, "Concepts." On Glückel's attitude

toward non-Jews, see Robert Liberles, "Die Juden und die anderen: Das Bild des Nichtjuden in Glikls Memoiren," in *Die Hamburger Kauffrau Glikl: Jüdische Exitenz in der Frühen Neuzeit*, ed. Monika Richarz (Hamburg: Christians, 2001), 135–46. On friendships between Jews and non-Jews in this period, see Daniel Jütte, "Interfaith Encounters Between Jews and Christians in the Early Modern Period: Toward a Framework," *American Historical Review* 118 (2013): 378–400 (reprinted in an abbreviated version in this volume).
58. Abrahams, *Glückel*, 83–84. See Joseph M. Davis, "Crossing the Name Barrier: Non-Jewish Names in the Memoirs of Glückel of Hameln and in Early Modern Ashkenazic Jewish Culture," in *Connecting Histories: Jews and Their Others in the Early Modern Period*, ed. Francesca Bregoli and David Ruderman (Philadelphia: University of Pennsylvania Press, 2019).
59. Abrahams, *Glückel*, 87, cf. 123, 169. My translation, based on Turniansky.
60. Abrahams, 150.
61. Glückel sometimes uses *fraynt* to mean specifically someone to whom she has turned for advice. See, for example, Abrahams, *Glückel*, 117–18. One aspect of her "friendship" with her first husband that Glückel stresses is that he relied on her advice (42). Many of her stories involve the bad advice that friends and family members give, another aspect of her skepticism of the overall value of friends.
62. Abrahams, 119. More than thirty unnamed individuals who are clearly non-Jews appear in the memoir. Is the unnamed woman who brings Glückel the mail a friend? She tells Glückel news, often a mark of friendship in the memoir. The news is false, but that is in line with Glückel's theme of the untrustworthiness of friends (60).

Was the unnamed president of Altona a friend? He allows Glückel's son Leib to stay in Altona under his protection. (Abrahams's translation [124] is misleading; see Turniansky, *Zikhronot*, 413n247.)
63. Abrahams, 55–59; Turniansky, *Zikhronot*, 189. The three disloyal friends in Glückel's story of the prince are also his *gute trink brider*, or "drinking companions." Turniansky, 377.
64. Abrahams, *Glückel*, 75.
65. Abrahams, 134. See also the anecdote about Glückel's stepsister (19–20).
66. Abrahams, 8–9. Love and friendship also appear in Glückel's descriptions of Jewish communities: in Hamburg, she writes, when she was a child, the Jews all loved one another: "They lived together in love and great affection [*ahavah ve-ḥibah rabah*]" (Turniansky, *Zikhronot*, 52; my translation). They lived "in peace together" (Abrahams, *Glückel*, 14). In Metz, in spite of the party divisions that split the community, Glückel wrote that the rabbi had only friends (*oyhevim*) and no enemies (*sonim*) (Abrahams, *Glückel*, 177; Turniansky, *Zikhronot*, 584).
67. Abrahams, *Glückel*, 111, 120, 175.
68. Cf. Abrahams, 39 and 68.
69. Abrahams, 159.
70. Abrahams, 159. See also 53–54, 78, 83, 95–96, and 158 for other lists of travel companions.
71. For hospitality, see Abrahams, 47, 56, 65, 76, 78, 81, 82, 83, 115, 116, 125, 140, and 157. Note particularly 116, where the connection between hospitality and Glückel's relationship of friendship with her in-law (Jachet's mother) is clear. An exception to the rule that hospitality always produces happy results is the story of Glückel's grandmother's hospitality toward victims of the plague, which leads to her death (21).
72. Abrahams, 81, cf. 14.

CHAPTER 6

"Got Yourself Some Friends? Now Build a Movement!"
Friendship in the Jewish Women's Movement in the United States

MARTHA ACKELSBERG

Friendship has been central to Jewish feminist groups and organizations in the United States from their beginnings in the 1970s until the present. Twentieth-century Jewish feminism arose at the intersection between the secular women's movement and countercultural Jewish student/progressive organizations, especially *ḥavurot*.[1] Those movements were at least partly formed in reaction to traditional family structures and practices, as well as to top-down organizational forms. In the secular context, this included organizations of the "Old Left" and, in the Jewish context, federations and suburban synagogues. The 1960s counterculture challenged the hierarchy, alienation, isolation, competition, and individualism of dominant liberal political and Jewish communal perspectives while championing visions of more egalitarian, mutualist, engaged, small-scale collaborations. None of these groups or movements would have existed or developed as they did without the friendships at their core.

THE PRACTICE OF FRIENDSHIP

When I speak of friendship, I borrow here from Danielle Allen, who describes friendship as a practice that we engage in in our daily lives and that provides citizens with "knowledge that can be carried into the political realm to good effect." She goes on to argue that "friendship is not an emotion, but a practice, a set of hard-won, complicated habits that are used to bridge trouble, difficulty, and differences of personality, experience, and aspiration."[2] Friend relationships are generally thought to be different from familial ones (though family members can certainly be friends) in that they are voluntary. They are also characterized by equality, reciprocity, and mutuality. While it is true that we do hear of friendships between people in positions of greater or lesser power in relation to each other, I take friendships, in general, to be relationships between relative equals. And again, while we may all know of friendships that are less than fully reciprocal, the expected *norm*, at least, is one of relative mutuality and reciprocity: friends are expected to care about, and for, each other.

This understanding of friendship was central to the creation of early Jewish feminist groups. Ezrat Nashim, for example, one of the very first Jewish feminist organizations of the second wave, began as a study group within the New York Havurah, which itself started as a collection of friends in New York City in 1969.[3] Weekly communal dinners and conversations, monthly weekend retreats, peer-led classes, informal davening (praying), and joint participation in antiwar activities soon turned that initially loose collection of friends into an intimate community. In turn, the practices of that community created new, and lasting, friendships. In fact, it was precisely a challenge to that intimacy that led to the establishment of what was to become Ezrat Nashim: at an informal Shabbat morning davening, one of the men present spoke about what he found so powerful in the *nishmat* prayer, describing it in very male sexual terms.[4] I was one of two women present (Dina Rosenfeld was the other), and we suddenly experienced ourselves as invisible in the conversation, went into another room, and started to talk about what had just happened. The shock of realizing that despite our communal intimacy, there were profound, unrecognized differences among us led to a decision to gather other women to discuss the situation of women in Judaism and to form a ḥavurah class on the topic. Indeed, the shock was probably intensified by the context: the ḥavurah had provided an opportunity to explore the prayers personally, yet it was precisely in that context that our very different experiences were somehow not noticed. We invited friends, both from within and from outside the ḥavurah, to join, and we explored biblical and Talmudic texts as well as those very few contemporary critiques that existed.[5] Late in 1971, we heard that a group of men (members of either the New York Havurah or Havurat Shalom—a similar group in Boston) were gathering for a weekend to discuss the future of the American Jewish community, but no women would be present.[6] So women from the class in New York contacted friends in Boston who had established a small women's group within Havurat Shalom, and we spent a weekend together.[7]

The Havurat Shalom women strongly encouraged those of us from New York to "go public" with the findings of our study group: in essence, to begin actively protesting the marginalization of women within Jewish life and communities. Some of us hesitated to do so, believing that simply asking for equality in a system that had been created by men would be too limited a goal but not yet knowing what it was we *should* be aiming for, what Judaism would look like if it took women's lives and experiences seriously. Others suggested that figuring out a new vision of Judaism would take a great deal of time, and meanwhile, Jewish women around the country should know that we were raising these issues.

In the end, we decided on the "go public" strategy, and when we returned to New York City, we contacted the Conservative movement's Rabbinical Assembly, asking for an opportunity to address the rabbis at their 1972 convention, scheduled for mid-March at the Concord Hotel in Kiamesha Lake, New York. When told that there was no room on the program, the group decided simply to go to the convention and attempt to speak anyway. Meanwhile, we needed a name for ourselves. After a short time, we agreed on Ezrat Nashim because we loved the double entendre (*Ezrat Nashim* literally means "help for women," but it was also the name for the area of the Temple in Jerusalem that was set aside for women). In preparation for our trip to the Concord, we composed a document, "Jewish Women Call for Change," which listed a number of demands ranging from the counting of women in a *minyan* (a quorum of ten adults required for public prayer) and the admission of women to rabbinical and cantorial schools to the full membership of women in synagogues and Jewish communal organizations.[8] In addition to the "Call," we photocopied articles by Trude Weiss-Rosmarin and Rachel Adler to bring with us for distribution. And we alerted the *New York Post* and the *New York Times* to our plans.[9]

The trip to the Concord was as much an adventure of friends as it was a protest expedition: two carloads of us (roughly a *minyan* of women) arrived on March 14, 1972, and we presented ourselves to the organizers of the conference. Much to our surprise and delight, they set aside a room for us to meet with the rabbis and another room (and time) for us to meet with the rabbis' wives (there were no women rabbis at the time, and the activities for wives were generally on the order of shopping trips and flower arranging).[10] At least one hundred rabbis came to the rabbinic session, some quite supportive (asking for information they could bring back to their synagogues) and others quite combative (arguing that we would destroy Judaism if women took equal roles in the synagogue). At the session for the rabbis' wives, we encountered a generally favorable reception, the most notable comment coming from Adele Ginsburg, who stood up and, with a quavering voice, said, "What I want to know is . . . where have you been all these years?" When it began snowing heavily late in the day, the organizers refused to let us attempt to drive home and instead offered us room and board at the Concord until the next morning. They were clearly treating us like their daughters, and we were happy to accept.

Our appearance at the Concord, and subsequent publicity, put our small group of friends onto the Jewish communal map. Ezrat Nashim (which was, at that point, simply eight to ten women who were meeting once a week to study together) started receiving letters from women all over the country, asking to join the organization and for more information. We responded to all of them, explaining that we were not a membership organization and encouraging them to start study or discussion groups in their own communities. Meanwhile, the group changed and grew as some members left the area and others invited friends and then more friends. Members of the group were invited to speak both in and around New York City and more broadly. We began writing pieces for Jewish newsletters and journals, and we started collecting and writing naming ceremonies for girls and putting them into a form (a typescript booklet) that could be distributed. Elizabeth Koltun edited a special issue of *Response* magazine on Jewish women, which was soon expanded into the first published anthology, *The Jewish Woman: New Perspectives*.[11] We began connecting with women friends in the North American Jewish Students' Network to plan the first National Jewish

Women's Conference, which would take place at the McAlpin Hotel in New York City in the spring of 1973. Soon, Jewish women's groups (secular and religious) were springing up in synagogues and communities around the country; a movement had begun. Although Ezrat Nashim did not continue to engage in movement activism as a collective for much longer, many of the friendships within the group broadened and deepened. Some of these friends continued to meet—in the context of both the New York Havurah and then beyond it—for many more years.

The further effort to imagine what a Judaism that takes women's experience seriously would look like however, did not really find a home until 1981, with the founding of B'not Esh, a Jewish feminist spirituality collective that also had its roots in the *ḥavurah* movement. At the National Havurah Conference held in Hartford, Connecticut, in the summer of 1980, there were three classes related to women and Judaism. A number of women friends, having taken two of the three courses, started talking about creating a similar sort of study experience, but this time focused entirely on women.[12] Some of those women met that fall and continued talking, but probably nothing would have happened had not two of them met the following spring at the wedding of another mutual friend. They sent invitations to friends who were committed to both Judaism and feminism. An initial group of sixteen attendees has grown over the years through widening friendship circles. Roughly fifty people have been part of the collective at one point or another.[13] In the process, many new close friendships have formed.

B'not Esh celebrated its thirty-seventh anniversary in 2018, having met every year (except one), generally on Memorial Day weekend at a retreat center in New York's Hudson Valley.[14] In conversations and workshops focused on images of God, new liturgies, politics and spirituality, sexuality and spirituality, class, race, white supremacy, age, militarism, parenting, Israel, and many other topics, we have explored both what traditional texts have had to say about issues and how we can use our own lives as texts to generate new visions and new liturgies and challenge ourselves individually and as a community. Although its membership remains small, the group's impact on the Jewish community has been substantial—members of B'not Esh, together with others, have contributed significantly to new liturgical works, *siddurim*, *maḥzorim*, and *haggadot* and to commentaries on Torah and Talmud. Members have composed music, which is now fully incorporated into the liturgies of nonorthodox congregations around the country and beyond. As rabbis, professors, social workers, and community activists, they have brought feminist insights and perspectives into communities and Jewish communal organizations in the United States, Israel, and Europe.

Meanwhile, of course, many other groups and organizations have arisen to take up one or another aspect of the work of transforming Judaism and Jewish communal life, including entities as varied as the Jewish Orthodox Feminist Alliance, RitualWell.org, Rosh Hodesh: It's a Girl Thing, Ma'ayan, the Women's Rabbinic Network, the Creative Jewish Women's Alliance, and the Maharat program at Yeshivat Chovevei Torah in New York City, to name just a few. Many of these groups also have roots in friendship networks. Esther Broner's *The Telling*[15] explores the ways just one group of Jewish women writers and artists supported one another's efforts to draw on Jewish themes and traditions in their creative work. Conferences, anthologies, journals, and multiple other forms have served as venues for the creation and presentation of Jewish women's creative energies.[16] In many of these cases as well, friendship networks formed the basis of organizing.

THE POWER OF A FRIENDSHIP MODEL

Of the many ways that feminism posed a challenge to mainstream U.S. culture and Jewish feminists challenged Jewish traditions, I want to explore here three interconnected perspectives. Each is related to the power and importance of friendship within Jewish feminism: (1) insisting that gender is a social construction, thus challenging the naturalness of family and other communal institutions, (2) questioning the (necessity of the) patriarchal structure of Jewish institutions and arguing for the possibility of greater equality, and (3) exploring the pervasiveness of a separation between a so-called public (read: male) and a so-called private (read: female) domain.

One of the signal contributions of feminism to contemporary culture has been its insistence that gender is "socially constructed," that institutions and practices formerly thought of as natural and necessary—such as the notion that some activities are "women's work" and others are properly "men's work"—are the product of social conditioning and legal regulation. While the assumptions that women's domain is the home and men's is the world beyond can be traced back at least to Aristotle and, in Jewish tradition, to early rabbinic Judaism,[17] feminists argued that "women's subordinate position was not natural but socially, economically, and culturally constructed. Understanding sexism as *learned*—taught, like racism, to children from their earliest years—meant that it could be unlearned."[18] Thus feminists, Jewish and otherwise, questioned many institutions that had seemed to be natural—most important, perhaps, the family.

Questioning the structure and functioning of heterosexual nuclear families was a radical act for any feminist. Nevertheless, given the particular power of family in Judaism, when Jewish feminists challenged the naturalness of the traditional, male-led family, they found themselves accused of undermining a central institution of Jewish life. Many feminists challenged the assumption that it was every woman's destiny and responsibility to marry and to give birth to and raise children—in other words, to be the guardians of the family.[19] But defenders of the Jewish status quo argued that for women to question the primacy of the roles of wife and mother was to put the future of Judaism at risk. Many within the Jewish community greeted critiques of the family with fear and anger. For example, when the women of Ezrat Nashim made their presentation to the rabbis at the Concord, more than one male rabbi predicted that if women were to take on equal roles in the synagogue and other so-called public sites, Judaism would be threatened at its core.[20]

Interestingly, I think this fear about the dangers of questioning the naturalness of traditional family structures was, and remains, a function of the individualism of U.S. culture. As we see all too clearly even today, many cultural critics and defenders of a more hierarchically structured, communitarian vision seem to assume that the only alternative to a so-called traditional family is isolated individualism.[21] Thus, as Benjamin Barber suggested, "our great modern free world is all too often a world in which men and women do not exist for others.... In this world, there can be no fraternal feeling, no general will, no selfless act, no mutuality, no species identity, no obligation, no social empathy, no love or belief or commitment that is not wholly private."[22] Or, as Michael Walzer wrote: "Liberal theory... deprives us of any ready access to our own experience of communal embeddedness."[23] In contrast, communitarians argue, "it is through his or her membership in a variety of social groups that the individual identifies himself or herself and is identified by others. I am brother, cousin and grandson, member of this household, that village, this tribe. These are not characteristics that belong to human beings accidentally, to be stripped away in order to discover 'the real me.' They are part of my substance.... Individuals inherit a particular space within an interlocking set of social relationships; lacking that space, they are nobody."[24] Families, as Christopher Lasch and his collaborators famously argued, are thought to provide a "haven in a heartless world."[25]

Both feminists in general and Jewish feminists in particular share *some* aspects of this communitarian critique of liberalism. Of course, Judaism is *not* a liberal tradition of the sort these critics decry; it is, rather, deeply communal. Many of the critiques that communitarians make of U.S. society could be—and have been—articulated by Jewish thinkers and activists as well. Jewish defenses of the primacy of the family fit well into this perspective: families are the primary relationships that form us and, Jews have argued, the primary context for instilling and passing on Jewish tradition. In such a context, any challenge to the family could easily be construed as a challenge to the continuity of Judaism.[26] And yet, as Penny Weiss has argued, "while feminists, like communitarians, do take issue with liberalism for its neglect of the family, feminists are more interested in bringing the familial experiences of women and children into the conversation, and the attention they want paid to the family is far more critical [than that of communitarians]."[27]

Thus in questioning the centrality of "the traditional Jewish family," Jewish feminists were throwing into relief other aspects of that institution, for families in the United States are, at least by law, hierarchical and male-dominated institutions. Both U.S. and Jewish law have traditionally defined families as male-headed, even if they have also been considered the domain in which women are "in charge."[28] Families *may* provide a sense of place and belonging for their members, but they do so in the context of reflecting and reinforcing multiple dimensions of hierarchy and social inequality, as well as "harbor[ing] social roles and structures which have been highly oppressive for women."[29] It may well be that—particularly for members of groups that are otherwise marginalized in this society, such as African Americans, Latinos, immigrants, and Jews—families are crucial to children's development of the capacities and abilities they need to survive, and even thrive, in a hostile social and political environment.[30] But feminists have insisted that families can fill that function without denying the personhood and full humanity of women.

For many Jewish feminists, friendships and collectives rooted in friendships have provided alternative spaces for creating social bonds. Women have always had ways of connecting with one another, both within and outside of families—whether drawing water at communal fountains, quilting, cooking in communal kitchens, or caring for one another's children—and often such extrafamilial friendships helped sustain the traditional family.[31] Traditionally constituted families are not, after all, the only alternative to isolated individualism. Rather, friendship networks can also create lasting bonds of love and support and, in many circumstances, may be *more* supportive and tolerant (particularly of nonnormative life choices) than are traditional families.[32] Indeed, increases in recent decades in the numbers of women living alone—or apart from families of origin—in urban settings has created an even greater need for such networks of support.[33]

Further, friendship, almost by definition, is a relationship of *equality* (often we question even the possibility of friendship between people viewed as unequal within a given culture). As Marilyn Friedman suggests, friendships can offer models of relationships of care and nurturance that are not, at the same time, relationships of hierarchy and dominance: "Friendship is more likely than many other relationships, such as those of family and neighborhood, to be grounded in and sustained by shared interests and values, mutual affections, and possibilities for generating mutual respect and esteem.... Friendship is more likely than many other close personal relationships to provide social support for people who are idiosyncratic, whose unconventional values and deviant life-styles make them victims of intolerance from family members and others who are unwillingly related to them."[34] Women's groups and collectives of many sorts did provide such alternative sources of nurturance and community during the early years of the women's movement, and in many cases, they still do.[35] Importantly, they provided a basis rooted in experience for a questioning of traditional norms and practices.

It was not only the supposed naturalness of the Jewish family that Jewish feminists challenged; they also highlighted the almost total control by men of major communal institutions—especially synagogues, Jewish community centers (JCCs), philanthropic organizations, and the like—and the assumption that it was simply normal and natural for men to be at the helm. When Jewish feminists began to voice these concerns in the 1970s and 1980s, the norm in many communities was that synagogue membership was a male prerogative: wives were considered to be included in a husband's membership, and single women were virtually ignored. Synagogue leadership operated in similar ways. Federations were always headed by men (except for those that had "women's campaigns"), as were JCCs and other major communal organizations. Women had virtually no official roles in Jewish communal life other than in specifically women's organizations such as Women's League, Hadassah, the Organization for Rehabilitation through Training (ORT), and synagogue sisterhoods. Many Jewish leaders also accepted the perspectives of contemporary communitarian thinkers (such as Alisdair McIntyre, Michael Sandel, and Benjamin Barber) that hierarchically structured families and communal institutions were essential to the continuity of Judaism.

Of course, in the years since, many congregations have changed their membership policies so that women are now full members along with men. Women have also moved into congregational leadership positions around the country. Many federations and JCCs have women in executive/leadership positions, though hardly in the largest ones, and not anywhere near their numbers in the population. Male friendship networks helped create and sustain this pattern, while female friendship networks have helped challenge it.[36] Friendships and other more egalitarian/feminist networks have been critical to forcing changes within the community and have helped nurture the women who have moved into those positions. And neither Jewish communal life nor its central organizations have collapsed—although it is also true that in nonorthodox Jewish communities, as in the culture more generally, as women have moved into these arenas, men have tended to move out.

Another—and also related—way in which the experiences of friendship among Jewish feminists challenged central institutions and practices of the Jewish community is reflected in a dismantling of the assumptions of the necessity of the so-called public/private split. In the larger U.S. context, it is important to recognize that the supposed ideological separation between a private, or home-based, arena (that is primarily the domain of women) and the arena of economics and politics outside the home (thought of as primarily the domain of men) is central to classical liberal political theory and the structuring of political and economic roles.[37] Thus although poor and working-class women and women of color in the United States have virtually always engaged in paid work to support their families, the presumption that men would earn a "family wage" to support a wife and children at home was widespread and used to justify higher wages for men and discrimination against women in the labor market.

Yet friendships, although they may be understood to be rooted in the so-called private sphere, often cross the domestic/public divide. In fact, as I have argued elsewhere, "friendship itself poses a potential challenge to that dichotomization, and stands as a model of the unity of the personal and the public": "The things that matter most about a person, his [sic] unique biography, his flaws and his virtues ... are his most significant private possession. Yet every effort is made to prevent the intrusion of this private world into a person's public role system. Thereby the unique quality of the personal is suppressed. It is, however, precisely this personal quality on the basis of which friendships become possible."[38] Friendships may be formed at home or at work, and not all friendships stay within the sphere in which they originated. It is certainly the case that friendships rooted in school, in the community, or at work can provide the basis for engagement in the broader public or political arena. Similarly, friendships formed elsewhere (and the experience of equality, mutuality, and reciprocity within them) can—and did—affect women's expectations of how they were and are treated in the home or workplace. As the contemporary uproar about sexual harassment makes clear, we are still a long way from experiencing gender equality in homes, workplaces, or public spaces. But women's friendships that bridge a presumed gap between public and private have helped erode the sense that different behavioral norms obtain in the more closed domains of homes and offices. They also challenge the presumption that the two spheres must remain separate and distinct.

It is also the case, as Paula Hyman notes, that in the eastern European Jewish context, it was *women* who were often the breadwinners, at least in those households headed by men who spent their time in prayer and study. Many of those practices changed with the Americanization of immigrant families, when Jewish women took on more traditional American roles, such as keepers of the children and the household.[39] In either case, however, the norm was the expectation of different roles for men and women; as the oft-quoted statement went, "*kol kevudah bat ha-melekh penimah*"—a woman's place (and her realm) was in the home.

Thus demands by Jewish women to take their places not only in the workplace but also in synagogues and communal institutions challenged Jewish institutions that had seen themselves not just as male-led but effectively as separate male domains. What would it mean for women to enter the house of study as equals when the house of study was defined as a male space? What would it mean for women to claim a place in synagogues—not just behind a *mehitzah* (the partition used to separate men and women) but on the *bimah* (the reader's platform in the synagogue)—when these spaces had been understood to be exclusively male, almost "*mi d'oraita*"?[40]

Jewish feminists argued, of course, that rather than weakening those institutions, equalizing roles within them (as well as within homes) would strengthen both Judaism and Jewish attachment. Even within the context of a traditional Jewish home, enabling women to receive a serious Jewish education and allowing them to participate more fully in communal life would provide more—and potentially different—role models for new generations of Jews. Even if, overall, men and women have different talents to contribute to the community, why not let particular individuals contribute in whatever ways *they* wish? Why should limiting each to one domain be better for either of them or for their children? And since even married women with children (let alone those who are single or not raising children) are not necessarily engaged full time with home and child-rearing for the whole of their adult lives, there is no legitimate reason to prevent their equal participation in religious or communal life. Would it not be good for both young Jewish boys and young Jewish girls to see men, as well as women, taking more active roles in child-rearing and the upkeep of the home? Indeed, many studies of role changes over the past few decades have found that children growing up in more egalitarian households fare as well, if not better, in their lives than those growing up in more hierarchical, gender-divided ones. Other studies have reported similar findings with respect to children raised in households headed by lesbian or gay couples. And surely the Jewish community has been enriched by the individual and collective contributions of all those women who have entered the "Jewish public sphere" as rabbis, cantors, and synagogue leaders, as well as heads of federations, JCCs, and the like.

PROBLEMS WITH THE FRIENDSHIP MODEL

While I have focused so far on some of the ways that friendship models have strengthened Jewish feminism and on continuities between Jewish feminist and secular feminist organizations and perspectives, it is also important to acknowledge some significant differences and some limits to friendship as a ground for organizing. One has to do with the relationship between "internal" versus "external" positioning. While some secular feminists, in criticizing traditional communal or institutional structures as patriarchal, tried to separate from them and create women-only spaces, those who defined themselves as *Jewish* feminists generally refused to abandon their communities. Rather, these women insisted on transforming Judaism from within.[41] Most Jewish feminists maintained friendships and activist relationships with secular feminists and others engaged in the multiple political and social movements that roiled the country in the 1960s and 1970s as well as with other Jews, family members, and members of their religious communities. From their positions within both the secular feminist and Jewish worlds, Jewish feminists refused to choose between or among the various components of their identities, insisting that truly inclusive communities must make room for complexity and multiplicity, whether of gender, sexuality, race, or ethnicity.[42]

Nevertheless, this issue of the complexity of identities also points to some of the significant limits or problems with a movement based on friendship networks, for in a society such as that of the United States—one highly stratified by race, ethnicity, and class despite an ideological commitment to equality of rights, opportunity, respect, and dignity—friendship networks themselves tend to be limited by class, ethnic, and racial factors.[43] As studies have repeatedly shown, large percentages of those who identify as white in the United States live and socialize in overwhelmingly white contexts created by governmental policies that have, over the years, either enforced or allowed for residential segregation.[44] Consequently, the educational experiences of many children in the United States are also racially segregated. For many people, the years of college and university life are the first—and sometimes the last—opportunity for living closely with others of different racial or ethnic backgrounds. While it is true that many workplaces are becoming more multiethnic and multiracial, friendships are often formed more on the basis of geographical or neighborhood proximity rather than at the workplace. Thus friendship networks may well be as segregated by race, ethnicity, and class as are neighborhoods and communities.

Further, as Iris Young and others have noted, our understandings of community in the United States tend to emphasize homogeneity rather than diversity. Young argues that we tend to understand "community" as unity and that the desire to "bring things into unity generates a logic of hierarchical opposition," creating a sense of us versus them, insider versus outsider.[45] The achievement of such unity—which she describes as the goal of "shared subjectivity"—is, however, an impossibility. We can *never* be known by others as we (think we) are known to ourselves. But the hope for such intersubjective knowledge fuels the desire for homogeneous communities and leads to "racism, ethnic chauvinism, and class devaluation."[46]

Regardless of the source of the problem, however, the fact that so many of our friendship networks have been framed in the context of segregated communities means that building organizations and movements on the basis of them results in organizations and movements that are themselves effectively segregated and more homogeneous than Jewish communities as a whole. We have seen evidence of this in the overwhelming maleness of early havurah communities in Boston and New York City, in the exclusively male invitation lists to many Jewish communal events (even in the so-called Jewish counterculture), and in the continued underrepresentation and devaluation of women within Jewish communal life.[47] But significantly, despite the focus of much early feminist activism and writing about the importance of recognizing "equality within diversity," we also see it in the overwhelming whiteness of many contemporary Jewish organizations, including Jewish feminist groups. Progressive organizations throughout the Jewish community are now attempting to address this issue by exploring their own histories and practices of white hegemony and by striving to "center the leadership and activism of people of color" within their communities.[48] The fact that these organizations feel the necessity to undertake such steps, however, while reflecting an important shift in awareness, is also an indication that deliberate action is necessary. Friendship networks alone have not led to the creation of organizations that are at all reflective of the existing diversity of the community. And as a result, the agendas of these organizations—again, including feminist organizations that place a high value on acting and theorizing from personal experience—reflect a necessarily limited vision of what it is "the community" needs and wants.

Another difficulty arising from the grounding of organizations or movements in friendships, however, is that those groups may become as volatile as familial ones. Issues of competition for official notice—what Jo Freeman and others initially referred to as "trashing"—arose within feminist organizations almost from the beginning, ironically *because* the antihierarchical ideology of the early movement easily led to a "tyranny of structurelessness" that made it difficult to either choose leaders or hold accountable those who took on leadership.[49] The assumption was that friends could manage everything informally, that no formal roles or responsibilities were needed. But as many of these organizations discovered, if tasks are to be accomplished, there needs to be some mechanism for assuring that necessary steps are taken. Formal hierarchical structures are not the only way of achieving such assurance—and, of course, they do not guarantee that those with responsibility will follow through in any case—but most organizations or groups will require some system of allocating duties and assuring that those who have undertaken them meet their commitments. In the first flush of excitement about nonhierarchical organizing, many groups either forgot about accountability or did not recognize that there are a variety of ways to encourage it. Almost every feminist organization suffered from some aspect of these issues in the early years, and Jewish feminist groups were not immune. As Esther Broner writes of the "Seder Sisters" in New York City, "Because we are so grand in our gestures, so often, it is even more hurtful when we are petty, which we are—covetous of the other's success, impatient, judgmental."[50]

Friendship, that is to say, provides no guarantee of successful, nonhierarchical organizing. Nevertheless, the equality, reciprocity, and mutuality at the core of our common understandings of friendship have offered important challenges and correctives to the unspoken and unacknowledged patriarchal and exclusivist character of much of Jewish communal life. While we are far from having achieved true equality, even within Jewish feminist organizations themselves, the models presented by friend relationships and the groups and movements that have grown from them make clear that there are alternatives to hierarchical structures. At least one of the continuing goals of Jewish feminism must be to develop ways not only to acknowledge but also to welcome and celebrate the diversity of the Jewish community while not succumbing to the assumption that there is only one way for that community (or communities) to organize itself or make decisions about its future.

NOTES

I am very grateful to Judith Plaskow and Dina Rosenfeld, both dear friends and cotravelers on this feminist journey, for helpful comments on earlier versions of this chapter.

1. These are small, intentional, lay-led Jewish communities.
2. Danielle S. Allen, *Talking to Strangers: Anxieties of Citizenship Since Brown v.*

Board of Education (Chicago: University of Chicago Press, 2004), xxi.
3. The author became a member of the New York Havurah in 1970.
4. *Nishmat* is part of the Shabbat morning liturgy that is highly evocative and filled with sensual imagery.
5. For example, Trude Weiss-Rosmarin, "The Unfreedom of Jewish Women," *Jewish Spectator* 35, no. 7 (October 1970): 2–6; and Rachel Adler, "The Jew Who Wasn't There: Halacha and the Jewish Woman," in *The Jewish Woman: An Anthology, Response* 18 (Summer 1973): 77–82.
6. When we inquired, we were told that the invitation was sent simply to "a group of friends," so the fact that no women were included was of no significance.
7. This experience points to both the strengths and the *limits* of friendship networks as building blocks for social movements. The men met with their friends, who "just happened to be men." In a society divided along a variety of (stratified) lines of cleavage, relatively few friendships cross such lines. Thus building organizations and movements through existing social relationships tends to reinforce, rather than challenge, existing hierarchies. I will examine this in greater depth later in the chapter.
8. "Jewish Women Call for Change," March 14, 1972, https://jwa.org/teach/livingthelegacy/documentstudies/jewish-women-call-for-change.
9. The *New York Post* published an article, "10 Orthodox Feminists Confronting the Rabbis," by Barbara Trecker, which appeared on the day we arrived at the Concord, March 14, 1972; an article in the *New York Times* appeared a few weeks later.
10. The invitation to the rabbis' wives, "To All Women at the R.A. Convention," Jewish Women's Archive, accessed April 6, 2020, http://www.jwa.org/feminism/hyman-paula.
11. Published by Schocken Books in 1976.
12. A similar conversation took place among women who had attended the Conference on Alternatives in Jewish Education (CAJE) that same summer.
13. For explorations of the founding and early years of B'not Esh, see Martha Ackelsberg, "Spirituality, Community, and Politics: B'not Esh and the Feminist Reconstruction of Judaism," *Journal of Feminist Studies in Religion* 2, no. 2 (Fall 1986): 109–20. On the spiritual/liturgical/personal work of B'not Esh, see also Barbara E. Breitman, "Social and Spiritual Reconstruction of Self Within a Feminist Jewish Community," *Women and Therapy* 16, no. 2/3 (1995): 73–82; and Merle Feld, "Brigadoon: A Place for Dreams to Grow," in *A Spiritual Life: Exploring the Heart and Jewish Tradition* (Albany: SUNY Press, 2007), 283–96.
14. In 2018, we moved our retreats to a different center on the West Coast.
15. Esther Broner, *The Telling: The Story of a Group of Jewish Women Who Journey to Spirituality Through Community and Ceremony* (San Francisco: Harper San Francisco, 1993).
16. Conferences in California, initiated by Marcia Cohn Spiegel, included God, prayer, and the Jewish woman (1982); feminism, creativity, and spirituality (1985 forward); and old symbols, new rituals. I am grateful to Marcia Cohn Spiegel for information on these and many other ventures. Personal communication, January 2, 2018.
17. Aristotle wrote in *The Politics* that some people are "by nature" slaves and others are meant to rule (1254b and 1255a), that "the relation of male to female is naturally that of the superior to the inferior" (1254b), and that "it is the function of the one to acquire, and of the other to keep and store" (1277b). The analogous perspective in Judaism is captured by the Hebrew phrase *kol kevudah bat melekh penimah* (Ps. 45:14, "all of the honor of the daughter of the King is within"). This biblical passage was employed in later tradition to argue

that a woman's place is in the home rather than the public sphere as well as for women's modesty more generally.
18. Linda Gordon, "The Women's Liberation Movement," in *Feminism Unfinished: A Short, Surprising History of American Women's Movements*, by Dorothy Sue Cobble, Linda Gordon, and Astrid Henry (New York: Liveright, 2014), 85.
19. See, for example, Barrie Thorne and Marilyn Yalom, eds., *Rethinking the Family: Some Feminist Questions* (New York: Longman, 1982), especially essays by Thorne, Rapp, and Zaretsky; Irene Diamond, ed., *Families, Politics and Public Policy: A Feminist Dialogue on Women and the State* (New York: Longman, 1983); and Martha Ackelsberg, "Families and the Jewish Community: A Feminist Perspective," *Response* #48, 14, no. 4 (Spring 1985): 5–19.
20. Mortimer Ostow, "Women and Change in Jewish Law," *Conservative Judaism* 29 (1974): 5–24. Reuven Kimelman makes related arguments about the importance of heterosexuality within the context of traditional family structure and how it is women's task to "domesticate" male sexuality in "Homosexuality and Family-Centered Judaism," *Tikkun* 9, no. 4 (July/August 1994): 53, http://www.tikkun.org/article.php/jul1994_kimelman. See also my exchange with Susan Handelman in *Sh'ma*, reprinted as Handelman, "Family: A Religiously Mandated Ideal," 319–25; and Ackelsberg, "Family or Community?," 326–30, both in *Jewish Marital Status*, ed. Carol Diament (Northvale, NJ: Jason Aronson, 1989). See also Yaakov Levado's reply to Reuven Kimelman, "Family Values: A Reply to Reuven Kimelman," *Tikkun* 9, no. 4 (July/August 1994): 57, http://www.tikkun.org/article.php/jul1994_levado.
21. See, for example, David Brooks, "America: The Redeemer Nation," *New York Times*, November 23, 2017; "When Politics Becomes Your Idol," *New York Times*, October 30, 2017; and "When Life Asks for Everything," *New York Times*, September 17, 2017.
22. Benjamin Barber, *Strong Democracy: Participatory Politics for a New Age* (Berkeley: University of California Press, 1984), 71–72, cited in Penny A. Weiss, "Feminism and Communitarianism," in *Feminism and Community*, ed. Penny A. Weiss and Marilyn Friedman (Philadelphia: Temple University Press, 1995), 171.
23. Michael Walzer, "The Communitarian Critique of Liberalism," *Political Theory* 18 (February 1990), cited in Weiss and Friedman, *Feminism and Community*, 171.
24. Alisdair McIntyre, *After Virtue*, 32, cited in Weiss and Friedman, *Feminism and Community*, 168.
25. Christopher Lasch, *Haven in a Heartless World: The Family Besieged* (New York: Basic Books, 1977).
26. See, for example, Kimelman, "Homosexuality and Family-Centered Judaism."
27. Weiss, "Feminism and Communitarianism," 174.
28. On some important *differences* between the "traditional" (eastern European) Jewish family structure and that which became dominant in the United States, see Charlotte Baum, Paula Hyman, and Sonya Michel, *The Jewish Woman in America* (New York: Dial Press, 1976), especially chaps. 1, 3, and 4.
29. Marilyn Friedman, "Feminism and Modern Friendship: Dislocating the Community," in *Feminism and Political Theory*, ed. Cass R. Sunstein (Chicago: University of Chicago Press, 1990), 145. See also Ackelsberg, "Sisters or Comrades? The Politics of Friends and Families," in *Families, Politics and Public Policy*, ed. Irene Diamond (New York: Longman, 1984), 339–56.
30. See, among many others, Patricia Hill Collins, *Black Feminist Thought: Knowledge, Consciousness, and the Politics of Empowerment* (Boston: Unwin Hyman, 1990), especially chaps. 3–4; bell hooks, *Feminist Theory: From Margin to Center* (Boston: South End Press,

1984), especially chap. 10; Ta-Nehisi Coates, *Between the World and Me* (New York: Spiegel and Grau, 2015); Blu Greenberg, *On Women and Judaism: A View from Tradition* (New York: Jewish Publication Society of America, 1981), 11–16; and many of the essays in Gloria Anzaldúa, *Making Face, Making Soul: Haciendo Caras: Creative and Critical Perspectives by Women of Color* (San Francisco: Aunt Lute, 1990).

31. See, for example, Laurel Thatcher Ulrich's comment that "self-sufficient households were atypical [among seventeenth- and eighteenth-century New England families], and that relationships between women were far more crucial than most scholars have supposed," in "A Friendly Neighbor: Social Dimensions of Daily Work in Northern Colonial New England," *Feminist Studies* 6, no. 2 (Summer 1980): 392. See also Mary P. Ryan, "The Power of Women's Networks: A Case Study of Female Moral Reform in Antebellum America," *Feminist Studies* 5, no. 1 (Spring 1979): 66–86.

32. Ackelsberg, "Sisters or Comrades?," 343–46; Caroline F. Pukall, "Family Matters, but Sometimes Chosen Family Matters More: Perceived Social Network Influence in the Dating Decisions of Same- and Mixed-Sex Couples," *Canadian Journal of Human Sexuality* 24, no. 3 (2015): 257–70. For a review of recent studies in this area, see "LGBTQ & Chosen Families," A Better Balance, March 15, 2017, http://www.abetterbalance.org/resources/lgbtq-and-chosen-families.

33. I am grateful to Dina Rosenfeld for pointing this out to me and for thoughtful suggestions about so many aspects of this chapter.

34. Friedman, "Feminism," 154.

35. Nancy J. Knauer, "LGBT Older Adults, Chosen Family, and Caregiving," *Journal of Law and Religion* 31, no. 2 (July 2016): 150–68.

36. See, for example, Linda Maizels, "The Old Boys Club Is Keeping Women out of Leadership Roles in the Jewish World," *The Forward*, December 26, 2017, http://forward.com/opinion/national/390572/gender-gap-jewish-world-lack-of-female-experts-in-old-boys-network; Steven M. Cohen, Shifra Bronznick, Didi Goldenhar, Dr. Sherry Israel, and Dr. Shaul Kelner, *Creating Gender Equity and Organizational Effectiveness in the Jewish Federation System: A Research-and-Action Project* (New York: Advancing Women Professionals and the Jewish Community, 2004); and Shifra Bronznick, Didi Goldenhar, and Marty Linsky, *Leveling the Playing Field: Advancing Women in Jewish Organizational Life* (New York: Advancing Women Professionals and the Jewish Community and Cambridge Leadership Associates, 2008). Also, for a recent exploration of the gender gap in both positions and salaries, see Larry Cohler-Esses, "The Gender Gap Is Getting Worse at Jewish Non-Profits," *The Forward*, December 11, 2017, https://forward.com/news/389448/the-gender-gap-is-getting-worse-at-jewish-non-profits.

37. Carole Pateman, "Feminist Critiques of the Public/Private Dichotomy," in *The Disorder of Women* (Stanford: Stanford University Press, 1980), 118–40; and Stephen T. Leonard and Joan C. Tronto, "The Genders of Citizenship," *American Political Science Review* 101, no. 1 (February 2007): 33–46. See also Martha Ackelsberg and Mary Lyndon Shanley, "Privacy, Publicity and Power: A Feminist Rethinking of the Public-Private Distinction," *Revisioning the Political: Feminist Reconstructions of Traditional Concepts in Western Political Theory*, ed. Nancy Hirschmann and Christine DiStefano (Boulder, CO: Westview Press, 1996), 213–33.

38. Ackelsberg, "Sisters or Comrades?," 351, citing Horst Hutter, *Politics as Friendship* (Waterloo, ON: Wilfred Laurier University Press, 1978), 183.

39. See, for example, Baum, Hyman, and Michel, *Jewish Woman*.

40. The literal translation is "from the Torah," but it is more colloquially translated as "legally required."
41. For a recent work exploring the variety of ways Jewish women engaged in feminist activism during the early years of second-wave feminism, see Joyce Antler, *Jewish Radical Feminism: Voices from the Women's Liberation Movement* (New York: New York University Press, 2018).
42. This perspective—also articulated powerfully by feminists of color and working-class feminists in the early years of the second wave—has recently been termed *intersectionality*. But the insistence on the interconnectedness of identity categories, and the refusal to separate them, has been a critical feature of the activism of many feminists on the margins of U.S. society almost from the beginning. See, among many others, the Combahee River Collective, "A Black Feminist Statement," in *Capitalist Patriarchy and the Case for Socialist Feminism*, ed. Zillah Eisenstein (New York: Monthly Review Press, 1979), 362–72; Judith Plaskow, "Jewish Feminist: Conflict in Identities," in *The Jewish Woman: New Perspectives*, ed. Elizabeth Koltun (New York: Schocken, 1976), 3–10; María C. Lugones and Elizabeth V. Spelman, "Have We Got a Theory for You! Feminist Theory, Cultural Imperialism, and the Demand for 'the Woman's Voice,'" *Women's Studies International Forum* 6, no. 6 (1983): 573–81; Iris Marion Young, "The Ideal of Community and the Politics of Difference," *Social Theory and Practice* 12, no. 1 (Spring 1986): 1–26; Iris Marion Young, "Polity and Group Difference," in *Throwing like a Girl and Other Essays in Feminist Philosophy and Social Theory* (Bloomington: Indiana University Press, 1990), 114–37; Martha Ackelsberg, "Identity Politics, Political Identities: Thoughts Toward a Multicultural Politics," *Frontiers: A Journal of Women's Studies* 16, no. 1 (1996): 87–100; Kimberlé Crenshaw, "Mapping the Margins: Intersectionality, Identity Politics, and Violence Against Women of Color," *Stanford Law Review* 43, no. 6 (1994): 1241–99; and Marla Brettschneider, ed., *The Narrow Bridge: Jewish Views on Multiculturalism* (New Brunswick: Rutgers University Press, 1996).
43. Deborah L. Plummer, Rosalie Torres Stone, Lauren Powell, and Jeroan Allison, "Patterns of Adult Cross-Racial Friendships: A Context for Understanding Contemporary Race Relations," *Cultural Diversity and Ethnic Minority Psychology* 22, no. 4 (October 2016): 479–94.
44. See, for example, Mary Fischer and Douglas Massey, "The Ecology of Racial Discrimination," *City and Community* 3, no. 3 (September 2004): 221–41; Douglas Massey and Mary Fischer, "How Segregation Concentrates Poverty," *Ethnic and Racial Studies* 23, no. 4 (July 2000): 670–91; Douglas Massey and Mary Denton, *American Apartheid* (Cambridge, MA: Harvard University Press, 1993); Erica Frankenberg and Gary Orfield, "The Resegregation of Suburban Schools: A Hidden Crisis in American Education," Civil Rights Project, October 6, 2012, http://www.civilrightsproject.ucla.edu/research/k-12-education/integration-and-diversity/the-resegregation-of-suburban-schools-a-hidden-crisis-in-american-education; and Deirdre Pfeiffer, "The Opportunity Illusion: Subsidized Housing and Failing Schools in California," Civil Rights Project, December 2009, http://www.civilrightsproject.ucla.edu/research/metro-and-regional-inequalities/housing/the-opportunity-illusion-subsidized-housing-and-failing-schools-in-california/pfeiffer-opportunity-illusion-2009.pdf.
45. Iris Marion Young, "Ideal of Community and the Politics of Difference," in Weiss and Friedman, *Feminism and Community*, 235.
46. Young, "Ideal of Community," 244.

47. See, for example, discussions of gender issues in *New Jewish Agenda* and *Breira*, available at American Jewish Peace Archive: http://ajpeacearchive.org/initiatives/breira-a-project-of-concern-in-diaspora-israel-relations-1973-1978; "Women in Breira," AmericanJewishPeaceArchive, October 3, 2016, YouTube video, http://www.youtube.com/watch?v=0GnosIfh_Yg; and "A Dialogue Across Generations: If Not-Now (founded 2014) and New Jewish Agenda (1980–1992)," AmericanJewishPeaceArchive, October 3, 2016, YouTube video, http://www.youtube.com/watch?v=mU4EC3Ynk70. See also Maizels, "Old Boys Club."

48. This specific formulation comes from Jews for Racial and Economic Justice (JFREJ) in New York City.

49. "Trashing: The Dark Side of Sisterhood," *Ms.*, April 1976, 49–51, 92–98, http://www.jofreeman.com/joreen/trashing.htm. See also Joreen (Jo Freeman), "The Tyranny of Structurelessness," *The Second Wave* 2, no. 1 (1972), http://www.jofreeman.com/joreen/tyranny.htm.

50. Broner, *Telling*, 162. See also Susan Faludi, "American Electra: Feminism's Ritual Matricide," *Harper's Magazine*, October 2010, 29–42, although I think Faludi overstates the case.

PART 3
Friendship and Its Challenges

CHAPTER 7

Jacob and Esau
Twinship, Identity, and Failed Friendship

GEORGE SAVRAN

In the ancient world, the birth of twins was seen as an exceptional event that represented a basic paradox. On the one hand, twins represent a miracle of unusual fecundity—multiple births from the same source that encompass an essential unity, two in one (especially if they are identical). But at the same time, the twins themselves are two distinct individuals whose separate development is the very embodiment of duality, confounding the initial impression of unity. In the face of this anomaly, some societies have sought to rid the twin identity of its power by doing away with the simultaneity of twinship and normalizing the birth by declaring one the elder and the other the younger.[1]

Despite such efforts, the bipartite nature of twinship remains a vital force. In the biblical world, this two-sidedness can be seen in the contrast between narrative depictions of twinship and figurative representations elsewhere. In the Song of Songs, twinning is seen as a form of flawless identity. In Song of Songs 4:5 and 7:4, the pairing of twin fawns is a descriptor for parts of the body, here the perfect symmetry of the breasts of the beloved. In Exodus 26:24 and 36:29, twin language describes architectural congruence in the building of the tabernacle.[2] But the narrative accounts of twin birth in Genesis 25 and 38 emphasize their duality by focusing on the sense of rivalry between brothers: Peretz and Zerah battling to be the first to emerge from the womb as well as Jacob and Esau in lifelong contention for primacy and blessing.[3] Thus the array of twin language in the Bible expresses the essential paradox of twinship. It indicates both an indissoluble identity that radiates harmony and an axis of fracture and division that points to tension and duality.

Twinship is both a societal and an interpersonal phenomenon, often accompanied by difficulties in identity formation. Given the potential for exceptional intimacy between twins, it is not surprising that the sense of rivalry between them is equally intense.[4] How much room is there in such a competitive relationship for the mutual trust and empathy that is essential to friendship? Because they share their identities in an unusually close manner, twins have the potential to become the kind of friends who display deep concern for each other's welfare and well-being. Yet the narratives of twin relations in Genesis describe actions that undercut the likelihood of such mutuality. In what follows, I explore how the twinship of Jacob and Esau bears out this tension and how the opportunity for friendship arises briefly toward the end of the cycle only to be rejected by Jacob.

Brotherly relations in Genesis go awry almost immediately with Cain's murder of Abel.[5] There is a slight improvement in the relationship between Isaac and Ishmael, but things become complicated with Jacob and Esau and turn violent once more in the interaction between Joseph and his brothers.[6] One is hard-pressed to find instances of friendship in Genesis, as sibling rivalry casts a shadow over all the patriarchal narratives. There are some positive moments of cooperation and reconciliation in kinship relations, such as sons coming together to bury their fathers and Abraham's rescue of his nephew Lot in Genesis 14.[7] Far more noticeable are the cases of sons deceiving their fathers, such as Jacob stealing the blessing from Isaac in Genesis 27 and Jacob's sons lying to their father in Genesis 37. Mothers and daughters do not fare any better: Rebecca deceives Jacob in promising to send for him in Haran, and Rachel steals the *terafim* from Laban.[8] Despite the many statements about filial loyalty and responsibility found in wisdom literature, familial relationships in Genesis are rife with conflict and deception.[9]

The texts that describe the intensity of the youthful twin relationship between Jacob and Esau are found in Genesis 25 and 27. While these chapters are often read in light of the conflict and competition between the brothers,

I prefer to focus on how the text reflects their proximity to each other: Jacob and Esau exchange roles and characteristics as they grow up, even going so far as to imitate each other. The stories in these chapters refer to early stages in the development of the brothers, in which the formation of identity is very much a work in progress. Difficulties in the establishment of individual identity in twins have been studied at length and likely play a role in the incidents in these narratives. The problem of unstable identity is not uncommon in the development of twins. Each twin is caught between the desire to remain bonded with their twin and at the same time the need to separate from their twin, to recognize and assert their individuality.[10] Some twins manage this well, while others experience complications. In this case, fluidity of identity is more noticeable in the character of Jacob as reflected in his relations with Esau; his obedience to his mother, Rebecca; and his passivity with regard to Laban and his wives in Genesis 29–30.

TWINSHIP AND IDENTITY

Brotherly conflict may be endemic to the book of Genesis, but the relationship between Jacob and Esau is unique in its complexity. Their intertwined relationship begins, naturally, in their mother's womb. The unusual turmoil inside her body during pregnancy is described as a struggle between the twins, but the divine oracle that she seeks in response to this (25:23) also describes the twins' commonality:[11]

> Two nations are in your womb,
> Two peoples from within you shall be separated.
> One people shall be mightier than the other
> *Verav ya'avod tsa'ir.*

The repetition of "two" (*shenei*) in the first lines of the oracle highlights the twins' essential similitude, for both are "nations" and both are "peoples."[12] But the last word of the second line (*yippareidu*) states that what has been together in the womb will be separated from each other in the world.[13] The separation into two peoples refers to the division between Israel and Edom and is not coterminous with the twins' emergence from the womb. This process of detachment takes place only gradually as their story unfolds, first as individuals and later as nations.[14] The third line again refers to both with the same word (*le'om*) without specifying which people will dominate. This is followed by the ambiguous expression *verav ya'avod tsa'ir*, which can be understood as either "the older will serve the younger" or "the younger shall serve the older" (biblical Hebrew often does not mark subject and object grammatically). Many readers feel that the plain sense of the text is that the elder will serve the younger, for there would be little point in restating the obvious claim of the elder over the younger. But the ambiguity built into the poetic parallelism hints at the narrator's subtext—namely, the fundamental *linkage* between the twins. This concluding line of the oracle with its reversible syntax reflects the essential ambiguity in the text. At times Jacob will be subservient to Esau, and at other times Esau will be bested by Jacob. Indeed, which of the two is "greater" (*rav*)—the younger or the elder?[15]

The description of Jacob grasping the heel of his brother in the womb (Gen. 25:26) is another significant point of connection. This is most often read as Jacob's attempt to supplant Esau, in keeping with the other twin account in Genesis (38:27–30) concerning Perez and Zerah. Additional support for this reading can be found in the accepted understanding of the description of Jacob struggling with his brother in the womb in Hosea 12:4.[16] But the verb *ahaz* itself may convey a somewhat different picture. It most often implies grasping with the intent of keeping hold of something, whether to gain protection as in 1 Kings 1:51 (the horns of the altar) or to guide and support as in Psalms 73:23 and 139:10, where God holds the hand of the psalmist. It is with this intention that the woman grasps her lover in Song of Songs 3:4—"I held him fast; I would not let him go"—and Ecclesiastes 7:18 urges holding fast to two paths without releasing either. Jacob grips his brother's heel because he refuses to be left behind; as far as Jacob is concerned, Esau is not going anywhere without him. In the words of the nineteenth-century commentator Malbim, "The two are permanently tied to one another."[17] Despite the prediction of separation in the oracle, these twin brothers are inseparable at this point, bound to each other despite the differences between them. If Esau exits the womb first, it is only a matter of minutes till Jacob catches up with him, challenging the technical claim of Esau's firstborn status.

A second way the connection between the brothers is articulated is by the presentation of contrasting descriptions after their birth in Genesis 25:27. At first sight, the differences between them could not be clearer: Esau is the hunter, the planner, the successful brother who knows how to trap his quarry. Jacob is "quiet," a "plain man," staying close to home, perhaps tending the flocks.[18] They are physically distinct from each other as well. Esau's red skin and hairiness are mentioned explicitly (Gen. 25:26), and later on we learn that Jacob is smooth-skinned (Gen. 27:11).[19] Yet in the story that follows these descriptions, the sale of the birthright, the brothers' roles are abruptly reversed.

Esau returns from the field famished, exhausted, and empty-handed, for here he is a failed hunter.[20] Moreover, he shows himself to be gullible and short-sighted regarding the future value of his birthright. The description of Esau after his birth marked him as the one meant for leadership. His abundant hair is a sign of power and virility; both temperamentally and physically, he prefers the hunt to the pasture. Esau is also clearly the beloved of his father.[21] Yet in Genesis 25:29–34, Jacob shows himself to be skilled in culinary matters as well as in cutting a deal to his own advantage. He is sharply contrasted with Esau, the unsuccessful huntsman, who cannot see beyond satisfying his immediate needs. He is no longer the "innocent" person described earlier, just as Esau is no longer the triumphant man of the field. Has Jacob become Esau while Esau has turned into Jacob? What appeared to be clear lines of definition between the brothers have become blurred.

The question of identity is brought into focus in a different way in Genesis 27, the theft of the birthright. The structure of the narrative reveals an overriding symmetry in the actions of the characters. There are two sons and two parents; each parent has a favored son who wants the paternal blessing. In strikingly similar language, the command to bring food is first told to Esau by Isaac and then retold to Jacob by Rebecca.[22] This retelling underscores the parallel situation in the family dynamic. While the story is ultimately about the fate of the sons, the parents are the principles who hold the cards, even though they never address each other in the story. The idea of twinship is reflected clearly in the analogous behavior of the sons. Both sons act in response to the wishes of the beloved parent, and both bring specially prepared food (*mat'amim*) to their father. Both sons receive a blessing from their father after an extended interrogation about each son's identity. Both sons seek a wife at the end of the story: Esau weds the daughter of Ishmael, and Jacob sets out for Paddan-aram to marry Laban's daughters.[23] Their introductory speeches to Isaac are strikingly similar: Jacob's request to feed his father in Genesis 27:19 is remarkably like Esau's opening statement in 27:31, and Jacob's opening words and Esau's self-identification are nearly identical in their language.[24] The similarities in the blessings they receive have been noted carefully and further reinforce the connection between the brothers.[25]

But the difference in their actions clarifies the disparity between them. Here they do not exchange roles. Esau remains the hunter and faithful son of his father, while Jacob simply mimes his brother in words and deeds. The scene of Jacob dressing up in Esau's clothing and goatskins, pretending to be his brother, would be almost comic were it not for the seriousness of Jacob's duplicity. He may be following his mother's initiative, but he is certainly a willing participant in this deceit. The main point here is the graphic representation of Jacob's desire to become Esau, of which the birthright is only one aspect. In Genesis 27, he tries to become like him physically: his smell, his touch, and even the taste of his food is that of Esau. The physical description of Jacob dressed in Esau's clothes, wrapped in goatskins to mimic his brother's hairiness, reifies the fluidity of Jacob's identity here. He is Jacob, the beloved son of his mother, but he is simultaneously "Esau, your firstborn" to his father. This is summed up well in Isaac's comment in 27:22: "The voice is Jacob's but the hands are Esau's." But what is Jacob's voice here? His introductory speech to Isaac in Genesis 29:19 is essentially a reworking of both Isaac's request to Esau in verse 4 and Rebecca's demand to Jacob in verse 10. When asked again by his father if he really is Esau, his response is *ani*—"It is I." Who is Jacob here if not a changeable character pulled in different directions by mother, father, and brother?

By contrast, Esau's sense of self is more clearly delineated in the continuation of the chapter, expressed first by his harsh comment on the meaning of Jacob's name in Genesis 27:37 and then by his intention to take his brother's life. If Esau's identity wavered briefly in Genesis 25, he seems more clearly defined by the end of this story, both in his anger at his brother and in his attempt to please his father by marrying a descendant of Abraham (Gen. 28:9). We may have a clearer sense of Esau, but we still do not truly know who Jacob is. From Esau's perspective, we have a signal example of a failed friendship (the reader has no access to Jacob's perspective on this). Such unsuccessful relationships are not infrequent in the Bible. They are discussed at length by Saul M. Olyan, who identifies a number of central tropes: rejection, paying back good with evil, adversarial behavior, and disloyalty.[26] Such themes are particularly noticeable in psalms of individual lament, such as Psalms 28, 35, 38, and 88. In Jeremiah 9:3, this idea of failed friendship with a play on Jacob's name is used to address the wider societal problem of distrust:

> Beware, every man of his friend
> Trust not even a brother!
> For every brother acts like a Jacob (*akov ya'akov*).

Yet despite this mistrust between brothers, there is no disowning one's own kin, as much as Esau's desire to kill his brother may hint at this: "A brother does not typically cease to be a brother, even if he has behaved dreadfully."[27]

IN LABAN'S HOUSE

At this point, Esau disappears from the narrative for the next twenty years, and we expect that Jacob's separation from his brother and parents will compel him to develop his own individuality. But he falls in with a family no less dysfunctional than his own, with relatives who have their own problems of individuation—particularly Rachel and Leah. Genesis 29–30 describes the sisters' conflict in detail, focusing on Jacob's love of Rachel and Leah's success in childbearing. Like Jacob and Esau, they are physically distinct, but each wants what the other has; Leah craves Jacob's love, and Rachel desires Jacob's children. The sisters' competition clearly serves as a foil for the brothers' rivalry in the previous chapters. But the text also assumes a deep intimacy between the sisters, for how could the bed trick of Genesis 29 work without Rachel's cooperation?[28] This substitution of the older sibling for the younger is the sisters' version of Jacob's theft of the blessing, and the fluidity of boundaries between the sisters is graphically reflected by Leah "becoming" Rachel in bed. Throughout this section, Jacob remains remarkably passive. Despite a few brief moments of assertiveness at the well in Haran—rolling away the stone and kissing Rachel (in public!)—Jacob demonstrates a lack of clearly defined boundaries of self-definition in his negotiations with Laban. Is he primarily a hired hand, a son-in-law, or a nephew? Clearly he is all three, but his inability to define himself forcefully as one or the other leads to a further period of identity moratorium in which Laban takes advantage of him and his wives struggle for his favor. I understand Jacob's passivity here as a deliberate withdrawal from involvement, whether because of his inability to measure up to the demands of the family or because his sense of self is not yet fully formed.

A combination of social limitations and psychological factors contribute to this dilemma. First, Jacob's uncertain position in Laban's house weakens his ability to negotiate for better conditions. His status as a penniless dependent also leaves him at Laban's mercy, since asserting his rights in the face of his father-in-law at this stage would be socially unacceptable. On a psychological level, his sense of self is deeply compromised by both the past and the present. These might include Jacob's desire to achieve parity with his brother, his anxiety about being a stranger in a new land without the support of his family, the shame of having been deceived by Laban after leaving himself vulnerable by declaring his love for Rachel, and his lack of feeling for Leah despite her clear desire for his love. All these factors coalesce to depict a young man who has not yet settled into a clear identity of his own.

Jacob's distinctive adult identity begins to emerge consistently only in the second half of Genesis 30, after eleven of his twelve sons are born. We see this in the renegotiation of the terms of his employment with Laban and in his successful plan to multiply his own flocks. From Genesis 30:25 onward, Jacob first speaks and then acts decisively on his own behalf. The wish to return to his homeland and the references to "his wives" and "his children" describe a fuller expression of Jacob's awareness of self than we have seen before. The contrast with his earlier negotiation in Genesis 29:15 is striking. In both cases Laban asks Jacob what his wages will be, but whereas the young and naïve Jacob placed himself at a disadvantage by asking for Rachel (and nothing more), in Genesis 30:29–33 he is more seasoned and more conscious of his own needs. He begins by calling attention to his success in increasing Laban's flocks, describing himself as a conduit for divine blessing and only then making reference to "myself and my household." In Genesis 30:33 he invokes his own character for the first time as a guarantee of his worthiness: "Let my honesty toward you testify for me." It would not be out of the question to see this as a response to Esau's description of him as a "heel-sneak" in Genesis 27:36.[29] The proliferation of his flocks in Genesis 30:37–43 is the complement to the birth of his sons, but whereas Jacob's role in their birth is not stressed by the narrator, his accumulation of wealth is portrayed as entirely the product of his own actions.

The clearest emergence of the "new" assertive Jacob is found in Genesis 31. In this chapter we see Jacob taking decisive action in a number of ways. He encourages his wives to leave Laban's house and return with him to Canaan.

He is more aware of his situation, taking note of the change in Laban's attitude toward him and giving voice to his resentments about Laban's exploitation of him. He explains this to his wives in Genesis 31:7–13, after which he confronts Laban with an even more powerful argument in Genesis 31:36–42. In both texts, he describes the mistreatment he has suffered at Laban's hands, but in the second speech, one gets a clearer impression of Jacob's consciousness, as he calls on his memory of the past to bolster his case against Laban. Jacob protests his innocence in a way that shows an accounting of himself as the primary actor (God is mentioned only briefly here). Most of the speech is given over to self-description and self-vindication: "What is my crime and what is my guilt.... Your ewes and she-goats never miscarried, nor did I feast on rams from your flock." Jacob explicitly notes the boundaries of his own property, which Laban has violated, as he accuses him of having "rummaged through all my things." His call for an independent, objective reckoning in Genesis 31:37 further marks his sense of separation from Laban. Jacob has gained perspective on himself and his life that he did not display before, making use of one of the clearest markers of a more firmly established sense of self: his awareness of the importance of the past for defining the present and the future.

REUNION

Just as the sisters reach a certain degree of cooperation and agreement in Genesis 31:14–16, we might expect the brothers to do the same (or better) in their reunion in chapter 33.[30] Having followed Jacob's growth and maturation in chapter 31, there is good reason to believe that he will continue in the same vein in his meeting with Esau. But relations between siblings are rarely harmonious in biblical narrative. While there is a desire for reconciliation on Esau's part, Jacob does not fully reciprocate. The tension between affection and competition in their adult selves is expressed most clearly here. When Jacob receives the news of Esau's impending arrival, he is seized with fear, and most of Genesis 32 is taken up with his preparations for the meeting. He prays to God for protection, develops strategies for defense and escape, and arranges an elaborate gift to win Esau's favor. Having become used to Jacob's perspective in chapter 31 as reliable and realistic, readers expect Jacob to be met with hostility from Esau. But the reality that Jacob encounters is different.

Esau begins the meeting with an exceptional display of affection toward his brother. The language of Genesis 33:4 describes an emotional intensity that is unmatched in the Jacob story, except perhaps for Esau's deeply painful reaction to the theft of the blessing in chapter 27.[31] No fewer than five terms of emotional attachment are used here, certainly an unusual surfeit of expression for such greetings in biblical narrative. Esau "ran to greet him, embraced him, fell on his neck, kissed him, and they wept" (Gen. 33:4). Only at the high point of this display of affection does Jacob indicate something of his own feelings as he joins in the weeping. Esau's running toward his brother to greet him recalls other positive receptions, such as Abraham's welcome to his anonymous guests (Gen. 18:2) and Abraham's servant's acknowledgment of Rebecca (Gen. 24:17). In all cases, it is the sign of a most eager greeting.[32] Embracing can be a sign of erotic attachment or indicative of the warm reception of a family member, as it is here.[33] Falling on the neck occurs twice elsewhere in Genesis, both in the context of Joseph's reunion with his family: with Benjamin (Gen. 45:14) and with Jacob (Gen. 46:29). One recalls Isaac's blessing to Esau in Genesis 27:40: "You shall break his yoke *from your neck*" (emphasis mine), but here the neck is a physical manifestation of reconnection with a loved one rather than a trope for servitude.[34] The final expression, the kiss, is most often bestowed in familial contexts, including the reunion of brothers (Exod. 4:27). In addition to its affective sense, the kiss recalls and reverses the deceptive kiss Jacob gave his father in Genesis 27:27. The mutual shedding of tears speaks for itself as an emotional outburst. It, too, can be seen as a reversal of Esau's bitter cry (Gen. 27:38). While all these terms are found elsewhere in the Bible, the exceptional concentration of expressions for welcoming and warmth in this verse bespeaks Esau's desire for more than formal reconciliation with his brother.[35] It would not be unfair to suggest that Esau is seeking a deeper relationship with his brother—indeed, friendship—as the continuation of the chapter will show.

Esau's display of emotion seems to have little effect on Jacob. Despite the mutual crying (Gen. 33:4), Jacob remains in a pose of showing deference to an overlord. As he bows down to Esau seven times (Gen. 33:3), he continues to relate to his brother with the respect and fear one might show to an all-powerful potentate. He presents his family before Esau in perfect alignment, approaching, bowing down, never speaking. When Esau inquires as to the meaning of the elaborate gift Jacob has prepared, he answers ceremoniously "to find favor in the eyes of my lord"—not "my brother" but a lord to be feared, honored, and lavished with tribute. Esau's initial refusal of this gift in Genesis 33:9 is not a rejection of his brother but a reflection of his intent not to play the game of stronger versus weaker. When he says "I have much, my brother," he is not refusing out of disrespect or slighting Jacob in order to provoke an incident. Esau seeks true reconciliation here; he is not simply paying tribute to an angry lord or exchanging gifts out of obligation. Only when Jacob appeals to him at length in Genesis 33:10–11 does he realize the depth of his brother's anxiety. The fawning style of Jacob's address, in which he compares seeing Esau's face to seeing God, and the exaggeration of his own self-assessment ("I have everything") make clear to Esau just how important this gift is to Jacob; this is what compels him to acquiesce.

Moreover, once Esau has decided to accept the gift, he seeks to draw Jacob closer, hoping that the acceptance of the gift will be strengthened by proceeding to a common destination and displaying his hospitality. Hence Esau's request for Jacob to join him in traveling to Seir is phrased in the plural: "Let *us* travel together." The mutuality of the request reflects Esau's desire for parity. The phrase *aylekhah negdekha* can mean either "I will go in front" or "I will proceed at your pace," but the sense of traveling together is best captured by R. David Kimchi's comment: "Sometimes I will go in front but I will always be close by."[36] Nonetheless, Jacob refuses. Even after Esau modifies the offer, suggesting that Jacob bring along some of his men as guides or as protection, Jacob's response is again negative. The language of his refusal is deferential: "Why should I find favor in my lord's eyes?" (Gen. 33:15). It recalls the same formal language Jacob used in Genesis 33:8, 10, but here it signals a rejection rather than a request.[37] Esau's overtures here go beyond mere reconciliation, but Jacob is unable or unwilling to break away from the hierarchical language of lord and servant by which he has addressed Esau throughout the chapter. Even more disturbing, Jacob's excuses turn out to be another case of deception. Whether he ever had any intention of going to Seir we cannot know; Esau returns to Seir, perhaps in expectation of his brother's visit, while Jacob continues westward toward Sukkot.

Jacob rebuffs Esau's offer, apparently convinced that with his oversized gift, he has repaid his brother for the earlier theft of the blessing.[38] The scene ends in disappointment; it is another example of failed friendship even though it does not lead to a renewal of hostilities between the brothers.[39] Kinship and twinship brush up against each other to create friction and tension rather than cooperation and good relations. Esau makes distinct moves toward goodwill and friendship, but Jacob keeps himself at a distance. The mutuality that is essential for friendship is hypothetically present in the twinship bond, but it does not come to fruition. Rather, it is the *burden* of twinship that has left its mark on Jacob. This is a different sort of failed friendship than those described by Olyan. It is not a violent betrayal but a turning away, an unwillingness to respond with mutual favor and shared concern. It is more of a frustrated attempt at friendship, the refusal of a brother to respond positively to the initiative of his twin. This is not abandonment in a time of need so much as an unwillingness to live up to the potential for friendship embodied in the idea of twinship.

THE LIMITS OF FRIENDSHIP

Why is Jacob unable or unwilling to respond positively to his brother's initiative? One possibility is that there may be something inherent in his character that resists intimacy. Throughout Genesis 25–35, Jacob does not enter into close mutual relations with the other characters in the narrative. Rebecca loves Jacob, but what, besides respect and obedience, does Jacob feel toward his mother? Isaac's preference for Esau apparently keeps Jacob at a distance from his father, except for the moment of deception and the theft of the blessing. His relationship with Laban is lengthy but not positive; Jacob's accusations in Genesis 31 reveal a deep mistrust that leads him to try to escape surreptitiously in order to avoid dealing with his father-in-law. Jacob certainly shows no positive sentiment toward Leah, and it is never clear how much his love for Rachel is reciprocated. The unpleasant interchange between them in Genesis 30:1–3 does not leave the reader with the impression of mutual affection. In light of this (and their previous relations), we should not be surprised by Jacob's fearful and evasive responses to Esau's overtures.

Perhaps Jacob's reluctance or inability to bond with others is a reflection of the dilemma he faces as Esau's twin. His difficulty in establishing the boundaries of his identity in his earlier life may have left a permanent mark. Having formed his sense of self only with great effort, he is reluctant to bond more closely with Esau for fear of losing that hard-won self-confidence. In this case, friendship and twinship do not go hand in hand but remain at odds with each other. The intense competition between the twins as described in Jacob's boyhood and adolescence is never fully overcome. Jacob has matured in many ways and has surmounted earlier struggles, but the encounter with Esau reawakens his earlier experience and prevents him from responding to Esau's opening in a positive way.

A third possibility, probably the most likely, is that Jacob's turning away from Esau is the result of his newly won identity as Israel, as the father of a national entity that will go its separate way. Dalit Rom-Shiloni has shown how Jacob's national identity comes to the fore in distinct ways from Genesis 31 onward.[40] Like Israel and Aram, Jacob and Laban speak different languages and worship different gods according to Genesis 31:47–53. The establishment of the *gal 'eid* in Genesis 31:47 separates Israel from Aram in territorial terms. There is a strong emphasis on the ethnic separation between Israel and others in the story of the rape of Dinah (Gen. 34). We also see a clear rejection of idolatry in the demeaning treatment of Laban's *terafim* and in the disposal of foreign gods (Gen. 35:4). In all these ways and more, Jacob as Israel now stands at the head of a people that distinguishes itself from Aram and Edom in clear and unmistakable ways. There can be no journey to Seir, no intercourse with the Edomites other than passing through their territory on the way to Canaan, as we see in Numbers 20 and Deuteronomy 2. Jacob remains Esau's kin, but he can never become his friend.

We can see in the relationship of Jacob and Esau the anger and fear, the competition and jealousy that characterize nearly all kinship ties in the patriarchal narratives, but here they are supercharged by the intensity of the twin relationship. As with other sibling relations, there may be room for partial reconciliation, but the reciprocity that is essential for a deeper sense of friendship does not develop. One need only look at the interaction of Joseph and his brothers to see how tensions within the family are never fully resolved.[41] Genuine friendship in biblical narrative is rare and seems to work best outside the nuclear family. The most enduring examples of biblical friendship—David and Jonathan as well as Naomi and Ruth—are an unusual mixture of friendship and kinship. David and Jonathan are brothers-in-law (the only such relationship developed in the Bible), and Ruth and Naomi are mother-in-law / daughter-in-law (also unique in biblical narrative).[42] Growing up in the same household is not a sure formula for close bonding, as the relations between Jacob and Esau clearly demonstrate. Despite the possibilities for intimacy in twinship, it seems that the sibling aspect of twin relations, at least in the Bible, does more to hinder friendship than to promote it.

NOTES

1. Elizabeth A. Stewart, *Exploring Twins* (New York: St. Martin's, 2000), 13–26. The process of normalization may even go as far as removing the twins from society either symbolically or physically. See Victor Turner, *The Ritual Process: Structure and Anti-Structure* (Ithaca: Cornell University Press, 1969), 44–50.
2. Karolien Vermeulen, "Two of a Kind: Twin Language in the Hebrew Bible," *Journal for the Study of the Old Testament* 37 (2012): 135–50.
3. On the relation between these two texts, see Yair Zakovitch, *Jacob: Unexpected Patriarch* (New Haven: Yale University Press, 2012), 17–20.
4. Stewart, *Exploring Twins*, 68–76.
5. Interestingly, some rabbinic traditions see Cain and Abel as twins. See *Genesis Rabbah* 22:3; and *Yalkut Shim'oni* 35.
6. This depends on how one understands *metsaḥek* in Genesis 21:9. See Claus Westermann, *Genesis 12–26* (Minneapolis: Fortress Press, 1995), 339.
7. Sons bury their fathers in Genesis 25:9, 35:29, and 50:13. Saul M. Olyan discusses the relationship between kinship and friendship at length in his important monograph *Friendship in the Bible* (New Haven: Yale University Press, 2017), 11–37, where he demonstrates that most biblical texts emphasize the primacy of kinship. A notable exception can be found in Proverbs 18:24: "There are companions to keep one company, and there is a friend more devoted than a brother." Family members have special obligations incumbent upon them: redeeming land (Lev. 25) and acting as *levir* (Deut. 25), as well as burial and mourning of family members. At the same time, what we find in legal and wisdom texts contrasts sharply with the strained and conflict-ridden kinship relations in biblical narrative.
8. Rebecca in Genesis 27:45; Rachel in Genesis 31:19.
9. For a summary of kinship responsibilities, see Olyan, *Friendship*, 14–24. On brotherly conflict in Genesis, see Frederick E. Greenspahn, *When Brothers Dwell Together* (New York: Oxford University Press, 1994), 111–40.
10. Barbara Schave and Janet Ciriello, *Identity and Intimacy in Twins* (New York: Praeger, 1983); Mari Siemon, "The Separation-Individuation Process in Adult Twins," *American Journal of Psychotherapy* 34 (1980): 387–400; Stewart, *Exploring Twins*, 66–76, 101–4, 166–67; Muriel C. Winestein, "Twinship and Psychological Differentiation," *Journal of the American Academy of Child Psychiatry* 8 (1969): 438–40.
11. The verb *vayyitrotsetsu* can indicate fighting between the two or simply vigorous movement with no sense of struggle, as in the Septuagint. Cf. Rashbam ad loc.; and Bradford A. Anderson, *Brotherhood and Inheritance* (New York: Bloomsbury, 2011), 22.
12. Karolien Vermeulen, "Two of a Kind," 143, notes the language of *sh-n-y* either as "two" or as "scarlet" that occurs repeatedly within twin language contexts for the purpose of paronomasia.
13. On the poetic weight of this term, see Jan P. Fokkelman, *Narrative Art in Genesis* (Eugene: Wipf and Stock, 1991), 89.
14. On the personal/national dichotomy implied here, see Anderson, *Brotherhood*, 23–33.
15. See the discussion in Anderson, 26–27; John E. Anderson, *Jacob and the Divine Trickster* (Winona Lake, IN: Eisenbrauns, 2011), 59–65; and Zakovitch, *Jacob*, 16.
16. But compare Francis I. Anderson and David Noel Freedman, *Hosea* (Garden City, NY: Doubleday, 1980), 607.
17. Meir Leibush ben Yehiel Mikhel Weiser (Malbim), *Ha-Torah ve-ha-mitsvah*, comment on Genesis 25:26.
18. See the similar phrase in Genesis 4:20.
19. Esther Hamori points out some interesting parallels with Gilgamesh

and Enkidu: Gilgamesh is a fair-skinned civilized man, whereas Enkidu is a hairy creature at home in the field. While they are not twins, Enkidu is described as Gilgamesh's double (*zikru*). See Esther Hamori "Echoes of Gilgamesh in the Jacob Story," *Journal of Biblical Literature* 130, no. 4 (2011): 633–34. One noteworthy difference between the texts is that Enkidu and Gilgamesh begin their relationship with a wrestling match and end up being the best of friends.
20. The term *ayeif* is repeated twice as a description of Esau and can also connote failure or defeat—cf. Judges 4:21; Isaiah 5:27; and 2 Samuel 17:29.
21. Susan Niditch, *"My Brother Esau Is a Hairy Man": Hair and Identity in Ancient Israel* (New York: Oxford University Press, 2008), 114–18.
22. On this repetition, see the discussion in George Savran, *Telling and Retelling Quotation in Biblical Narrative* (Bloomington: Indiana University Press, 1988), 41–42, 127n8; and Fokkelman, *Narrative Art*, 102.
23. On the question of the separation of Genesis 27:1–45 from 27:46–28:9, cf. Elie Assis, *Identity in Conflict* (Winona Lake, IN: Eisenbrauns, 2016), 31n24; Westermann, *Genesis 12–26*, 435, 446; and Gerhard von Rad, *Genesis* (Philadelphia: Westminster, 1972), 281–82.
24. Jacob: "I am Esau your firstborn"; Esau: "I am your son, Esau, your firstborn."
25. Cf. Anderson, *Brotherhood*, 56–73; Assis, *Identity in Conflict*, 30–37; Fokkelman, *Narrative Art*, 107–12; and Westermann, *Genesis 12–36*, 441–43.
26. See the discussion in Olyan, *Friendship*, 38–60.
27. Olyan, 50. Cf. also 59: "But if the tie is familial . . . some texts seem to suggest that such a relationship very likely survives . . . even the worst offenses, while a few others suggest the possibility of the termination of family members."
28. This idea is elaborated on in a midrash from Lamentations Rabbah (Proem 24), where Rachel reveals to her sister a set of secret signs intended as a means of secure communication between her and Jacob, all out of her love for Leah. Even without this midrashic expansion, it is reasonable to assume Rachel's complicity in Jacob's deception for the sake of her sister.
29. Thus Everett Fox renders Jacob's name in *The Five Books of Moses* (New York: Schocken, 1995), 127. The term is a play on *ya'akov* and *ya'akveini* in Genesis 27:36.
30. Note also the story of the mandrakes in Genesis 30:14–16.
31. The anguish in Esau's response to Jacob's deception in 27:34–39 is unique in the Jacob cycle—"He cried an exceptionally great and bitter cry," followed by the pathos of his thrice-repeated plea to his father for a blessing of his own. This contrasts sharply with the absence of any mention of Jacob's feelings.
32. Laban's equally energetic greeting of Jacob in Genesis 29:13 uses the same language, though from the beginning we have doubts about the nature of Laban's intentions.
33. See erotic love in Song of Songs 2:6 and 8:3; Proverbs 5:20; familial connection in Genesis 29:13 and 48:10.
34. Jacob's neck was mentioned previously in Genesis 27:16 as one of the places Rebecca covered with goatskin to disguise him as Esau. That Esau falls on Jacob's neck here continues the process of reversal.
35. Elsewhere we usually find two expressions of affection (e.g., Gen. 45:15) and on a few occasions three (e.g., Exod. 18:7), but nowhere else do we find a consecutive string of five terms as we find here.
36. Cf. David Kimchi (Radak), commentary on Genesis 33:12.
37. The use of the phrase here is unusual. In nearly every other occurrence, it is used to preface a request; only here does it serve as a refusal. On the double refusal here, see George Savran, "Doubled Request and Doubled Refusal," in *Doubling and Duplicating in the Book*

of Genesis, ed. Elizabeth R. Hayes and Karolien Vermeulen (Winona Lake, IN: Eisenbrauns, 2016), 14–15.

38. This idea is based on Jacob's plea to Esau, "Please take my *berakhah*," in 33:11. Cf. Michael Fishbane, *Text and Texture* (New York: Schocken, 1979), 52; and Anderson, *Brotherhood*, 119.
39. Cf. Olyan, *Friendship*, 49.
40. Dalit Rom-Shiloni, "When an Explicit Polemic Initiates a Hidden One: Jacob's Aramean Identity," in *Words, Ideas, Worlds: Biblical Essays in Honor of Yairah Amit*, ed. Athalya Brenner and Frank H. Polak (Sheffield: Sheffield Phoenix Press, 2012), 210–14.
41. The character of Jacob as he appears in the Joseph story is freer with his emotions. Compared with his reactions to Rachel's death, he mourns the loss of Joseph more extensively (Gen. 37:34–35), shows exceptional pleasure at seeing Joseph again (Gen. 46:29–30), and describes his own life to Pharaoh in surprisingly emotional terms (Gen. 47:9).
42. One might also mention the positive relations between Moses and Jethro as father/son-in-law in Exodus 18, despite the absence of further information.

CHAPTER 8

Hebraica Amicitia
Leon Modena and the Cultural Practices of Early Modern Intra-Jewish Friendship

MICHELA ANDREATTA

> Commend me to your honorable wife.
> Tell her the process of Antonio's end,
> Say how I loved you, speak me fair in death;
> And, when the tale is told, bid her be judge
> Whether Bassanio had not once a love.
> Repent but you that you shall lose your friend.
> And he repents not that he pays your debt.
> —WILLIAM SHAKESPEARE, *THE MERCHANT OF VENICE*, 4.1.268–74

Extant in the library of the Jewish Theological Seminary in New York is a voluminous manuscript preserving a complete Judeo-Italian glossary of the Bible.[1] Copied in 1567 in the town of Alba, Piedmont, by an anonymous scribe, the manuscript passed, at some point, through the hands of the seventeenth-century Venetian rabbi Leon Modena (1571–1648), who apparently used some blank pages between the biblical sections as a commonplace book.[2] At folio 369v, at the end of the section on the *Latter Prophets*, the manuscript preserves a Hebrew rendition of a stanza of the *Orlando Furioso*, the most celebrated romance epic of the Renaissance, by Ludovico Ariosto (1474–1533).[3] This translated fragment is not the only surviving sample of early modern attempts at rendering Ariosto's work into Hebrew nor the most significant. After its first publication in 1516, thanks to the impact of print, Ariosto's poem became an instant best seller whose reception crossed social and religious boundaries. In fact, Modena himself had successfully tried his hand at translating two more sizable parts of the *Orlando Furioso* into Hebrew in his early years as part of his education in Hebrew prosody and poetic versification.[4] This single stanza, though, is of special interest in view of the topic it deals with: the ambiguous nature of friendship and the risk of insincerity, especially within a relationship of vertical amity (i.e., between unequal friends).

In the Italian original, this stanza and the following one formed the proem—that is, the introduction to canto 19, one of the most famous of the entire poem, in which the heroic loyalty of the young Saracen soldier Medoro to his king, Dardinello, is retold.[5] In the poem, proems are often the place in which Ariosto offers the reader bits of sententious advice on the most varied of topics. In the case of canto 19, he evokes the proverbial figure of the inconstant friend, who is ready to forgo the ties of friendship as soon as misfortune strikes. In particular, the opening octave—the same one that drew Modena's attention—offers a reflection on the ethical value of friendship and on loyalty as its fundamental attribute. It also encapsulates a typical Renaissance conception, according to which amity within a patron-client relation is not only possible but even morally superior to other forms of association.[6]

Recurrent warnings against the figure of the fickle or unreliable friend and its contrary, praises of the loyal and devoted companion, have been programmatic elements not only of popular wisdom and works of belles lettres but also of theoretical treatments devoted to friendship since antiquity.[7] Philosophical and ethical works extolled the two attributes of sincerity and faithfulness as indispensable virtues of the ideal friend. The idealized concept of friendship they often promoted, which derived from classical writers, combined with the pragmatic acknowledgment of the role played by friendship and sociability in strengthening and maintaining group relations and communal structures.[8] Also, didactic and devotional manuals often included disquisitions around the nature and value of friendship, thus signaling the role attributed to it in the program of self-edification that this specific literature aimed to imprint on the believers' interiority and moral practice. Such inclusion also evinced that friendship was perceived as a vital and powerful force in society—a force that, insofar as it contributed to securing the social order, needed to be disciplined and channeled into accepted patterns of behavior.

FRIENDSHIP IN LEON MODENA'S *TSEMAḤ TSADDIK*

A similar conceptual deployment of friendship is found, for example, in the overwhelmingly popular Italian compilation titled *Fior di Virtù* (Flower of virtue), an anonymous moralizing work structured as a catalog of virtues and vices supplemented with exempla and theoretical commentary. Its earliest versions date to the early fourteenth century, but its countless manuscript copies, early modern printings, adaptations, and translations into other languages testify to its enduring appeal in the following centuries.[9] Endowed with patent Christian religious character but neither doctrinal nor theological in nature, *Fior di Virtù* was the first book read after the primer in sixteenth-century vernacular schools in Venice, and it held a secure place in the book market of Counter-Reformation Italy, which was bursting with devotional compilations and moral guides.[10]

The Hebrew adaptation of *Fior di Virtù* was the work of the versatile pen of the very same Leon Modena. As a teacher and an author who was well aware of the role of print in education, Modena aspired to equip his coreligionists with a book that inculcated a moral alignment of behaviors and values. He thus sought to reaffirm the implicit adherence of individuals to those practices and feelings that were considered as required in order to sustain collectivity in both Jewish and non-Jewish camps. Modena, who probably based his version on the Italian original printed by Giovanni di Gara in Venice in 1588, eventually had it published in 1600 under the title of *Tsemaḥ Tsaddik* (Shoot of a righteous man) at the press of Daniele Zanetti.[11] Modena's adaptation mostly retains the structure and material organization of the Italian original and, in its printed version, even some of the external features of the work, such as several of the original woodcut illustrations.[12] Yet beyond being written in Hebrew, it offers a distinctive Jewish adaptation, which Modena achieved mainly by substituting some of its original exempla with quotations from the ethical sayings of the rabbis, the Talmud, and less frequently from midrashic literature, as well as by selectively expurgating explicit Christian elements or omitting the attribution of statements to Christian writers.[13]

The virtue of friendship is the topic of chapter 3 of *Tsemaḥ Tsaddik*, and here, as in the case of other chapters in the book, Modena retains most of the original treatment of the subject included in *Fior di Virtù* while Judaizing some parts of the text by integrating the views of Jewish authors. In the almost total absence of extensive Jewish theorizations of friendship, his reelaboration is of particular significance, as it shows Jewish adherence to a conception of friendship and, more generally, sociability that dated back to the classical period, persisted throughout the Middle Ages, and was eventually revisited and expanded by Renaissance and early modern humanists and authors, as the aforementioned octave by Ariosto well exemplifies.[14] Modena's discourse on friendship in *Tsemaḥ Tsaddik* in fact reflects the general ideas of amity persisting in his days, confirming that among Jews as well friendship was conceived as both a guiding ideal and a practical element, a component able to shape and govern that variety of social and affective reciprocities that lay at the foundations of both individual and communal life.

Closely following in the steps of the Italian original, in chapter 3 of *Tsemaḥ Tsaddik*, Modena classifies friendship as a subcategory of the overarching virtue of love, which includes, besides the love of friends (*ahavat ḥaverim*), also love for God (*ahavat ha-Shem*); love for parents or next of kin (*ahavat kerovim*); sensual love, or love for women (*ahavat nashim*); and "natural love"—that is, the attraction of like for like (*ahavah tiv'it*). This conceptual organization is rooted in Aristotle's views of friendship as expounded in books 8 and 9 of the *Nicomachean Ethics*, where the Greek term *philia* is used as an umbrella for a variety of human relationships, including the marital bond between husband and wife. The Aristotelian notion of sociability as an innately human propensity and the consequent emphasis on the pleasures and positive repercussions of friendly associations, two elements that both figure in the Italian original, are highlighted in Modena's rendition too. Likewise, he maintains the idea of virtuous friendship as characterized by a concern for each other's well-being for its own sake, an idea that, while still hinging on the *Nicomachean Ethics*, was also receptive to Cicero's more exclusive vision of friendship.[15] As in *Fior di Virtù*, in Modena's resulting exposition in *Tsemaḥ Tsaddik*, friendship is articulated as an elective and voluntary relationship characterized by reciprocity and implying a commitment to ongoing mutual service. This special bond is immune to changes of fortunes and alterations in the friends' condition, verges on self-sacrifice, and lasts even beyond death:

> The third [type of love] is also called friendship, or fraternity, or accord, or companionship. It consists of pursuing [together] things that are honest and right. The foundation of this kind of love lies in that delectable union and bond of affection that people like to establish among them. According to its motivation, though, [friendship] can be of three different kinds: the first one springs from the benefit and profit that a man hopes to receive from his friend, and this is the kind of friendship about which the sages have said: "Any love that is dependent on something—when that thing ceases, the love also ceases" (*Pirkei Avot* 5:16); hence this kind of friendship is inferior and mediocre. The second kind [springs from the desire] to benefit each other, like two hands that wash each other, and a friendship of this kind can be called "good." The third kind springs from the desire of the friend to benefit his companion in any way, even if he will suffer loss and damage because of him, and this is the perfect friendship, and nothing is above this. And the proof of such friendship is given when one loves his friend with all his heart and strives to do all that he thinks might please him, and refrains from all that he dislikes or that might damage him. In fact, one acquires and keeps a friend by doing three things: by honoring him in his presence, by praising him in his absence, and by supporting him in times of need. Besides, he won't be one of those friends who loves you in time of prosperity, but flees and disappears in time of adversity, as is known that "at the gate of the store [i.e., during a time of prosperity] there are many brothers and friends; at the gate of loss there are neither brothers nor friends" (BT *Shabbat* 32a). And it is known that the highest example of faithful friends were David and Jonathan, whose bond was extraordinary both in life and in death,[16] as described in the book [of Samuel].[17]

Closely adhering to the idealized formulation of friendship conveyed in the Italian original, Modena's own articulation views the amical relationship as depending on integrity and selflessness rather than on personal advantage and control: true friends are not driven by greed or vanity and are characterized by constancy, liberality, and utter altruism. Later in chapter 3 of

Tsemaḥ Tsaddik, friendship is described as necessary not only to create bonds of affective and disinterested reciprocity but also to the establishment of a balanced, hierarchical society. It is also postulated as the site for what we could call the "sociability of the mind"—that is, intellectual exchange based on elective affinity:

> And a sage said, "There are three things that are better when they are old rather than new: wine, fish, and oil; but above all is a friend." As Aristotle put it, "The bigger the tree, the more it needs much support; similarly, the man of high standing is more in need of many friends." This because there is no happiness for men in this world in being by themselves; on the contrary, they need the companionship of friends, as it is said: "Either friendship, or death (BT *Ta'anit* 23a)." Of the same opinion was the philosopher Archita [of Taranto] who said that if a man were to go to heaven and behold the sun as it rises and then sets, and the gloriousness of the moon and the stars as they shift in the firmament and all the other celestial wonders, and then he were to return to earth and contemplate the beauty of the world and of all it contains, he would not feel any joy, but rather bitter sorrow, if he were by himself and could not relate all this to his friends.[18]

Chapter 3 of *Tsemaḥ Tsaddik* concludes with the recommendation for the reader to acquire a good friend, test his loyalty and affection, and then, if he stands the test, love him devotedly. Modena does not expand upon what the test should consist of, but the exemplum that seals the chapter makes it clear that the true friend is expected to meet the highest criteria. This narrative section, which Modena retains from the original, although shifting its position, retells the story of a man who, having been condemned to death, asks for a delay of eight days to set his home and his affairs in order before the sentence is executed.[19] The delay is granted on the condition that the man finds someone who would be beheaded in his place should he not return. The man sends for "his friend and companion whom he loved like himself and by whom he was loved in return very much" (*ohevo ve-re'o asher ke-nafsho ve-gam hu ahuv me-ito me'od*). The man departs and his friend takes his place in prison. As the eight days pass, people mock the foolish man who agreed to be sent to death in his companion's place, but "he did not fear, because his heart trusted his loyal friend" (*lo hayah mityare kelum, ki bataḥ libbo be-ohevo ha-ne'eman*). On the very last day, the convict comes back and is eventually pardoned in acknowledgment of the bond of "such immense and devout love" (*ahavah atsumah ve-ne'emanah ka-zo 't*) tying him to his companion.[20]

According to the ethics conveyed in *Fior di Virtù*, true friendship is thus measured by the willingness to die for one's friend in an altruistic act of self-sacrifice that affirms the exclusive, total, and almost holy nature of amity, an assumption to which Modena, in his Hebrew adaptation, seems to subscribe. Indeed, the examination of Modena's language of friendship as deployed in *Tsemah Tsaddik* seems to confirm the central role that friendship played in the sentimental education of early modern Italian Jews. The array of Hebrew terms that Modena provides at the beginning of the chapter in order to render the multifarious concept of amity is clearly aimed at exhausting all the emotional and affective nuances with which a bond of friendship can be endowed. Thus the love between friends is also termed *ahavah* (fraternity), *shalom* (accord), and *re'ut* (companionship)—a variety of definitions whose cumulative list conveys the complexity, richness, and indispensability of such an alliance in a man's personal life.

THE INTIMACY OF FRIENDSHIP BETWEEN MALES

Conceived as a constructive and even salvific force, this special bond is described in *Tsemah Tsaddik* as exclusive—involving only two people— and in terms verging on the erotic in a language that consciously borrows from the biblical account of David and Jonathan's relationship.[21] Thus the friends are termed *ohev* (lover) and *ahuv* (beloved), and their attachment has the quality of a union of kindred souls. The erotic nature of friendship is explicitly acknowledged in the woodcut inserted at the beginning of chapter 3 of *Tsemah Tsaddik*, one of the five extra woodcuts that do not appear in the corresponding chapter of Di Gara's edition of *Fior di Virtù* and whose insertion in the Hebrew adaptation was probably Modena's own initiative (figure 8.1).[22] In the woodcut, two friends, supposedly the biblical David and Jonathan, are depicted as they embrace while a chubby Cupid, equipped with his distinguishing attributes of bow and arrow, gazes at them.[23]

Modena's *Autobiography* confirms the idea that in contemporary perception and practice, historical male-male friendship could share a trait with passion and consequently also be associated with heartbreak and sometimes even death. He recounts the cold-blooded murder of his son Zebulun by

צמח צדיק

הב' אחכ'חאד' אביו ואמו
וכל קרוביו כי עצם
מעצמיו ובשר מבשרו הם ּ
והטבע יטה הרצון להקדים
אהבתם לאחרים ּ וחוב אהבת
וכבוד אב ואם כבר ידענו נגדל'
כמו שאמר שלמה בן חכם
ישמח אב וכסיל אדם בוזה ּ
אמרּ ואם זל שהרבה הועיל
לעשו מה שכבד יצחק ורבקה
על כל האדם ּ וספדו בפק
דקדושין צאו וראו מה עשדה
גו' אח' באשקלון לאביו ודמא
בן נתינה שמו פעם אחּ בקשו
ממנו חכמים אבנים לאפוד
בששי'רבוא שכר והיה מפתח
תונא תחת ראשותיו של אביו
ולא צערו ּ לשנה אחרת נתן
לו הקב'ה שכרו שנולדה לו
פרה ארומ' כעדרו נכנסו חכמי'
ישראל אצלו אמ'להם יודע אני
בכם שאם מבקש אני מכב
כל ממון שבעולם אתה נותנים
ל' אין אני מבקש מכם אלא
אותו ממון שהפסדתי בשביל
בבוד אבא ּ וכששמעו חכמים

צדיק ט

בדברו ּ אמרו ומה מי שאינו
מצווה כך מי שמצווה עאכו ּ
ואחר זה ראוי לאהוב אחיו
וקרוביו כי כנד אמרו החכמים
אין עוני כעוני שאר בשר כי
סוף כל סוף הדם לא יהפך
למים ואיש את קרובו יעזור
ויושיע לעת הצורך ּ ואמרו
דזל במסכת יבמות פרק שני
תנו רבנן האוהב את שכניו
והמקרב את קרוביו ונהנשא
בת אחותו והמלוה סלע לעני
בשעת דוחקו עליו הכחו'אומ'
אז תקרא וה'יענה תשוע ואמ'
הנני'ועניך ועני' עירך עניך
קודם ּס כי הדם הוא הנפש
מאהבת הידידיס וגעים פרק ד

השלישית הנקר'
גס בן
אהב ּ

FIGURE 8.1 Woodcut, in Leon Modena, *Tsemaḥ Tsaddik: Sefer Keton ha-Komah u-Gedol Ḥokhmah*, published by Daniel Zanetti, Venice, 1600.

the hands of Jewish hooligans and the profound grief that his tragic death caused to the many who had known and loved him, both inside and outside of the ghetto: "Even Christians and Turks grieved. At the cemetery there was an eighteen-year-old Christian citizen from the Dolfin family who had known him, and he grieved so much that immediately after returning home he took to his bed and died within four days."[24] Modena's words could be easily dismissed as hyperbole, the outpouring of a bereaved father who is vouching for the exceptional character of his lost son. In fact, the episode, as it is recounted, perfectly fits contemporary cultural constructions of friendship, pointing rather to the acceptability and normalcy of bonds based on attachments that were deemed even stronger than brotherly kinships—the latter often being fraught with rivalry—and, as such, could stand the supreme test of fidelity.[25]

Thus it seems that the ideal features of friendship as described in *Tsemaḥ Tsaddik* did not just pose a high moral standard to which individuals must aspire and strive to conform; they also provided a framework against which attitudes toward the practice of friendship were construed and explicated. Certainly, actual friendship was much more varied and complex than ethical manuals could theorize, but early modern representations of friendship, especially literary ones, are notably consistent. The notions of self-denial and abnegation also dictate, for example, Antonio's willingness to suffer, in the name of his feelings for Bassanio, the penalty of the bond imposed on him by Shylock in Shakespeare's *The Merchant of Venice*, possibly the most famous example of an exclusive bond such as this in early modern discourse on friendship.

In fact, Antonio's passionate and explicit words of farewell to his beloved friend in act 4 of Shakespeare's play—which provide the epigraph to this essay—are particularly significant, as they also seem to point to a tension between friendship and marriage, or between amical love and sensual love, obliquely suggesting that the former involves a deeper and purer form of affection than the love between a man and his wife.[26] Antonio's words reflect commonly held opinions at the time: while both friendship and marriage were seen as drawing on the same emotional source, male-male attachments were frequently considered as ethically and morally superior to heterosexual relations.[27]

In this regard, Modena's conception of love in *Tsemaḥ Tsaddik* is no exception, and at least in its theoretical deployment, the bond of friendship, with its combination of intimacy and mutual aid, is similarly construed as exclusively male. This is implicitly posed as a *conditio sine qua non* to friendship's ethical value; by contrast, sensual love between a man and a woman, which is the topic of chapter 5 of *Tsemah Tsaddik*, is described as a blind force compromised by materiality and essentially incapable of fully ennobling a man's mind and emotions. True, Modena retains the idea of sensual love as a refraction of divine love, a concept he endorses by means of reference to traditional Jewish sources. But this does not compensate for the underlying misogynistic sentiment conveyed by the subsequent list of aphorisms in favor of and against women found in the original Italian work, upon which Modena largely draws.[28] Significantly, chapter 5 of *Tsemah Tsaddik* concludes with the exhortation to cultivate intellectual rather than sensual love.

WOMEN AND FRIENDSHIP: THEORY AND PRACTICE

That friendship and marriage could be perceived as alternative sites of affection does not come as a surprise. Their competing roles originated in contemporary social norms that prescribed the segregation of sexes and imposed limitations on female speech, behavior, and public activity. Particularly among members of middle-class and upper-class families, the opportunities for male-female socialization were scant outside the domestic realm. On the contrary, by virtue of the public role played by men, many important social, political, and economic relations were homosocial among Jews and Christians alike. Besides, although marriage was a common institution, particularly among Jews, unions formed primarily on the basis of love or physical attraction were discouraged, while other more pragmatic concerns guided the choice of a partner, such as financial considerations, social status, and parental approval.[29] Modena himself fell victim to this logic when, as he recounts in his *Autobiography*, his betrothed died and he reluctantly agreed to marry the dead girl's sister at the insistence of his mother, even though he found the personality of his future bride less congenial.[30]

Furthermore, from the classical period through the early modern era, women were most often deemed by nature incapable of friendship.[31] This notion, rooted in Aristotle's statement that true friendship was possible only between men—as only men could be virtuous—confirmed women's theoretical exclusion from the physical and emotional intimacy of friendship. It also explains why early modern discourse on friendship focused exclusively on male relationships. Certainly, friendship among women did exist, but it had less prominent public visibility, being mainly circumscribed to the realm of the household and family relationships.[32] Besides, female-female friendship—and even the less plausible male-female relationships—had little basis in biblical and classical models (which featured primarily male friendships) and, as a consequence, unsurprisingly provided no conceptual framework for Modena's discourse on friendship. Yet we are left wondering to what extent theory reflected everyday practice.

If we look at evidence from Modena's profuse writings outside of *Tsemaḥ Tsaddik*, we find scant reference to elective friendship among women or between men and women. His *Autobiography* is silent concerning any activity that could point to an engagement of female members of Modena's family in the realm of sociability. Although articulated with some emotional restraint, Modena's bond of affection for his daughters is evident from the *Autobiography*. Even so, Modena does not record any episode that could shed light on the emotional and affective lives of Diana and Esther. He does not even indicate if his daughters were provided any education as were his sons. Finding a suitable match and the money necessary to furnish a dowry for them seems to have been Modena's main concern when it came to his daughters, and the task, given the constant financial strictures in which he led his adult life, was a source of no small anxiety for him. Significantly, while Modena's daughters apparently led a secluded and quiet life, his sons moved freely within a wide and variegated network of friends, acquaintances, and lovers, in some cases embarking on relationships and activities of which their father was less than approving.[33]

In the vast circles of kin, neighbors, and patrons within which Modena led most of his adult life, we know of only a single friendship between him and a woman, the Venetian poetess and salonierre Sara Copia Sullam (or Sarra Copia Sullam, ca. 1592–1641).[34] While this relationship was in many respects unequal, there was nevertheless a degree of intimacy. The only extant document revealing some details concerning the nature of their relationship is the dedicatory letter that Modena inserted in the printing of his Italian play *L'Ester*, published in 1619 by Giacomo Sarzina. In the letter, Modena addresses her as "my most respectful patroness," who "deemed me worthy of her honorable and genteel conversation."[35] He also refers explicitly to the several occasions in which he and the poetess did "fall into a discussion of that most unusual poem"[36]—that is, Ansaldo Cebà's *Reina*

Esther, a dramatic poem similarly inspired by the eponymous biblical heroine, which Copia Sullam particularly admired.[37] Modena's own play was a reworking of an earlier play by Salomon Usque that had first been performed in Venice in 1559. In dedicating his reelaboration to Copia Sullam, Modena was overtly attempting to provide her a poetically sound Jewish alternative to Cebà's poem. The general tone of Modena's dedicatory letter is obliging yet friendly. Its prevailing manner is devoid of any flattery or servile attitude, but it rather conveys sincere concern for Copia Sullam. Predicated on direct interlocution, it addresses the specific circumstances that saw the unfolding of their unusual friendship. It attests to a relationship that, while based on service, also included a level of exchange between "equals" in spite of the differences in status, gender, and age. In fact, Modena's dedication acknowledges much more than a binding duty that needed to be honored. It is the public recognition and endorsement of Copia Sullam's intellectual standing and how exceptional she was by a loyal friend who wishes—in Modena's own words—"to show her some sign of how much I respect and revere her: just as I recognize her worth and her virtue, so I would like them to be recognized by the world at large."[38]

In her short and unconventional life, Copia Sullam showed a proclivity to cultivate relations with otherwise unequal individuals who were removed from her in terms of socioeconomic standing or religious affiliation but with whom she felt compatible in character and comparable in intellectual accomplishments. Most of these friendships were possible insofar as they were framed as patronage relationships. Copia Sullam's public role eventually led to her betrayal and slander by several men, some of whom had been previously part of her circle of friends and protégés, showing the hazards of friendship across gender and religious lines and, more generally, the harm to which nonconforming femininity could be exposed when stepping into male-dominated areas.[39] It is noteworthy that at her death, Modena composed an epitaph for her as dignified as it was conventional. In it he extolled, and thus vindicated, her female virtues as a modest and discerning wife and as a solicitous community benefactor; this was certainly the best proof of his enduring affection and alliance.[40]

Modena's dedicatory letter to Copia Sullam demonstrates that in seventeenth-century Jewish Italy, the patron-client relation could still offer a safe space for friendship between individuals otherwise separated by unbridgeable differences. It also demonstrates that material obligations did not prevent the development of bonds based on devotion and sincere reciprocal concern—thus apparently contradicting the assumptions repeated in *Tsemaḥ Tsaddik*, according to which true friendship could exist only between equals—and implied an association exclusively by choice. In fact, although refracting contemporary perceptions of the amical bond, it seems that the moralizing, highly idealistic delineation of friendship in *Tsemaḥ Tsaddik* is not an entirely accurate mirroring of the reality of contemporary amity, nor does it exhaust its many applications.

MODENA'S OTHER FRIENDSHIPS

In everyday life, Modena's experience of friendship was often more pragmatic and overlapped with kinship and a variety of other ties. An examination of his quite candid *Autobiography*, his letters, and his poetic oeuvre offer a catalog of sociability applied to a variety of relationships that can all be traced to a flexible, widely intended notion of friendship. These relationships included juvenile ties of friendship among peers, affections (not exempt of dissonances) inside the immediate and the extended family, intellectual affinities and professional collaborations, teacher-disciple associations, the already mentioned patronage bonds, and some exploitative relations forged around the gambling table. Some of these relationships included utilitarian arrangements motivated by material interest and revolved around the exchange of services and reciprocal advantage.[41] Others implied a disinterested affective bond between equals somehow resembling the idealistic articulation of virtuous friendship displayed in *Tsemaḥ Tsaddik*. To the first type we can ascribe, for example, Modena's relationship with several members of the influential Copio family, who sponsored the publication of some of his works and commissioned him with the composition of a number of occasional poems.[42] The merchant and insurer Moses Copio, who, together with his brother, sponsored the printing of Modena's collection of sermons, *Midbar Yehudah*,[43] was a relative of Modena's wife, and as recounted in the *Autobiography*, in 1607, after sojourning in Ferrara, Modena moved into Moses's house to teach his son, Abraham, and other students. The cohabitation soon revealed itself difficult due to Moses's unpleasant personality, a circumstance that within months forced Modena to look for another residence in the ghetto, as "no one could live cooped up with such a wild person."[44] Moses was later to convert to Christianity, which in part explains Modena's harsh remarks, but the relationship between the two nevertheless exemplifies a specific yet common form of patronage—the one extended to relatives—and the entangled notions of friendship and service, individual and familial, private and public in the early modern period.[45]

Sara Copia Sullam and Moses Copio were not the only patrons who, at different times, supported Modena.[46] Modena's life and intellectual activities indeed confirm the key role played by patronage in social and occupational contexts in seventeenth-century Italy. Most of his adult life, though, was also marked by relationships that fell rather into the category of "private friendship" or "companion friendship."[47] An example of an exclusive, long-lasting bond based on reciprocal esteem, mutual support, and loyal affection is the one that Modena forged with Solomon Shemaiah Sforno, a friendship whose beginnings probably dated back to the late 1580s and that continued until the latter's death in 1616.[48] Sforno was a rabbi and a salaried employee of the Italian synagogue in the ghetto; his main job, like Modena's, included teaching and preaching. He was several years Modena's senior and played a decisive role in supporting him when he was granted the rabbinical title of *ḥaver*. But he was much more than a colleague. References scattered in the *Autobiography* testify that Modena's attachment to Sforno was, in many respects, a sort of kinship: the younger rabbi turned to his friend for guidance at momentous times in his life, while Sforno also entertained close relations with other members of Modena's family, particularly his son Mordechai.[49] A firm believer in signs and omens, Modena saw his own life and Sforno's bound together by a common fate, something that becomes manifest when he recounts how, after Sforno's death, he went to live in the house previously occupied by his friend's family, one in which Mordechai was also destined to die a year after.[50] Modena and Sforno's bond was also cemented by intellectual affinities fostered by a comparable intellectual background and similar training: evidence from Modena's collection of letters shows that he used to seek Sforno's advice in matters related to his own poetical writing and trusted his friend's erudition in both Hebrew and Italian belles lettres. Thus, for example, in a letter dating to 1590, Modena told Sforno he had written an elegy to mark Pope Sixtus V's death and inquired if it was appropriate to use the expression "may peace be upon him" (*alav ha-shalom*) in referring to a dead pope, especially since in his ministry Sixtus V had shown a tolerant attitude toward the Jews. To strengthen his argument, Modena quoted a line from canto 1 of the *Orlando Furioso* in his own Hebrew translation, evidently relying on Sforno's ability to recognize Ariosto's words even if disguised in Hebrew garb.[51]

Modena's letters to Sforno and, more generally, his large correspondence corroborate the role that interpersonal relations and affections played in his life, offering a panoramic view of forms of individual friendship and a window into the ways in which friendship was conceptualized, articulated, and negotiated in the early modern period. His letters allowed him to create and sustain fundamental emotional bonds with friends and relatives, from whose proximity he found himself removed by the circumstances of life. Letter writing had been part of Modena's training since his early years under the guidance of Samuel Archivolti (1515–1611), the Jewish scholar from Padua who authored a major manual on epistolary writing in Hebrew.[52] It should not come as a surprise, therefore, that Modena's letters, especially the ones he penned in his youth, are composed in a formulaic, ornate style, which, while well serving the semiprivate/semipublic nature of these exchanges, nonetheless allows the expression of the writer's sentiments. In fact, the interlocutory mode typical of letter writing helps the young Modena achieve a "conversational" tone, which, despite some mannerisms, attests to the bond of reciprocal trust, closeness, and intimacy between him and his correspondents.

The letters Modena exchanged with other young men from small towns in the Veneto region while he was still in his teens provide particularly illuminating examples of the forms in which juvenile sociability among young, well-educated males was experienced. This correspondence allowed Modena to exchange current news, insights on scholarly matters, and sometimes also poetical compositions with his friends and thus overcome the isolation of his dull life in Montagnana, a small town in which he had very few peers.[53] But some of his early letters also constitute deeper conversations with absent friends with whom Modena clearly shared a uniquely affectionate bond. Some of them can be read as oblique treatises on friendship whose lexicon and rhetoric of intimacy are strikingly similar to those operating in *Tsemaḥ Tsaddik* and in which the language of exclusive male-male amity is similarly deployed. One letter that Modena penned in 1588 soon after the death of his beloved half-brother Abraham Parenzo in Ancona, is particularly exemplary of the degree of friendship between the correspondents and the ways in which reciprocal feelings could be articulated. The addressee is Jacob Cohen da Este, whom Modena sorrowfully reprimands for having failed to write to him since his last visit in Venice after he had come back from Ancona:

> I drank the cup of sufferance to its drags, I sunk into its depths, and when I was thirsty for pure water, that is the water of solacing words, water sweeter than honey to console me, and [for] the words of my friend and companion (*ohevi ve-re 'i*) to stand in front of me, no one said a word.... And you, *Signor mio*, who among my friends are the king, and among my companions are the prince, and among my beloved ones are the first, to whom among all my friends (*doday*) I have offered my heart: the fountain of your gentle words has dried up, the tree that bore the fruit of your loving writ has been cut; you have placed your hand on your mouth, and have no more to say.[54]

Modena's letter to his elusive friend deals with the fragility of friendship and the resulting heartbreak when the trust of love and loyalty fails. With his language of love, its manner of entreaty, and the ideal of loyalty underlying it, this brief epistolary excerpt brings us back to the notion of friendship as an elective spiritual bond that was deemed an indispensable element in the life of any early modern (young) man.

A short occasional poem by Modena, similarly dating back to his early years, gives expression to the positive nature of a close and trusting friendship. It also shows how the rhetoric of friendship, as conventional as it was, nonetheless played a role in the rituals governing real-world social interactions, of which occasional poetry, like letter writing, was an important element:

> O friend (*ohev*) pure at heart,[55] and fair in your words;[56] / Joseph, you're the sweetest honey, you're flavor and savor.
> Your mind is all beauty and wisdom; / humble and patient, you know how to curb anger.[57]
> My soul is thirsty for your friendship (*yedidotekha*): / why should I care for anybody else, as once I did,
> If my heart is yours? Therefore, / let's make a covenant of brothers the two of us![58]

Modena's short poem encapsulates the idealized conception of friendship transmitted by ethical and moral works, as well as works of belles lettres, as an exclusive bond of affection based on the acknowledgment of the other's virtues and on reciprocal commitment. Its binding language, culminating in the final plea for an oath to be sworn, exemplifies the contractual nature attributed to friendship with its corollary of commitment and obligation, emotional investment, and consequent expectations. As we have seen, this was just one of the many configurations that friendship assumed in Modena's personal experience and works. His life and personality, his profuse writings and interests, and his self-consciousness as a man of letters offer a wonderful example of the variegated and multivalent scope of friendship in early modern Jewish culture. The exploration of his conception of friendship serves to expand our understanding of contemporary ideas and practices related to loyalty, family ties and kinship, patronage and elective bonds, masculinity and the youthful articulation of emotions, and individual and group identity.

NOTES

I thank Howard Adelman for his many insightful remarks on the first draft of this chapter.

1. New York, Jewish Theological Seminary, MS L701 (838); Jewish National and University Library / The National Library of Israel, Institute of Microfilmed Hebrew Manuscripts, F 23942. For a description of the manuscript, see Aharon Maman, *Otsrot Lashon: The Hebrew Philology Manuscripts and Genizah Fragments in the Library of the Jewish Theological Seminary of America* (New York: Jewish Theological Seminary of America, 2006), 23–24. The glossary is briefly described in Lily Kahn and Aaron D. Rubin, *Handbook of Jewish Languages* (Leiden: Brill, 2015), 302.

2. One of the most fascinating and, in many respects, elusive figures of early modern Venice, Leon Modena (Yehudah Aryeh mi-Modena in Hebrew) served as a rabbi, cantor, teacher, and preacher in the ghetto while authoring a variety of works, including the first autobiography in Hebrew ever written, several sermons and rabbinical responses, a critique of Kabbalah, the first exposition of Jewish rites and customs composed by a Jew for a non-Jewish readership (in Italian), a polemical treatise against Christianity and Christian Kabbalah, and a collection of more than four hundred poems in Hebrew. On Modena, see *The Lion Shall Roar: Leon Modena and His World*, ed. David Malkiel (Jerusalem: Magnes; Ben-Zvi Institute, 2003), and the bibliographical citations included in the historical notes to the English translation of his memoir: Modena, *The Autobiography of a Seventeenth-Century Venetian Rabbi: Leon Modena's Life of Judah*, trans. and ed. Mark R. Cohen (Princeton: Princeton University Press, 1988), 183–273. Further updated bibliographical citations can be found in Talya Fishman, *Shaking the Pillars of Exile: "Voice of a Fool," an Early Modern Jewish Critique of Rabbinic Culture* (Stanford: Stanford University Press, 1997), and Yaacob Dweck, *The Scandal of Kabbalah: Leon Modena, Jewish Mysticism, Early Modern Venice* (Princeton: Princeton University Press, 2011).

3. I thank Howard Adelman for confirming that the marginalia match Modena's hand. The existence of this translation

was first signaled by Max Berenblut, "A Comparative Study of Judeo-Italian Translations of Isaiah" (PhD diss., Columbia University, 1949), 10; and then, on the basis of Berenblut, by Howard Adelman (Modena, *Autobiography*, 20n10). For a brief analysis of the Hebrew text and its comparison with the Italian original, see Chiara Benini, "Leone Modena e la sua versione di parti dell'Ariosto: Per una nuova ricerca su testi e contesto," *Materia Giudaica* 20/21 (2015): 425–30. While the language and style of the translation match Modena's, the absence of cross-outs raises the questions of why, if this translation was indeed his, Modena did not include it in the collection of his poetical works but rather opted to copy it down in a manuscript he apparently used as a reference work.

4. Modena's autographed collection of poems preserves his Hebrew renditions of portions of canto 1 and canto 28 of the *Orlando Furioso* (Oxford, Bodleian Library, MS Mich. 528 [*olim* 759], fols. 55r–58v, nos. 338–39), which the author asserts having accomplished at the precocious age of twelve. Both portions have been published in Modena, *The Divan of Leo De Modena: Collection of His Poetical Works Edited from a Unique MS. in the Bodleian Library*, ed. Simon Bernstein [in Hebrew] (Philadelphia: Jewish Publication Society of America, 1932), 33–45.

5. The story begins in canto 18: after Medoro and his friend Cloridano have sneaked into the Christian camp and moved the corpse of Dardinello to give it proper burial, they are pursued by a group of enraged Scottish knights. Cloridano suggests they should leave the corpse behind, but Medoro refuses and is eventually encircled by the enemies and left wounded on the ground while Cloridano makes his escape.

6. Remains, nor after death does he depart.

The following quotation is taken from Barbara Reynolds, trans., *Orlando Furioso (The Frenzy of Orlando): A Romantic Epic by Ludovico Ariosto* (Harmondsworth: Penguin, 1975–77), 1:584:

No man can know by whom he's truly loved
When high on Fortune's wheel he sits, serene.
His friends surround him, true and false, unproved,
And the same loyalty in all is seen.
When to catastrophe the wheel is moved
The crowd of flatterers passes from the scene;
But he who loves his lord with all his heart

As Ariosto's commentators have variously noted, the octave recasts a famous Latin proverb (Tempore felici multi numerantur amici, / si fortuna perit, nullus amicus erit; In happy times we reckon many friends, but if fortune fails, we will have no friends). This octave possibly reflects the proverb's reformulation by Ovid (Donec eris felix, multos numerabis amicos; / tempora si fuerint nubila, solus erit; As long as you are fortunate, you will have many friends; if cloudy times come, you will be alone [*Tristia*, I ix, 5–6]). On the fortune of this topos in the Italian literature of the Renaissance outside of Ariosto, see the historical note by Emilio Bigi in Ludovico Ariosto, *Orlando Furioso*, ed. Cristina Zampese (Milan: BUR Rizzoli, 2016), 635n1.

7. For an overview of the historical development of theorizations on friendship in European culture, see Barbara Caine, ed., *Friendship: A History* (London: Equinox, 2009).

8. On this, see Ullrich Langer, *Perfect Friendship: Studies in Literature and Moral Philosophy from Boccaccio to Corneille* (Geneva: Droz, 1994).

9. On *Fior di Virtù*, see the still fundamental studies by Carlo Frati, "Ricerche sul 'Fiore di Virtù,'" *Studi di filologia romanza* 6 (1893): 247–447; and Maria Corti, "Le fonti del 'Fiore di virtù' e

la teoria della 'nobiltà' nel Duecento," *Giornale storico della letteratura italiana* 136 (1959): 1–82.

10. Paul F. Grendler, "What Zuanne Read in School: Vernacular Texts in Sixteenth Century Venetian Schools," *Sixteenth Century Journal* 13, no. 1 (1982): 44–45, 46. On the printing of Christian devotional literature in early modern Italy, see Amedeo Quondam, "La letteratura in tipografia," in *Letteratura italiana* (Turin: Giulio Einaudi Editore, 1983), 2:594–96.

11. On the work, see Steinschneider, "Jehuda (Leon) Modena und *Fior di virtù*," *Monatsschrift für die Geschichte und Wissenschaft des Judentums* 40 (1897): 324–26; Howard E. Adelman, "Success and Failure in the Seventeenth Century Ghetto of Venice: The Life and Thought of Leon Modena, 1571–1648" (PhD diss., Brandeis University, 1985), 340–46; Joanna Weinberg, "Leon Modena and the *Fior di virtù*," in *The Lion Shall Roar: Leon Modena and His World*, ed. Robert Bonfil and David Malkiel (Jerusalem: Hebrew University Press, 2003), 137–57; and Vered Tohar, "Ẓemaḥ Ẓaddik by Leon Modena: Between Two Worlds," in *Religious Stories in Transformation, Conflict, Revision and Reflection*, ed. Alberdina Houtman, Tamar Kadari, Marcel Poorthuis, and Vered Tohar (Leiden: Brill, 2016), 353–75.

12. On the cultural significance of the illustrations included in *Tsemaḥ Tsaddik* in the context of contemporary attitudes toward the figurative arts among Italian Jews, see Shalom Sabar, "'The Right Path for an Artist': The Approach of Leon Modena to Visual Art," in *Hebraica Hereditas: Studi in Onore di Cesare Colafemmina*, ed. Giancarlo Lacerenza (Naples: Università degli Studi di Napoli "L'Orientale," 2005), 254–90, especially 268–69.

13. Weinberg, "Leon Modena," 146–54.

14. On the persistence of classical and medieval discourses on friendship in the Renaissance, see Reginald Hyatte, *The Arts of Friendship: The Idealization of Friendship in Medieval and Early Renaissance Literature* (Leiden: Brill, 1994).

15. Aristotle, *Nicomachean Ethics*, 8.5. This position is echoed by many commentators, including Thomas Aquinas in the *Summa Theologiae* (IIa IIae q. 30, art. 2). On this, see Constance J. Mews and Neville Chiavaroli, "Latin West," in Caine, *Friendship*, 100–101. On the blending of Aristotelian and Ciceronian theoretical approaches to friendship, particularly in the Renaissance, see Carolyn James and Bill Kent, "Renaissance Friendships: Traditional Truths, New and Dissenting Voices," in Caine, *Friendship*, 111–64. In general, on ancient and medieval discourses on friendship, see Daniel T. Lochman and Maritere López, "Introduction: The Emergence of Discourses: Early Modern Friendship," in *Discourses and Representations of Friendship in Early Modern Europe, 1500–1700*, ed. Daniel T. Lochman, Maritere López, and Lorna Hutson (Farnham: Ashgate, 2011), 3–9.

16. The idea of true friendship as an everlasting bond, a covenant between kindred souls that is able to overcome death, figures prominently also in contemporary emblematic literature, likely by virtue of its powerful moral symbolism and highly didactic potential. In Andrea Alciato's *Emblematum Liber*, the first and most widely disseminated collection of emblems, which was first published in Augsburg in 1531 and then was the object of numerous reprints, adaptations, and imitations, the faithful friend is represented by the image of a vine enveloping the trunk of an elm, grateful for the support it receives. The Latin motto reads "Amicitia etiam post mortem durans" and the explanatory text accompanying the *pictura* closes with the following exhortation: "By the example it offers, the vine tells us to seek friends of such sort that not even our final day will uncouple them from the bond of friendship" (Exemploque

monet, tales nos quaerere amicos, / Quos neque disiungat foedere summa dies). *Andree Alciati... Emblematum Liber* (Augsburg: Heinrich Steyner, 1531), fol. 6r–v; the English translation is based on the one available on the website of the project Alciato at Glasgow, sponsored by Glasgow University: http://www.emblems.arts.gla.ac.uk/alciato/emblem.php?id=A31a012.
17. Yehudah Aryeh mi-Modena (Leon Modena), *Tsemah Tsaddik: Sefer Keton ha-Komah ve-Gedol Hokhmah* (Venice: In casa di Daniele Zanetti, 1600), fol. 6v (my translation throughout).
18. Modena, *Tsemah Tsaddik*, fol. 6v.
19. Modena, fol. 7r. In the Italian original, this novella is placed after the chapter devoted to sensual love that concludes the treatment of the overarching virtue of love. See Weinberg, "Leon Modena," 149.
20. Modena, *Tsemah Tsaddik*, fol. 7r.
21. See 1 Samuel 18: 1–4.
22. Weinberg, "Leon Modena," 143–46.
23. Modena, *Tsemah Tsaddik*, fol. 6r.
24. Modena, *Autobiography*, 121.
25. On early modern discourse on death for love as culturally given, see Clark Lawlor, *Consumption and Literature: The Making of the Romantic Disease* (Basingstoke: Palgrave Macmillan, 2006), 15–27.
26. Janet Adelman, "Male Bonding in Shakespeare's Comedies," in *Shakespeare's "Rough Magic": Renaissance Essays in Honor of C. L. Barber*, ed. Peter Erickson and Coppélia Kahn (Newark: University of Delaware Press and Associated University Presses, 1985), 73–103.
27. On the tension between homoerotic and heterosexual relationships in early modern culture and perception, see Michael Rocke, "Gender and Sexual Culture in Renaissance Italy," in *Gender and Society in Renaissance Italy*, ed. Judith C. Brown and Robert C. Davis (London: Longman, 1998), 150–70.
28. For a discussion of the subsection of *Tsemah Tsaddik* on sensual love, or love for women, see Weinberg, "Leon Modena," 149–51. Weinberg points out that although the list of aphorisms mostly follows the one in the Italian original, the author of the *Fiore* displays a clearly philogynist attitude that is missing from Modena's version (150).
29. On Jewish marriage in early modern Italy, see Howard Adelman, *Women and Jewish Marriage Negotiations in Early Modern Italy: For Love and Money* (New York: Routledge, 2017); and Roni Weinstein, *Marriage Rituals Italian Style: A Historical Anthropological Perspective on Early Modern Italian Jews* (Leiden: Brill, 2003). Common concerns governing matchmaking and marriage and the ensuing conflict between parents and children are at the center of the sixteenth-century play *Tsahot Bedihuta de-Kiddushin* by Mantuan playwright Leone de' Sommi (ca. 1525–ca. 1590), on which see Yair Lipshitz, *The Holy Tongue, Comedy Version: Intertextual Dramas on Stage in "A Comedy of Betrothal"* [in Hebrew] (Ramat Gan: Bar-Ilan University Press, 2010). The edition of the Hebrew text is available in de' Sommi, *Tsahot Bedihuta de-Kiddushin: Komediah be-hamesh ma'arakhot me-et Yehudah Sommo Ish Mantovah*, ed. Hayyim Schirmann (Jerusalem: Sifrei Tarshis, 1965). For an English translation, see Leone de' Sommi, *A Comedy of Betrothal (Tsahot Bedihutha de-Kiddushin)*, ed. and trans. Alfred S. Golding (Ottawa: Dovehouse Edition Canada, 1988).
30. Modena, *Autobiography*, 90–92.
31. Caine, *Friendship*, xii–xiii.
32. One notable exception were female confraternities, which certainly provided affiliated women an important venue for sociability, and possibly also for friendship, outside of the household. The phenomenon of Jewish female confraternal devotion in early modern Italy still needs to be thoroughly explored. On female confraternities in eighteenth-century Modena, see Federica Francesconi, "Confraternal

Community as a Vehicle for Jewish Female Agency in Eighteenth-Century Italy," in *Faith's Boundaries: Laity and Clergy in Early Modern Confraternities*, ed. Nicholas Terpstra, Adriano Prosperi, and Stefania Pastore (Turnhout: Brepols, 2012), 251–76. On early modern devotional confraternities and sociability in their male configuration, see Elliott Horowitz, "Coffee, Coffeehouses, and the Nocturnal Rituals of Early Modern Jewry," *AJS Review* 14, no. 1 (1989): 17–46; and Horowitz, "The Eve of the Circumcision: A Chapter in the History of Jewish Nightlife," *Journal of Social History* 23, no. 1 (1989): 45–69. In general, on Jewish confraternities in early modern Italy, see Bracha Rivlin, *Arevim zeh la-zeh ba-geto ha-Italki: Hevrot gemilut ḥasadim, 1516–1789* (Jerusalem: Magnes, 1991).
33. See, for example, Modena, *Autobiography*, 108, 113, 114, 118, and 168.
34. The figure of Sara Copia Sullam has attracted the attention of several scholars. For a first survey of her life with reference to previous scholarship, see Howard Adelman's encyclopedic entry "Sarra Copia Sullam," in Jewish Women's Archive, accessed April 6, 2020, https://jwa.org/encyclopedia/article/sullam-sara-coppia; and Adelman, "Jewish Women and Family Life, Inside and Outside the Ghetto," in *The Jews of Early Modern Venice*, ed. Robert C. Davis and Benjamin Ravid (Baltimore: Johns Hopkins University Press, 2001), 146–49. For an English translation of Copia Sullam's writings, see *Jewish Poet and Intellectual in Seventeenth-Century Venice: The Works of Sarra Copia Sullam in Verse and Prose, Along with Writings of Her Contemporaries in Her Praise, Condemnation, or Defense*, trans. and ed. Don Harrán (Chicago: University of Chicago Press, 2009).
35. Leon Modena, *L'Ester, tragedia tratta dalla Sacra Scrittura* (Venice: Giacomo Sarzina, 1619), 3.
36. Modena, *L'Ester*, 3.
37. On Copia Sullam's fateful encounter with the poem and her subsequent correspondence with Cebà, see Adelman, "Sarra Copia Sullam"; and Copia Sullam, *Jewish Poet*, 115–267.
38. Modena, *L'Ester*, 4.
39. Adelman, "Sarra Copia Sullam."
40. The Hebrew text of Modena's epitaph was published in *Luḥot avanim: Hebräische Grabschriften in Italien: Erster Theil. 200 Inschriften aus Venedig, 16. u. 17. Jaharhundert*, ed. Abraham Berliner (Frankfurt: J. Kauffmann, 1881), no. 159, as well as in *La Comunità Ebraica di Venezia e il suo antico cimitero*, ed. Aldo Luzzatto (Milan: Il Polifilo, 2000), 1:246–50. An English translation of the epitaph with commentary is provided in Copia Sullam, *Jewish Poet*, 519–22.
41. On the "utilitarian" concept of friendship as a paramount declination of *amicitia* in early modern society, see Lochman, López, and Hutson, *Discourses and Representations*. On friendship and service in this period, see Lorna Hutson, *The Usurer's Daughter: Male Friendship and Fictions of Women in Sixteenth-Century England* (London: Routledge, 1994). On friendship and the practice of gift giving, see Natalie Zemon Davis, *The Gift in Sixteenth-Century France* (Madison: University of Wisconsin Press, 2000), 18–22.
42. Modena, *Divan*, no. 185; *Luḥot avanim*, no. 156.
43. Modena, *Autobiography*, 212, note *m* and 224, note *y*.
44. Modena, 105.
45. On Moses's conversion, see Modena, 213, note *n*.
46. On Modena's relationships with Christian patrons, see Michela Andreatta, "Praising the 'Idolater': A Poem for Christians by Rabbi Leon Modena," in *Connecting Histories: Jews and Their Others in the Early Modern Period*, ed. Francesca Bregoli and David Ruderman (Philadelphia: University of Pennsylvania Press, 2019), 115–28.
47. I am borrowing these definitions from James and Kent, "Renaissance Friendships," 132.
48. Modena, *Autobiography*, 109.
49. Modena, 99–100.

50. Modena, 112–13.
51. Modena, *Letters of Rabbi Leon Modena*, ed. Yacob Boksenboim [in Hebrew] (Tel Aviv: Chaim Rosenberg School of Jewish Studies and Tel-Aviv University 1984), no. 15.
52. Samuel Archivolti, *Ma'yan ganim: ... hamishim iggerot ... hokhmah u-musar* (Venice: Alvise Bragadin, 1553).
53. On this, see Howard Adelman's remarks in Modena, *Autobiography*, 21. For Modena's juvenile compositions for friends, see, for example, Modena, *Divan*, nos. 88, 90, and 91. For a brief overview on poetry of friendship in the Hebrew sonnet of the Renaissance and the Baroque, see Dvora Bregman, *The Golden Way: The Hebrew Sonnet During the Renaissance and the Baroque*, trans. Ann Brener (Tempe: Arizona Center for Medieval and Renaissance Studies, 2006), 220–23. A thorough investigation of discourses and representations of friendship in Hebrew poetry from Italy still remains a desideratum.
54. Modena, *Letters*, no. 6 (my translation).
55. Cf. Proverbs 22:11.
56. Cf. Psalm 45:3.
57. Cf. Isaiah 10:25; Daniel 11:36.
58. Modena, *Divan*, no. 88 (Oxford, Bodleian Library, MS Mich. 528 [*olim* 759], fol. 37v, no. 245) (my translation). Modena's introductory note to the poems reads as follows: "To a bloke whose name is Joseph: words of greeting and friendship." I thank Matti Huss and Yonatan Vardi for their remarks and suggestions on the Hebrew text of Modena's poem.

CHAPTER 9

Friendship and Betrayal
Hasidism and Secularism in
Early Twentieth-Century Poland

GLENN DYNNER

The Jewish community in the small Polish town of Przytyk (pron. "PSHI-tik") is usually remembered for its members' fierce self-defense tactics during the infamous pogrom on July 9, 1936. But for Dr. Shalom Honig, writing after the Holocaust, Przytyk's Jewish community was best defined by its members' close friendships. This was particularly true of the town's Hasidic community: "In one's *own shtibl* [small prayer house], with its homey company," Honig recalls, "everyone knew each other, related to each other in a friendly manner, and was as close as family." Similarly, in the region's Hasidic courts an "atmosphere of comradery" reigned, and every Hasid was received as a "member of the family."[1] At the same time, Honig admits, there was an unspoken contingency to these close friendships: in interwar Poland's atmosphere of ideological factionalism, only someone who belonged to one's own subculture was considered a "true friend."[2] Of course, friends were often drawn to similar subcultures.[3] But what happened when ideological choices put them on opposing sides of the emerging traditionalist/secularist divide?

In the case of Hasidic friendships, the sense of contingency was particularly acute. Hasidic youths were repeatedly admonished to guide each other along a common spiritual path and to warn each other against straying into evil, increasingly defined as secularism. One friend's experimentation with a secularist Jewish alternative could spell the end of the relationship. At first, Hasidic leaders tended to publicly ostracize wayward youths, forbidding all contact with them and effectively ending their friendships. By the interwar period, as youth defections became more widespread and ostracism lost much of its terror, some Polish Hasidic leaders began to experiment with more positive retention initiatives, such as the creation of political youth groups and apolitical spiritual circles. However, this more benign approach did little to diminish the inherent spiritual functionalism of Hasidic friendships.

DEFINING FRIENDSHIP IN HASIDIC SOCIETY

Conventional ideals of friendship in the Western tradition tend to conform to the Aristotelian conception of an authentic relationship of mutual care and concern that is devoid of ulterior motives.[4] The notion of an ostensibly "pure" relationship, valorized by Western humanist and Enlightenment thinkers, seems to have entered Jewish culture through the autobiographical writings of *maskilim* ("enlightened" Jews) such as Solomon Maimon (1753–1800).[5] However, for Hasidim and other traditionalists, friendship was usually conceived as an intimate relationship between individuals who, crucially, abetted each other's piety, education, and spirituality in addition to forming an emotional bond.[6] This does not mean that Hasidic friendships lacked spontaneity, affection, mutual respect, and trust. In fact, the spiritual imperative may have deepened and intensified the relationships between fellow believers. But Hasidic friendship ultimately demanded the subversion of each friend's own will to the will of the divine as defined by the Hasidic community. Therefore, few Hasidic friendships could withstand one friend's abandonment of the communal mission.[7]

The underlying spiritual imperative in Hasidic friendships is made explicit in later Polish Hasidic homiletic literature. In such works, one finds a striking shift away from descriptions of the spiritually perfect Hasidic master (*tsaddik*), the centerpiece of most early Hasidic literature, toward prescriptions for the rank-and-file Hasid's cultivation of piety and humility as well as interpersonal and communal bonds.[8] There were some earlier precedents for the latter concern: leaders of eighteenth-century

Tiberian Hasidism, once they had immigrated to the Land of Israel, placed new emphasis on the importance of friendships among their followers back in eastern Europe, urging them to transform their friendships into proxies for a connection to the absent *tsaddik*.[9] However, in the case of twentieth-century Polish Hasidic communities, where the *tsaddik* was usually accessible, relationships between followers were reconceived as alliances against emerging secularist formations. In a certain sense, the stakes became even higher.

The predominant category of friendship in Polish Hasidic literature is collective, what we would call *comradery*.[10] The preeminent Polish Hasidic master Yehuda Aryeh Leib Alter of Ger (1847–1905) conceived of comradery as a lateral mystical union: an act of connecting (*leḥaber*) groups of individuals that mirrors the *tsaddik*'s act of vertically connecting (*leḥaber*) heaven and earth or God and man. The pinnacle of comradery had been achieved during communal worship at the ancient divine sanctuary (*mishkan*), but in post-Temple times comradery is still attainable through communal ritual acts, such as Sabbath observance, study sessions on Shavuot eve, celebrations of the festival Shemini Atseret, and dwelling together in the Sukkah.[11] Connectedness among the "totality of Israel" (*klal yisrael*), he taught, helped dispense holiness throughout the world.[12]

R. Yerahmiel Yisrael Yitzhak Danziger (1853–1910), the Alexander rebbe, similarly emphasized the importance of "love and unity," presenting the commandment to "love your neighbor" as the basis of all other commandments and assuring his followers that evil, including physical assaults on Jewish communities, only occurs when there is a "division of hearts."[13] In his view, the Exodus from Egypt was an event that unified the nation's flawed individual members behind a spiritually perfect *tsaddik*—Moses—signifying their collective triumph over senseless hatred and enslavement to materiality. The wickedness displayed by the "wicked son" of the Passover Haggadah lay in his self-removal from the exilic community. Such defections can be remedied through acts that inspire love for all of Israel—studying the laws governing relations between neighbors, praying communally, and learning to discern the holy spark that resides within every fellow Jew. "When we unite ourselves with a complete *tsaddik*, who is primary, and with the simple folk, and we join together to unite our hearts in Truth," it is possible to elevate even "souls of lesser quality" who are marred by impure thoughts and deeds and achieve complete, collective redemption.[14]

R. Kalonymous Kalman Shapira (1889–1943), the Piaseczner rebbe, warned his students against self-isolation, exhorting them to "love each other" and to contribute a portion of their "self-love" to their friends. He had personally witnessed how arrogance—that is, inflation of self and denigration of one's comrades—could ruin promising young scholars. No one can rightfully say "I am for myself, my friend is secondary," he warned, for we all are "emissaries of God" and "hosts of God." In these dark times (the 1930s), the battle for light, like any battle, is a collective effort that must be waged within an army of peers.[15] Comradery was also critical for conquering one's own spiritual stagnation. A particularly effective method was drinking liquor with "Hasidic soul mates" in order to "stir up spiritual passion and serve God with an open soul (*be-nefesh galuyah*)." Communal drinking "with proper intention and mental preparation and within a celebration of Hasidic companions" rouses the spirit. Formerly, one's divine service was merely rote; now one could "feel it enclothed in a holy garment; a passion for divine service, for faith, for awe, for fear, and for love of God." It is of course difficult to imagine a similar sanctification of comradeship within secularist Polish Jewish subcultures.[16]

Polish Hasidic literature addresses personal friendships between two individuals less frequently but with a similar emphasis on their spiritual function. A true friend is your spiritual partner and guide, someone able to rebuke you, encourage you in your studies, push you to visit the courts of *tsadkikim*, and help you maintain a strict standard of piety, Danziger insisted. Intimate male friendships often blossomed within devotional (Torah) study partnerships: "By means of the union of one Jew with his friend, one nullifies himself within the other in complete self-abnegation, and they speak among themselves qualitatively and substantially about matters of the spirit, and one person shares in the sorrows of his friend amid powerful love. And by means of this they attain the attribute of Truth."[17] By discussing "matters of the spirit," the hearts and minds of each study partner begin to merge, deepening their insight into divine truth while emotionally binding themselves to each other. The erotically charged sessions cause each partner to realize that "by himself he has nothing at all, he is but a partial form, and he yearns and desires to cleave to the second form," his friend. The study partners become at once exalted and humbled, elated and burdened with each other's sorrows, empowered yet mutually dependent. The spiritual imperative only strengthens their bond.[18]

EARLY CASUALTIES:
THE FRIENDSHIP OF HERSHEL NOVAK AND ZALMAN HOROWITZ

When one partner abandoned the Hasidic path, however, it was quite another story. A vivid case of mutual betrayal during the early twentieth century is found in a Yiddish autobiography by Hershel Novak (1892–1952) entitled *Fun meine yunge yorn* (From my younger years). Like many authors of autobiography who were raised Hasidic, Novak had already left the traditionalist community when he began to write.[19] Despite occasional bitterness, however, his autobiography evinces a seemingly genuine appreciation of the traditionalist community that cast him out. "If only the youth of today could experience the joy" of Sabbaths and festivals, he exclaims wistfully, and the "sublime atmosphere of the Polish Hasidic court!"[20]

Novak's hometown of Piotrków grew from a typical early twentieth-century *shtetl* into an industrialized town with its first "assimilationist" Jews, yet it remained a "Hasidic fortress." Its main study house (*bet midrash*) adopted the Hasidic liturgy, and its *shtiblekh* (small houses of worship) were affiliated with major Polish Hasidic dynasties—Alexander, Radomsko, Chechanov, Radzyn, and the most popular of all, Ger. The town rabbi was a Kotzker Hasid (Ger was an outgrowth of Kotzk). In Novak's family's new neighborhood, the predominately Gerer *shtibl* became the town's "central institution," and Novak's father served as its beadle (*gabbai*).[21] Novak relished his days in the local clandestine *heder* (traditional elementary school), and he emphatically rejected the well-known Haskalah (Enlightenment) trope of the *ḥeder* as a place of terror and tedium. The texts he studied there "fulfilled and inspired" the students, and the Talmudic chants "strummed our heartstrings."[22] His days on the "hard benches of the study house" were the most beautiful of his life, and inside their walls one still finds the "future light and eternal life of the people." Yeshivot (talmudic academies) like Vlozhyn, Slobodka, Lomza, and the Gerer *shtiblekh*, he insists, were "our Harvard, Oxford, and Sorbonne."[23]

It was in the Gerer *shtibl* that Hershel met his best friend, Zalman Horowitz. The "two prodigies," as they were soon called, were the youngest boys to be admitted to R. Yankele Dayan's legendary Talmud class, and they naturally became study partners (figure 9.1). "We always 'learned' together, the same Talmudic volumes in the same classes in the same study houses," Novak recalls. A good Hasidic friend, Horowitz prodded Novak along his

FIGURE 9.1 Two young Hasidic boys studying together. On the right, Menahem-Mendel Horowitz, the seven year-old son of Rabbi Tuvia Horowitz (1931), Rzeszow, Poland. United States Holocaust Memorial Museum, courtesy of Marilka (Mairanz) Ben Naim, Ita (Mairanz) Mond, and Tuvia Mairanz.

spiritual path and warned him about the pitfalls of the increasingly secularizing Polish society that surrounded them: "In our friendship—in life, in Talmud and commentaries, in hair-splitting arguments, in behaving in the childlike Gerer Hasidic manner, and in spirited study house games—he constantly motivated me.... In short, he begged and admonished me to not allow myself to be drawn to the 'other side,' Heaven forfend."[24] Horowitz's concern for Novak's general well-being merged almost imperceptibly with a concern for Novak's spiritual well-being.

Thanks to their mutual encouragement, the two friends progressed rapidly in their studies and were asked to teach classes for the "simple folk." Under Horowitz's influence, Novak would sneak off to various Hasidic courts, sampling the rapture of each court's distinctive melodies and reveling in the "spiritual bonding" that occurred between each rebbe and his followers. The court comradery made such an impression on Novak that he began to become something of a fanatic. His parents were bursting with pride.[25]

In the Gerer *shtibl*, Novak also befriended Nehemele Mortenfeld, with whom he embarked on lighter adventures and misadventures, like sneaking into orchards to steal fruit. Sometimes they got caught and had their hats confiscated by the angry owners and were forced to return home bareheaded and ashamed. Undaunted, they pulled off pranks in the *shtibl* as well, sometimes with serious consequences (Novak sliced off part of his finger when he fell from the *shtibl*'s attic). Novak and Mortenfeld's friendship was clearly based more on the pursuit of fun than on mutual intellectual and spiritual development.[26] Yet it was Mortenfeld who first betrayed Novak, informing his teachers and parents about his heretical reading habits.[27]

Meanwhile, Novak was excelling in his Talmudic studies with Horowitz. The two young scholars were now asked to co-lead an advanced class on the most difficult Talmudic commentaries, codifications, and casuistry (*pilpul*) for the top students in town. At times, they still behaved like children, trying to persuade the local water carrier to march like a soldier or to marry the local "crazy woman." But usually they were consumed with more weighty matters, such as battling the secularist Jewish heresies beginning to mushroom across Poland.[28] It was this very militancy that was to prove Novak's undoing.

The turning point was a disputation with a Jewish Socialist activist who was frequenting local study houses in search of potential converts. Novak, having already been exposed to Socialist arguments by his older brother, felt sufficiently confident to challenge the activist to a public debate. Invoking pietistic (*musar*) tracts by the Hafetz Hayyim (R. Israel Meir Kagan [d. 1933]), he overwhelmed the Socialist with his righteous zeal and became the hero of the study house. But the novel ideas he had so handily dispensed with during the debate began to gnaw at him. Novak began to experience doubt.[29]

He fell in with a group of local *maskilim* and began to follow their leader, Pinḥas, who became his "new rebbe." He debated Zionists and Socialists; discovered libraries, lectures, and the theater; and inhaled philosophy, grammar, and modern Yiddish fiction. He read the forbidden works in hiding, beneath the *shtibl*, and began to lead a double life. Novak was convinced that he could solve all the problems of his people and give them a new existence. The most important and learned merchant in town, Moshe Yankel, was savvy enough to sense that something was amiss with the young prodigy. He began to study with Novak, coaxing him back onto the right path. But Moshe Yankel suddenly passed away, and Novak sank deeper into the mire.[30]

People in town began to whisper about Novak, and the rumors inevitably reached his home. Novak's "good friends" reported solemnly to his parents that he no longer studied in the study house and that he was no longer seen in the Gerer *shtibl*. Mortenfeld provided sordid details about their son's new reading habits. Novak's mother fell ill from despair, and his cheerful, outgoing father became gloomy and withdrawn. The *shtibl* members tried to rescue Novak by means of an auspicious marriage arrangement. The town rabbi—a revered eighty-year-old Kotzker "Hasidic genius"—invited Novak to see him. But the stubborn fifteen-year-old refused. "I knew that this was foolish audacity (*chutzpah*)," he admits. Some *shtibl* members resolved to teach the rebellious youth a lesson with their fists; as a result, Novak became afraid to enter the *shtibl*. Finally, one Sabbath day, it was announced in every *shtibl* in town that Novak had been placed under a ban (*ḥerem*). His closest friends were forbidden to have anything to do with him, and they all complied.[31]

None of this caused Novak to back down. Bitter over his friends' betrayal, he became more militant in his secularism. He moved in with a fellow former Gerer Hasid and joined a group composed of Hasidic exiters, Polonized Jews, and non-Jewish Socialists. They would meet secretly in forests, plot the transformation of society, and take oaths of fidelity to Spinozist beliefs while trying to ignore their poverty and hunger. Novak made the transition to a Socialist, then to a Zionist, and then to a Jewish cultural autonomist (diaspora nationalist). But all the intellectual projects suddenly began to weary him. Reckoning himself to be more of a "doer" than a thinker, Novak purchased a steamship ticket to America. On his departure day, his old friend and study partner Horowitz came to see him off despite lingering fears of being seen in public with him. Horowitz's sole parting wish, one last expression of Hasidic spiritual functionalism, was that Novak at least "remain a Jew and not convert as many others like him had."[32]

What makes this account so poignant is the goodwill reflected throughout much of the narrative. Novak engaged in genuine soul searching and intellectual experimentation, but he continued to conceive the atmosphere at Hasidic courts as "sublime." He confessed that the Hasidic melodies are "still with me to this day" and that he remained a "spiritual Hasid."[33] Though he had initially felt betrayed by Horowitz, who did not stand up for him, Novak now grasped Horowitz's difficult position and chastised himself for being insensitive. Horowitz, he came to realize, could not conceive of friendship outside the bounds of the Hasidic spiritual quest. For Horowitz, loyalty to the communal mission, not personal friendship, remained paramount.

MOBILIZING FRIENDSHIP: A NEW RETENTION STRATEGY

The ideals of friendship imparted in Polish Hasidism's prescriptive literature were put to a more severe test during the interwar period. In the absence of the older mechanisms of compulsion and control, which included state-sanctioned censorship, Jewish youth in the Second Polish Republic could sample cultural alternatives that had by now taken on highly institutionalized forms and virtually become total subcultures. The first watershed had occurred after the 1905 revolution, which heralded bourgeoning Zionist-Hebraist and Socialist-Yiddishist parties, press, and schools. After 1918, Jewish cultural movements became further politicized as members of various Jewish subcultures vied for seats in the Kehillah (Jewish communal self-government), the town council, and the Polish parliament (*Sejm*).[34]

Certain Hasidic communities began to organize politically too. The Polish branch of the Orthodox political organization Agudat Yisrael, formed in 1912 under the sponsorship of the Gerer rebbe, now became active.[35] For a time, the main course of action against wayward youths remained intimidation and ostracism.[36] Hasidic youth formed "Sabbath Guardians" groups and were willing to resort to violence.[37] However, as the secularist threats continued to grow, Hasidic leaders began to conceive more positive retention strategies.

Ita Kalish, a daughter of the Otwock rebbe, who left the community in 1919, was ostracized from her community and prevented from bringing her infant son with her to Warsaw. Kalish and her sister moved into a humble apartment and, like Novak, joined a circle of former Hasidim, eccentric Yiddish poets, and Polanized and Russified Jews, a motley group that was united most of all by their love of modern literature. In Kalish's view, the transition to a secularist existence was somewhat easier for Hasidic women, whose lack of direct access to Hasidic discourses and religious melodies made them miss the lifestyle a little less.[38] But most of Kalish's fellow former Hasidim, male and female alike, found themselves in a predicament: their lack of a formal secular education made it difficult to land a satisfying job. One scion of an important Hasidic family committed suicide (he was also disappointed in love). Another found he could only make a good living by composing steamy exposés for Yiddish tabloids about children of Hasidic rebbes who had gone astray. His former friends regarded such journalism as sheer betrayal, but Kalish reacted graciously when she read his spurious claim that she had run away from her father's court with a Gentile—after all, she reasoned, the former Hasid had to make a living. She soon provided him with plenty of real material: denied custody of her son, Kalish resorted to kidnapping him and fleeing to Germany. Many other former Hasidim seem to have left Poland, an indication that post-Hasidic communities lacked stability and permanence.[39]

The next two decades witnessed the emergence of more positive retention methods by Hasidic leaders. The most prominent methods were political, such as the establishment of Aguda-sponsored youth groups like Tseirei Aguda, Basya, and Bnos Agudas Yisroel (Daughters of Agudas Yisroel). Political affiliation meant institutional support, enabling the creation of "orthodox" libraries, summer camps, nature outings, choirs, and periodicals. A young memoirist using the pseudonym "Damaszek" claimed that his Tseirei Aguda youth group enabled him to remain "one hundred percent a religious Jew and avoid following the trends of the time." Damszek became an ardent activist for his well-funded local chapter, building its library, delivering Talmudic lectures, collecting charitable funds, and helping edit and publish its Hebrew periodical and Polish supplement. Tseirei Aguda was, in his estimation, both intellectual and "completely in the spirit of ancient Hebrew literature." It also nourished his intimate friendship with his cousin, though the latter soon emigrated to America and refused to write—suggesting his abandonment of traditional observance.[40]

The spiritual functionalism of Orthodox youth groups could threaten certain friendships. A woman named Esther noted bitterly that her close friend's decision to leave the Beys Yaakov school "caused the leaders of Bnos to denounce our friendship."[41] The groups' political affiliation could, furthermore, undermine solidarity in unexpected ways. Contemporaneous police reports demonstrate that spies and informants regularly attended Aguda meetings, meaning that some youth group members were furtively reporting on speeches and discussions for the benefit of the police.[42] Even more seriously, politicization bred dissension and open physical altercations, both among members of rival youth groups and within the Tseirei Aguda chapters themselves. Police reports include accounts of all-out brawls at Tseirei Aguda chapter meetings.[43]

Some Hasidic leaders began to conceive of less politicized approaches to youth retention.[44] The most well-articulated program was that of the aforementioned Piaseczner rebbe (Shapira), who urged Polish Hasidic youth to unify and organize purely spiritual, expressly apolitical circles. For Shapira, such circles hearkened back to the generation of Hasidism's founders. He began his pitch by paraphrasing a passage from *Ma'or ve-shemesh* by Kalonymous Kalman Epstein of Krakow (1751–1823) that repudiates the inherent isolationism of pre-Hasidic asceticism. Hasidism's innovation, Epstein had explained, was to recognize that repentance is best achieved in a social setting because one is humbled by his friend's "blazing heart and burning passion for divine service" and forced to recognize his own crookedness. It was even preferable to interrupt your own private connection (*devekut*) with God in order to connect with a friend and set him on the divine path, for such generosity spreads divine illumination. The help of friends, Shapira himself added, was needed even more in the current generation, which lacked the asceticism of old.[45]

Shapira encouraged Hasidic youth to establish a local circle (*ḥevrayya*) in each town for communal study, prayer, drinking, singing, and dancing. Such a circle must refrain from collective involvement in communal affairs and function without formal leaders, not even a secretary. It must be selective—members who were overly ambitious, unreliable, self-deceptive, or only there for appearances could corrupt the entire circle. Members must meet in a permanent space with a place for ritual immersion (*mikveh*) and agree on a single Hasidic text to study deeply and communally, heeding the insights that happened to occur to each participant. The communal third meal of the Sabbath (*seudah shelishit*) must be treated with extra sanctity, since the meal occurs when the soul is most removed from the cares of the workaday week and the "roar of the crowd." From time to time, members should drink together—"not to the point of drunkenness and wantonness, God forbid, but in the Hasidic manner: to bond with each other more deeply and raise up the animal spirit (*nefesh ha-behemit*) from its slovenliness." After drinking, they should sing an inspiring song. If their spirits are roused and they are moved to dance together, then they should also dance.[46]

Shapira also encouraged the cultivation of one-to-one friendships within this structure but highlighted their spiritual function: "Though everyone should join together in comradely love, and everyone should love each other with great love, each should nevertheless select a friend for himself before whom he shall reveal his entire inner heart, both spiritual and material matters, his worries and joys, his failure and success. And his friend who is listening shall comfort and counsel him, and cheer him as much as possible. Also in spiritual matters he should counsel and lead him according to his knowledge and condition, and vice versa."[47] Shapira's attempt to institutionalize and mobilize friendship was ambitious and well developed. Whether it would have succeeded in stemming youth defections cannot be known, however, since time ran out for the Jews of Poland.

This chapter proposes that Hasidic friendships in modern Poland contained a vital spiritual function and could not countenance the decision by one partner to embark on a different, especially secularist, path. Personal friendships were never to be preserved at the expense of the collective sacred ethos. While such constraints had probably always existed, they became more frequently tested owing to the successes of new secularist alternatives. By the interwar period, Hasidic leaders experimented with new ways to control and deploy their followers' friendships.

Formerly Hasidic men and women who decided to join secularist subcultures frequently evinced shock at their ostracism. Perhaps they had only intellectually understood the costs of breaking their community's social contract and were jarred by the reality of lost friendships. On the other hand, self-discovery, liberation, secular education, and the pursuit of secularist utopias were simply intolerable for Hasidic communities, where self-realization and agency were attained, paradoxically, through a *subversion* of autonomous selfhood and *self-integration* into the sacred community with the aid of one's peers. The tragedy of Jewish modernity in eastern Europe was not simply what Max Weber termed a "disenchantment of the world" but rather the coexistence of multiple ideologically charged subcultures, each advocating its own modes of transcendence and resistance in the midst of a largely inhospitable Polish majority.[48]

NOTES

1. Dr. Shalom Honig, "Maflagot ve-hivei Yehudei Pshitik," in *Sefer zikharon Pshitik*, ed. David Sztokfisz (Tel Aviv: Irgune yotse Pshitik, 1973), 44–49. On interwar Polish Jewry, see Ezra Mendelsohn, *The Jews of East Central Europe Between the Wars* (Bloomington: Indiana University Press, 1983), 11–84; and Antony Polonsky, *The Jews in Poland and Russia*, 3 vols. (Oxford: Littman Library of Jewish Civilization, 2010–12), vol. 3. On female Hasidic comradery, see, for example, Malkah Shapiro, *The Rebbe's Daughter: Memoir of a Hasidic Childhood*, ed. Nehemia Polen (Philadelphia: Jewish Publication Society, 2002). For examples of women petitioning Hasidic leaders, see Yizhak

Isaac Yehudah Jehiel Safrin, *Megilat Setarim*, ed. Naftali Ben-Menahem (Jerusalem: Mossad ha-Rav Kuk, 1944), 9; Eleazar Hakohen of Pułtusk, "Ets Avot," in *Ḥidushei Maharakh* (Warsaw, 1898), 1; and Yaakov Aryeh of Radzymin, *Maʾasyot noraʾim* (Piotrków: Be-hotsaat Avraham Yosef Klaiman, 1914), for example, 7–8.
2. Honig, "Maflagot ve-hivei Yehudei Pshitik," 44–49.
3. See, for example, YIVO Archives, *Youth Autobiographies*, RG 4: #3512, T. S., Ostrow Mazowiecka (near Siedlce); #3513, B. M., Rudnik (near Ostrowiec Swietokrzyski); #3514, F. J., Ostrowiec; #3515, G. S., Ostrolenka; #3536, L. A. Bialystok; #3552, Z. A., Bialystok, Grodno; #3559, S. R., Grojec.
4. Aristotle, *Aristotle: Nicomachean Ethics*, trans. Christopher Rowe (New York: Oxford University Press, 2002), book 8.3–6. On secularism, see Dipesh Chakrabarty, *Habitations of Modernity* (Chicago: University of Chicago Press, 2002), 26; Chakrabarty, *Provincializing Europe: Postcolonial Thought and Historical Difference* (Princeton: Princeton University Press, 2000), 46; Saba Mahmood, *Politics of Piety: The Islamic Revival and the Feminist Subject* (Princeton: Princeton University Press, 2005); and Jose Casanova, *Public Religions in the Modern World* (Chicago: University of Chicago Press, 1994). On traditionalism, see Jacob Katz, "Orthodoxy in Historical Perspective," *Studies in Contemporary Jewry* 2 (1986): especially 3–4; Mordecai Breuer, *Modernity Within Tradition: The Social History of Orthodox Jewry in Imperial Germany*, trans. E. Petuchowski (New York: Columbia University Press, 1992); Adam Ferziger, *Exclusion and Hierarchy: Orthodoxy, Nonobservance, and the Emergence of Modern Jewish Identity* (Philadelphia: University of Pennsylvania Press, 2005); and Michael Silber, "The Emergence of Ultra-Orthodoxy," in *The Uses of Tradition: Jewish Continuity in the Modern Era*, ed. Jack Wertheimer (New York: Jewish Theological Seminary, 1992).
5. See Maimon's description of his "bosom friend" Moses Lapidot in *Solomon Maimon: An Autobiography* (Champaign: University of Illinois Press, 2001), 138–44. On Maimon's tendency to model episodes of his life on Rousseau's writings, see Marcus Moseley, *Being for Myself Alone: Origins of Jewish Autobiography* (Stanford: Stanford University Press, 2006), 56–57.
6. See, for example, Lawrence Fine, "Spiritual Friendship: 'Go Among People Who Are Awake and Where a Light Shines Brightly,'" in *Jewish Mysticism and the Spiritual Life: Classical Texts, Contemporary Reflections*, ed. Lawrence Fine, Eitan P. Fishbane, and Or N. Rose (Woodstock, VT: Jewish Lights, 2013), 112–18; Tsippi Kauffman, "Doctrine of the Distant Tsaddik—Mysticism, Ethics, and Politics" (forthcoming in *Jewish History*); and Aubrey Glazer, "From Tiberias with Love: Hermeneutics of Imbrication in Letters of Love" (forthcoming in *Jewish History*).
7. On defections, see David Assaf, *Untold Tales of the Hasidim: Crisis and Discontent in the History of Hasidism*, trans. Dena Ordan (Waltham: Brandeis University Press, 2010), especially 154–235; and Moriah Herman, "Ha-yaḥas livnei ha-noʾar be-ḥasidut be-tekufah shebein milḥamot ha-olam" (PhD diss., Bar Ilan University, 2014).
8. See, for example, *Yismaḥ Yisrael*, parshat Pekudei, 1:105–7, and parshat Terumah (Rosh Hodesh), 1:64–65; Yehuda Leib Alter, *The Language of Truth: The Torah Commentary of the Sefat Emet*, trans. Arthur Green (Philadelphia: Jewish Publication Society, 2012), for example, Commentary to Passover, 390; and Shmuel Borenshtein of Sochaczew, *Shem mi-Shmuel* (repr., Jerusalem: n.p., 1950), parshat Toldot, 201. This shift appears first in Schneur Zalman of Liady's *Tanya* (1797) with its emphasis on the "intermediary man" (*beinoni*).
9. Kauffman, "Doctrine."

10. On the distinction between comradery and personal friendship, see Fine, "Spiritual Friendship," 113.
11. Yehuda Aryeh Leib of Ger's *Sefat Emet*, 5 vols. (Piotrków: n.p., 1905). See 2:150, 2:222, 4:37, 4:52, 4:57, 4:67, and 5:194.
12. Yehuda Aryeh Leib of Ger's *Sefat Emet*, 3:184. Citing *Zohar*, Leviticus 33b. A similar teaching is found in *Sefat Emet*, 3:198.
13. Yerahmiel Yisrael Yitzhak Danziger of Alexander, *Yismaḥ Yisrael*, 2 vols. (n.p., 1911; repr., Brooklyn: n.p., 1991), 2:52. On physical attacks, see 2:57.
14. Danziger of Alexander, *Yismaḥ Yisrael*, 3:34–35. See also 4:110 on collective prayer.
15. Kalonymous Kalman Shapira of Piaseczno, *Ḥokhmat Talmidim* (Warsaw: Bi-defus shel ha-aḥim Feder, 1931), 32–33 (chap. 6).
16. Kalonymous Kalman Shapira, *Sefer Hakhsharat ha-avrekhim, mevo ha-she'arim (le-Ḥovat ha-avrekhim): Tsav ve-zeruz* (Jerusalem: Va'ad ḥasidei Pyasetsnah, 1965), chap. 9, p. 47. See also Menachem Ekstein's description of the "influences and forces that pass between people" during Hasidic gatherings in Daniel Reiser, "The Encounter in Vienna: Modern Psychotherapy, Guided Imagery, and Hasidism Post–World War I," *Modern Judaism* 36, no. 3 (2016): 8.
17. *Yismaḥ Yisrael*, 2:78.
18. *Yismaḥ Yisrael*, 2:79. Similarly, his grandson Yitzhak Menahem Mendel Danziger (1880–1943) said, "One's friend strengthens him in serving the Holy One Blessed be He and in all endeavors, and does not let him succumb to despair, God forbid." See Danziger, *Akedat Yitzhak* (Jerusalem, 1953; repr., Bnei Brak, Israel: Haidei Aleksander, 2005), 19. See also the earlier admonition in Asher of Stolin's *Hanhagot Tsaddikim* 2:474: "See that you have a good friend, someone who can be depended upon and who is able to keep a secret. You should talk with this person half an hour every day about everything in your heart and your innermost thoughts that flow from the evil inclination." See Fine, "Spiritual Friendship," 116. Note also S. Ansky's description of two "friends in the same yeshiva" whose "souls were connected in a precious friendship," in the play *Der Dybuk* (first performed 1920); and S. Etonis's observation that "in very rare instances you find a friend who is well suited to you, with whom you have a bond, both for study and for friendship, for intimate companionship," in Jeffery Shandler, ed., *Awakening Lives: Autobiographies of Jewish Youth in Poland Before the Holocaust* (New Haven: Yale University Press 2002), 15.
19. This tendency was probably due to a higher tolerance for secular education in the case of girls. See Shaul Stampfer, "Gender Differentiation and the Education of Jewish Women," in Stampfer, *Families, Rabbis, and Education: Traditional Jewish Society in Nineteenth-Century Eastern Europe* (Oxford: Littman Library, 2010), especially 169; and Iris Parush, *Reading Jewish Women: Marginality and Modernization in Nineteenth-Century Eastern European Jewish Society* (Waltham: Brandeis University Press, 2004). For female traditionalist autobiographies, see Shulamith Soloveitchik Meiselman, *The Soloveitchik Heritage: A Daughter's Memoir* (Hoboken: KTAV, 1995); Chaja Finkler, *Lives Lived and Lost: East European History Before, During, and After World War II as Experienced by an Anthropologist and Her Mother* (Boston: Academic Studies Press, 2012); and Gutta Sternbuch, *Gutta: Memories of a Vanished World* (New York: Feldheim, 2013), with David Kranzler. See also Joanna Lisek, "'To Write? What's This Torture For?': Bronia Baum's Manuscripts as a Testimony of the Formation of a Writer, Activist, Journalist," special issue of *Jewish History*, "Jewish Women in Eastern and East Central Europe," *Jewish History* 33 (2020): 61–113.

20. Hershel Novak, *Fun meine yunge yorn* (New York: Workmen's Circle, 1957).
21. Novak, 11–24, 31–37. As the building belonged to a tavernkeeper named Nisanzohn, the *shtibl* was temporarily transformed into a tavern every Sunday and Christian holiday, something that did not faze the worshippers. However, when Nisanzohn's daughter married a Gentile, converted, and opened a tavern nearby, the members decided it was time to relocate. According to Marcin Wodzinski, there were 281 Gerer *shtiblekh* in the region of central Poland alone. See "Space and Spirit: On Boundaries, Hierarchies, and Leadership in Hasidism," *Journal of Historical Geography* 53 (2016): 63–74, especially table 1.
22. There were three public schools in Piotrków before World War I. See Mojesz Feinkind, *Dzieje Żydów w Piotrkówie i Okolicie* (Piotrków: n.p., 1930), 50.
23. Novak, *Fun meine yunge yorn*, 46–48.
24. Novak, 50. Horowitz was the son of a Kotzker Hasid and descendant of the renowned R. Isaiah Horowitz (1555–1630).
25. Novak, 51–53, 60–63.
26. This is a less durable category of friendship according to Aristotle's taxonomy. See Aristotle, *Nicomachean Ethics*, book 8.3.
27. Novak, *Fun meine yunge yorn*, 54–56.
28. Novak, 67–71.
29. Novak, 79–87.
30. Novak, 86–93.
31. Novak, 101–6.
32. Novak, 118–35.
33. Novak, 62–64.
34. See Scott Ury, *Banners and Barricades: The Revolution of 1905 and the Transformation of Warsaw Jewry* (Stanford: Stanford University Press, 2012); and Ury, "In Kotik's Corner: Urban Culture, Bourgeois Politics and the Struggle for Jewish Civility in Turn of the Century Eastern Europe," in *Warsaw: The Jewish Metropolis*, ed. Glenn Dynner and Francois Guesnet (Leiden: Brill, 2015), 206–27; and Jack Jacobs, *Bundist Counterculture in Interwar Poland* (Syracuse: Syracuse University Press, 2009).
35. Gershon Bacon, *The Politics of Tradition: Agudat Yisrael in Poland, 1916–1939* (Jerusalem: Magnes, 1996), especially 72, 79–80, 84, and 87; and Robert Moses Shapiro, "Jewish Self-Government in Poland: Lodz, 1914–1939" (PhD diss., Columbia University, 1987), 108–227. On Orthodox party politics in prewar Galicia, which may have preceded secularist Jewish politics there, see Rachel Manekin, *Yehude Galitsyah ve-ha-ḥukah ha-Ostrit: Reshitah shel politikah Yehudit modernit* (Jerusalem: Merkaz Zalman Shazar, 2015); and Manekin, "Orthodox Jewry in Kraków at the Turn of the Twentieth Century," in *Polin 23: Jews in Kraków*, ed. Michał Galas and Antony Polonsky (Oxford: Littman Library of Jewish Civilization, 2011), 165–98.
36. According to Gauri Viswanathan, defectors are seen as threatening because they are "undoing the concept of fixed, unalterable identities," and tempting others to follow suit. See Viswanathan, *Outside the Fold: Conversion, Modernity, and Belief* (Princeton: Princeton University Press, 1998), 16. For expressions of panic, see Bacon, "Prolonged Erosion, Organization and Reinforcement: Reflections on Orthodox Jewry in Congress Poland (up to 1914)," in *Major Changes Within the Jewish People*, ed. Yisrael Gutman (Jerusalem: Yad Vashem, 1996), 71–91; and Mordechai Breuer, "Orthodox German Jewry and the Political Changes of the Early Twentieth Century," in Gutman, *Major Changes*, 59–69. However, the sense of panic was usually tempered by optimism about the power of devotional "Torah" education to bring secularist youth back into the fold.
37. In 1924, the Lublin chapter of Sabbath Guardians felt it necessary to admonish members to "battle the Yiddish newspaper *Tagblat*, which derides the Jewish religion and to fight against

the impious not with physical force but by means of moral, holy writings." This appeal for peaceful methods was read aloud in every prayer house in the Lublin District. *Archiwum Państwowe w Lublinie, Komenda Wojewódska Policji Państwowej w Lublinie* 551 (1924–25): n.p. See also Asaf Kaniel, "Al milḥamah ve-shmirat mitsvot: Vilna, 1914–1922," *Gal Ed* 24 (2015): 37–74.
38. Ita Kalish, *Etmoli* (Tel Aviv: Ha-kibbutz ha-meyuḥad, 1970), 92–100.
39. Kalish, *Etmoli*, 100–107.
40. The Tseirei Aguda chapter was established after a visit by R. Tsvi Hirschhorn. See YIVO Archives, *Youth Autobiographies*, RG 4, #3819, 8–10. See also "T. Y.," in YIVO Archives, *Youth Autobiographies* RG 4, #3668.
41. "Esther," in Shandler, *Awakening Lives*, 334. See also Bacon, *Politics of Tradition*, 118–41; Naomi Seidman, "A Revolution in the Name of Tradition: Orthodoxy and Torah Study for Girls," *Polin* 30 (2018): 329–30; and Ido Bassok, "Jewish Youth Movements in Poland Between the Warsaw as Heirs of the *Kehilah*," *Polin* 30 (2018): 299–320.
42. Reports on meetings of *Shlomei Emunei Yisrael*, renamed *Agudat Yisrael*, were reassuring, since attendees openly and consistently declared their support for the new government. See, for example, United States Holocaust Memorial Museum (USHMM) Archives, RG 15 457, p. 263; Archiwum Państwowe w Warszawie (APW), Urząd Wojewódzki Warszawskim (UWW) 22, p. 46 (January 21, 1928); APW, UWW 38, p. 445 (January 11, 1930).
43. In a 1930 Tseirei Aguda meeting in Szydlowiec, several Zionists attempted to "start to stir up the meeting but were afraid of the police, who were there to keep order." Urząd Wojewódzki Kielecki I, s. 3172, 21/100, p. 28. In 1929, a meeting of Tseirei Aguda erupted into a brawl when members of a competing faction attacked a speaker. Archiwum Państwowe w Lublinie (APL), Urząd Wojewódzki Lubelski Wydział Społeczno-Polityczny (UWL) 485, p. 18 (November 3, 1929). In a meeting of Tseirei Aguda, opponents of the chapter's president, Joseph Hertz, beat him and his followers until the police broke up the meeting. UWL 1896 (1934), 259.
44. See Herman, *Ha-yaḥas livnei ha-no ʾar.*
45. Kalonymous Kalman Epstein, *Ma ʾor ve-shemesh* (Warsaw, 1857/9), parshat Ki Tetsei, p. 43. See also parshat Kedoshim, teachings 1 and 2 (30–31).
46. Shapira, *Mevo ha-sheʾarim (le-Ḥovat ha-avrekhim)*, in *Sefer Hakhsharat ha-avrekhim, mevo ha-sheʾarim (le-Ḥovat ha-avrekhim): Tzav ve-zeruz* (Jerusalem: Vaʾad ḥasidei Pyasetsnah, 1965), 60–62. See also Zvi Leshem (Blobstein), "Hasidism Confronts Modernity: Spiritual Societies of the Piaseczner Rebbe," Academia, n.d., http://www.academia.edu/8916424/Hasidism_Confronts_Modernity_Spiritual_Societies_of_the_Piaseczner_Rebbe, 1–25; Daniel Reiser, "The Study of Jewish Mysticism: Imagery Techniques in the Teachings of Rabbi Kalonymus Kalman Shapira as a Case Study," *Modern Judaism* 36, no. 1 (2016): 1–16; and Reiser, *Ha-marʾeh kaʾmarah: Tekhnikat ha-dimiyun ba-mystikah ha-yehudit be-meʾah ha-esrim* (Los Angeles: Cherub, 2014), 107–42.
47. Shapira, *Mevo ha-sheʾarim (le-ḥovat ha-avrekhim)*, 62.
48. See Jason Ānanda Josephson-Storm, *The Myth of Disenchantment: Magic, Modernity and the Birth of the Human Sciences* (Chicago: University of Chicago Press, 2017). On communities of resistance, see John Clarke, Stuart Hall, Tony Jefferson, and Brian Roberts, "Subcultures, Cultures and Class: A Theoretical Overview," in *Resistance Through Rituals: Youth Subcultures in Post-war Britain*, ed. Stuart Hall and Tony Jefferson (London: Routledge, 1993), 12 and 47–48.

PART 4

Crossing Boundaries

Friendship Between Women and Men, and Between Jews and Gentiles

CHAPTER 10

Interfaith Encounters Between Jews and Christians in the Early Modern Period and Beyond
Toward a Framework

DANIEL JÜTTE

The study of Jewish history has come a long way since Salo Baron, in a seminal 1928 essay, demanded a break with the "lachrymose conception" of the history of the Jews in premodern Europe.[1] Today, pre-Enlightenment Jewish history is no longer depicted as an uninterrupted chain of conflict and oppression—although, of course, those aspects cannot and should not be overlooked. On the other hand, it has been rightly stated that Baron's "challenge was not really taken up by scholars in any systematic fashion," and there are significant lacunae in the study of Jewish-Christian encounters and relations.[2] In particular, we lack a framework for surveying the entire spectrum. While conflict and persecution were on one end, what exactly was on the other? This issue can be explored by way of a simple but perhaps unexpected question: Were there amicable relations and friendships between Jews and Christians in medieval and early modern Europe? And if so—leaving aside for the moment the question of their frequency—how do we integrate them into our understanding of Christian-Jewish relations? By raising these questions, we can begin to outline a framework for the historical study of interfaith relations. In the process, we can shed new light on the general nature, perception, and practice of friendship in premodern Europe. The issue is thus not only the *fact* of interfaith friendships but also how these particular friendships, characterized as they were by religious difference, fit into the spectrum of practices and expectations associated with friendship.

The question of premodern Jewish-Christian friendship has been tackled by scholars only reluctantly; some have even rejected it outright. Nearly half a century ago, Jacob Katz declared sweepingly that "the outside world did not overly occupy the Jewish mind" during that period.[3] In this "outside world," according to Katz, interaction between Jews and Christians was almost entirely "governed by the immediate purpose of business" and was generally marked by "social barriers to intimacy and friendship."[4] To be sure, Katz's methodological approach—that is, his reliance on normative sources such as halakhic texts—has been challenged.[5] However, his and other scholars' similar conclusions still inform a number of standard accounts of Jewish life at the time. A comprehensive history of Jewish daily life in Germany states that "for a long time Jews and Christians only mixed for economic reasons and had few friendly ties."[6] Another standard account informs us that even in the small villages of early modern and modern Germany, where Jews had lived for centuries, the proximity of Gentiles did not lead to more than "occasional friendships" and that "as a result of the hesitancies on both sides, ongoing social contact between Jews and Christians was not common."[7] Yet another scholar states bluntly that "interreligious friendship [was] impossible, if not unthinkable, in Germany" before the Enlightenment and that friendship between Christians and Jews was thus "out of the question."[8] Not surprisingly, then, there is no entry for "friendship" in the *Dictionary of Jewish-Christian Relations*.[9]

Such examples could easily be multiplied, but even these few instances make it clear that the question of friendship has not ranked high on the agenda of historians working on premodern European Jewry. In studies of the Ashkenazic world, the term has been largely avoided. While these authors agree that there was economic interaction between Christians and Jews, business, in their view, seems to have more or less excluded any form of sincere social relationship or friendly reciprocity. However, this assumption oversimplifies the reality of Jewish-Christian relations and also distorts the nature of business in that period.

In studies of the Italian and the Sephardic world during the Renaissance, the term *friendship* appears more often, but primarily in relation to intellectual encounters in the context of Christian Hebraism or the early modern Republic of Letters.[10] While these studies point to a certain intellectual rapprochement, they rarely engage in a systematic discussion of the word and its historical meaning. The reader is therefore left wondering whether *friendship* is used consciously or merely slipped into what some later historians have criticized as an unclouded image of the Renaissance that harkens back to Jacob Burckhardt.[11] Interestingly, the situation is different for the historiography of Jewish life under Islamic rule. Historians of Ottoman Jewry, in particular, have demonstrated that "relations between Muslims and Jews were not a one-way street," and in everyday life, friendly relations crossed religious divides.[12] Indeed, the political framework of Jewish life tended to be more favorable in the Ottoman Empire than in most parts of Christian Europe, but this does not mean that the Ottoman authorities encouraged intermingling. Yet physical proximity, daily encounters, and shared leisure-time activities "led to the establishment of social relationships, even friendship, between Jews and Muslims."[13] It is hard to believe that similar relations were completely nonexistent in daily life in Christian lands.

Of course, it would be ludicrous to claim that there is—or ever was—a "conspiracy of silence" among historians regarding the question of friendship in premodern Jewish-Christian relations. In fact, some historians have explicitly written about interfaith friendships, but with respect to a much later period: the second half of the eighteenth century. From that perspective, the focal point—one historian has even called it "a breakthrough"—is usually the relationship between Moses Mendelssohn and Gotthold Ephraim Lessing, the two influential Enlightenment thinkers.[14] Their relationship, famously portrayed in Moritz Daniel Oppenheim's later painting *Lavater and Lessing Visit Moses Mendelssohn* (1856), has often been described and can serve as a good example of the particular Enlightenment type of male intellectual friendship.[15] But is there no evidence of friendly relations between Christians and Jews before Lessing, that "most tolerant of the German enlighteners"?[16] Is it true that in the early modern period, often described as an age of religious conflict, "certain friendships were no longer possible," or were impossible from the outset, as some historians claim?[17] It seems misleading to assume that interfaith friendship became conceivable only after the idea of tolerance and secularism gained currency.

If, then, this whole area is still underresearched, it is because of a preoccupation with the question of whether, where, and when tolerance emerged in premodern Europe.[18] No one would deny that this field of research has yielded valuable studies; at the same time, it can be hard to overlook its methodological limits and somewhat ahistorical nature. As Stuart Schwartz notes, studies of this subject have often "focused exclusively on educated ideas [and] on great intellectual turning points"—with the result that the history of tolerance is rarely studied from the bottom up.[19] And even though some studies argue that it existed in practice in certain situations, it is indisputable that the concept of "tolerance" as we commonly understand and advocate it today was neither universally accepted nor a guiding principle in early modern governance and thought. For this reason, the complexity of early modern interfaith encounters should not be studied solely in conjunction with the concept of tolerance (or lack thereof); it must be explored as a phenomenon in its own right.

While instances of interfaith friendship may not have been widespread, they raise important methodological questions that can help us challenge established narratives. Quite apart from the classical and humanist discourse about *amicitia*—which set the bar for friendship quite high, even between Gentiles—there were situations in which amicable relations with Jews were clearly within the realm of the conceivable. In fact, if we take a closer look at some causes célèbres often invoked as evidence of intolerance and prejudice, we see that they actually originate in familiarity and close relationships. For instance, there is the well-known case of the humanist and Hebraist Johannes Reuchlin (1455–1522), who became the target of a campaign spearheaded by the Dominicans, at least in part because of his close relationships with Jewish scholars.[20] Another example is the famous eighteenth-century court Jew Joseph Süß Oppenheimer ("Jud Süß"), whose surviving letters to the Duke of Württemberg reveal a degree of intimacy that can be called friendship. Indeed, Oppenheimer even used the second-person address "Du" in those letters—an extremely rare privilege reserved mainly for fellow sovereigns and immediate family members.[21]

One can, of course, object that these cases were exceptional because they involved two unrepresentative protagonists: a scholar and a court Jew. To counter this argument, it is necessary to examine the dimension of everyday life. This does not imply an irenic concept of daily life—indeed, prejudice and hatred were a common feature of premodern social life in all strata of society. On the other hand, recent studies of hatred as a social institution in premodern Europe show that except in times of crisis, everyday Jewish-Christian relations were quite the opposite of what one might expect. Daniel Lord Smail has convincingly shown that in late medieval Marseilles, "Jew-Christian confrontations were relatively infrequent." By contrast, cases of "intracommunity confrontations among Jews" were far more frequent, given the small size of the Jewish community.[22] In light of this, consigning minorities such as Jews to an "otherly status" in premodern society is debatable.[23]

Early modern Jewish history is generally viewed within a coordinate system with only two axes: one Christian, the other Jewish. As with the scholarship on tolerance, however, there is something unsatisfying in the underlying premise that when Jews and Christians met, they did so primarily as "Jew" and "Christian" rather than as individuals embedded in a multifaceted reality. Adding further axes might enable us to situate Jewish history, especially interfaith encounters, within a more multidimensional space. The complexity of this enterprise becomes particularly apparent on a microhistorical level, as can be shown in a case study based on the memoirs of a German merchant. In this context, the heightened role of travel and mobility, the effects of the confessionalization of Christianity, and the importance of local identity as commonality emerge as particularly important factors in expanding the spectrum of Christian-Jewish relations during the early modern period. In addition, probing the various meanings of friendship in early modern Europe shows that in practice, it clearly existed as part of interfaith relations. This leads to a number of methodological challenges and desiderata that need to be addressed if we wish to achieve a more differentiated understanding of interfaith relations in the early modern period and thereafter.

JAILHOUSE ENCOUNTERS:
A JEWISH-CHRISTIAN TALE FROM SIXTEENTH-CENTURY TRIPOLI

The experiences of Hans Ulrich Krafft (1550–1621), a merchant from the region of Swabia in southern Germany, provide a fascinating case study in this regard both because they elude simple classification and because Krafft's memoirs have remained largely unknown to historians.[24] One reason for this is that the original German text is fairly challenging, even for native speakers, because of its Swabian dialect and early modern syntax.[25] Written mostly around 1615—about five years before his death—Krafft's handwritten memoirs were intended mainly for his three sons, and it is clear that he used detailed notes and records from the past. The manuscript was eventually published in 1861 under the title *Reisen und Gefangenschaft Hans Ulrich Krafts* (The travels and captivity of Hans Ulrich Krafft).[26]

Krafft was born in Ulm, in southern Germany, to a patrician family who had played an important role in the political, economic, and religious life of the prosperous imperial city for generations.[27] His father served as an alderman on the city council and was also the mayor of Ulm for a few years. Krafft was raised as a devout Lutheran; in fact, later in life he collected autographs of Luther and Melanchthon almost like relics and kept them in his Bible, in Luther's German translation.[28] As it was planned that he would go into commerce, he never attended an institution of higher learning. After apprenticeships in Lyon and Florence, he was hired by the Augsburg-based Manlich Trade Company, which sent him to the Levant as the head factor.[29]

Along with a few other Manlich employees, Krafft arrived in the Levant in the fall of 1573. Based primarily in Tripoli (a city in northern Lebanon), he was well known to the French and Venetian merchants in this major port city. He also had extensive dealings with local Ottoman subjects, especially Turks and Jews. Krafft quickly realized that the latter were indispensable as translators and business brokers. For the most part, he got along well with them. He recorded, for instance, his respect for a Jewish translator named Elias, who spoke Italian, Greek, Arabic, and Turkish and was highly respected by the French merchant community in Tripoli.[30] At some point, Krafft was even invited to Elias's house, where he spent a delightful evening: "It was," he recalled, "so beautiful a setting that I cannot remember having ever been to such a pleasant place."[31]

Life might have gone on this way if dramatic news had not arrived from Europe: the Manlich Trade Company had gone bankrupt. In the summer of 1574, the news spread like wildfire in Tripoli, and it was not long before Krafft and two colleagues were taken to court there by numerous local creditors.[32] As Krafft did not have the means to pay off the debts he had guaranteed on behalf of his employers, the court decided to keep him in jail. He was twenty-four years old at the time.

This dismal situation lasted for three years, during which Krafft faced moments of real crisis. One problem was that in order to manage his legal and business affairs from inside the prison, he often had to pay outside parties and officials large amounts of *baksheesh* (bribes). His financial reserves were soon depleted; as a result, he had to find a way to earn some money. At this point, he became acquainted with a fellow prisoner, a Levantine Jewish button-maker who had received permission to continue making cords, ribbons, and buttons in prison.[33] The craftsman spoke some Italian, so the two were able to communicate. This Jew—whose name Krafft unfortunately did not record—taught Krafft the skills necessary for making buttons. Interestingly, the student was soon outproducing his master, but the Jew—who by then had been released from jail—remained an important adviser and supporter. He served as Krafft's translator, warned him of imminent intrigues, and was of vital help in selling the buttons Krafft made. Sometime later, Krafft was transferred to the prison in the citadel of Tripoli (considered by his creditors to be more secure), where he suddenly found himself no longer able to make buttons because the warden there prohibited the use of scissors and knives in the cells. This restriction was eased only after the Levantine Jew made a special petition and personally vouched for Krafft. No less important, he eventually managed to convince the authorities to transfer Krafft back to the municipal prison, where he was able to work more easily and received better food. The Jew even went so far as to incur a small debt in order to return to prison and be with Krafft (it was a minor enough offense that he was permitted to sleep at home). Such a sense of solidarity was beyond anything that Krafft—and probably most historians today—could have expected. "I did not seek the friendship [*freindtschaft*] of this Jew," he wrote, "but I accepted it with gratitude." When Krafft was eventually released from prison in 1577 and was preparing to return to Europe, he made sure to give the button-maker a significant sum of money for "the numerous troubles that he experienced on my behalf." In return, he was given a "beautiful, gold-embroidered purse made of crimson satin"—which, to his great regret, was taken from him when a Neapolitan patrol boarded his ship in the Mediterranean a few weeks later.

Another example involving Krafft also shows the complexity of early modern Christian-Jewish relations. In this case, a relationship was forged on the basis of a common place of origin.[34] On May 23, 1575, during Krafft's second year of imprisonment, he received an unexpected visit from a fellow German. The stranger said that he had heard about Krafft's misfortune and had decided to make contact. Meeting in Krafft's gloomy cell, the two

Germans quickly discovered that they both spoke the Swabian dialect, and the stranger remarked with great satisfaction that they were "fellow countrymen." They were even more surprised to learn that they were both from the same region of Swabia: the stranger introduced himself as being from Neuburg, a small hamlet on the Kammel River, some thirty miles from Krafft's home city of Ulm. Apparently, it was only then that the two men exchanged names, at which point Krafft realized that his fellow countryman was a Jew named Mayer Winterbach.[35] "When he said that he was a Jew, I became sad [*trawrig*]," Krafft recorded bluntly in his memoirs. Winterbach rushed to "console" him, saying that he could understand the reason for Krafft's antipathy, since several of Krafft's creditors were Jews. As it turned out, it was those creditors who had urged Winterbach to go to the jail and find out more about the personal circumstances of the foreign prisoner. Having met Krafft, however, Winterbach had changed his mind. Invoking God in heaven, he declared that he would not be involved in any schemes against his Swabian fellow countryman. He also said that many of the creditors who had sent him were "Oriental Jews," and he admitted that German Jews disliked "Oriental Jews" even more than most Christians did. Winterbach went even further: he explicitly offered Krafft his support and help. He explained that he was about to leave for Safed in the Galilee, where he had to deliver a message. But once that mission was fulfilled, he would return to Germany, at which time he would be happy to deliver a letter to Krafft's family in Ulm. (It even emerged that Winterbach knew Krafft's father well from mutual business dealings.) Winterbach also proposed a scheme in which he would use his report to the creditors to downplay Krafft's role in the hierarchy of the Manlich Trade Company and to present him as the son of an impecunious family. Solemnly insisting on his trustworthiness, he even encouraged Krafft to trust him "like a brother." Krafft hesitated at first but was eventually convinced.

Winterbach kept his promise: he led the creditors to believe that Krafft was only a minor figure in the business, as Krafft quickly learned with great satisfaction. And on his return from the Galilee, he visited Krafft regularly in jail. For Krafft, this must have been a welcome distraction from his grim life in prison; in turn, Winterbach apparently enjoyed the opportunity to share stories—particularly the less pleasant ones—of his journey to Safed. By the sixteenth century, Safed had become a major center for the study and transmission of Jewish mysticism as well as for Hebrew printing; it was also a place of Jewish settlement and pilgrimage in the Holy Land. It had eight synagogues, and Winterbach recalled seeing "a huge number of Jews" there who had come from all over Europe and the Middle East. Yet here again the German Jew had not gotten along with the "Oriental Jews" who formed the majority of the Galilee Jewish community. According to Winterbach, they were arrogant and cunning and had cheated him. Hearing these complaints, Krafft could not help but laugh at his new acquaintance, recommending that Winterbach return to Germany, for he was clearly too naïve for life in the Levant. Winterbach agreed, adding that his experiences in the Galilee confirmed the old saying "The closer to Safed, the worse the Jews; the closer to Rome, the worse the Christians."[36] Under these circumstances, it is not surprising that Winterbach did not wish to stay in the Levant any longer than necessary. A few days later, he left Tripoli on a ship bound for Venice. As soon as he arrived in Ulm, as Krafft learned later, he delivered the letter and personal items that had been entrusted to him.

The story of their relationship, however, does not end there. Following a protracted legal deal, Krafft was finally released from prison in 1577. He returned safely to Europe, but it was not until 1585 that he moved permanently back to Ulm, where he later married. In 1587 he accepted the position of bailiff (*Pfleger*) in the small Swabian town of Geislingen. We know that Winterbach eventually learned that Krafft was back in Swabia, but we do not know exactly how or when he received that information. In August 1590, fifteen years after the two men had met in the prison in Tripoli, a gray-bearded stranger turned up on Krafft's doorstep in Geislingen.[37] "Do you remember me?" he asked. At first Krafft shrugged his shoulders, but he then "recognized the man's way of speaking": it was Winterbach.

What stands out in this account is the affection with which Krafft described the reunion twenty-five years later. In his memoirs, he admits that he had already given up hope of ever seeing Winterbach again. But when the two men met, they rejoiced "in a way that every good-hearted reader can imagine" and spent time in "cheerful, merry conversation." In response to the gifts Winterbach had brought all the way to Geislingen, Krafft offered hospitality to his Jewish friend, who stayed at his house for two days. The gifts included a "beautiful big nautilus" and a "beautiful blackish-brown hollow nutmeg." Soon after, Krafft commissioned a skilled artisan to make him an expensive drinking cup, with the nutmeg—shaped like a turtle—at the top.

Winterbach and Krafft may well have maintained a correspondence that has not survived. But even from the extant evidence, it is clear that they kept up their friendly relationship, even though Winterbach was about to embark on major journeys to Italy and Portugal. "I do not know a Christian who has traveled as much as he did," Krafft recalled with admiration.[38] In a certain sense, Winterbach's extraordinary mobility actually facilitated their friendship. Three years later, for example, while traveling through the south of Germany, he visited his Christian friend in Geislingen again. And it was apparently only his relocation to Prussia that caused them to lose track of each other at some point after 1593. Krafft was probably right in assuming that his friend Winterbach, who was older than he, died soon thereafter or, rather, that "his life was placed into God's hand," as he put it in a tellingly empathic way.[39]

We get an even fuller picture of Krafft's warm feelings for Winterbach if we place the story of their relationship within the broader context of Krafft's memoirs. Indeed, his purpose in writing them was to give an account of his imprisonment and his travels preceding and following it.[40] Thus Krafft, who was over sixty at the time of writing, recorded almost nothing of the last three decades of his life, with two notable exceptions: one is the account of his reunions with Winterbach right at the end of the book, and the other is a far less detailed account of his meeting with a French merchant in Ulm nineteen years after they met in Aleppo.[41] The latter was a chance encounter, and Krafft's rather terse description of it underscores how much deeper his relationship with Winterbach was.

No less significant is the insight that we gain from one of the appendixes to Krafft's memoirs. It lists the objects that his sons would find in an old locked chest with the manuscript after his death.[42] Most of these approximately twenty objects were mementos of his travels and imprisonment in the Levant. At the top of the list are two objects that were apparently very dear to him: his Lutheran prayer book (in German and, interestingly, "in a binding made by a Jew") and the "beautiful nautilus" given to him by Mayer Winterbach in 1590.[43] Clearly, this relationship was very important to Krafft.

What is the historian to make of this story? In order to answer this, it is necessary to look at certain aspects of the broader historical framework. Indeed, such relationships, and the constellations that enabled them, were not as uncommon as one might think. Generally speaking, we can identify three factors that contributed to an increase in Jewish-Christian interaction and that became particularly prominent in the early modern period.

THE ROLE OF TRAVEL AND MOBILITY

The first factor is the overall increase in travel and mobility during the early modern period.[44] This does not mean that travel, whether private or commercial, was necessarily connected to tolerance or even openness. Tolerance was certainly not a precondition for travel, and conversely, travel did not necessarily result in tolerance toward other religious, social, or ethnic groups.[45] But in a conspicuous number of cases, travel aroused curiosity and played a role in creating situations that might not have been common, desirable, or even possible in the traveler's country or region of origin. For instance, the Dominican friar Felix Fabri from Ulm, who went on a pilgrimage to the Holy Land in the 1480s, describes an encounter, during his stay in Jerusalem, with his Christian hosts: "[They] invited me and two of the Minorite fathers, two Jews, one Saracen and one Mameluke, to sup with them, and we supped merrily together—albeit we were of different faiths and customs." It was, as Fabri added, precisely "because of this converse with the infidels that a man is obliged to get leave from our lord the Pope when he wishes to make a pilgrimage to Jerusalem."[46]

Of course, interreligious encounters could also take place when one was traveling in Europe. The case of Krafft's famous contemporary Michel de Montaigne is a case in point. It is well known that in his account of his journey to Italy (1580–81), Montaigne included a detailed and fairly unbiased description of his visit to the Jewish community in Rome, including a circumcision ceremony (*brit milah*) that he attended at a Jewish house.[47] This would have been almost impossible in France, where Jews—with few exceptions—were not allowed to settle at that time. Travelers less prominent and learned than Montaigne and Fabri had similar experiences. Sometimes their willingness to mingle with Jews was the result of curiosity, as we see in many accounts of early modern Christian visitors to the Venetian ghetto, which express attitudes ranging from traditional hostility to sincere and positive interest.[48]

At other times, encounters between Christian travelers and Jews were a matter of necessity or practicality. For example, Christian travelers on their way to the Levant often used local Jews as translators. Sometimes they also depended on the hospitality of Jews and lodged in their homes—occasionally even in their synagogues.[49] The fact that they usually paid for this hospitality does not mean that it did not leave an impression, and there is evidence that such situations created opportunities for cordial interaction.

"We lodged heare 3 nyghtes in the house of a Jew, who is by Inglishe men caled the honeste Jew, for he is verrie lovinge unto Inglishe men," recalled the English traveler Thomas Dallam of his stay in the Greek port city of Lepanto in 1600.[50] Dallam was a fairly representative sixteenth-century Englishman, for he was neither a diaspora-based merchant nor an eccentric intellectual but rather an ordinary artisan who had been sent to Constantinople to deliver an organ to the Ottoman sultan.[51] There is evidence that he did not have particularly positive feelings toward Jews as a group, but that did not keep him from establishing good relations with individual Jews whom he met on his journey.

It was even more common throughout the early modern period for Jewish travelers and merchants to lodge in the homes of Christians.[52] Such arrangements were unavoidable given that Jewish settlement was scattered and a number of major European cities had no Jewish community that could accommodate traveling coreligionists. The fact that such arrangements were unavoidable, however, does not mean that they were necessarily unwelcome to the Jewish traveler. In fact, rabbinical complaints about the presence of Jews in Christian houses and taverns (even on the Sabbath) are not at all rare.[53] Nor should we underestimate the extent of the interaction between Christians and Jews on the road.[54] This was also true on ships. It had been a widespread practice since the Middle Ages for ships owned by Christians to carry Jewish passengers, although periodically this angered the Christian authorities, some of whom even tried to stop the practice.[55] We also know that cramped conditions on early modern ships and the religious zeal of some Christian pilgrims occasionally led to conflicts between the two groups.[56] However, we have to balance these tensions against the fact that life on ships called for unusual arrangements, for what else can we make of the little-known evidence that on some early modern Christian ships, Jews were allowed to blow the *shofar* during their High Holidays?[57]

Within the context of increased travel, we should also remember that Christians traveling to the Levant experienced something that Jews knew well: what it meant to be a religious minority. Indeed, it is well known that in Islamic countries, Christians and Jews shared the minority status of *dhimmī*.[58] Thus there was an imposed commonality to which both groups had to adjust. The case of Krafft confirms this observation with an interesting twist, for during his travels, he not only experienced what it meant to be treated *like* a Jew; he was also taken *for* a Jew. In 1577, the galley that carried him back to Marseilles was stopped by a Spanish patrol ship near Sicily. The Spaniards, who wanted to find out whether all the passengers aboard were good Catholics, soon became suspicious of Krafft's seemingly "Jewish" outfit: "For I wore a red nightcap on my head and (because of my lack of money) instead of a vest, a red woolen shirt as well as red woolen pantaloons." Explaining the reason for his unusual appearance, Krafft only aroused new doubts: "Now they took me for a Jew because I was able to speak more languages than just my mother tongue."[59] Of course, the experience of commonality through travel was neither a linear nor a teleological development. Rather, empathy and mutual understanding were both selective and situational. In Krafft's case, we can see how his years in the Levant changed his attitude toward Jews or, more precisely, toward individual Jews.

CONFESSIONALIZATION: CHRISTIAN AND JEWISH

The second contextual factor in which we need to embed Krafft's relationship with Mayer Winterbach is the process of sixteenth-century confession-building—that is, the rift between Protestants and Catholics and the emergence of different confessions within post-Reformation Christianity, often referred to as "confessionalization."[60] Here, too, Krafft's memoirs are illuminating. Even in an Ottoman jail, Krafft complained bitterly about the influence of "jaundiced papists" and also expressed his resentment toward Greek Orthodox inmates—two groups that were, after all, composed of fellow Christians.[61] At the same time, such diversification of resentment could deflect attention from the Jewish minority. As Benjamin Kaplan has noted, "the splintering of Western Christendom gave Europeans a whole new set of enmities." Unlike the various Christian confessions, "Jews and Muslims were not diseased limbs of the corpus Christianum, they simply stood outside it."[62] Thus the authorities often considered radical Christian movements such as the Anabaptists to be a far greater threat to the Christian polity.[63] In fact, following the Peace of Augsburg (1555), it was not uncommon for Jews in the territorial states of the Holy Roman Empire to enjoy more privileges than the members of an unwanted Christian denomination. In England during the Interregnum, the influence of Puritan and millenarian beliefs was one of the factors that led to the idea of national "friendship" toward the Jews, which resulted in the famous Whitehall Conference (1655) and Cromwell's subsequent decision to readmit Jews to the country. While this controversial decision did not prompt a large-scale return of Jews to England, we know that some of its Christian supporters forged personal friendships with Jews.⁶⁴ But even if we put the English case aside, we cannot fail to observe that from the late sixteenth century onward, there was a shift in Christian-Jewish relations from exclusion to reintegration, at least partly because of "the unresolved deadlock [and] ceaseless triangular conflict between Catholics and the competing Lutheran and Calvinist confessional blocs."⁶⁵ One can certainly say that "the coming of multiconfessionalism created, by analogy, more room for the Jews."⁶⁶

A similar splintering can be observed on the Jewish side. The reasons were different, of course, than in post-Reformation Christianity, but the results were comparable. The reality of early modern Judaism presents itself as highly diversified and heterogeneous (and even included sectarian movements). Suffice it to recall the antipathy that the Ashkenazi Jew Winterbach harbored toward "Oriental Jews," which he did not hesitate to share with the Lutheran Krafft. This diversification—whether or not we call it "Jewish confessionalization"—is certainly one of the reasons Winterbach felt culturally and personally closer to his Lutheran fellow countryman than to his Levantine coreligionists. From examples such as these, it becomes clearer how the two axes—Jewish and Christian—in which the study of early modern Jewish history is situated were not as neatly drawn in reality as is commonly presented.

LOCAL IDENTITY AS COMMONALITY

There are other axes unrelated to the religious sphere that should also be considered. One of these is local identity—and this constitutes the third contributory factor. In the case of Krafft and Winterbach, their Swabian background was a shared local identity, and for them this meant more than that they had lived in the same region for most of their lives. They also shared the same dialect, Swabian. At a time when German (like most other major European languages) was far from standardized, such dialectal factors—which also included a shared vocabulary—were important and could even outweigh religious differences.⁶⁷

In this respect, Krafft and Winterbach were not an exception. Take the case of Michael Heberer, a German Christian adventurer and seaman captured by Turks in the 1580s, who spent several years as a prisoner and galley slave in the Ottoman Empire. During his time in Cairo, he and another German slave met a Jewish tax farmer who "spoke Swabian German as well as if he had been born in the city of Augsburg."⁶⁸ Heberer himself was not actually from Swabia; he came from the nearby region of Kraichgau. However, the fact that both he and the Jew came from southern Germany outweighed the difference in social, religious, and economic status. Although Heberer did not stay long in Cairo, a sense of solidarity developed between the two men. The Jew, whose name remains unknown, gave him and the other German slave money as well as advice, and they responded with "friendly gratitude."⁶⁹ Heberer also encountered other Jews who offered assistance.⁷⁰ In significant contrast, his fellow Germans at the imperial embassy in Constantinople made little effort to help him—for Heberer was a Protestant, while the embassy officials were Habsburg-appointed Catholics (another reminder of the effects of confessionalization).

Thus historians should not underestimate how essential a shared regional background was in creating common ground—even a bridge—between Christians and Jews. Winterbach and Krafft shared not only the same Swabian background and dialect but also overlapping social circles: Krafft knew the lords of Neuburg (the protectors [*Schutzherren*] of the small Jewish community from which Winterbach came), and Winterbach had personally known Krafft's father. The two men were quick—and glad—to make note of these common elements. Krafft's account of the food he ate in prison in Tripoli provides further insight into the importance of origin. For him, even in the Levant, Swabian cuisine served as the measure of quality.⁷¹ We have no similar record for Winterbach, but we do know that he ate in the houses of non-Jews—as when he stayed with Krafft for two days in 1590—and thus shared the local food culture.⁷² His experience was not unusual. Throughout the early modern period, Jewish communities across Europe developed culinary tastes that were similar to, if not derived from, those common to their non-Jewish environment. And even if they had not been aware of it before, many European Jews realized this as soon as they traveled abroad, especially to the Levant.⁷³

Recent research has shown the importance that the Jews of early modern Swabia placed on their local identity. In fact, they considered themselves to be genuinely Swabian long before their legal emancipation in the nineteenth century. In sixteenth-century Jewish and Christian documents, the official term "Jews of Swabia" (Gemeine Jüdischheit in Schwaben) was relatively common both in and beyond southern Germany. Given the fact that Swabia had ceased to exist as a duchy in the mid-thirteenth century, this was more than just a political designation—it reflected the Jews' embeddedness in local culture and everyday life. Indeed, in early modern Swabia, as in many other regions across Europe, everyday life offered a variety of opportunities for interaction between Jews and Christians. Throughout this period, a significant number of Jews in *Medinat Schwaben*—the Hebrew term for the Land of Swabia—lived among Gentiles in small villages. At times they were more than 50 percent of the local population, creating a reality that was marked not only by tension and religious difference but also by a large degree of daily contact and sometimes friendship.[74]

This background, together with the story of Winterbach and Krafft, thus fits well into recent approaches to medieval Jewish history. Jonathan Elukin, for instance, has argued that "Jews of the Early and High Middle Ages were deeply integrated into the rhythms of their local worlds," and in light of the above, it is possible to extend his observation to the early modern period.[75] One could even go further and argue that Jewish culture in general "is always a *local* phenomenon" and therefore cannot be analyzed without reference to its immediate environment.[76]

REASSESSING INTERFAITH RELATIONS BETWEEN VIOLENCE AND FRIENDSHIP

How are we to classify a Christian-Jewish encounter such as the one between Hans Ulrich Krafft and Mayer Winterbach? Krafft himself used the word "friendship" (*freindtschaft*) to describe the bond that developed between him and the Jewish button-maker in Tripoli, and it can safely be assumed that he would have described his relationship with Winterbach the same way. Historians today may feel more comfortable using a different term, and they have a wide range of scholarly terms to choose from, including *coexistence, toleration, cross-cultural contact, cultural intermediation,* and *hybridity*. These terms are valuable tools for historical analysis and discussion. Yet when we use them, we must be careful not to elide the personal dimension of relationships such as Krafft's and Winterbach's. In order to capture their full extent and complexity, we should thus take Krafft's use of the word *friendship* seriously. Of course, in the medieval and early modern world, the term *friendship* had a wide range of meanings.[77] It was used to describe relationships not only between individuals but also between groups and even political entities such as states. It can also be found in the context of kinship alliances, and the terminological line between "friend" and "kin" was not always sharply drawn.[78] In addition, the word *friend* sometimes appears in the context of patronage relationships and, more specifically, courtly language.

Alongside this variety of meanings, there was also *friendship* as we commonly understand it today: a "friendly feeling or disposition felt or shown by one person for or towards another."[79] The Swabian word that Krafft used, *freindtschaft*, clearly encompassed this meaning.[80] In general, as Lorna Hutson notes, *friend* in early modern usage "tends to denote both a relation of affection and the understanding that one is able to do good on behalf of another, and there is rarely a sense that the latter assumption alone renders the former insincere."[81] It should be added that then, as now, friendship did not necessarily imply the absence of differences or tensions. Modern sociologists tend to regard friendship as a relationship that can reach different levels of intensity rather than as a universally uniform type of social bonding, and the idea of such "differentiated friendships" (Georg Simmel's words) was not unknown to early modern people.[82] While many early modern thinkers glorified the ancient ideal of unconditioned and altruistic *amicitia* (at least between men), they also realized that such perfect friendships rarely occurred in everyday life. In his famous essay "On Friendship," Montaigne praised the ancient notion of "sovereign and masterful friendship" yet admitted that in reality, "ordinary and customary friendships" also existed.[83] Such friendships were primarily "acquaintanceships and familiarities formed by some chance or convenience"; nevertheless, they deserved to be termed friendship.[84] Francis Bacon went a step further when he noted, in an essay first written in 1597, "There is little friendship in the world, and least of all between equals, which was wont to be magnified. That [friendship] that is, is between superior and inferior, whose fortunes may comprehend the one the other."[85]

The case of Krafft, who was imprisoned in the Levant around the same years that Montaigne and Bacon were reflecting on the nature of friendship—both ideal and actual—finely illustrates the differentiated notion of the term in the early modern period. Krafft explicitly used the word *friendship* to characterize his relationship with the Jewish button-maker, but the modern reader can sense that his description of that connection is slightly less affectionate than his memories of Winterbach. This may have been because the button-maker was also Krafft's employer in jail, or it may have come from purely personal feeling. For whatever reason, Krafft felt friendship toward both men, but in the case of Winterbach, the relationship clearly outlasted the crisis in which it began. We should not, however, confuse these friendly connections with a more general philo-Semitism. It is important to emphasize that Krafft did not like *all* Jews and that he did not even like his two Jewish "friends" to the same degree. It is the task of the historian to carefully study these different degrees of friendship.

One could, of course, argue that the friendship between Krafft and Winterbach resulted mainly from the unusual setting in which they met: an Ottoman jail thousands of miles from home. This is a legitimate objection but a rather narrow one, for there were also prisons in Europe as well as many other more positive sites where Jews and Christians could meet in everyday life. Taverns and roads, fairs, princely courts, and doctors' houses come immediately to mind. These sites, however different, share an important feature with prisons—namely, a common "heterotopic" character. As Michel Foucault has noted, prison is a typical "heterotopia" that often suspends, neutralizes, or reverses given or imposed sets of relations and is thus fertile ground for historical observation.[86] In fact, the tales and written accounts of captives in the early modern and modern period "were never simply stories about individuals under stress, but commentaries on, and by-products of changing power relations over time."[87]

There is as yet no comprehensive history of early modern Jewish-Christian relations. A study of this sort would need to be embedded between two poles: extreme violence, including recurrent anti-Jewish riots and pogroms, on the one hand, and the possibility of friendship, in varying degrees and modes, on the other. Between those poles, one can find a vast and highly nuanced array of social interactions and contacts. The picture that emerges may be bewildering, chaotic, and sometimes even paradoxical: at one end, one would have to grapple with the fact that friendship did not necessarily hinge on or translate into an abstract notion of "tolerance," and at the other, one would have to make sense of the observation that rites of violence sometimes served to stabilize coexistence.[88] In order to explore this complex world, it is necessary to use "thick descriptions"—to adopt Clifford Geertz's term—rather than neat and general categorizations, for the historian can reach a balanced and nuanced picture of premodern interfaith relations only by taking into account the multidimensionality of everyday life and its inherent dynamics of entanglement.

In this endeavor, microhistory is an extremely valuable tool, but it cannot be expected to provide exhaustive answers. Rather, its purpose is to raise questions that prompt us to further explore the complexity of interfaith relationships and to scrutinize the assumptions that have often been taken for granted in the study of relationships between Jews and Christians. Even though friendship between the two groups may not have been widespread during the early modern period, the very fact that it occurred—and in addition to the aforementioned examples, there may well be others yet to be uncovered—must be taken seriously and incorporated into our understanding of Christian-Jewish relations. The question, then, is not about the representativeness of the case of Krafft and Winterbach—it would be misleading to expect microhistory to yield primarily or only stories that are "representative." Suffice it to mention the long-forgotten tale of the sixteenth-century Italian miller Menocchio—a truly unrepresentative and enigmatic individual, but at the same time a story that can teach us, as Carlo Ginzburg has demonstrated, to challenge established narratives about high and low culture in early modern Europe.[89]

The case of Hans Ulrich Krafft and Mayer Winterbach shows similar potential in terms of the way we think about interfaith relations. If we dismiss the two men's amicable relationship as an exception to the rule, we need to ask ourselves, Which rule, precisely? By reading the past solely through the lens of the two categories of "Christian" and "Jewish," the historian imposes a clear-cut grid that does not capture the complexity of everyday life.[90] It is entirely legitimate to describe Krafft and Winterbach's encounter as a meeting between fellow Swabians, for their shared local background was of great importance to them. In the premodern period, there were, of course, many other commonalities (such as gender) and shared experiences (for instance, unusual environmental conditions) that could generate interaction, solidarity, and sometimes even friendship between Christians and Jews.[91] Being a Christian or a Jew may have played an important role in religious and legal disputes, but clearly less so on the road, at a patient's bedside, or in prison, to mention but a few examples. The situation with respect to economic life was equally complex: while religion mattered in certain economic sectors (one need only look at the guilds, most of which did not admit Jews), it was far less important among merchants and traders.

Indeed, business in the premodern world was largely an ongoing "game of trust," and precisely because many of the institutions that govern economic life today were either weak or nonexistent then, there was great reliance on friendship, kinship, and patronage. The humanist ideal of unconditioned and "total" *amicitia* cannot really serve as a touchstone here for the historian. Rather, situational and social friendship, with their own vocabularies and array of practices, were available to tradesmen and helped them build alliances and trust.[92] Friendship was a field of practice and compromises. Its foundations were complex and at times unstable, but business could not have functioned without it.

The Republic of Letters can serve as another example, as can be seen from recent works on Christian Hebraism.[93] In fact, we know that Jewish intellectuals were familiar with the humanist concept of *amicitia* and considered it an important part of building and fostering scholarly communities.[94] At the same time, it would be problematic to depict learned ideas as the primary or only site for Jewish-Christian interaction. First, such intellectual encounters—whether scholarly or theological—affected primarily a small elite. Second, we have seen that the friendly relationship between Krafft and Winterbach was based neither on a shared library nor on particular books they had read. In short, commonalities could exist or emerge without the exchange of learned ideas. An equally important form of exchange was the exchange of gifts, which had immense social and cultural significance among all strata of early modern society.[95] And this takes us back to Hans Ulrich Krafft. For him, the crimson purse and the precious nautilus were more than just tokens of civility from Jews—they testified to a particular form of friendship. Unfortunately, these gifts have not come down to us, and the same is undoubtedly true of many other objects that connected Christians and Jews. However, we can and should explore the everyday life stories behind them in an attempt to achieve a more differentiated, multidimensional understanding of the past.

NOTES

This is an abbreviated and slightly revised version of an article that appeared under the same title in the *American Historical Review* 118, no. 2 (2013): 378–400.

1. Salo Baron, "Ghetto and Emancipation," *Menorah Journal* 14, no. 6 (1928): 515–26.
2. Jonathan Elukin, *Living Together, Living Apart: Rethinking Jewish-Christian*

Relations in the Middle Ages (Princeton: Princeton University Press, 2007), 5.

3. Jacob Katz, *Out of the Ghetto: The Social Background of Jewish Emancipation, 1770–1870* (Cambridge, MA: Harvard University Press, 1973), 26.

4. Katz, *Out of the Ghetto*, 42; Jacob Katz, *Tradition and Crisis: Jewish Society at the End of the Middle Ages*, trans. Bernard Dov Cooperman (New York: New York University Press, 1993), 22.

5. Azriel Shohet, *Im chilufe tekufot: Reshit ha-haskalah be-yahadut Germanyah* (Jerusalem: Bialik Institute, 1960). See also the summary of early reviews of Katz's work in Cooperman's afterword to Katz, *Tradition and Crisis*, 237, 243–46.

6. Steven M. Lowenstein, "The Beginnings of Integration, 1780–1870," in *Jewish Daily Life in Germany, 1618–1945*, ed. Marion A. Kaplan (Oxford: Oxford University Press, 2005), 164. A more nuanced assessment can be found in Robert Liberles, "On the Threshold of Modernity, 1618–1780," in Kaplan, *Jewish Daily Life*, 87–92.

7. Michael A. Meyer, "Judaism and Christianity," in *German-Jewish History in Modern Times*, ed. Michael A. Meyer and Michael Brenner, vol. 2, *Emancipation and Acculturation, 1780–1871* (New York: Columbia University Press, 1997), 191–92.

8. Klaus L. Berghahn, "On Friendship: The Beginnings of a Christian-Jewish Dialogue in the 18th Century," in *The German-Jewish Dialogue Reconsidered: A Symposium in Honor of George L. Mosse*, ed. Klaus L. Berghahn (New York: Peter Lang, 1996), 12.

9. Edward Kessler and Neil Wenborn, eds., *A Dictionary of Jewish-Christian Relations* (Cambridge: Cambridge University Press, 2005).

10. Moses Shulvass, for instance, notes that "sometimes a genuine friendship developed between rabbis and Christian clergymen"; Shulvass, *The Jews in the World of the Renaissance*, trans. Elvin I. Kose (Leiden: Brill, 1973), 209.

On p. 347, he speaks again of "personal friendships ... between rabbis and priests." Cecil Roth uses the term *friendship* in a similar way in his *The Jews in the Renaissance* (Philadelphia: Jewish Publication Society of America, 1959), most particularly in chap. 6, "With the Humanists of Florence," 129–30, and chap. 7, "The Christian Hebraists," 149. On the Republic of Letters, see also Shohet, *Im chilufe tekufot*, 49. This was actually not disputed by Katz, *Out of the Ghetto*, 43.

11. See especially Robert Bonfil, *Jewish Life in Renaissance Italy*, trans. Anthony Oldcorn (Berkeley: University of California Press, 1994), 8–10. A more nuanced view is taken by David B. Ruderman, "Cecil Roth, Historian of Italian Jewry," in *The Jewish Past Revisited: Reflections on Modern Jewish Historians*, ed. David N. Myers and David B. Ruderman (New Haven: Yale University Press, 1998), 128–42.

12. Yaron Ben-Naeh, *Jews in the Realm of the Sultans: Ottoman Jewish Society in the Seventeenth Century* (Tübingen: Mohr Siebeck, 2008), 126.

13. Ben-Naeh. One could also point here to S. D. Goitein's *A Mediterranean Society: The Jewish Communities of the Arab World as Portrayed in the Documents of the Cairo Geniza*, 5 vols. (Berkeley: University of California Press, 1967–93). On the basis of documents from the Cairo Geniza, Goitein claimed that "relations of mutual trust and cooperation" between Jews and Muslims were "by no means exceptional" as early as in the medieval period (2:289–99, quotations from 295). As Mark Cohen reminds us, however, until a few decades ago, it was standard fare among medievalists to claim that "Jews living 'under the crescent' enjoyed substantially greater security and a higher level of political and cultural integration than did Jews living 'under the cross.'" Cohen, *Under Crescent and Cross: The Jews in the Middle Ages* (Princeton: Princeton University Press, 1994), xv.

As Cohen has demonstrated, this "myth of an Islamic interfaith utopia" in the Middle Ages is no less a distortion of history than the "lachrymose conception" of Jewish history in Europe. Both myths were used by historians in the nineteenth and twentieth centuries for similar—and often political—reasons (Cohen, chap. 1). In this context, studies such as Goitein's have not been spared criticism. However, regardless of the underlying premises, Goitein's account can, I think, still serve as a model of applied history of everyday life. It also offers one of the few detailed treatments of what friendship actually meant *within* the Jewish community (Goitein, *Mediterranean Society*, 5:272–97), a topic that clearly deserves more research but is beyond the scope of the current chapter.

14. Berghahn, "On Friendship," 12. See also Meyer, "Judaism and Christianity," 169. Shohet dates the beginning of proto-*haskalah* friendships slightly earlier, but not before 1700; *Im hilufe tekufot*, 51. Marion Kaplan, in contrast, has chosen a much later starting date—the second half of the nineteenth century—for her study of friendship between Jews and Christians. In her view, it was not until the last decades of the nineteenth century that Jews reached "a new high point of social integration," and even then "these friendships maintained a degree of reserve, avoiding certain areas of intimacy, interest, and feeling." Kaplan, "Friendship on the Margins: Jewish Social Relations in Imperial Germany," *Central European History* 34, no. 4 (2001): 500.

15. Berghahn, "On Friendship." For a general discussion of the Enlightenment cult of friendship, see, for instance, Friedrich H. Tenbruck, "Freundschaft: Ein Beitrag zu einer Soziologie der persönlichen Beziehungen," in Tenbruck, *Die kulturellen Grundlagen der Gesellschaft: Der Fall der Moderne* (Opladen: Westdeutscher Verlag, 1989), 227–50.

16. Meyer, "Judaism and Christianity," 169.

17. Laura Gowing, Michael Hunter, and Miri Rubin, introduction to *Love, Friendship and Faith in Europe, 1300–1800*, ed. Gowing, Hunter, and Rubin (New York: Palgrave Macmillan, 2005), 6.

18. On toleration as a social practice in the early modern period, see the important study by Benjamin J. Kaplan, *Divided by Faith: Religious Conflict and the Practice of Toleration in Early Modern Europe* (Cambridge, MA: Harvard University Press, 2007). On the gradual historical emergence of the ideal of tolerance, see especially Hans R. Guggisberg, *Religiöse Toleranz: Dokumente zur Geschichte einer Forderung* (Stuttgart-Bad Cannstatt: Frommann-Holzboog, 1984); and Henry Kamen, *The Rise of Toleration* (New York: McGraw-Hill, 1967).

19. Stuart B. Schwartz, *All Can Be Saved: Religious Tolerance and Salvation in the Iberian Atlantic World* (New Haven: Yale University Press, 2008), 3–4.

20. See, for instance, the contributions to Wilhelm Kühlmann, ed., *Reuchlins Freunde und Gegner: Kommunikative Konstellationen eines frühneuzeitlichen Medienereignisses* (Ostfildern: Thorbecke, 2010).

21. Gudrun Emberger and Robert Kretzschmar, *Die Quellen sprechen lassen: Der Kriminalprozess gegen Joseph Süß Oppenheimer 1737/38* (Stuttgart: Kohlhammer, 2009), 56.

22. Daniel Lord Smail, "Hatred as a Social Institution in Late-Medieval Society," *Speculum* 76, no. 1 (2001): 118.

23. Smail, "Hatred as a Social Institution," 120. On this tendency in historical scholarship, see Elukin, *Living Together*, 4–5.

24. The autograph manuscript is preserved today in the Stadtarchiv Ulm, Bestand H (Handschriften/Nachlässe: Krafft, Hans Ulrich).

25. To the best of my knowledge, the only historical study that acknowledges the riches in Krafft's memoirs as a source of cultural history (although it uses it only marginally) is Axel Gotthard, *In*

der Ferne: Die Wahrnehmung des Raums in der Vormoderne (Frankfurt: Campus, 2007), especially 66.
26. Krafft, Reisen und Gefangenschaft Hans Ulrich Kraffts, ed. Konrad Dietrich Haßler (Stuttgart: Litterarischer [sic] Verein, 1861). All subsequent quotations of Krafft are taken from this edition; all translations into English are mine.
27. The biographical information here is taken primarily from the introductions to extant editions of Krafft's book. A valuable compilation of available biographical information on Krafft can also be found in the relevant entry in an online databank of German ego-documents (Selbstzeugnisse im deutschsprachigen Raum) maintained by the Free University of Berlin: http://www.geschkult.fu-berlin.de/e/jancke-quellenkunde/verzeichnis/k/hu_krafft/index.html.
28. Krafft's Bible survives in the Herzog August Bibliothek in Wolfenbüttel.
29. The company's success was based mainly on its ore and copper dealings in Habsburg-ruled lands, and during those years it set itself the ambitious goal of expanding to the Orient.
30. Krafft, Reisen und Gefangenschaft, 98.
31. Krafft, 98.
32. Krafft, 98, 143–45.
33. For the following information and quotes, see Krafft, 160–61, 184, 281, 285–86, 313.
34. Krafft, 189–90.
35. Despite extensive research, I have been unable to find any information on Winterbach other than what is in Krafft's account.
36. This is Winterbach's own extension of a popular medieval and early modern saying, also occasionally quoted by Luther in his assaults on papal power. The traditional version is "The closer to Rome, the worse the Christians." See *Thesaurus proverbiorum medii aevi*, 13 vols. (Berlin: De Gruyter, 1995–2002), 9:56, 356–57.
37. For a description of the following events, see Krafft, *Reisen und Gefangenschaft*, 417.
38. Krafft, 417.
39. Krafft, 417.
40. Krafft, 416–17.
41. Krafft, 417–18.
42. Krafft, 421.
43. Unfortunately, these objects, along with the other items from the list, seem to have been lost.
44. The role of travel in the "change in modes of thought in regard to the Jews" has also been noted by Myriam Yardeni in her *Anti-Jewish Mentalities in Early Modern Europe* (Lanham: University Press of America, 1990), especially chaps. 3 and 6; quotation from 72. However, Yardeni limits her study to trading nations such as England and Holland, while in the case of French travelers, she actually notes that "their hatred and contempt keep mounting and gathering strength as they meet their first live Jews" (140). Yardeni's approach here is somewhat simplistic, and she devotes little attention to the role of travel and mobility on the Jewish side. On the latter, see especially David Ruderman, *Early Modern Jewry: A New Cultural History* (Princeton: Princeton University Press, 2010), chap. 1.
45. Guggisberg, *Religiöse Toleranz*, 59.
46. Felix Fabri, *Evagatorium in Terrae Sanctae, Arabiae et Egypti peregrinationem*, ed. K. D. Hassler, 3 vols. (Stuttgart: Litterarischer Verein, 1843–49), 2:129. The English translation is taken from Felix Fabri, *The Wanderings of Felix Fabri*, trans. Aubrey Stewart, 2 vols. (New York: AMS Press, 1971), 2:132.
47. Michel de Montaigne, *The Complete Works*, trans. Donald M. Frame (New York: Knopf, 2003), 1152–54.
48. These sources have been handily compiled in Benjamin Ravid, "Travel Accounts of the Jews of Venice and Their Ghetto," in *Between History and Literature: Studies in Honor of Isaac Barzilay*, ed. Stanley Nash (Tel Aviv: Ha-Kibuts ha-me'uchad, 1997), 118–50.
49. Wolfgang Treue, "'Ich verlangte sehr, sie in ihren Synagogen zu sehen . . .': Juden und jüdisches Leben im Spiegel christlicher Reiseberichte des 16. und

17. Jahrhunderts," in *Selbstzeugnisse und Ego-Dokumente frühneuzeitlicher Juden in Aschkenas: Beispiel, Methoden und Konzepte*, ed. Birgit E. Klein and Rotraud Ries (Berlin: Metropol, 2011), 332.
50. Thomas Dallam, *The Diary of Master Thomas Dallam, 1599–1600*, in *Early Voyages and Travels in the Levant: With Some Account of the Levant Company of Turkey Merchants*, ed. J. Theodore Bent (London: Hakluyt Society, 1893), 86.
51. Introduction to Bent, *Early Voyages*, i–xlii, especially xv–xviii.
52. Shohet, *Im hilufe tekufot*, 49–51.
53. Shohet, 49–51; Liberles, "On the Threshold," 87.
54. For a focus on the lower classes (albeit not entirely satisfying), see Yacov Guggenheim, "Meeting on the Road: Encounters Between German Jews and Christians on the Margins of Society," in *In and Out of the Ghetto: Jewish-Gentile Relations in Late Medieval and Early Modern Germany*, ed. R. Po-chia Hsia and Hartmut Lehmann (Cambridge: Cambridge University Press, 1995), 125–36. For a fuller treatment, see Rudolf Glanz, *Geschichte des niederen jüdischen Volkes in Deutschland: Eine Studie über historisches Gaunertum, Bettelwesen und Vagantentum* (New York: Waldon Press, 1968).
55. See, for instance, Shlomo Simonsohn, "Divieto di trasportare ebrei in Palestina," in *Italia Judaica: Atti del II convegno internazionale* (Rome: Ufficio centrale per i beni archivistici, 1986), 39–53.
56. See, for instance, the case of the Italian Jewish traveler Meshullam da Volterra, who in 1487 decided to disembark from a French galley in the Mediterranean as a result of the hostility he faced from the ship's crew after a quarrel with one of the seamen. These events are reported in a contemporary Hebrew travelogue: Obadiah di Bertinoro, *Me-Italyah li-Yerushalayim: Iggerotav shel R. Ovadyah mi-Bartenura me-Erets Yisrael*, ed. Menachem Emanuele Artom and Abraham David (Ramat Gan: Hotsaʾat Proyekt Yerushalayim, 1997), 43.
57. See an early seventeenth-century letter by an Italian Jewish traveler, reproduced in Abraham David, "Mekorot hadashim al haflagat ha-yehudim mi-Venetsyah la-mizrach ve le-Erets Yisrael [...] ba-meot ha-15 veha-17," *Shalem* 6 (1992): 331.
58. On the concept of *ahl al-dhimmah* (protected people) and the practical ramifications of *dhimmī* status in Islamic society, see, for example, Cohen, *Under Crescent and Cross*, especially 112.
59. Krafft, *Reisen und Gefangenschaft*, 312.
60. The literature on confessionalization is vast. A useful introduction can be found in Ute Lotz-Heumann, "Confessionalization," in *Reformation and Early Modern Europe: A Guide to Research*, ed. David M. Whitford (Kirksville: Truman State University Press, 2008), 136–57. See also Heinz Schilling, "The Confessionalization of European Churches and Societies: An Engine for Modernizing and for Social and Cultural Change," in Schilling, *Early Modern European Civilization and Its Political and Cultural Dynamism* (Hanover, NH: University Press of New England, 2008), 11–32.
61. Krafft, *Reisen und Gefangenschaft*, 297–99.
62. Kaplan, *Divided by Faith*, 327.
63. Elukin, *Living Together, Living Apart*, 133.
64. Andrew Crome, "Friendship and Enmity to God and Nation: The Complexities of Jewish-Gentile Relations in the Whitehall Conference of 1655," in *Friendship in the Middle Ages and Early Modern Age: Explorations of a Fundamental Ethical Discourse*, ed. Albrecht Classen and Marilyn Sandidge (Berlin: De Gruyter, 2010), especially 776.
65. Jonathan I. Israel, *European Jewry in the Age of Mercantilism, 1550–1750*, 3rd ed. (London: Littman Library of Jewish Civilization, 1998), 10.

66. Thomas A. Brady Jr., "Germans with a Difference? The Jews of the Holy Roman Empire During the Early Modern Era—a Comment," in Hsia and Lehmann, *In and Out*, 290.
67. As has been noted, in passing, by Gotthard, *In der Ferne*, 86.
68. Michael Heberer, *Aegyptiaca Servitus: Das ist / Warhafte Beschreibung einer Dreyjährigen Dienstbarkeit / So zu Alexandrien in Egypten jhren Anfang und zu Constantinopel jhr Endschafft genommen* [. . .] (1610; repr., Graz: Akademische Druck- und Verlagsanstalt, 1967), 136.
69. Heberer, *Aegyptiaca Servitus*, 136.
70. Heberer, 121–22.
71. Krafft, *Reisen und Gefangenschaft*, 282.
72. There were no Jews living in Geislingen at that time. The last record of their presence there is in the 1540s and 1550s. See Joachim Hahn, *Erinnerungen und Zeugnisse jüdischer Geschichte in Baden-Württemberg* (Stuttgart: Theiss, 1988), 193. I would like to thank Stefan Lang for confirming this fact.
73. The Jewish merchant Meshullam da Volterra, who traveled from Tuscany to the Levant in 1481, was not the only European Jew to complain about the food served by his Levantine coreligionists. He clearly preferred to adhere to Italian *diete*—the Italian term he used. He was also fairly appalled by the eating habits of Jews in Islamic countries. Having observed them eating while they sat on the ground, Meshullam compared them to "swine." See Meshullam da Volterra, *Massa Meshullam mi-Volterrah be-Erets Yisrael bishenat 1481*, ed. Avraham Yaari (Jerusalem: Mosad Bialik, 1948), 75–76. Similarly, an Italian Jew in Prague made explicit arrangements to be served Italian rather than Bohemian food (he said nothing about *kashrut*). See Giuseppe Jarè, *Abramo Colorni: Ingegnere di Alfonso d'Este—Nuove ricerche* (Ferrara: Premiata Tipografia Sociale, 1891), 28.
74. Sabine Ullmann, *Nachbarschaft und Konkurrenz: Judenpolitik und jüdisches Leben in Württemberg und im "Land zu Schwaben" (1492–1650)* (Ostfildern: Thorbecke, 2008), especially 345–49, 470–72. In-depth research on *Landjuden*—Jews who lived in rural areas—has long been neglected by historians, who have tended to study Jewish society in central Europe as a primarily urban phenomenon. On more recent interest in this topic as well as some continuing lacunae, see Monika Richarz, "Ländliches Judentum als Problem der Forschung," in *Jüdisches Leben auf dem Lande: Studien zur deutsch-jüdischen Geschichte*, ed. Monika Richarz and Reinhard Rürup (Tübingen: Mohr Siebeck, 1997), 1–8.
75. Elukin, *Living Together, Living Apart*, 6. In a similar vein, see Ivan G. Marcus, "A Jewish-Christian Symbiosis: The Culture of Early Ashkenaz," in *Cultures of the Jews: A New History*, ed. David Biale (New York: Schocken, 2002), 449–516, especially 449–51.
76. This assumption is essential to what Moshe Rosman defines as the postmodern approach to Jewish history. Rosman, *How Jewish Is Jewish History?* (Oxford: Littman Library of Jewish Civilization, 2007), 97. Rosman also offers a critical evaluation of such approaches (53).
77. Gowing, Hunter, and Rubin, introduction, especially 4. See also Daniel T. Lochman, Maritere López, and Lorna Hutson, eds., *Discourses and Representations of Friendship in Early Modern Europe, 1500–1700* (Farnham: Ashgate, 2011). These two studies are useful recent introductions to the growing number of historical studies on the meaning and practice of friendship and *amicitia* in late medieval and early modern Europe. Another important study is Reginald Hyatte, *The Arts of Friendship: The Idealization of Friendship in Medieval and Early Renaissance Literature* (Leiden: Brill, 1994). On the various layers of the term *amicitia*, see Maurice Aymard, "Friends and Neighbors," in *Passions of the Renaissance*, ed. Roger Chartier (Cambridge,

MA: Harvard University Press, 1989), 447–58, especially 453.
78. Klaus Oschema, *Freundschaft oder "amitié": Ein politisches Konzept der Vormoderne im zwischensprachlichen Vergleich (15.–17. Jahrhundert)* (Berlin: Duncker and Humblot, 2007), especially 82–89.
79. *Oxford English Dictionary*, 6th ed., s.v. "friendship" (Oxford: Oxford University Press, 2007).
80. Hermann Fischer, ed., *Schwäbisches Wörterbuch* (Tübingen: Laupp, 1904–36), s.v. "Freundschaft."
81. Lorna Hutson, afterword to Lochman, López, and Hutson, *Discourses and Representations*, 242.
82. Simmel, however, restricted his observations to modernity, noting that "modern sensitivity tends more towards differentiated friendships, i.e., to such that have their realm associated typically with only one pertinent aspect of the personalities and in which the rest plays no role." Georg Simmel, *Sociology: Inquiries into the Construction of Social Forms*, trans. Anthony J. Blasi, Anton K. Jacobs, and Matthew Kanjirathinkal, 2 vols. (Leiden: Brill, 2009), 1:320–21; see also Tenbruck, "Freundschaft," especially 231–32.
83. Montaigne, *Complete Works*, 171.
84. Montaigne, 169.
85. Francis Bacon, "Of Followers and Friends" (Essay 48), in *The Works of Francis Bacon*, ed. James Spedding, Robert Leslie Ellis, and Douglas Denon Heath, 14 vols. (London: Longman, 1861–79), 6:494–95.
86. Michel Foucault, "Different Spaces," in *The Essential Works of Michel Foucault*, vol. 2, *Aesthetics, Method, and Epistemology*, ed. James D. Faubion (New York: New Press, 1998), 180.
87. Linda Colley, *Captives: Britain, Empire, and the World, 1600–1850* (New York: Anchor Books, 2004), 98.
88. On the sometimes "constructive relationship between conflict and coexistence" in medieval Spain, see David Nirenberg, *Communities of Violence: Persecution of Minorities in the Middle Ages* (Princeton: Princeton University Press, 1996), especially 9.
89. Carlo Ginzburg, *The Cheese and the Worms: The Cosmos of a Sixteenth-Century Miller*, trans. John and Anne Tedeschi (Baltimore: Johns Hopkins University Press, 1980).
90. I differ on this point from Robert Bonfil's overly polarizing—though stimulating—*Jewish Life in Renaissance Italy*. A more nuanced approach is offered by Kenneth Stow, "Jews and Christians—Two Different Cultures?," in *Interstizi: Culture ebraico-cristiane a Venezia e nei suoi domini dal Medioevo all'età moderna*, ed. Uwe Israel, Robert Jütte, and Reinhold C. Mueller (Rome: Edizioni di Storia e Letteratura, 2010), 31–32.
91. For the former, see Debra Kaplan, "'Because Our Wives Trade and Do Business with Our Goods': Gender, Work, and Jewish-Christian Relations," in *New Perspective on Jewish-Christian Relations: In Honor of David Berger*, ed. Elisheva Carlebach and Jacob J. Schacter (Leiden: Brill, 2012), 241–61. On the fascinating case of a spiritual friendship between a Jewish poetess and a monk in seventeenth-century Venice, see Umberto Fortis, *La bella ebrea: Sara Copio Sullam, poetessa nel ghetto di Venezia del '600* (Turin: Zamorani, 2003). For the shared experience of environmental crises, see Dean Philip Bell, "The Little Ice Age and the Jews: Environmental History and the Mercurial Nature of Jewish-Christian Relations in Early Modern Germany," *AJS Review* 32, no. 1 (2008): 1–27; and Herman Pollack, *Jewish Folkways in Germanic Lands, 1648–1806: Studies in Aspects of Daily Life* (Cambridge, MA: MIT Press, 1971), 13.
92. Francesca Trivellato, *The Familiarity of Strangers: The Sephardic Diaspora, Livorno, and Cross-cultural Trade in the Early Modern Period* (New Haven: Yale University Press, 2009), 181–84, 192.

93. See especially Anthony Grafton and Joanna Weinberg, *"I Have Always Loved the Holy Tongue": Isaac Casaubon, the Jews, and a Forgotten Chapter in Renaissance Scholarship* (Cambridge, MA: Harvard University Press, 2011). See also Allison P. Coudert and Jeffrey S. Shoulson, eds., *Hebraica veritas? Christian Hebraists and the Study of Judaism in Early Modern Europe* (Philadelphia: University of Pennsylvania Press, 2004).
94. As has been demonstrated by Bernard Dov Cooperman, "*Amicitia* and Hermeticism: Paratext as Key to Judah Moscato's *Nefutsot Yehudah*," in *Rabbi Judah Moscato and the Jewish Intellectual World of Mantua in the 16th–17th Centuries*, ed. Giuseppe Veltri and Gianfranco Miletto (Leiden: Brill, 2012), 79–104.
95. The classic study of the importance of gifts in society is Marcel Mauss, *The Gift: The Form and Reason for Exchange in Archaic Societies*, trans. W. D. Halls (1990; repr., New York: Norton, 2000). Mauss's approach has recently been applied to early modern history. See especially Natalie Zemon Davis, *The Gift in Sixteenth-Century France* (Madison: University of Wisconsin Press, 2000); and Gadi Algazi, Valentin Groebner, and Bernhard Jussen, eds., *Negotiating the Gift: Pre-modern Figurations of Exchange* (Göttingen: Vandenhoeck and Ruprecht, 2003).

CHAPTER 11

Friendship, Jewish Female Philosophers, and Feminism

HAVA TIROSH-SAMUELSON

Friendship is a philosophically rich topic because it entails the crossing of boundaries, whether between self and others, between humans and God, between Jews and non-Jews, or between men and women. Before the modern period, true or perfect friendship was considered for men only because friendship was believed to be grounded in intellectual capacities that women presumably lacked. In chapter 3, I discussed the ways in which philosophy has marked both the limits and potential possibilities for women. This chapter continues to explore the connection between friendship, philosophy, and gender but focuses on modern and contemporary philosophy. It highlights the differences between the premodern and modern conceptions of friendship, which renders the modern discourse on friendship necessarily ambiguous.[1] Modernity has transformed life for Jews, who became citizens in their country of residence and equal under the law. The spread of the democratic ideal also meant the inclusion of women in many areas of life from which they had been previously excluded. In the modern period, Jews and women wrestled with the same paradox: how to be equal and different at the same time. Whereas the desire for equality has led women and Jews to emphasize sameness at the expense of distinctiveness, the determination to retain their distinct identity has entailed emphasis on difference and otherness. Friendship is the type of human relation that accommodates equality and difference simultaneously. This chapter considers the contribution of Jewish philosophers, both men and women, to modern understandings of friendship.

MODERNITY:
FRIENDSHIP AND THE INCLUSION OF JEWS AND WOMEN

For upper-class Jewish women in Renaissance and baroque Italy, philosophy and broad secular learning offered new educational opportunities. These opportunities would become a reality in the modern period with the spread of Enlightenment ideology, the secularization of European culture, the emancipation of the Jews, the modernization of Judaism, and Jewish acculturation and assimilation into Western society and culture. In the modern period, philosophy would open up new possibilities of inclusion for Jews as well as for women because philosophy insisted on the universality of reason and the inherent equality of all humans endowed with reason. At the same time, philosophy also set the boundaries that excluded Jews and women from egalitarian participation in society and culture. Whereas the exclusion of Jews was rooted in age-old anti-Semitism that was now given a racial, presumably scientific basis, the exclusion of women was rooted in age-old misogyny and patriarchy. Thus the heated debates about the "Jewish question" and the "women question" were two sides of the same debate about the meaning of being human and the scope of human rationality. Modernity signified the corrosion of social boundaries between Jews and non-Jews and the inclusion of Jews, as well as women, in many aspects of life from which these groups were previously excluded, even though equality between Jews and non-Jews and between men and women remained contested. The growing integration of Jews into Western culture also problematized the meaning of Jewish identity, as Judaism was variously defined as a "religion," an "ethnicity," a "nationality," or a "people."

As social, religious, and cultural boundaries became more porous in the modern period, new types of friendships between Jews and non-Jews and between men and women emerged. This phenomenon was evident first among wealthy Jews, some of whom held official positions in princely courts and rendered services to the state. In particular, wealthy and educated

Jewish women in Berlin and Vienna were responsible for new paradigms of socialization and new types of intellectual friendships between Jews and non-Jews and between men and women. Rahel Varnhagen (d. 1833) was a case in point. Born Rahel Levin, the daughter of a wealthy Prussian Jew, Marcus Levin, she was brought up in an Orthodox home where Yiddish was spoken, but she acquired knowledge of European languages, philosophy, and literature. Between 1790 and 1806, she ran a literary salon in her sumptuous home where leading intellectuals of the day—the Humboldt brothers (Alexander and Wilhelm), Friedrich Schlegel, Friedrich Schleiermacher, Friedrich August Wolfe, the Tieck brothers, Heinrich Heine, and many other talented members of German society—were entertained.[2] Rahel Levin had several friendships and love affairs with non-Jews, eventually marrying the diplomat Karl August Varnhagen, a marriage that required her to convert to Christianity and change her name to Antoine Friederike Varnhagen. Despite her desperate effort to assimilate into what she termed "high society" or "aristocratic society," she was tormented by her inescapable Jewishness, which she regarded as the "misfortune," "shame," and "misery" of her life. Rahel Varnhagen was not a professional philosopher, but she and other Jewish salonnièrs were intellectually well informed, and they even shaped the direction of culture in German-speaking countries by promoting certain intellectual trends, such as Romanticism.

The salons of wealthy Jewish women, where art, philosophy, and literature were cultivated as an expression of the German ideal of *Bildung*, were crucial to the emergence of the modern conception of friendship.[3] The salons, as Seyla Benhabib describes them, "forged bonds across classes, religious groups, and the two sexes, creating the four walls within which the new forms of sociability and intimacy could develop among members of an emergent civil society."[4] In the salons, Benhabib goes on to explain,

> the joy of speech culminates in friendship, in that meeting of the hearts, minds, and tastes between two individuals. Particularly in the case of the German salons, the search for *Seelensfreund*, a friend of one's soul, one who understands oneself perhaps better than oneself, is predominant.... With friends one shares one's soul, however, to share the soul—an entity that itself comes to be discovered in this new process of individuals—one has to project a certain depth of the self, one has to view the self as a being whose public presence does not reveal all.[5]

The salons created a new social space between the public and the private in which writers, artists, civil servants, and aristocrats mingled, exchanged ideas and texts, and formed emotional bonds and romantic attachments. These intersubjective relations were very different from the civic friendships between virtuous men of antiquity or the intellectual love of God in the Middle Ages and the early modern period.

MODERN CONCEPTIONS OF FRIENDSHIP

The modern discourse on friendship both built on its premodern antecedents and also departed from them. In the nineteenth century, friendship was understood as a private, intimate, emotional bond between men and/or women. They did not need to share the same social status, but they were expected to reveal themselves to each other and provide mutual emotional support for one another in the highly fragmented modern world obsessed by utility, productivity, and consumption. As Montaigne was first to note, the emotional attachment to the friend could not be explained by citing objective facts about the friend or listing his objective virtues.[6] Rather, friendship could only be justified through a creative understanding of the dynamic interaction with the friend and his or her irreducible uniqueness. If the premodern conception of friendship insisted on the sameness and similarity between good men of virtue, the modern understanding recognized the otherness and uniqueness of the friend, and that facilitated friendship between men and women as well as friendship among women.[7]

That friendship should be among equals who are also different would become the focus of postmodern reflections as exemplified by Jacques Derrida and Maurice Blanchot.[8] But as we shall see, the first person to argue for such an understanding of friendship would be the Jewish female philosopher Hannah Arendt (d. 1975). To appreciate her contribution to the philosophic discourse on friendship, we need to realize that friendship did not fit well into the dominant theories of moral philosophy in the nineteenth century, theories that emphasized rationality, universality, and impartiality. In fact, friendship often conflicted with modern moral reasoning, a tension that did not exist in the premodern period.

Both deontology and consequentialism could not easily accommodate the notion of friendship. In deontology, whose major theorist was Immanuel Kant (d. 1804), duty rather than virtue determines the rightness of the act.⁹ Kant, who distinguished between duties of love and duties of respect, treats friendship separately because in friendship, love and respect are combined on equal footing.¹⁰ But Kant thought that the perfect form of friendship, "friendship of disposition," was *unachievable* because of the gap between the phenomenal and noumenal worlds. In Kant's deontological moral theory, the rightness or wrongness of actions depends not on the consequence but on whether they fulfill our *duty* to the moral law—the categorical imperative—which acts on all people regardless of their interest or desires. Friendship did not fit neatly into Kant's moral theory because friendship is based on emotions; it pertains to particular individuals, and it is inherently partial.

Consequentialism holds that the moral agent ought to do whatever action produces the greatest aggregate happiness for all human beings so that the good deeds that a friend does for his or her friend would be morally justified only if they were to bring about the most good for everyone. Because this moral theory is concerned with universal happiness, within consequentialist moral theory, it is difficult to explain the deeds that good friends do for each other, for true friends seem to love each other for their own sake, and they seem to regard the good that they do for each other valuable in its own right. Since friendship has a dubious moral standing in deontology and consequentialism, this topic remained marginal in modern moral philosophy.[11] This was the case until the second half of the twentieth century, when moral theorists, following the lead of the British (female) philosophers Philippa Foot and G. E. M. Anscombe, revived Aristotle's virtue ethics as an expressed alternative to deontology and consequentialism.[12] The revival of virtue ethics meant a new interest in Aristotle's conception of civic friendship and a realization that notwithstanding his negative view of women, Aristotle's analysis could even be useful to feminists.[13]

FRIENDSHIP AND JEWISH PHILOSOPHERS OF DIALOGUE

Jewish philosophy in the nineteenth century stood under the sway of Kantianism. Jewish philosophers—most notably Hermann Cohen (d. 1918)—contributed to the flourishing of Kantianism in German academe and the recasting of Judaism in terms of Kantian philosophy.[14] Since friendship did not fit neatly into Kantian philosophy, it is understandable that Jewish philosophers in the nineteenth century showed little interest in friendship, although Cohen's theory of correlation could be seen as laying the foundation for a new Jewish philosophy of dialogue that accommodated the notion of friendship.[15] At the turn of the twentieth century, the totalizing style of European philosophy was challenged by existentialist philosophers (e.g., Kierkegaard, Nietzsche, Schopenhauer, Husserl, and Heidegger), who rejected any system that sought to explain the meaning of being human, be it scientific, materialist, historicist, or idealist. In existentialist thought, truth is not theoretical and abstract but a value that people are willing to live by and even die for. Human existence itself takes priority over the contemplation of abstract theoretical truths, and truth is not about the correspondence between cognition and reality but about the meaning of life as experienced by the self. Truth is subjective, a synonym to authenticity, and truth is personal and relates to the subjectivity of the philosopher and the life that he or she calls on others to lead. Because existentialist philosophy was more attuned with the dynamics of real human life, it could conceptualize friendship anew as a dialogical relationship.

Two Jewish philosophers—Martin Buber (d. 1965) and Franz Rosenzweig (d. 1929)—were at the forefront of dialogical philosophy, or philosophy of encounter, in which to be human does not mean to contemplate abstract truths but to engage in intersubjective relations.[16] In his *I and Thou* (1923), Buber insightfully distinguished between two primary relations: I-It and I-Thou. The former is conditional, instrumental, and mediated, treating the Other as a means to an end, whereas the latter is unconditional, noninstrumental, and immediate, treating the other as an end. In *I-Thou* relations, "when Thou is spoken, the speaker stands in mutual relation to the other, without aim, desire or means. The *I* addresses the *Thou* with his whole person and encounters him in the full freedom of his otherness, while the It is encountered with only part of the person.... In the I-Thou relations there is no purpose or desire but only spaceless and timeless 'present'—a present in which everything indirect is irrelevant."[17] Buber recognized the difficulty of retaining openness and presence in I-Thou relations, which often turn into objectification, but it is precisely the dialogical encounter characteristic of I-Thou relations that enables humans to cross boundaries of religion, class, nationality, race, and gender. Buber's dialogical philosophy offered a new conceptual framework for friendship among men, between men and women, and between Jews and non-Jews, although it is well known that Buber had difficulty living out his own dialogical philosophy. Relevant to this essay is the fact that Buber fell in love and married Paula Winkler (d. 1958), a non-Jew by birth who converted to Judaism. Winkler, Buber's intellectual equal, whom he met at the University of Zürich, became deeply involved in Buber's work. She is rarely remembered today as an independent scholar in her own right, in part because she published her work under the male pseudonym "Georg Munk."[18] It was with Winkler that Buber succeeded in establishing an I-Thou relationship.

Franz Rosenzweig, Buber's friend and collaborator in the translation of the Bible into German, is another example of a Jewish dialogical philosopher who had a deep intellectual friendship, as well as deep romantic attachment, with a non-Jewish woman, Margrit (Gritli) Rosenstock-Huessy (d. 1959), the wife of his best friend, Eugen Rosenstock-Huessy (d. 1973), himself a convert to Christianity. Rosenzweig came from an assimilated Jewish family and was himself on the verge of conversion, but after a transformative experience on the Day of Atonement in 1913, he became a *ba'al teshuvah* of sorts and gradually returned to traditional Judaism. Rosenzweig's love affair with Gritli (who married Eugen in 1914) lasted from 1918 to 1922, but the friendship with her lasted later until 1925, when Rosenzweig's advanced paralysis made the relationship between them untenable. As we now know from the published correspondence between Rosenzweig and Gritli, she was much more than a mere sounding board for the deep philosophical ideas expressed in his masterpiece *Star of Redemption*.[19] Rather, Rosenzweig's "new thinking" developed out of his love for Gritli, a Christian art historian who accepted Rosenzweig's commitment to Judaism and shared his growing involvement with traditional Jewish life.[20] Unlike her husband and Rosenzweig's converted cousins, Rudolph and Hans Ehrenberg, who pressured Rosenzweig to convert, "Gritli was a careful, attentive listener who paid attention to her lover's alterity, something that her husband Eugen Rosenstock hardly respected."[21] As Ephraim Meir puts it, the correspondence between Rosenzweig and Gritli was itself an example of "a stimulating, confirming and dialogical thinking which constituted Part III of the *Star*."[22]

The key person who remained outside Rosenzweig's intimate community of friends was his lawful wife, Edith Hahn, whom Rosenzweig married (in 1920) because she was Jewish rather than out of love.[23] Edith functioned as the typical Jewish "woman of virtue," especially after Rosenzweig fell ill in 1922. She ran the household where his famous Lehrhaus was convened, she arranged for his nursing, and she implemented the system that enabled him to dictate his ideas despite his gradual motoric decline. It was Edith rather than Gritli who was the main figure in Rosenzweig's life at the end, functioning as "a wife, a mother, a secretary and the principal nurse."[24] Rosenzweig's philosophy, which was a dialogical philosophy of love, could not have been written without these two women, although Edith, who was the executor of Rosenzweig's estate, did her best to erase Gritli's presence from Rosenzweig's legacy and public memory.[25]

Intellectual friendships between male Jewish intellectuals and non-Jewish educated women, of which there are numerous examples, were possible because of the admission of Jews and women to European universities. For women as well as for Jews, admission to the universities offered new paths toward self-fulfillment, new ways of being "modern" people, and new opportunities for employment and professional careers outside the home. From the end of the nineteenth century until the rise of Nazism, whose race-based laws expelled Jews from universities, the liberal professions, and civic organizations, Jewish women could experience a whole new way of being in the world. In the secular university, Jewish women enrolled in the natural sciences, the social sciences, the humanities (including philosophy), and medicine and law, becoming teachers, lawyers, social workers, nurses, or physicians.

In her comprehensive study of university-educated Jewish women in central Europe, Harriet Freidenreich has documented the challenges these Jewish women faced. They experienced both academic misogyny and anti-Semitic prejudices even as they tried to resolve the tension between their desire for an academic career and the Jewish bourgeois gender expectations of marriage and children.[26] A good number of university-educated Jewish women did not follow gender expectations and remained either unmarried or married without children. The university experience also complicated the Jewish identity of many women. Some converted to Christianity, becoming what Freidenreich calls "former Jews," while others were "just Jews"—namely, "they accepted their Jewishness as a fact of life, even though this aspect of their personal identity did not always play an important role in their lives before the advent of Nazism. For such women, being Jews was simply what one was, not what one did or believed."[27] Still others were "Jewish Jews"—that is, "being Jews was central to their personal identity," and they "actively affirmed their Jewishness, whether by perpetuating Jewish observances in their homes, becoming involved in Jewish voluntary organizations, acknowledging a Jewish nationality, or seeking to acquire and spread advanced Jewish knowledge."[28] These university-educated "Jewish Jews" came to identify themselves with Zionism more than Judaism.[29]

HANNAH ARENDT: A JEWISH FEMALE PHILOSOPHER OF FRIENDSHIP

Hannah Arendt illustrates Freidenreich's second category. Arendt came from an assimilated Jewish family, but she identified herself all her life as a Jew, which she understood in secular, ethnic terms.[30] Arendt wrote extensively about Jewish history and worked in the Zionist organization Youth Aliyah and later for Schocken, the important European Jewish publishing house. Arendt's association with Zionism (which she also rigorously critiqued) allowed her to define herself as a "conscious pariah," a person who chooses to be a social outsider rather than a social climber, or parvenu.[31] That posture, Arendt claimed, was derived from none other than Rahel Varnhagen, the subject of Arendt's habilitation thesis, which she was researching before fleeing Nazi Germany to France in 1933.[32] In Paris, where Arendt belonged to a group of displaced intellectuals, she met and eventually married Heinrich Blücher, a communist non-Jewish intellectual. Blücher became her second husband in 1940 after she and her first husband, Günther Stern (who, like her, was a Jewish student of Edmund Husserl and Martin Heidegger) divorced. Importantly, with Blücher, Arendt would develop the intellectual friendship that she craved and that would sustain her for the rest of her life.[33]

In America, Arendt became one of the most influential Jewish intellectuals of her generation.[34] Arendt is pertinent to our exploration of friendship in modern Jewish philosophy because she articulated a full-fledged philosophy of friendship and had a talent for cultivating lifelong friendships with men and with women, with Jews and with non-Jews. Reminiscent of the salon of Rahel Varnhagen in Berlin, Arendt's small apartment in New York, first on Morningside Drive and later on Riverside Drive, became an intellectual hub where leading scholars and intellectuals regularly convened (figure 11.1). Among them were Paul Tillich, Salo and Jeanette Baron, Helen and Kurt Wolff, Hans Morgenthau, Alfred Kazin, Mary McCarthy, Lotte Kohler, Elizabeth Hardwick, Randall Jarrell, Robert Lowell, W. H. Auden, and Lionel and Diana Trilling, along with many other writers, artists, and critics. Arendt, however, was always at the center. Her capacity for friendship was legendary, and friendship was not only the basis for a vast social

FRIENDSHIP, JEWISH FEMALE PHILOSOPHERS, AND FEMINISM   221

FIGURE 11.1 Standing, left to right: Heinrich Buchler, Hannah Arendt, Dwight Macdonald, Gloria Lanier. Sitting, left to right: Nicola Chiramonte, Mary McCarthy, Robert Lowell. Courtesy of Archives and Special Collections, Vassar College Library, Ref. #6.83.

network that replaced family or communal affiliation but also the center of her political theory and her critique of modernity. Friendship through free intellectual dialogue was central to Arendt's life and political theory.

Arendt was a professionally trained philosopher, receiving a doctorate in philosophy in 1929 from the University of Heidelberg. She preferred, however, to call herself a political theorist rather than a philosopher because she was critical of speculative philosophy, which dominated German intellectual life. Arendt privileged the *vita activa* over the *vita contemplativa*—that is, politics over philosophy. She articulated her political theory through dialogue with past philosophers, including Socrates, Plato, Aristotle, Augustine, Kant, Kierkegaard, and Nietzsche, and especially her own two mentors, Heidegger (with whom she had a brief passionate love affair in 1926)[35] and Karl Jaspers (with whom she had a lifelong friendship).[36] Contrary to the focus on subjectivity and interiority characteristic of German philosophy,

Arendt focused on "the world"—namely, on the political and the social sphere. Arendt saw friendship as "the expression of betwixt and between the human world emblematic of politics,"[37] referring to this "in-between" space as "inter-est," a solidarity that "lies between people and therefore can relate and bind them together."[38]

Friendship, for Arendt, was different from other bonds, such as familial kinship, institutional affiliations, or erotic love. Echoing both Aristotle and Kant, she understood friendship as a lifelong commitment based on respect of what is good in us, since each one wants that goodness in the other to grow. For this reason, she never initiated a breakup in her relationships (although Gershom Scholem, the great scholar of Jewish mystical tradition, terminated his friendship with her after Arendt published her controversial book on the Eichmann trial). And she was able to remain committed to Heidegger despite his obvious character flaws and his pathetic failure to act morally by way of his association with German Nationalist Socialism during World War II. After the war, Arendt resumed her friendship with Heidegger and his wife, Elfried, and was crucial in rehabilitating Heidegger's intellectual reputation. In "dark times," as she characterized the challenges of totalitarianism and radical evil, Arendt found that only committed friendship, in which friends accept each other despite their flaws and bare themselves to each other through conversation, can enable us to be "humanized by discourse."[39] Arendt saw friendship as an ongoing dialogue based on equality and mutual respect that does not erase otherness and difference.

Difference and otherness are precisely what totalitarian regimes sought to erase, reducing human plurality to sameness. Arendt was among the earliest critics of modern science and technology; she understood how they facilitated the erasure of plurality through mass production, which in the Holocaust became the mass production of death. In her profound exploration of totalitarianism, Arendt hailed the ancient philosophic idea of public happiness based on public freedom, the very freedom denied to her and all other Jews by the Nazis. As Jon Nixon puts it, "Through public happiness friendship finds its own place within that structure and contributes to the sustainability of political freedom."[40] Friendship is primarily a free, open dialogue between intellectual equals who explore the truths of their opinion through the give and take of verbal exchanges. In this regard, friendship is the *microcosm* of the polity, and it is fundamentally different from erotic desire, in which self-sacrificial union is expected. Friendship is based on trust between free agents, and it has the potential to transform the partners, but unlike erotic love, which seeks to erase difference, friendship retains and protects the otherness and uniqueness of the partners. Friendship protects the plurality that gives us the freedom to be who we truly are and gives us agency, or capacity to act, even though plurality means that there is no certainty about the outcomes of our actions.

Arendt was most attentive to the vulnerability of friendship and its inherent uncertainty, insecurity, and indeterminacy. She experienced these in her deep friendships with men (e.g., Gershom Scholem, Hans Jonas, and Kurt Blumenfeld) and with women (e.g., Mary McCarthy, Lotte Kohler, Hilde Fränkel, and Rosalie Colie)[41] because she appreciated the inherent promise of friendship. Friendship is always a promise of continuity and stability in a world of discontinuity and instability, exacerbated by modern science and technology. In friendship, both men and women, Jews and non-Jews, can find "an isolated island of certainty in an ocean of uncertainty."[42] In friendship, human beings can be simultaneously equal and different as they experience the truth of dialogue.

Arendt was a Jewish female philosopher, but she was no feminist. In the 1920s while still in Germany she did not identify herself with German feminism or with the struggle of the suffragettes. In the United States, she did not join the second-wave feminist movement of the 1960s, launched by another Jewish, secular social thinker, Betty Friedan.[43] Arendt died in 1975, just as feminist philosophy began to take off, focusing on sex and gender as the key analytical categories of the human condition—two categories Arendt had ignored. Arendt insisted that perfect friendship is not sexual, and friends do not lose themselves as romantic lovers do; rather, friends gain affirmation of their distinct identity. More importantly, whereas the feminists declared that the "personal is political," Arendt sharply differentiated the personal and the political spheres. Although she was a celebrated public intellectual nationally and internationally, she was a very private person. In the first two decades of the feminist movement, feminist theorists were disappointed in her, but since the 1990s, feminist theorists have recognized her analysis of plurality and difference, of public and private—especially in her biography of Rahel Varnhagen—as especially useful to feminist theorizing of equality and difference.[44]

FRIENDSHIP IN FEMINIST MORAL THEORY

Friendship looms large in feminist moral theory, as feminists critiqued traditional philosophy's ideals of impartiality, impersonality, and universality. Instead, feminists have argued for partiality, recognized that identity is always relational, highlighted the value of care and caring relationships, and appreciated friendship as a particular kind of caring relationship based on equality, mutuality, and trust. A revolutionary movement, feminism "aimed to overturn what many consider the most entrenched hierarchy there is: the hierarchy of gender."[45] Feminism is committed to the equality of women, although it offers diverse and even conflicting interpretations of the meaning of equality. The point of departure for feminist thought is the experience of women, "the lived experience of feeling as well as of thinking, of performing actions as well as receiving impression, and of being aware of our connections with other persons as well as of our own sensations."[46] Validating women's experiences, feminist theorists have rejected the dominant moral theories of deontology and consequentialism, focusing instead on the relevant experience of women in the social sphere, especially within the family. Family relations—above all, mothering—and the interaction with friends became the focal point of feminist moral theory known as "ethics of care," a normative moral theory that holds that moral action centers on interpersonal relationships and care. Ethics of care takes the practice of care, which tends to fall mainly on women, as the paradigm of ethical relations: ethics is not about autonomy, independence, self-determination, fairness, or rights (as the dominant moral theories have insisted). Rather, ethics is about interdependence, relatedness, and positive involvement in the lives of others, precisely as friends act toward each other. Family relations and friendship, especially friendship among women, take places of honor in a feminist ethics of care.[47]

It is no coincidence that three major contributors to feminist ethics of care are Jewish women—Carol Gilligan (b. 1936), Joan Tronto (b. 1952), and Marilyn Friedman (b. 1945). Their highly influential work has been excluded from the story of contemporary Jewish philosophy because they do not engage Jewish texts. This is problematic because feminist Jewish philosophers reflect the secularization of Judaism in modernity that has impacted all modern and contemporary Jews. In this sense, secular Jews are no less part of the modern Jewish experience than observant Jews.

Moreover, the ethics of care has much in common with the modern Jewish philosophy of dialogue.

Gilligan, the founder of the concept of the ethics of care, broke new ground in ethics when she showed empirically that girls (and later women) reason differently from boys: instead of focusing on abstract rules, fairness, and justice, girls think in terms of protecting interpersonal relationships. There is no one morality but different moral voices; the female voice is rooted in women's experience as primary caretakers of children, the sick, the infirm, and the old, either within the family or within social institutions. Since Gilligan's pioneering work, the feminist discourse of ethics of care has developed greatly, becoming philosophically more nuanced but also mired in heated debates. The most relevant to our discussion is the debate about the relationship between ethics of care and politics. Joan Tronto, a political theorist, argues that "feminists ignore the political setting of their moral arguments at their peril."[48] Her subtle analysis of the concept of care shows that care "will lead to some type of action"[49] and that care consists of four interconnected phases: "caring about, taking care of, care-giving, and care receiving."[50] The better we understand care, the more we appreciate care as a particular and universal practice and a disposition governed by responsibility—indeed, a central value in Jewish ethics, especially as espoused in the highly influential philosophy of Emmanuel Levinas.[51] The ethics of care teaches a deep truth about human beings—namely, that they are "best described as interdependent," contrary to the myth of the rational, autonomous man, the characteristics of liberalism, and certain modern moral theories. Care as a practice and as a disposition should inform the practices of democratic citizenship, a point Tronto develops in her most recent book.[52]

Within the ethics of care, friendship has received special attention, and the major theorist is Marilyn Friedman, a daughter of Holocaust survivors.[53] She argues that friendship is a voluntary relationship that "offers personally as well as socially transformative possibilities usually lacking in other important tradition-based close relationships, such as familial ties."[54] Friedman also rejects the autonomous view of the self, asserting instead a conception of the self as inherently social and hailing friendship as "a model of community that usefully counterbalances the family-neighborhood-nation complex favored by communitarians."[55] Friendship facilitates the transformation of the self, when "the needs, wants, fears, experiences, projects and dreams of our friends can frame for us new standpoints from which we can explore the significance and worth of moral values and standards."[56] Friendship is so precious in contemporary life because of the dissolution of traditional social bonds, especially in urban settings. In friendship, individuals re-create themselves anew and build voluntary social relations outside family and ethnic ties, "often in opposition to the expectations and ascribed roles of their found communities."[57] Friedman promotes friendship, and especially friendship between women, as a vehicle for critique not only of reigning moral theories but also of the conventional conception of ethnic community.

In conclusion, in the modern period, Judaism underwent profound transformations due to the emancipation of the Jews and their subsequent assimilation, acculturation, and secularization. The integration of Jews into society at large yielded various levels of acculturation and assimilation so that the meaning of being Jewish became a matter of subjective choice, often contested or ambiguous. The meaning and scope of Jewish philosophy became even more difficult to ascertain in the modern period as Jewish philosophers wrestled with the paradoxes of equality and difference. Since philosophy, the most abstract of intellectual activities, was no longer predicated on the religious idiom of Judaism, the Jewishness of the philosopher could be easily occluded, suppressed, or erased.

In this essay, I wish to expand the boundaries of modern Jewish philosophy by including women philosophers who were born Jews but who philosophized without explicit reference to Judaism. The inclusion of female philosophers and the attention to feminist theory indicate that in the modern period, gender is even more central to understanding friendship than it was in the premodern period. Modern (male) Jewish philosophers contributed to theories of friendship, as we have seen, by articulating the relational concept of the self and dialogical philosophy. Jewish female philosophers developed these ideas in different directions, either in the context of secular political theory or within the feminist embrace of ethics of care. Feminists who are committed to Jewish life—and who are informed by Jewish philosophy—could greatly expand their scope by generating a fruitful dialogue between the canon of Jewish philosophy and feminist theories.[58]

To date, contemporary Jewish philosophers have not paid sufficient attention to friendship, even though friendship has been a persistent theme of Jewish philosophy.[59] Friendship matters because it enables us to cross the boundaries that we construct between individuals, communities, cultures, and traditions. Friendship negotiates between the public and private spheres, between self and others, between Jews and non-Jews, between men and women.

NOTES

1. This point is argued most persuasively by Alexander Nehamas, *On Friendship* (New York: Basic Books, 2016).
2. For close analysis, see Deborah Hertz, *Jewish High Society in Old Regime Berlin* (New Haven: Yale University Press, 1988).
3. The term *Bildung* stood for a broad education of the citizenry, echoing the educational ideals of ancient Greek *paideia* as well as Renaissance humanism. Goethe's version of the Bildung tradition combined the Romantic notion of Sturm und Drang with Enlightenment rationalism, thus insisting that Bildung should include thought and feeling, mind and body. Goethe initiated the literary genre of the bildungsroman, the story of self-cultivation and character formation; Rahel Varnhagen was personally responsible for "Goethe's cult" in the early nineteenth century. On the Bildung tradition among German-speaking Jews, see George Mosse, *German Jews Beyond Judaism* (Bloomington: Indiana University Press, 1985).
4. Seyla Benhabib, *The Reluctant Modernism of Hannah Arendt* (Lanham, MD: Rowman & Littlefield, 2000), 16.
5. Benhabib, *The Reluctant Modernism of Hannah Arendt*, 17.
6. Michel de Montaigne, "Of Friendship," in *Other Selves: Philosophers on Friendship*, ed. Michael Pakaluk (Indianapolis: Hackett, 1991), 187–99. Montaigne's essay echoes many themes of the premodern thinkers, especially Aristotle and Cicero, while paving the way for the modern understanding of friendship.
7. See Marilyn Yalom with Theresa Donovan Brown, *The Social Sex: A History of Female Friendship* (New York: HarperCollins, 2015).
8. Jacques Derrida, *The Politics of Friendship*, trans. George Collins (1997; repr., London: Verso, 2005); Maurice Blanchot, *Friendship*, trans. Elizabeth Rottenberg (Palo Alto: Stanford University Press, 1997), especially the essay "Friendship," 289–92. Derrida and other postmodern philosophers rejected binary distinctions that underlie traditional logocentrism and the "metaphysical" approach of Western philosophy. As the title of his book indicates, Derrida suggested that a nonbinary conception of friendship, freed from exclusionary tendencies could be the foundation of a new politics of democracy.
9. Kant discussed friendship in *Tugendlehre*, translated into English as *The Doctrine of Virtue* by Mary J. Gregor (New York: Harper and Row, 1964). For a very useful summary of Kant's theory of friendship, see H. J. Paton, "Kant on Friendship," in *Friendship: A Philosophical Reader*, ed. Neera Kapur Badhurar (Ithaca: Cornell University Press, 1995), 132–54.
10. Paton, "Kant on Friendship," 135.
11. Indeed, most anthologies of primary sources about friendship consist of literary rather than philosophic sources. For example, see D. J. Enright and David Rawlinson, eds., *The Oxford Book of Friendship* (Oxford: Oxford University Press, 1991). The reason is quite obvious: prose narrative and drama are better at representing the complex and fluid relationships between friends. Yet in the past few decades, academic philosophers have also paid more attention to friendship, a development directly indebted to the revival of virtue ethics in moral philosophy and the rise of feminist philosophy.

12. See Arthur Flemming, "Reviving the Virtues," *Ethics* 40 (1980): 587–95; Stephen M. Gardinaer, *Virtue Ethics, Old and New* (Ithaca: Cornell University Press, 2005); and Daniel C. Russell, ed., *The Cambridge Companion to Virtue Ethics* (New York: Cambridge University Press, 2013).
13. A good example of this trend is Sibyl A. Schwarzenbach, *On Civil Friendship: Including Women in the State* (New York: Columbia University Press, 2009). See also Cynthia A. Freeland, ed., *Feminist Interpretations of Aristotle* (University Park: Penn State University Press, 1998).
14. On the impact of Kant's "religion of reason" on Judaism, see Alan Mittleman, *Between Kant and Kabbalah: An Introduction to Isaac Breuer's Philosophy of Judaism* (Albany: SUNY Press, 1990).
15. Michael Zank, *The Idea of Atonement in the Philosophy of Hermann Cohen* (Providence, RI: Brown Judaic Studies, 2000). According to Cohen, we discover the "I" only by means of the "Thou." We recognize our moral self by recognizing our moral failures toward others.
16. On Jewish philosophy of dialogue, see Michael D. Oppenheim, *Encounters of Consequence: Jewish Philosophy in the Twentieth Century and Beyond* (Boston: Academic Jewish Press, 2009). The literature on Buber and Rosenzweig is too extensive to be cited here.
17. Sandra Lynch, *Philosophy and Friendship* (Edinburgh: University of Edinburgh Press, 2005), 72.
18. See Kenneth Paul Kramer, *Martin Buber's I and Thou: Practicing Living Dialogue* (Mahwah, NJ: Paulist Press, 2003), 84–85. The intellectual collaboration between Martin Buber and Paula Winkler was not exceptional. There were other marriages of male Jewish scholars and university-educated Jewish women in which the wife was very involved in the intellectual work of her husband, often at the expense of her own academic career. The historian Selma Stern-Täubler was involved in the work of her husband, the classical historian Eugen Täubler, as much as she published independently of him, and Jeannette Meisel Baron, an economist by training, was the writing partner of her husband, the historian Salo W. Baron, but did not publish on her own.
19. See Franz Rosenzweig, *F. Rosenzweig, Die "Gritli"-Briefe: Briefe an Margrit Rosenstock-Huessy*, ed. Inke Ruhle and Reinhold Mayer, with a preface by Rafael Rosenzweig (Tübingen: Bilam Verlag, 2002). The publications of the letters generated enormous scholarly attention. For an initial assessment of this published correspondence, see Michael Zank, "The Rosenzweig-Rosenstock Triangle, or, What Can We Learn from the Letters to Gritli? A Review Essay," *Modern Judaism* 23 (2003): 74–78. Zank is rather critical of Rosenzweig's personality—"a brilliant and elegant snob given to bouts of pettiness and vanity" (75). A much more positive evaluation of Rosenzweig's personality, as well as the significance of the letters to the interpretation of Rosenzweig's philosophy, is offered in Ephraim Meir, *Letters of Love, Franz Rosenzweig's Spiritual Biography and Oeuvre in Light of the Gritli Letters* (New York: Peter Lang, 2006).
20. Gritli's acceptance of Rosenzweig's rediscovered Jewishness is akin to a therapist's acceptance of a patient. The growth of the psychoanalytic movement during the 1920s, in which women and especially Jewish women were deeply involved, might be relevant to our understanding of the relationship between Gritli and Rosenzweig. Friendship within the psychoanalytic movement requires a separate study, but let me only note that Freud had a deep intellectual friendship with Lou Andreas-Salomé (d. 1937), a very talented novelist and essayist who (like Gritli) was also a great listener. See Andreas-Salomé, *The Freud Journal of Lou Andreas-Salomé*, trans. Stanley A. Leavy (New York: Basic Books, 1964). As psychoanalysis delved into

the psychology of love and self-love and the dynamic of erotic fantasies, it would become harder to differentiate between "friendship" and "love." One element of differentiation could be the presence of sex or lack thereof. For example, whereas Andreas-Salomé had friendships with Freud and with Nietzsche that did not include sex, she had a very passionate love affair with Rainer Maria Rilke, notwithstanding the huge age difference between them (when they met, she was thirty-six and he was twenty-one). The affair lasted several years (1897–1900), turned into friendship after Rilke's marriage in 1901, and lasted until Rilke's death in 1926.

21. Meir, *Letters of Love*, 82.
22. Meir, 82.
23. Meir, 149.
24. Meir, 166. For Meir, who looks at Edith through the lens of traditional Judaism, Edith was the ideal "fitting helper" (Gen. 2:18), or *ezer kenegdo*. A feminist reading of the marriage between Edith and Franz could be more critical.
25. See Zank, "Rosenzweig-Rosentsock Triangle," 76–77.
26. Harriet Pass Freidenreich, *Female, Jewish, Educated: The Lives of Central European University Women* (Bloomington: Indiana University Press, 2002); Harriet Pass Freidenreich, "How Central European Jewish Women Confronted Modernity," in *Women and Judaism: New Insights and Scholarship*, ed. Frederick E. Greenspahn (New York: New York University Press, 2009), 131–52.
27. Freidenreich, *Female, Jewish, Educated*, 141.
28. Freidenreich, 142.
29. Freidenreich, 144.
30. Ron H. Feldman, *The Jew as Pariah: Jewish Identity and Politics in in the Modern Age* (New York: Grove Press, 1978); Jerome Kohn and Ron H. Feldman, eds., *Hannah Arendt: The Jewish Writings* (New York: Schocken, 2007), especially Ron H. Feldman, "The Jew as Pariah: The Case of Hannah Arendt," xli–lxxvi; Richard J. Bernstein, *Hannah Arendt and the Jewish Question* (Cambridge, MA: MIT Press, 1996).
31. The use of the terms *pariah* and *parvenu* as two human types was proposed by the French Jewish journalist Bernard Lazar to analyze modern anti-Semitism. His analysis framed Arendt's interpretation of Varnhagen's and her own Jewishness. See Bernstein, *Hannah Arendt*, 14–45.
32. The book was completed only after she settled in the United States and was published first in English (1958) and then in German (1959). Hannah Arendt, *Rahel Varnhagen: The Life of a Jewish Woman*, rev. ed. (New York: Harcourt Brace Jovanovich, 1974).
33. See Lette Kohler, ed., *Within Four Walls: The Correspondence Between Hannah Arendt and Heinrich Blücher, 1936–1968* (New York: Harcourt, 1996).
34. The secondary literature on Arendt is too extensive to be cited here. The standard intellectual biography is Elisabeth Young-Bruehl, *Hannah Arendt: For the Love of the World* (New Haven: Yale University Press, 1982).
35. For a detailed and subtle analysis of the relationship between Arendt and Heidegger, see Antonia Grunenberg, *Hannah Arendt and Martin Heidegger: History of Love*, trans. Peg Birmingham, Kristina Lebedeva, and Elizabeth von Witzke Birmingham (Bloomington: Indiana University Press, 2006). Arendt was not oblivious to Heidegger's moral failings. She recognized his weakness and the presence of "a clearly pathological streak" (Grunenberg, *Hannah Arendt*, 191) in him, and yet Arendt revived the friendship with Heidegger after the war, and she was instrumental in the rehabilitation of his philosophic reputation.
36. See Lotte Kohler and Hans Saner, eds., *Hannah Arendt / Karl Jaspers Correspondence, 1926–1969*, trans. Robert and Rita Kimmer (New York: Harcourt Brace Jovanovich, 1992). Arendt saw in Jaspers the embodiment of civilization,

and she eulogized him at his funeral as a man "who realizes human existence in an exemplary way, and is the bodily incarnation of something that we would otherwise know only as a concept or ideal. In a singular way Jaspers exemplified in himself, as it were, a fusion of freedom, reason, and communication." Cited in Marcus Raskin, "Philosophers and Friends, Review of *Hanna Arendt/Karl Jaspers Correspondence, 1926–1969*," *Washington Post*, November 29, 1992, 6. See also Jon Nixon, "Hannah Arendt and Karl Jaspers: The Time of Friendship," *Journal of Educational Administration and History* 48, no. 2 (2016): 160–72.

37. Jon Nixon, *Politics of Friendship* (London: Bloomsbury, 2015), 7. Although Arendt is not commonly viewed as a Jewish philosopher of dialogue, her ideas can be easily seen as a political extension of Buber's analysis of the "in-between."

38. Lisa J. Ditsch, "On Friendship in Dark Times," in *Feminist Interpretations of Hannah Arendt*, ed. Bonnie Honig (University Park: Penn State University Press, 1995), 288.

39. Ditsch, "On Friendship," 289. The focus on the "in-between" is quite similar to Buber's relational philosophy.

40. Nixon, *Politics of Friendship*, 36.

41. On her friendships with Scholem and Jonas, see Christian Wiese, "Zionism, the Holocaust, and Judaism in a Secular World: New Perspectives on Hans Jonas's Friendship with Gershom Scholem and Hannah Arendt," in *The Legacy of Hans Jonas: Judaism and the Phenomenon of Life*, ed. Hava Tirosh-Samuelson and Christian Wiese (Leiden: Brill, 2008), 159–93. On Arendt's friendships with women, see Kathleen B. Jones, *Diving for Pearls: A Thinking Journey with Hannah Arendt* (San Diego: Thinking Women Books, 2013).

42. Nixon, *Politics of Friendship*, 48.

43. Betty Friedan, *The Feminine Mystique* (New York: W. W. Norton, 1963). Many other secular Jewish women were at the helm of the feminist movement, but their social critique of patriarchy did not amount to a full-fledged philosophy, let alone Jewish philosophy.

44. For an assessment of the changed status of Arendt in feminist theory, see Bonnie Honig, "Introduction: The Arendt Questions in Feminism," in Honig, *Feminist Interpretations*, 1–16; and Mary G. Dietz, "Feminist Reception of Hannah Arendt," in Honig, *Feminist Interpretations*, 17–50.

45. Virginia Held, *The Ethics of Care: Personal, Political and Global* (Oxford: Oxford University Press, 2006), 23.

46. Held, *Ethics of Care*, 23.

47. See, for example, Janice G. Raymond, *A Passion for Friends: Toward a Philosophy of Female Affection* (Boston: Beacon Press, 1986).

48. Joan Tronto, *Moral Boundaries: A Political Argument for an Ethics of Care* (New York: Routledge, 1994), 3. Tronto offers excellent philosophical exposition of Gilligan's ideas on pp. 77–97.

49. Tronto, *Moral Boundaries*, 102.

50. Tronto, 106.

51. Responsibility is the central value of Emmanuel Levinas's philosophy. For a recent attempt to read Tronto's ethics of care in light of Levinas's philosophy, see W. Wolf Dietdrich, Roger Burggraeve, and Chris Gastmans, "Toward a Levinasian Care Ethics: A Dialogue Between the Thoughts of Joan Tronto and Emmanuel Levinas," *Ethical Perspectives: Journal of the European Ethics Network* 13, no. 1 (2006): 36–61. See also note 59.

52. Joan C. Tronto, *Caring Democracy: Markets, Equality and Justice* (New York: New York University Press, 2013).

53. Marilyn Friedman, *What Are Friends For? Feminist Perspectives on Personal Relationship and Moral Theory* (Ithaca: Cornell University Press, 1993).

54. Friedman, *What Are Friends For?*, 207.

55. Friedman, 234.

56. Friedman, 197.

57. Friedman, 248–49.

58. A good example is Leora Batnitzky "Dependency and Vulnerability: Jewish and Feminist Existentialist Construction of the Human," in *Women and Gender in Jewish Philosophy*, ed. Hava Tirosh-Samuelson (Bloomington: Indiana University Press, 2004), 127–52. The essay examines Buber's and Rosenzweig's understandings of the self in light of Tronto's ethics of care. For an overview of feminist Jewish philosophy, see also Hava Tirosh-Samuelson, "Feminism and Gender," in *The Cambridge History of Jewish Philosophy in the Modern Era*, ed. Martin Kavka, Zachary Braiterman, and David Novak (Cambridge: Cambridge University Press, 2012), 154–89.

59. An exception to this generalization is Yudit Kornberg Greenberg, ed., *Encyclopedia of Love in World Religions*, 2 vols. (Santa Barbara: ABC-CLIO, 2007). Her interest in the topic developed out of her scholarship on Rosenzweig's philosophy. See Yudit Kornberg Greenberg, *Better Than Wine: Love, Poetry, and Prayer in the Thought of Franz Rosenzweig* (Atlanta: Scholars Press, 1996).

CHAPTER 12

A Friendship in the Prophetic Tradition
*Abraham Joshua Heschel and
Martin Luther King Jr.*

SUSANNAH HESCHEL

The long tradition of prophetic rhetoric in the United States reached an extraordinary peak with Martin Luther King Jr., who made the Hebrew prophets central figures of the civil rights movement. King's voice, imbued with the words of Amos and Isaiah, was enhanced by a radical innovation in the understanding of the Hebrew prophets introduced by the Jewish theologian Abraham Joshua Heschel. The friendship between King and Heschel and their shared theological sensibilities extended across the differences in their backgrounds and religious beliefs. What brought them together were the prophets: the rhetoric of indictment and hope, irony and promise, but above all, the prophetic understanding of God.

The photograph of the front row of marchers crossing Selma's Pettus Bridge in March 1965 has become an iconic image in Jewish circles. A multicultural, multifaith mélange, the photograph represents an eschatological dream: a religious Jew, a rabbi from a Hasidic family in Poland, walking arm in arm with Rev. Martin Luther King Jr., Ralph Bunche, Ralph Abernathy, John Lewis, and other civil rights leaders to demand that Congress pass the Voting Rights Act and to protest Jim Crow laws and racism. The rabbi was Abraham Joshua Heschel, professor of Jewish ethics and mysticism at the Jewish Theological Seminary in New York City.

AN UNUSUAL FRIENDSHIP

King and Heschel met in Chicago in January 1963. They both participated in civil rights and antiwar demonstrations and lectured together in Jewish, Christian, interfaith, and university settings. Heschel had arrived in the United States as a refugee from Hitler's Europe in March 1940, "plucked as a brand from the fires," as he wrote.[1]

A few months after that momentous 1965 Selma march, Heschel founded Clergy and Laymen Concerned About Vietnam (CALCAV), the organization responsible for a major event at Riverside Church in April 1967, at which Dr. King spoke out against the war. CALCAV also organized a prayer vigil against the war at Arlington National Cemetery, held in February of 1968, in which they both participated. Indeed, photographs of Dr. King and Rabbi Heschel standing in silent witness at the cemetery are often mislabeled as a civil rights demonstration—though by 1968, opposition to the war was defined as part of the movement for civil rights and against racism (figure 12.1).

Unusual for the time, the friendship between Heschel and King surprised many, but it also inspired people because the two came from such different backgrounds. The pair found an intimacy that grew out of their religious commitments and transcended the growing public rifts between their two communities. Heschel brought King and his message to a wide Jewish audience, and King made Heschel a central figure in the struggle for civil rights. Often lecturing together, they both spoke about racism as the root of poverty and its role in the war in Vietnam. Both also addressed issues concerning Zionism and Israel, as well as the struggles of Jews in the Soviet Union. The transcendent issue, though, was "saving the soul of America," the motto of the Southern Christian Leadership Conference (SCLC).

Their first meeting in Chicago took place at the 1963 Conference on Religion and Race, planned by an interfaith organization, the National Conference of Christians and Jews (NCCJ), where each gave a keynote lecture. They had known of each other, and the bond between them after meeting in person was immediate. King's speech at that occasion, "A Challenge to Justice and Love," was straightforward, affirming that the struggle against racism was an interfaith effort: "The churches and synagogues have an opportunity and a duty to lift up their voices like a trumpet and declare unto the people the immorality of segregation. We must affirm that every human life is a reflex of divinity, and every act of injustice mars and defaces the image

FIGURE 12.1 Rabbi Abraham Joshua Heschel and Dr. Martin Luther King, protesting the Vietnam War, Arlington National Cemetery. Courtesy of John C. Goodwin Photo Catalog.

of God in man. The undergirding philosophy of segregation is diametrically opposed to the undergirding philosophy of our Judeo-Christian heritage, and all the dialectics of the logicians cannot make them lie down together."[2] Heschel opened his speech by bringing his audience into a dramatic biblical narrative: "At the first conference on religion and race, the main participants were Pharaoh and Moses.... The outcome of that summit meeting has not come to an end. Pharaoh is not ready to capitulate. The exodus began, but is far from having been completed. In fact, it was easier for the children of Israel to cross the Red Sea than for a Negro to cross certain university campuses."[3]

Heschel's speech electrified the audience, as did King's speech the next day. Heschel's tone was passionate and emotional and strikingly different from the typical dry sociological analyses of racism common in that era, as James Cone notes.[4] Rather than analyzing racism in legal or political terms, Heschel developed a theological approach that Cornel West has called the strongest condemnation of racism by a white man since William Garrison. In his speech, Heschel declared, "Racism is Satanism, unmitigated evil. . . . You cannot worship God and at the same time look at man as if he were a horse." Religion cannot coexist with racism, he said; it is a grave violation of the fundamental religious principle not to murder. Racism is public humiliation, which is condemned in the Talmud as tantamount to murder: "One should rather commit suicide than offend a person publicly." Heschel viewed racism as mired in institutional social structures for which individuals are responsible: "How long will I continue to be tolerant of, even a participant in, acts of embarrassing and humiliating human beings?" His critique extended to religious communities: "We worry more about the purity of dogma than about the integrity of love. . . . What is lacking is a sense of the monstrosity of inequality."[5]

Heschel's speech was not a jeremiad of denunciation; he drew instead on Jewish teachings regarding obligation. According to Heschel, "Religion is a demand, God is a challenge," making racism "the test of our integrity, a magnificent spiritual opportunity" for radical change. What is at stake, Heschel argued, is God: "Reverence for God is shown in reverence for man. . . . To be arrogant toward man is to be blasphemous toward God." Religion and race are two diametrically opposed words that cannot be uttered in the same sentence, he said.[6]

SHARED THEOLOGICAL SENSIBILITIES

What created the bond between Heschel and King was, in significant part, a shared theological sensibility. Both had disdain for the popular liberal Protestant thinkers of the era and a skepticism with respect to certain theological orthodoxies. They were dissatisfied with Paul Tillich's definition of God as the "ground of being" as uninspiring and unhelpful in the face of injustice. King wrote in his doctoral dissertation, "So Tillich ends with a God who is a sub-personal reservoir of power, somewhat akin to the impersonalism of Hindu Vedantism. He chooses the less than personal to explain personality, purpose, and meaning."[7] What was missing for both Heschel and King was God's transcendence. At the same time, both thought that Karl Barth's theology left "the average mind lost in the fog of theological abstractions," as

King wrote, and both appreciated Reinhold Niebuhr's analyses of American political culture and Niebuhr's deep awareness of human sin and national wickedness.[8] Both approached biblical scholarship with suspicion, feeling that scholars were more interested in historical criticism than elucidating its meaning. King would no doubt have agreed with Heschel's assertion on the opening page of his major book, *God in Search of Man*, that religion declined in the modern era not because of the challenges of philosophy or science but because the religious message of both liberalisms and orthodoxies had become "insipid."[9]

The reigning theological paradigms, both liberal and conservative, Christian and Jewish, were not helpful, and Heschel created a new theological approach that, like King's, combined a conservative theology with liberal politics. While his initial theological publications appeared during the first seven years after the end of World War II, his study of the prophets first appeared in English in 1962. The book was a major expansion of his German doctoral dissertation, completed in December 1932 and published in German under the title *Die Prophetie* in 1936. During the years Heschel was translating this book into English, he was attentive to Dr. King's activities and the civil rights movement, and his book reflects the political passions of the era.

The context was tense: the Birmingham campaign was underway during the first months of 1963. On June 11, 1963, George Wallace, governor of Alabama, attempted to block the enrollment of black students Vivian Malone and James Hood at the University of Alabama; federal troops forced him to step aside. That night, President John F. Kennedy delivered a major televised speech promising legislation and calling civil rights a "moral issue."[10] The next day, Medgar Evers, field secretary of the National Association for the Advancement of Colored People (NAACP) in Mississippi, was murdered.

COLLABORATIVE POLITICAL ACTIVITY

King was preparing that summer of 1963 for the March on Washington for Jobs and Freedom, organized by A. Philip Randolph and Bayard Rustin, a demonstration Kennedy was hoping to avert. Kennedy invited a group of civil rights leaders, including Heschel, to the White House for a meeting on June 20, 1963. Heschel replied to the invitation with a telegram dated June 16:

I look forward to privilege of being present at meeting tomorrow four PM. Likelihood exists that Negro problem will be like the weather. Everybody talks about it but nobody does anything about it. Please demand of religious leaders personal involvement not just solemn declaration. We forfeit right to worship God as long as we continue to humiliate Negroes. Church synagogue have failed, they must repent. Ask of religious leaders to call for national repentance and personal sacrifice. Let religious leaders donate one month's salary toward fund for Negro housing and education. I propose that you Mr. President declare state of moral emergency. A Marshall Plan for aid to Negroes is becoming a necessity. The hour calls for moral grandeur and spiritual audacity.[11] (See figure 12.2)

In this moment of violence, Heschel called on the president to declare a "state of moral emergency."[12] The phrase is unique; governments may declare a state of emergency that suspends political rights, abolishes a legislature, or imposes martial law. What Heschel demanded was something different: not an abolition of citizens' rights but a call to a moral obligation that transcends the state, the law, and the government. Based on his theology of Judaism, he called for recognition of a sphere rooted not in political interests but in what he believed to be a transcendent, divinely ordained bond of justice. His language was prophetic in the spirit of his just-published book, *The Prophets*.

The March on Washington took place in August 1963, with representatives of major religious and civil rights organizations participating. Rabbi Joachim Prinz, president of the American Jewish Congress and also a refugee from Nazi Berlin, was one of the speakers, and his words echoed those of King and Heschel. Prinz declared, "Bigotry and hatred are not the most urgent problem. The most urgent, the most disgraceful, the most shameful and the most tragic problem is silence."[13] Similarly, King had declared in a 1957 speech to the NCCJ, "It may well be that the greatest tragedy of this period of social transition is not the glaring noisiness of the bad people, but the appalling silence of the good people."[14] Heschel wrote in his study of the prophets that the opposite of good is not evil but indifference, and in a free society, some are guilty but all are responsible.

President Kennedy did not declare a state of moral emergency, nor did clergy donate a month of salary to housing for African Americans. If anything, the tensions in the United States grew even more dire. Just weeks

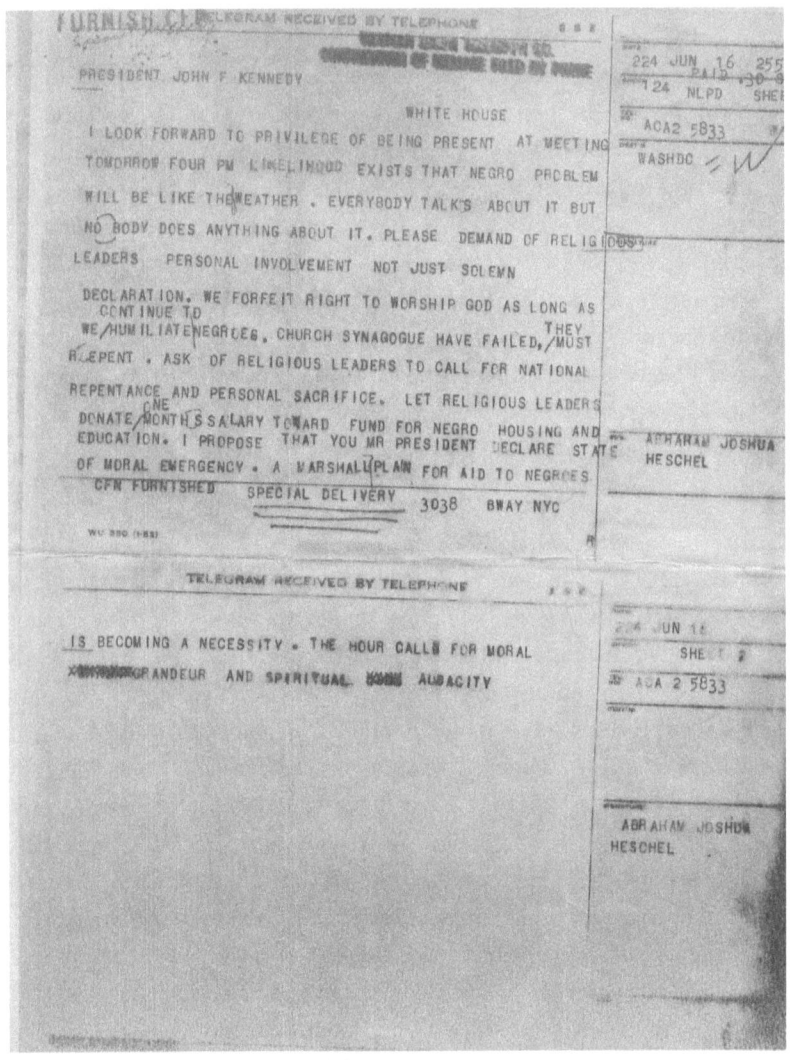

FIGURE 12.2 Telegram from Rabbi Abraham Joshua Heschel to President John F. Kennedy. Courtesy of Susannah Heschel.

later, on September 15, 1963, a church in Birmingham was bombed, killing four young black girls. That same day, James Bevel and Diane Nash launched the Alabama Project, which ultimately led to the famous march from Selma to Montgomery in March 1965. After the Montgomery bus boycott, the lunch counter sit-ins of 1960, and the vicious attacks on the Freedom Riders seeking to integrate the interstate transportation network that same year,

1964 saw numerous consequential, dramatic developments. These included congressional passage of the Twenty-Fourth Amendment ending the poll tax on voters; Freedom Summer in Mississippi, including the murder of James Cheney, Andrew Goodman, and Michael Schwerner in June; the passage of the Civil Rights Act on July 2; the assassination of Malcolm X on February 21, 1965; and Bloody Sunday on March 7, 1965.

Just a few months after they met, King joined Heschel at a hotel in the Catskills to speak to a convention of Jews affiliated with the Conservative movement, the first of many joint appearances. Both spoke about race and also about Israel and Zionism and the need to win religious freedom for Jews in the Soviet Union. A year later, in December 1964, King was awarded the Nobel Peace Prize. By 1965, now as close friends, they worked together on various projects, particularly on the growing opposition to the war in Vietnam. The year 1965 was a momentous and highly productive year for Heschel. In the fall of 1965, he became Harry Emerson Fosdick Visiting Professor at Union Theological Seminary. His inaugural address, "No Religion Is an Island," was delivered just a few weeks after the Vatican issued its landmark statement, *Nostra Aetate*, that redefined the Roman Catholic Church's relations with Jews and Judaism. Heschel had been active for several years as a consultant to Catholic cardinals, bishops, and theologians working on the document, and he served as a Jewish representative to the Second Vatican Council. At the same time, he was teaching and also completing a three-volume book in Hebrew on rabbinic theology in which he demonstrated the continuation of prophetic understandings of revelation within rabbinic thought.

HESCHEL, KING, AND THE HEBREW PROPHETIC TRADITION

The prophets—both Heschel's book and the biblical figures—drew Heschel and King together. Both men were trained theologians who also knew how to preach. King was the organizer and public figure, while Heschel was the theologian and scholar with the voice of a public intellectual. For both, the prophets were central to nearly all their speeches and writings. While prophetic rhetoric has a long public history in the United States, as the scholar Cathleen Kaveny demonstrates, it was not the rhetoric of the prophets alone that stood out for them.[15] For King and Heschel, the prophets were also extraordinary human beings with passionate emotional lives, people who knew how to pray and who also created powerful symbolic moments. The force of King's and Heschel's words also stemmed from their deployment of the emotive, poetic language of the prophets.

The passions of the prophets were also reflections, for King and Heschel, of the passion of God. Heschel wrote that God "has a stake in the human situation.... Man is not only an image of God; he is a perpetual concern of God."[16] Similarly, during the Montgomery bus boycott, King declared, "God is using Montgomery as His proving ground."[17] On January 30, 1956, just after learning that his home in Montgomery had been bombed, King stood outside to calm angry neighbors, assuring his followers, "Remember, if I am stopped, this movement will not stop because God is with the movement."[18] Later, in 1968, he said, "It is possible for me to falter, but I am profoundly secure in my knowledge that God loves us; He has not worked out a design for our failure."[19]

Not only did King integrate verses from the prophetic books of the Bible into his speeches; he also transferred the current moment into biblical time. He spoke of himself as Moses on the mountaintop, and he described civil rights activists as the burning bush: "Bull Connor next would say, 'Turn the firehoses on.' And as I said to you the other night Bull Connor didn't know history. He knew a kind of physics that somehow didn't relate to the transphysics that we knew about, and that was the fact that there was a certain kind of fire that no water could put out."[20]

Heschel spoke in similar terms in his 1963 speech "Religion and Race," reminding his audience that all white people, including Jews, were Pharaoh, denying freedom to African Americans. In another speech, "The White Man on Trial," delivered in February 1964 at a conference in New York City, Heschel reminded his audiences that the Israelites, just after leaving Egypt, had complained of the bitter water they found at Marah. They asked Moses, "What shall we drink?" Chiding his audience, Heschel said,

> This episode seems shocking. What a comedown! Only three days earlier they had reached the highest peak of prophetic and spiritual exaltation, and now they complain about such a prosaic and unspiritual item as water.... The Negroes of America behave just like the children of Israel. Only in 1963 they experienced the miracle of having turned the tide of history, the joy of finding millions of Americans involved in the struggle for civil rights, the exaltation

of fellowship, the March to Washington. Now only a few months later they have the audacity to murmur: "What shall we drink? We want adequate education, decent housing, proper employment." How ordinary, how unpoetic, how annoying! . . . We are ready to applaud dramatic struggles once a year in Washington. For the sake of lofty principles, we will spend a day or two in jail somewhere in Alabama. . . . The tragedy of Pharaoh was the failure to realize that the exodus from slavery could have spelled redemption for both Israel and Egypt. Would that Pharaoh and the Egyptians had joined the Israelites in the desert and together stood at the foot of Sinai![21]

Heschel's study of the prophets was multipronged. As noted, he delivered a devastating critique of Protestant biblical scholarship, developed new criteria for interpreting the prophetic texts, and brought to the fore a neglected but central Jewish theological tradition of understanding God, revelation, and the human. Because his book was initially published in 1936, in the midst of the Third Reich, it was neglected by European biblical scholars and garnered most of its attention from a few American scholars. The appearance of the expanded English edition, however, gained enormous attention among Bible scholars and theologians and especially among civil rights activists. Andrew Young, James Lawson, Vincent Harding, C. T. Vivian, and Bayard Rustin were among the young activists in the nonviolence movement who told this author that they carried a copy of the paperback edition in their back pockets for inspiration and consolation.

Where do Heschel and King fit into the understanding of the prophetic role in American politics and religion? In postwar American Jewish discussions, the prophets reemerged as figures of ethics in the political realm. The political scientist Michael Walzer presented the prophets as political figures, critics of the state presenting "an abnormal politics that is sometimes admirable and sometimes not."[22] In his book on the prophets, the conservative commentator Norman Podhoretz presented the central message of the prophets as attacks on paganism.[23]

By contrast, the Catholic theologian Cathleen Kaveny urged that the passionate jeremiad of the American prophetic tradition be reoriented as an affirmation of solidarity with those under indictment; she writes that prophetic admonition should be a form of "moral chemotherapy."[24] As chemotherapy, prophetic indictments may cure society of its moral cancers, but only when formulated constructively; otherwise, they can destroy the healthy body politic. This is certainly the spirit of King and Heschel, whose critiques always came with an affirmation of basic American values as well as specific demands for change, whether in legislation or political policies. The political theorist George Shulman captures an additional element of the prophetic nature of King and Heschel—namely, their focus on redemption. For Shulman, "To face race in America is to be compelled toward prophecy."[25] Prophecy speaks in the voices of rebuke, theodicy, and lamentation, but it also leads to redemption. In Shulman's view, redemption is the necessary means of purification to expunge America of racial domination. Redemption is the voice that renders historical suffering intelligible, lamentable, and bearable. More than moral indictment presented in religious language, King and Heschel promised redemption. They were powerful figures not only for what they preached but also for who they were as persons and, indeed, for their ability to forge a friendship that also seemed to promise redemption.

For both Heschel and King, what prophecy demands is an adherence to justice that transcends government and society. Each spoke of "maladjustment" as the prophetic goal. Heschel told an interviewer in 1972, "I would say about individuals [that] an individual dies when he ceases to be surprised. I am surprised every morning that I see the sunshine again. When I see an act of evil, I'm not accommodated. I don't accommodate myself to the violence that goes on everywhere; I'm still surprised. That's why I'm against it, why I can hope against it. We must learn how to be surprised. Not to adjust ourselves. I am the most maladjusted person in society."[26] In a 1957 speech, King also spoke of his maladjustment:

> I never intend to adjust myself to an economic system that will take necessities from the masses to give luxuries to the classes. I never intend to adjust myself to the madness of militarism and the self-defeating effects of physical violence. And my friends, I call upon you to be maladjusted to all of these things, for you see, it may be that the salvation of the world lies in the hands of the maladjusted. The challenge of this hour is to be maladjusted. Yes, as maladjusted as the prophet Amos, who in the midst of the tragic injustices of his day, could cry out in words that echo across the generations: "Let judgment run down like waters and righteousness like a mighty stream." ... The world is in desperate need of such maladjustment.

And through such courageous maladjustment, we will be able to emerge from the bleak and desolate midnight of man's inhumanity to man into the bright and glittering daybreak of freedom and justice.[27]

The civil rights movement introduced a new dimension of prophecy. What generated the power of the movement was not only prophetic rhetoric rooted in the preaching of the black Christian tradition and the classic American jeremiad but also the political use of the body—that is, responding to violence with nonviolence. The body became the symbolic representation of prophecy—the symbol as actor in its assertion of nonviolence. The presence of the nonviolent body, sitting or marching, made the teachings visible.

For Heschel, the claim that prophecy made upon its listeners assumes a mutual commitment to human life that is prior to the political; the human contract is prior to the social contract and necessary to constitute it. Prophetic speech is not simply to be admired, nor are we supposed to focus on the rhetoric. Rather, the prophet speaks to engage us ethically, to make it clear that we have a moral obligation to respond not simply to the prophet but to those who stand in suffering as a consequence of our immoral society. Prophecy is anchored in civic duty: we do not simply listen to the prophet. Instead, we are compelled to act because fundamental to prophecy is the awareness that we stand continually before choices framed by the state and society. In light of these convictions, what King and Heschel sought was to create a bond among us that was rooted in a commitment to a moral demand that stands apart from the laws of the state.

MARCHING TOGETHER FOR RACIAL JUSTICE

The march from Selma to Montgomery was a major event for both Heschel and King. A few days before, in mid-March 1965, Heschel led a delegation of eight hundred people to FBI headquarters in New York City to protest the brutal treatment demonstrators were receiving in Selma. There had been violence against the demonstrators in Selma earlier that month, and they had been prevented for two months from beginning the march. The New York delegation was not permitted to enter the FBI building, but Heschel was allowed inside, surrounded by sixty police officers, to present a petition to the regional FBI director. On Friday, March 19, two days before the Selma march was scheduled to begin, Heschel received a telegram from

King, inviting him to join the marchers in Selma. Heschel flew to Selma from New York on Saturday night and was welcomed as one of the leaders into the front row of marchers, with King, Bunche, and Abernathy. Each of them wore flower leis, brought by Hawaiian delegates. In an unpublished memoir written upon his returning from Selma, Heschel described the extreme hostility he encountered from whites in Alabama that week from the moment he arrived at the airport. He also described the kindness he was shown by Dr. King's assistants, particularly Rev. Andrew Young, who hovered over him during the march with great concern.

Heschel's presence in the front row of marchers was a visual symbol of religious Jewish commitment to civil rights and "stirred not only the Jewish religious community but Jews young and old into direct action, galvanizing the whole spectrum of activists from fund-raisers to lawyers."[28] Not everyone reacted as positively to the marchers; Alabama Republican representative William L. Dickinson asserted on the floor of the House of Representatives that the march was a communist plot and that "drunkenness and sex orgies were the order of the day."[29]

Upon his return home, Heschel described his experience in his diary:

> I thought of having walked with Hasidic rabbis on various occasions. I felt a sense of the Holy in what I was doing. Dr. King expressed several times to me his appreciation. He said, "I cannot tell you how much your presence means to us. You cannot imagine how often Reverend [C. T.] Vivian and I speak about you." Dr. King said to me that this was the greatest day in his life and the most important civil rights demonstration.... I felt again what I have been thinking about for years—that Jewish religious institutions have again missed a great opportunity, namely, to interpret a civil rights movement in terms of Judaism. The vast majority of Jews participating actively in it are totally unaware of what the movement means in terms of the prophetic traditions.[30]

Just before the march began, a service was held at Brown's Chapel, where Heschel read Psalm 27: "The Lord is my light and my salvation; whom shall I fear?"[31]

Heschel wrote in his diary, "I felt my legs were praying." Hasidism sought to endow all physical acts with the presence of the soul. To walk with a rebbe meant to experience the holy in the quotidian, to feel the divine radiance emanating from him, and recognize that walking, too, can be directed to heaven as prayer.

HESCHEL, KING, AND THE VIETNAM WAR

Whether Dr. King should speak out publicly against the war in Vietnam was a topic that preoccupied Heschel during the years between 1965 and 1967. Would his public opposition to the war hurt the civil rights movement? Which was the better political course, and which was the greater moral good? Lacking widespread support even within the SCLC for a public position against the war, King came under severe attack for his opposition. King's outspokenness against the war did not win approval from the major black organizations. Civil rights leaders, including Bunche, Whitney Young, Roy Wilkins, Jackie Robinson, and Senator Edward Brooke, publicly criticized him, and major newspapers within both the black and white communities editorialized against him.[32] King was attacked for possibly undermining President Lyndon Johnson's support for the civil rights movement. The Student Non-violent Coordinating Committee (SNCC) and the Congress of Racial Equality (CORE) opposed the war, but the Urban League and the NAACP defended it. Whitney Young stated, "The greatest freedom that exists for Negroes . . . is the freedom to die in Vietnam."[33] King's address against the war in Vietnam, one of his most important speeches, was delivered on April 4, 1967, to an enormous overflow audience at Riverside Church in New York City at a gathering organized by CALCAV. He was introduced by Heschel, who stated,

> Our thoughts on Vietnam are sores, destroying our trust, ruining our most cherished commitments with burdens of shame. We are pierced to the core with pain, and it is our duty as citizens to say no to the subversiveness of our government, which is ruining the values we cherish. . . . The blood we shed in Vietnam makes a mockery of all our proclamations, dedications, celebrations. Has our conscience become a fossil, is all mercy gone? If mercy, the mother of humility, is still alive as a demand, how can we say yes to our bringing agony to that tormented country? We are here because our own integrity as human beings is decaying in the agony and merciless killing done in our name. In a free society, some are guilty and all are responsible.

We are here to call upon the governments of the United States as well as North Vietnam to stand still and to consider that no victory is worth the price of terror, which all parties commit in Vietnam, North and South. Remember that the blood of the innocent cries forever. Should that blood stop to cry, humanity would cease to be.[34]

Echoing themes articulated by Heschel, King reminded his audience that the motto of the SCLC was "To save the soul of America," and he stated, "If America's soul becomes totally poisoned, part of the autopsy must read Vietnam.... A nation that continues year after year to spend more money on military defense than on programs of social uplift is approaching spiritual death."[35] King went on in his speech to call for a "revolution of values" in American society as the best defense against communism and "to remove those conditions of poverty, insecurity and injustice which are the fertile soil in which the seed of communism grows and develops."[36]

These were prophetic speeches and led to prophetic action. A few months later, CALCAV requested permission to hold a demonstration against the war at Arlington National Cemetery. Permission for a demonstration was denied, but a prayer service was permitted, with each person limited to one sentence. The event was held on February 6, 1968. The following month, on March 25, 1968, just ten days before he was assassinated, King returned to a hotel in the Catskills to deliver the keynote address at a birthday celebration honoring Heschel, convened by the Rabbinical Assembly of America, an umbrella organization of Conservative rabbis. This was their final meeting.

In his introduction of King to the audience, Heschel asked, "Where in America today do we hear a voice like the voice of the prophets of Israel? Martin Luther King is a sign that God has not forsaken the United States of America. God has sent him to us. His presence is the hope of America. His mission is sacred, his leadership of supreme importance to every one of us."[37] In response, King stated that Heschel "is indeed a truly great prophet. ... Here and there we find those who refuse to remain silent behind the safe security of stained glass windows, and they are forever seeking to make the great ethical insights of our Judeo-Christian heritage relevant in this day and in this age. I feel that Rabbi Heschel is one of the persons who is relevant at all times, always standing with prophetic insights to guide us through these difficult days."[38]

The death of King in April 1968 and of Heschel in December 1972 weakened the alliance between the African American and Jewish American prophetic traditions. Tensions between the two communities accelerated due to a variety of reasons, and no one had the stature of Heschel and King to help calm those tensions. In 1984, Jesse Jackson, who had been accused of anti-Semitism for a remark he made to a journalist about the Jewishness of New York City, addressed the country on live television at the 1984 Democratic National Convention. He asked for forgiveness and invoked the friendship that had become an American icon: "We are bound by Dr. Martin Luther King Jr. and Rabbi Abraham Heschel, crying out from their graves for us to reach common ground."[39]

The King-Heschel friendship has had an extraordinary afterlife as a source of profound inspiration for reconciliation across immense gulfs, especially as a source of hope to transcend the fraught political map of black-Jewish relations. Their friendship is a reminder of a great moment in which these two men, with radically different backgrounds, crossed immense gulfs of color, religion, and identity. Standing side by side, photographs of them are reprinted in publications about black-Jewish relations, and their friendship stands as a call for vision, hope, and transcendence of political conflict.

NOTES

1. Zechariah 3:2 and Amos 4:11.
2. The speech is reprinted in *Race: Challenge to Religion*, ed. Mathew Ahmann (Chicago: Henry Regnery, 1963), 161.
3. Abraham J. Heschel, "Religion and Race," in *The Insecurity of Freedom: Essays on Human Existence* (New York: Farrar, Straus and Giroux, 1966), 85.
4. James H. Cone, *The Cross and the Lynching Tree* (Maryknoll, NY: Orbis Press, 2011).
5. Heschel, "Religion and Race," 85–100.
6. Heschel, 85–100.
7. Martin Luther King Jr., "A Comparison of the Conceptions of God in the Thinking of Paul Tillich and Henry Nelson Wieman" (PhD diss., Boston University, April 1955), accessed via the King Institute, Stanford University, King Papers, https://kinginstitute.stanford.edu/king-papers/documents/chapter-iii-comparison-conceptions-god-thinking-paul-tillich-and-henry-nelson.
8. Clayborne Carson, ed., *The Papers of Martin Luther King, Jr.* (Berkeley: University of California Press, 2007), 6:103.
9. Abraham J. Heschel, *God in Search of Man* (New York: Farrar, Straus and Cudahy, 1955), 1.
10. "The President Faces the Racial Crisis," *CBS News*, June 11, 1963.
11. The text of the telegram is reprinted in Susannah Heschel, ed., *Moral Grandeur and Spiritual Audacity: Essays of Abraham Joshua Heschel* (New York: Farrar, Straus and Giroux, 1996), vii.

12. Heschel, *Moral Grandeur and Spiritual Audacity*.
13. Joachim Prinz, "I Shall Not Be Silent," speech delivered at the March on Washington, August 28, 1963, http://www.prinzdocumentary.org.
14. Martin Luther King Jr., "The Christian Way of Life in Human Relations," address delivered at the General Assembly of the National Council of Churches, December 4, 1957, in Carson, *Papers of Martin Luther King, Jr.*, 6:326.
15. Cathleen Kaveny, *Prophecy Without Contempt: Religious Discourse in the Public Square* (Cambridge, MA: Harvard University Press, 2016).
16. Abraham J. Heschel, *The Prophets* (New York: Harper and Row, 1962), 226.
17. *The Papers of Martin Luther King, Jr.*, vol. 3, *Birth of a New Age*, ed. Clayborne Carson, Steward Carson, Pete Holloran, and Dana L. H. Powell (Berkeley: University of California Press, 1997) 3:151.
18. Gary J. Dorrien, *Breaking White Supremacy: Martin Luther King, Jr., and the Black Social Gospel* (New Haven: Yale University Press, 2018), 294.
19. King, "A Testament of Hope," in *A Testament of Hope: The Essential Writings of Martin Luther King, Jr.*, ed. James M. Washington (New York: Harper and Row, 1986), 314.
20. Cited by Michael Osborn, "The Last Mountaintop of Martin Luther King, Jr.," in *Martin Luther King, Jr., and the Sermonic Power of Public Discourse*, ed. Carolyn Calloway-Thomas and John Louis Lucaites (Tuscaloosa: University of Alabama Press, 1993), 153.
21. Abraham J. Heschel, "The White Man on Trial," in Heschel, *Insecurity of Freedom*, 101–3.
22. Michael Walzer, *In God's Shadow: Politics in the Hebrew Bible* (New Haven: Yale University Press, 2012), 68, as cited in Kaveny, *Prophecy Without Contempt*, 254.
23. Norman Podhoretz, *The Prophets: Who They Were, What They Are* (New York: Free Press, 2002).
24. Kaveny, *Prophecy Without Contempt*, 287.
25. George Shulman, *American Prophecy: Race and Redemption in American Political Culture* (Minneapolis: University of Minnesota Press, 2008), xvii.
26. "Carl Stern's Interview with Dr. Heschel," in Heschel, *Moral Grandeur*, 395–412.
27. Martin Luther King Jr., "Don't Sleep Through the Revolution," in *Witnessing for the Truth* (Boston: Beacon Press, 2014), 34.
28. Murray Friedman with Peter Binzen, *What Went Wrong? The Creation and Collapse of the Black-Jewish Alliance* (New York: Free Press, 1995), 191.
29. "March on Montgomery—the Untold Story," recorded in the United States Congressional Record, 89th Congress, Session 1.111 (5): 6333–35, March 30, 1965.
30. Cited in Susannah Heschel, introduction to Heschel, *Moral Grandeur*, xxiii–xxiv.
31. He wrote in an unpublished memoir that he had originally intended to read Psalm 15 ("O Lord, who shall sojourn in thy tent?") but changed his mind after he arrived in Selma.
32. Frederick J. Antczak, "When 'Silence Is Betrayal': An Ethical Criticism of the Revolution of Values in the Speech at Riverside Church," in Calloway-Thomas and Lucaites, *Martin Luther King, Jr.*, 134–35.
33. Adam Fairclough, "The Southern Christian Leadership Conference and the Second Reconstruction, 1957–1973," *Southern Atlantic Quarterly* 80, no. 2 (Spring 1981): 177–94.
34. Text reprinted in Heschel, introduction to Heschel, *Moral Grandeur*, xxiv. See also Robert McAfee Brown, Abraham J. Heschel, and Michael Novak, *Vietnam: Crisis of Conscience* (New York: Association Press, 1967).
35. King, "A Time to Break Silence," in *Testament of Hope*, 234, 241.
36. King, 234, 241.
37. King, 397.

38. The texts of both speeches are reprinted in King, *Testament of Hope*, 657–79. For King's comments about Heschel, see p. 659.
39. Jesse Jackson, "Speech to the Democratic National Convention," reprinted in *The Will of a People: A Critical Anthology of Great African American Speeches*, ed. Richard W. Leeman and Bernard K. Duffy (Carbondale: Southern Illinois University Press, 2012), 385.

CONTRIBUTORS

MARTHA ACKELSBERG is the George R. Kenan Jr. Professor of Government and former chair of the Program for the Study of Women and Gender, emerita, at Smith College. She is the author of *Resisting Citizenship: Feminist Essays on Politics, Community, and Democracy* and *Free Women of Spain: Anarchism and the Struggle for the Emancipation of Women*, as well as many other studies on gender, feminism, and politics.

MICHELA ANDREATTA is an assistant professor of Hebrew language and literature at the University of Rochester. She is the author of *Gersonide, Commento Cantico dei Cantici nella traduzione ebraico-latina di Flavio Mitridate* and *Moses Zacuto's Tofteh Arukh: A Seventeeth-Century Poem on the Jewish Afterlife*, as well as other studies in the history of early modern Italian Jewry.

JOSEPH DAVIS is an associate professor of Jewish thought at Gratz College. He is the author of *Yom-Tov Lipmann Heller: Portrait of a Seventeenth-Century Rabbi* and *Eliezer Eilburg: The Ten Questions and Memoir of a Renaissance Jewish Skeptic*, as well as numerous other studies on early modern Ashkenazi Jewry.

GLENN DYNNER is a professor of religion at Sarah Lawrence College. He is the author of *Men of Silk: The Hasidic Conquest of Polish Jewish Society* and *Yankel's Tavern: Jews, Liquor, and Life in the Kingdom of Poland*, and other studies on the history of Hasidism.

LAWRENCE FINE is the Irene Kaplan Leiwant Chair of Jewish Studies and a professor of religion, emeritus, at Mount Holyoke College. He is the author and editor of numerous books, including *Physician of the Soul, Healer of the Cosmos: Isaac Luria and His Kabbalistic Fellowship, Judaism in Practice: From the Middle Ages Through the Early Modern Period*, and *Safed Spirituality*.

EITAN P. FISHBANE is an associate professor of Jewish thought at the Jewish Theological Seminary of America. He is the author of *As Light Before Dawn: The Inner World of a Medieval Kabbalist* and *The Art of Mystical*

Narrative: A Poetics of the Zohar, along with numerous other studies on Kabbalah and Hasidism.

SUSANNAH HESCHEL is the Eli Black Professor of Jewish Studies at Dartmouth College. She is the author of *Abraham Geiger and the Jewish Jesus* and *The Aryan Jesus: Christian Theologians and the Bible in Nazi Germany*, as well as numerous other studies on modern Jewish and Christian Theology.

DANIEL JÜTTE is an associate professor of history at New York University. He is the author of *The Age of Secrecy: Jews, Christians, and the Economy of Secrets, 1400–1800* and *The Strait Gate: Thresholds and Power in Western History*.

EYAL LEVINSON is a postdoctoral research fellow at the European Research Center at the Hebrew University, devoted to the study of daily life among medieval European Jews. His doctoral dissertation (Bar Ilan University) is entitled "Youth and Masculinities in Medieval Ashkenaz."

SAUL M. OLYAN is the Samuel Ungerleider Jr. Professor of Judaic Studies and a professor of religious studies at Brown University. He has authored numerous books, including *Biblical Mourning: Ritual and Social Dimensions* and *Friendship in the Hebrew Bible*.

GEORGE SAVRAN teaches Hebrew Bible at the Schechter Institute for Jewish Studies in Jerusalem and has also taught at the Rothberg International School at the Hebrew University. Among his many studies, he is the author of *Telling and Retelling: Quotation in Biblical Narrative* and *Encountering the Divine: Theophany in Biblical Narrative*.

HAVA TIROSH-SAMUELSON is a Regents' Professor of History and the Irving and Miriam Lowe Professor of Modern Judaism at Arizona State University. She is the author of numerous books, including *Between Worlds: The Life and Thought of Rabbi David ben Judah Messer Leon* and *Happiness in Premodern Judaism: Virtue, Knowledge, and Well-Being*. She is also editor-in-chief of the multivolume Library of Contemporary Jewish Philosophers.

INDEX

Abernathy, Ralph, 232, 244
Abravanel, Isaac, 66, 67
Abravanel, Judah, 9, 62
   Dialogues on Love, 55, 67–71
Adler, Rachel, 108–9
Aelred of Rievaulx, 47, 53n31
Alabama Project, 238
Alguades, Meir ben Solomon, 65
Allen, Danielle, 107
Almosnino, Moses ben Baruch, 66–67
Alter, Yehuda Aryeh Leib, 169
Altschul, Moses Hanokh, 90
amicitia, 188, 201, 204
anagnorisis, 40
Anscombe, G. E. M., 216
antiwar demonstrations, 233, 234, 245–46
Aquinas, Thomas, 65
Archivolti, Samuel, 159
Arendt, Hannah, 13, 14, 15, 215, 220–23
Ariosto, Ludovico, *Orlando Furioso*, 145–46, 158–59
Aristotle
   commentaries on *Nicomachean Ethics*, 65–67
   Nicomachean Ethics, 9, 56–58, 63, 148
   The Politics, 121n17
   virtue ethics of, 65–66, 216
Arlington National Cemetery, prayer vigil at, 233, 234, 246
Ashkenaz, medieval, conceptions of friendship in
   Ecclesiastes and, 23, 24, 25
   Judah b. Samuel and, 22, 27–28, 29–30
   love story of Shmuel and Yehiel and, 21–22, 26, 34, 35
   Torah study and, 5
   See also Eleazar b. Judah
Autobiography (Modena), 151, 153, 154, 155, 157, 158
Avot de-Rabbi Natan, 6, 7, 25, 31

Bacon, Francis, 201
Ballin, Elia, 98
Bamberg, Moses, 93
Barber, Benjamin, 112

Baron, Jeannette, 14, 220, 228n18
Baron, Salo, 14, 185
Barth, Karl, 235
behavioral parity, 83, 85
ben adam le-ḥavero, 3
Benhabib, Seyla, 214
Berlin, Judah (Jost Liebmann), 92, 93–94
Blanchot, Maurice, 16n9, 215
Blücher, Heinrich, 220
B'not Esh, 110–11
boundary-crossing
   friendships as, 12–15, 212, 226–27
   in I-Thou relations, 217–18
   See also Christian-Jewish friendships; interfaith relations; male-female relationships
Broner, Esther, 120
   The Telling, 111
Buber, Martin, 13–14, 217–18
Buchler, Heinrich, 221
Bunche, Ralph, 232, 244, 245
Burckhardt, Jacob, 187
Burgwinkle, William, 24
business networks, 96, 98, 204

CALCAV (Clergy and Laymen Concerned About Vietnam), 233, 245, 246
Cebà, Ansaldo, 71, 155–56
Chaim of Hameln, 89, 90, 93–94, 95, 97, 99, 100
challenges of friendship
   failed friendships, 32, 134–35, 139–41
   overview of, 11–12
   secularism, 171–78
   sharing secrets and, 32
   See also boundary-crossing
Chazan, Robert, 21
child-rearing and gender, 117
Chiramonte, Nicola, 221
Christian-Jewish friendships
   in early modern world, 200–201
   Glückel on, 98–99
   Krafft memoirs on, 190–94, 201–2
   limits on, 71
   premodern, scholarly views of, 186

Christian-Jewish friendships (*continued*)
  in Renaissance Italy, 68
  See also King-Heschel friendship
civil rights movement, 238–39, 241, 243–45
Clergy and Laymen Concerned About Vietnam (CALCAV), 233, 245, 246
Cohen, Hermann, 216–17
Cohen, Issachar, 97
Cohen da Este, Jacob, 159–60
communitarian critique of liberalism, 112–13
comradery, 169–70
Cone, James, 234–35
confessionalization and interfaith relations, 197–98
Congress of Racial Equality, 245
consequentialism, 216, 224
context of friendship, historical and cultural, 2–3
contractual nature of friendship, 161
Copia Sullam, Sara, 9, 10, 12, 71, 155–57
Copio, Moses, 157–58
cosmic isomorphic principle, 42
covenant-making, friendship through, 86
Cromwell, Oliver, 197
Crusades, Hebrew chronicles of, 21

Dallam, Thomas, 196
Danziger, Yerahmiel Yisrael Yitzhak, 169, 170
davak, 83
David and Jonathan
  as brothers-in-law, 141
  covenant-making and, 86
  language describing friendship of, 151
  as prototype in Western culture, 24–25
  sharing of secrets between, 31
  spiritual dimension of friendship of, 26
  unequal status of, 83, 85
Dayan, Yankele, 171
dead, responsibilities of friendship to, 96
deontology, 215–16, 224
Derrida, Jacques, 16n9, 215
dialogical philosophy, 217–19
dialogue, as literary genre, 68
Dialogues on Love (*Dialoghi d'amore*, J. Abravanel), 55, 67–71
Dickinson, William L., 244
Di Gara, Giovanni, 147

Ecclesiastes, 23, 24, 25
Egypt, Jews in, 59
Eleazar b. Judah, 5, 22, 26–27, 28, 30, 31
  Hokhmat ha-Nefesh, 33

Eliezer ha-Gadol b. Isaac, 31–32, 34
Elijah Interfaith Institute, 16n9
Elukin, Jonathan, 200
emblematic literature, 163n16
Epicureans, 58
Epstein, Kalonymous Kalman, 177
equality, friendship as relationship of, 24, 107, 114, 116, 120
eros, 56, 58, 70
eroticism and friendship, 12, 151, 170
ethics of care, 224–26
Evers, Medgar, 236
existentialism, 217
Ezrat Nashim, 107, 108–9, 110, 112

Fabri, Felix, 195
failed friendships, 32, 134–35, 139–41, 171–74
family
  ethics of care and, 224–26
  expressions of greeting in, 138
  friendship among members of, 10, 90–91, 107, 141, 201
  in Genesis, 129–31, 133–34, 135
  privileging of, in interpersonal sphere, 4
  questioning structure and functioning of, 112–14
  See also twinship
female confraternities, 164n32
feminism
  Arendt and, 223
  Aristotle and, 72n8
  groups and organizations of, 111
  moral theory of, 224–27
  power of friendship model in, 111–17
  practices of friendship in, 107–11
  problems with friendship model in, 117–20
  twentieth-century Jewish, 106
Ficino, Marsilio, 68
Fior di Virtù (anon.), 147, 151
Fishbane, Michael, 4
Foot, Philippa, 216
Foucault, Michel, 202
fraynt, 89, 90, 101n2, 105n61
Freeman, Jo, 119
Freidenreich, Harriet, 219–20
Friedan, Betty, 223
Friedman, Marilyn, 114, 224, 225–26
Fürst, Chaim, 100

Geertz, Clifford, 202
gemilut ḥasadim, 4

gender
    Aristotle on, 58
    friendship networks and, 121n7
    as socially constructed, 111–12
    in understanding friendship, 226
    See also women
gender and friendship
    boundaries in sharing of secrets and, 31–32
    in *Dialogues on Love*, 68–70
    Philo on, 59–60
    philosophical discourse on, 55–56
    See also men, friendships of; women, friendships of
Genesis
    family relations in, 129–31, 133–34, 135
    Jacob and Esau story in, 131–41
    Perez and Zerah story in, 132
Gilgamesh and Humbaba, 23
Gilligan, Carol, 224, 225
Ginsburg, Adele, 109
Ginzburg, Carlo, 203
Glückel of Hameln
    Berlin and, 92, 93–94
    experiences of friendship of, 99–101
    on family as friends, 90–91
    in-laws of, 92–93, 94–96
    memoir of, 10, 11, 89–90
    Mistress Jachet and, 94–96
    non-Jews and, 98–99
    nonkin friends of, 96–97
    parables of, 89, 99, 100
    second marriage of, 91–92
    See also Chaim of Hameln
God
    friendship with, 48–50, 59–60
    intellectual love of, 63–64
    passion of, 240
    relationship with, and well-being, 61
Goitein, S. D., 205n13

Hahn, Edith, 218–19
halakhic obligations, 3–4
happiness, Western discourses on
    Aristotle and, 56–58
    awareness of, by Jewish philosophers, 71
    Jewish philosophical reflections on friendship and, 55–56
    Nicomachean Ethics and, 65–67
    Plato and, 56
    Proverbs and, 65
    in rabbinic Judaism, 61

Harding, Vincent, 241
Harvey, Warren Zev, 64
Hasidic friendships
    in interwar Poland, 167–68, 175–76
    notions of, 168–70
    secularism and, 171–78
    Torah study and, 172
Hasidism, 171, 176–77, 244–45
ḥaver, 6
Havurat Shalom, 108
ḥavurot, 106
Heberer, Michael, 198–99
Heidegger, Elfried, 222
Heidegger, Martin, 220, 221, 222
Helmstadt, Moses, 97
Hermann III, 21
Heschel, Abraham Joshua
    career of, 239
    death of, 247
    God in Search of Man, 236
    invitation to White House of, 236–37, 238
    King on, 246
    at Pettus Bridge, 232
    The Prophets, 237
    as refugee, 233
    speeches of, 234–35, 240–41
    on surprise, 242
    on Vietnam war, 245–46
    See also King-Heschel friendship
Heszer, Catherine, 6, 7
ḥevrayya
    Luria and, 8
    Shapira and, 177
    Zohar and 40, 41, 44, 45, 48, 50
hierarchy
    of communal institutions, 114–15
    nonhierarchical organizations as reaction to, 119–20
    of traditional family, 113
Honig, Shalom, 167
Horowitz, Isaiah, 90
Horowitz, Menahem-Mendel, 172
Horowitz, Zalman, 171–72, 173, 174
humanism, 65, 68
humanness, conception of, in *Zohar*, 44
Husserl, Edmund, 217, 220
Hutson, Lorna, 201
Hyman, Paula, 116

Iberian cultural legacy, 66
Iberian letters, 40

256 INDEX

Iberian locales, 39
identities
　defections by Hasidic Jews and, 181n36
　friendship networks and, 118–19
　of Jacob, 135–37, 140–41
　local, as commonality in interfaith relations, 198–200
　twinship and, 129–30, 131–35
individualism of U.S. culture, 112–13
interfaith relations
　classification of, 200–204
　confessionalization and, 197–98
　continuum of, 202–3
　framework for historical study of, 185–89
　local identity as commonality in, 198–200
　in modern period, 213–15
　Muslim-Jewish, 187
　overview of, 12–13
　role of travel and mobility in, 195–97, 199
　tolerance in, 188, 189, 195
　See also Christian-Jewish friendships
interpersonal sphere, in Jewish religion and culture, 3–4
intersectionality, 124n42
Islam
　dhimmi status and, 196
　Jewish education of women and, 62
　Muslim-Jewish relations, 187
Israel, Jacob identity as, 141
Italy
　Counter-Reformation book market in, 147
　friendship in, 67–68
　humanism in, 65
　Jewish women in, 213
　Jewish writers in, 9
　medical practitioners in, 75n55
　Montaigne journey to, 195
　patron-client relation in, 156, 158
　Sephardic exiles in, 66
I-Thou relations, 217–18

Jachet, Mistress, 94–96
Jackson, Jesse, 247
Jaspers, Karl, 14, 221
Jephthah's daughter, friends of, 80–82, 85
Job, friends of, 81, 82
Judah b. Samuel, 5, 22, 27–28, 29–30
Judaism
　Catholicism and, 239
　diversification of, 198
　Greco-Roman, 59–60
　modernization of, 212–15
　rabbinic, in Middle Ages, 61–62
　Second Temple, 61
　secularization of, in modernity, 224–25
　See also Ashkenaz, medieval, conceptions of friendship in; Hasidism; Torah, study of
Judges 11, 80–82, 86

Kabbalah, love in, 70
kabbalistic fellowships in *Zohar*, 7–8, 39–40, 45, 50
Kagan, Israel Meir, 173
Kalish, Ita, 175–76
Kant, Immanuel, 215–16
Kantianism, 216–17
Kantor, Abraham, 97
Kaplan, Benjamin, 197
Katz, Jacob, 186
Kaveny, Cathleen, 239, 241
Kennedy, John F., 236
Kimchi, David, 139
King, Martin Luther, Jr.
　"A Challenge to Justice and Love," 233–34
　death of, 247
　Heschel on, 246
　on maladjustment, 242–43
　Nobel Peace Prize of, 239
　at Pettus Bridge, 232
　prophetic rhetoric of, 232, 240
　at Riverside Church, 245–46
　on silence of good people, 237
King-Heschel friendship
　bases for, 14
　marches for racial justice in, 243–45
　overview of, 233–35
　political activity in, 236–39
　prophetic tradition and, 239–43
　theological sensibilities in, 235–36
　Vietnam war in, 245–46
kiss, spiritual, 47, 53n31
Koltun, Elizabeth, 109
Krafft, Hans Ulrich
　on friendship, 201–2
　gifts given to, 194, 204
　interfaith friendships of, 12–13
　memoirs of, 189–94
　Swabian identity of, 198, 199
　as taken for Jew, 196–97
　on Winterbach, 200

"lachrymose conception" of Jewish history in Europe, 185, 206n13
"language" of friendship, 14–15

Lanier, Gloria, 221
Lasch, Christopher, 113
Laura (wife of Samuel ben Yehiel), 70–71
Lawson, James, 241
leadership
    of communal institutions, 114–15
    of feminist organizations, 119–20
learning, rabbinic culture of, 61–62
    See also Torah, study of
Lenzi, Mariano, 68
Leon, David Messer, 70–71
Lessing, Gotthold Ephraim, 187
letters
    interfaith friendships and, 188
    of Modena, 159–60
    rabbinic discourse in, 34–35
    of Rosenzweig and M. Rosenstock-Huessy, 218
Levant
    Christians traveling to, 195–96
    Krafft in, 190–94
Levin, Marcus, 214
Levinas, Emmanuel, 16n9, 225
Levy, Hirsch, 91–92, 95, 98
Lewis, John, 232
liberalism, communitarian critique of, 112–13
Liebes, Yehuda, 40
Lowell, Robert, 220, 221
loyalty, friendship as relationship of, 93–94, 146–47, 150–51
Luria, Isaac, 8

Macdonald, Dwight, 221
Maimon, Solomon, 168
Maimonides, Moses, 9, 15, 62–64
Malbim (Meir Leibush ben Yehiel Mikhel Weiser), 132
male-female relationships
    Arendt and, 220–21, 223
    intellectual, 217–19
    Modena, Copia Sullam and, 155–57
    in modern period, 213–15
    in *Zohar*, 41–44
    See also marriage
Manlich Trade Company, 190, 192
March on Washington for Jobs and Freedom, 236, 237
marriage
    friendship contrasted with, 153–54
    intellectual work of spouses in, 217–18
    sexual temptation and, 30
Matt, Daniel, 48
McCarthy, Mary, 220, 221

McGuire, Brian Patrick, 23–24
    Friendship and Community, 2
Meir, Ephraim, 218
Meir of Lublin, 92
mekhutonim, 92
men, friendships of
    biblical representations of, 23–25, 79, 85–86
    Eleazar b. Judah on, 26–27
    Modena on, 151, 153–54
    to overcome sexual temptation, 28–30
    overview of, 5–6, 33–34
    rabbinic friendship, 6–9, 27–28
    in rabbinic letters, 34–35
    in rabbinic treatises, 25–26
    sharing of secrets and, 31–32
    Shmuel and Yehiel, 21–22, 26, 34, 35
    as social institution, 22–23, 27
    Torah study and, 5–9, 27–30, 170
    wives compared to friends, 33
    See also David and Jonathan; King-Heschel friendship; male-female relationships; *Zohar*
Mendelssohn, Moses, 187
Merchant of Venice, The (Shakespeare), 153
mitsvot in interpersonal relationships, 3–4
Modena, Leon
    Autobiography, 151, 153, 154, 155, 157, 158
    Copia Sullam and, 155–57
    Fior di Virtù and, 147
    friendships of, 11–12, 157–61
    L'Ester, 155–56
    translations of Ariosto by, 145–46
    Tsemaḥ Tsaddik, 147–51, 152, 153–54, 157
modernity
    discourses on friendship and, 215–16
    in eastern Europe, tragedy of, 178
    secularization of Judaism in, 224–25
    as transforming life for Jews, 212–15
Montaigne, Michel de, 195, 215
    "On Friendship," 201
moral reasoning and friendship, 215–16
Mortenfeld, Nehemele, 172–73, 174
mourning rites, 81–82, 96
Muslim-Jewish relations, 187
mutuality, friendship as relationship of, 24, 107, 116, 120, 139–40
mysticism, Jewish, 39–40
    See also Zohar

Naples, 67, 69, 70
National Association for the Advancement of Colored People (NAACP), 236, 245

258 INDEX

National Conference of Christians and Jews, 233
National Jewish Women's Conference, 109–10
New York Havurah, 107–8, 110
Nicomachean Ethics (Aristotle), 9, 56–58, 63, 65–67, 148
Niebuhr, Reinhold, 236
Nissim of Pisa, Yehiel, 66
Nixon, Jon, 222
nonviolence movement, 241, 243
North American Jewish Students' Network, 109–10
Novak, Hershel, 171–74

Olyan, Saul, 134, 140
Oppenheim, Moritz Daniel, *Lavater and Lessing Visit Moses Mendelssohn*, 187
Oppenheimer, Joseph Süß, 188
Orlando Furioso (Ariosto), 145–46, 158–59
Ottoman Empire, 9, 66, 187, 190, 197–199

Paley, Grace, 11
patronage relationships, 156–58, 201
Peace of Augsburg, 197
pessimism about friendship, 102n8
philia, 56–58, 70, 148
Philo of Alexandria, 59–60
philosophical traditions and friendship
    J. Abravanel and, 67–71
    Arendt and, 220–23
    dialogical, 217–19
    existentialism, 217
    feminist moral theory, 224–26
    Kantianism, 216–17
    Maimonides and, 63–64
    in Middle Ages, 62
    in modern period, 213–15, 226–27
    moral reasoning, 215–16
    overview of, 9, 13–14, 55–56
    Philo and, 59–60
    post-Maimonidean, 64–67
    rabbinic Judaism and, 60–62
    virtue, happiness, and, 56–58
Pietist's Study House of Bet El, 8
Piotroków, Poland, 171
Pirkei Avot, 6, 15, 25
Plato and friendship, 38, 56
Platonism, in Renaissance Italy, 68, 70
Podhoretz, Norman, 241
Poland
    Hasidic dynasties of, 171
    interwar years in, 167–68, 175–76

retention methods in, 176–78
polity, friendship as microcosm of, 222–23
Portugal, 66, 194
practices of friendship
    culture and, 15n5
    persistence over time of, 15
    in women's movement, 107–11
Prinz, Joachim, 237
prison, as heterotopia, 202
prophetic tradition and King-Heschel friendship, 239–43
Proverbs, 29–30, 65, 79
Przytyk, Poland, 167
Psalm 55:21, 86
psychoanalytic movement and friendship, 228n20
public/private split, 115–17, 223

rabbinic discourse in letters, 34–35
rabbinic friendship, 5–9, 27–28
rabbinic notion of male bonding, 25–26, 30
racism
    civil rights movement and, 238–39, 241, 243–45
    Heschel on, 234–35, 237
    redemption and, 242
Randolph, A. Philip, 236
Rashi, 28, 29, 31
reciprocity, friendship as relationship of, 93–94, 107, 120, 141, 148–49
redemption and racism, 242
Republic of Letters, 204
Response magazine, 109
retention methods of Hasidic leaders, 176–77
Reuchlin, Johannes, 188
Ries, Hirschel, 93
Rome, 68, 69, 70, 195
Rom-Shiloni, Dalit, 141
Rosenstock-Huessy, Eugen, 218
Rosenstock-Huessy, Margrit "Gritli," 218–19
Rosenzweig, Franz, 13–14, 217, 218–19
Rustin, Bayard, 236, 241
Ruth and Naomi, 82–83, 84, 85–86, 141

Safed, Winterbach on, 192–93
Salonica, 66
salons, 13, 15, 71, 155, 214–15
Scholem, Gershom, 14, 17n21, 222
Schwartz, Stuart, 188
SCLC (Southern Christian Leadership Conference), 233, 245, 246

scriptures and Philonic approach to harmonization of Greek philosophy, 59–61
  See also specific books of Bible
secrets, sharing of, 31–32, 50
secularism and Hasidic friendships, 171–78
secularization of Judaism in modernity, 224–25
Sefer Ḥasidim, 29, 30, 31, 32
segregation and friendship networks, 118–19
selection of friends, 32
Selma, Alabama, 232, 243
Selma to Montgomery march, 238, 243–44
Sephardic intellectuals, discourse on friendship among, 66–67
Sephardic world during Renaissance, 187
sexism, as learned, 111–12
sexual norms and male friendship, 23
sexual urges, overcoming, and male friendship, 28–30
Sforno, Solomon Shemaiah, 158–59
Shapira, Kalonymous Kalman, 170, 176–78
Shekhinah, 41–43, 44, 45, 47–50
Shema Yisrael, 33
Shimon bar Yoḥai, 39
  See also *Zohar*
Shlomo ben Shimshon, 34
Shmuel ben Gedaliah, 21–22, 26, 34, 35
Shulman, George, 242
Smail, Daniel Lord, 189
sociability
  Aristotelian notion of, 148
  Glückel and, 91, 99–100
  in group relations and communal structures, 146
  of mind, 150
  Modena and, 157–61
Southern Christian Leadership Conference (SCLC), 233, 245, 246
Spain, 9, 17n19, 65
spiritual imperative in Hasidic friendships, 168–70, 176–78
Stern, Günther, 220
Stoics, 58, 59
Student Non-violent Coordinating Committee, 245
study of friendship, 1, 3–5
Swabian identity, 198, 199–200

"Therapeutae," 60
theurgic drama in *Zohar*, 41–42, 49–50
Thoreau, Henry David, *A Week on the Concord and Merrimack Rivers*, 1

Tif'eret, 41–43, 44, 49–50, 70
Tillich, Paul, 235
tolerance, 188, 189, 195
Torah, study of
  by boys, 172
  male friendship and, 5–9, 27–30, 170
  women as exempted from, 61–62, 63–64
totalitarianism, Arendt on, 222
travel and mobility, in interfaith relations, 195–97
Trilling, Diana, 14, 220
Trilling, Lionel, 14, 220
Tripoli, Lebanon, 190
Tronto, Joan, 224, 225
tsaddik, 168–69
Tseirei Aguda youth groups, 176
Tsemaḥ Tsaddik (Modena), 147–51, 152, 153–54, 157
twinship
  bipartite nature and paradox of, 129–30
  identity and, 131–35
  reunion of Jacob and Esau and, 137–40
  as societal and interpersonal phenomenon, 130

universities, admission of Jews and women to, 219–20
Urban League, 245
Usque, Salomon, 156
utility, friendship as relationship of, 64, 157

Varnhagen, Karl August, 214
Varnhagen, Rahel Levin, 13, 15, 214, 220
virtue ethics, 61, 65–66, 216
virtue friendship, 55–56, 57–58, 63–64
virtues
  cultivation of, and friendship, 56–58
  in *Fior di Virtù*, 147, 151
  of friendship, Modena on, 148–51
Vivian, C. T., 241, 244
Volterra, Meshullam da, 208n56, 209n73

Wallace, George, 236
Walzer, Michael, 112, 241
Weber, Max, 178
Weiss, Penny, 113
Weiss-Rosmarin, Trude, 108–9
West, Cornel, 235
Western culture
  David and Jonathan friendship as prototype in, 24–25

Western culture (*continued*)
  individualism in, 112–13
  integration of Jews into, 213
  See also happiness, Western discourses on
Whitehall Conference, 197
Winkler, Paula, 218
Winterbach, Mayer, 13, 192–94, 198, 199, 202
wives compared to male friends, 33
Wolfson, Elliot, 43
women
  admission of, to European universities, 219–20
  Aristotelian philosophy and, 62
  exclusion of, from Torah study, 60–62, 63–64
  Hasidic, transition to secularism by, 175
  life of contemplation and, 60
  Maimonides on, 63–64
  as medical practitioners, 75n55
  membership and leadership policies and, 114–15
  modernity and, 212–15
  negation of, in post-Maimonidean philosophy, 64–67
  as philosophers, 68–69
  salons of, 13, 15, 71, 155, 214–15
  study of philosophy by, in Italy, 70–71
  See also feminism; marriage
women, friendships of
  Arendt and, 220–23
  Aristotle and, 57–58
  biblical representations of, 85–86
  as crossing private/public divide, 116
  early modern discourse on, 154–55
  of Glückel, 94–96
  of Jephthah's daughter, 80–82, 85–86
  with men, 41–44, 155–57
  Modena and, 155
  modern conceptions of, 215–16
  as networks of support, 113–14
  overview of, 10–11
  philosophers of dialogue and, 216–20
  in philosophical tradition, 9
  Ruth and Naomi, 82–83, 84, 85–86, 141
  See also male-female relationships
women's movement. *See* feminism

Yankel, Moshe, 173
Yeḥiel ben Samuel, 21–22, 26, 34, 35
Yeḥiel of Pisa, Simon ben, 70
Yitzchak Ben-Menahem, 34
Yitzhak Bar Yitzhak, 34
Young, Andrew, 241, 244
Young, Iris, 118
Young, Whitney, 245

Zanetti, Daniele, 147
Zer-Kavod, Mordechai, 23, 24
Zohar
  devotional love in, 47–48
  dramatic speech and physical gesture in, 46–47
  face-to-face relations in, 41–45
  human-divine friendship in, 48–50
  kabbalistic fellowship in, 7–8, 39–40, 45, 50
  qualities of mystical friendship in, 45–46
  speaking of secrets in, 50
  spiritual life dramatized in, 40–41

www.ingramcontent.com/pod-product-compliance
Lightning Source LLC
Chambersburg PA
CBHW022044290426
44109CB00014B/979